AF396483

BBC
DOCTOR
WHO

INTO THE VORTEX

DOCTOR WHO MAGAZINE

EDITOR **MARCUS HEARN**
CONTRIBUTING EDITOR **ALAN BARNES**
ART EDITOR **ALISTAIR McGOWN**
SPECIAL THANKS
PERI GODBOLD
JONATHAN RIGBY

PANINI UK LTD
Managing Director
CHRIS CLOVER
Consultant MIKE RIDDELL
Managing Editor
ALAN O'KEEFE
Head of Production
MARK IRVINE
Circulation & Trade Marketing
Controller REBECCA SMITH
Head of Marketing
JESS TADMOR
Marketing Executive
SAMANTHA HAMMOND

**BBC STUDIOS,
UK PUBLISHING**
Chair, Editorial Review Boards
NICHOLAS BRETT
Managing Director, Consumer
Products and Licensing
STEPHEN DAVIES
Global Director, Magazines
MANDY THWAITES
Compliance Manager
CAMERON McEWAN
UK.Publishing@bbc.com

THANKS TO
Russell T Davies, Anju Dutta, Derek Handley,
BBC Wales, BBC Studios and *bbc.co.uk*

Email: dwm@panini.co.uk
Website: www.doctorwhomagazine.com
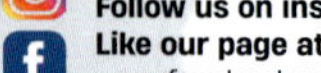
Follow us on X at: @DWMtweets
Follow us on instagram at: doctorwho_magazine

Like our page at:
www.facebook.com/doctorwhomagazine

Advertising Madison Bell
Telephone 0207 389 0859
Email jack.daly@madisonbell.com
Subscriptions telephone 01371 853619
Subscriptions email drwhomagazine@escosubs.co.uk

**Doctor Who Magazine™ Bookazine #35 – Into
the Vortex** published September 2024 by Panini UK
Ltd. Office of publication: Panini UK Ltd, Brockbourne
House, 77 Mount Ephraim, Tunbridge Wells, Kent, TN4 8BS.
Published every four weeks. BBC, DOCTOR WHO (word marks, logos and devices),
TARDIS, DALEKS, CYBERMAN and K-9 (word marks and devices) are trademarks of the
British Broadcasting Corporation and are used under licence. BBC logo © BBC 1996.
Doctor Who logo and insignia © BBC 1973. Dalek image © BBC/Terry Nation 1963.
Cyberman image © BBC/Kit Pedler/Gerry Davis 1966. K-9 image © BBC/Bob Baker/
Dave Martin 1977. Doctor images © BBC Studios 2024. Licensed by BBC Studios.
All other material is © Panini UK Ltd unless otherwise indicated. No similarity
between any of the fictional names, characters persons and/or institutions herein
with those of any living or dead persons or institutions is intended and any such
similarity is purely coincidental. All views expressed in this magazine are those of
their respective contributors and do not necessarily represent the views of **Doctor
Who Magazine**, the BBC or Panini UK. Nothing may be reproduced by any means
in whole or part without the written permission of the publishers. This periodical
may not be sold, except by authorised dealers, and
is sold subject to the condition that it shall not
be sold or distributed with any part of its cover or
markings removed, nor in a mutilated condition.
All letters sent to this magazine will be considered
for publication, but the publishers cannot be
held responsible for unsolicited manuscripts,
photographs or artwork. Panini and the BBC are not
responsible for the content of external websites.
Newstrade distribution: Marketforce (UK) Ltd, 3rd
Floor, 161 Marsh Wall, London, E14 9AP 020 3787 9001.
ISSN 0957-9818

Contents

Introduction

It was long ago, but there was a time when the only way to watch *Doctor Who* was to make sure you were in front of your television screen when the show was actually on. In the early 1980s, the BBC's entry to the home video market was partly galvanised by *Doctor Who* itself. In the years that followed, more and more episodes were liberated from the archive, giving some fans the opportunity to own stories they thought they'd never see again, and others the chance to finally discover the history of their favourite show.

Video and laserdisc gave way to DVD, which in turn was upgraded to high-definition Blu-ray. And then, in 2023, came another milestone. As part of the celebrations marking the series' 60th anniversary, the BBC added every available episode to its streaming service iPlayer. The stories from the show's 21st-century revival were already there, but from 1 November they were joined by countless episodes from its 20th-century run – all there at the touch of a button for UK viewers.

Never before has so much *Doctor Who* been so easily accessible. "I'd like to thank the BBC for all the hard work, to get this massive back catalogue under one roof, at long last," said showrunner Russell T Davies. "I'm so excited for new viewers – imagine being eight years old, spending winter afternoons exploring the 60s, 70s, 80s and beyond."

This iPlayer revolution has had a profound effect on viewing habits for fans of all ages. I've dipped into serials that I haven't watched for years, all because – I'm slightly ashamed to admit – it's so much easier to pick up a remote control than it is to cross to the other side of the house and rummage through a box of DVDs. The convenience of iPlayer has even prompted other members of my family to watch episodes that were originally broadcast years before any of us were born.

Doctor Who's arrival in the world of near-instant, digital accessibility is a wonderful thing. But it raises similar questions to those asked by people who have abandoned their CD collections in favour of music-streaming services. Namely: when presented with a bewildering amount of content, where on earth do you begin? Some of us will be able to indulge in the luxury of watching every available episode of *Doctor Who*, in order. If, however, you're planning a more selective, thematic journey through the Time Vortex, then this special publication has been designed as a guide. Whether you've been watching since day one, or you've just discovered the show, the following pages can satnav you through all 311 television stories, along with highlights of the spin-off series *The Sarah Jane Adventures* and *Torchwood*.

We have to mention that not every episode is on DVD, Blu-ray or the iPlayer. A stubbornly high number no longer exist as moving images at all. But we're not going to let the gaps in the archive spoil the fun. It's safe to say that more care has been lavished on *Doctor Who* than any other television series in history – if it's no longer possible to watch an episode, then there are soundtracks, photographic reconstructions and animations to choose from.

The opinions you'll read over the following pages are those of **Doctor Who Magazine**'s writers, and nothing's definitive. If you find yourself disagreeing with the choices in the *How to Watch* sections, then feel free to get in touch with your own recommendations for other readers. Everyone's welcome, and television's greatest adventure is now available to more of us than ever.

Marcus

Marcus Hearn
Editor

The FIRST DOCTOR

William Hartnell
Stories 1–29, 1963–66

Our first impression of the Doctor was of a suspicious character, determined to keep the time-and-space machine he'd parked in a London junkyard a secret. Later voyages in the fourth and fifth dimensions showed he had many sides: paternal and protective, crusading and compassionate, yearning to return to an unknown point of origin.

Susan (Carole Ann Ford), Barbara (Jacqueline Hill), Ian (William Russell) and the Doctor (William Hartnell) in *100,000 BC* (aka *An Unearthly Child*).

1 100,000 BC (aka An Unearthly Child)

(four episodes) by Anthony Coburn
Two schoolteachers are curious about the strange behaviour of one of their pupils, who lives with her grandfather in a junkyard. Entering a police box they find stationed there, the teachers are whisked away to a life-changing ordeal in the Stone Age…

■ **Where and When**
London, 1963 and Earth, 100,000 BC.
■ **The Baddies** Kal (Jeremy Young), an outsider who has notions of deposing Za (Derek Newark) – leader of the Tribe of Gum. But he's not the only one to be unfriendly to the time travellers.
■ **Introducing…** *Doctor Who*, an adventure in space and time. Everything is new, including the Doctor (William Hartnell), his police-box-shaped TARDIS, his granddaughter Susan (Carole Ann Ford) and her teachers Ian Chesterton (William Russell) and Barbara Wright (Jacqueline Hill). The Doctor can't reliably pilot his ship, so he

"Have you ever thought what it's like to be wanderers in the fourth dimension?"
THE DOCTOR

can't take Ian and Barbara back to London in 1963: they're stuck with each other.
■ **Look out for…** Not one, but *two* mentions of the show's title in dialogue – one from the Doctor, another from Ian.
■ **What they said** "Although *Dr. Who* is said to have been written for the 10-14 year olds, I feel sure that if it keeps up the high standard of the first two episodes it will capture a much wider audience. It has certainly captured me," said Marjorie Norris in *The Stage and Television Today*, on 5 December 1963.
■ **Arcs in Space** We'll learn more of what the Doctor was up to in London before this story in **148** *Remembrance of the Daleks* – which returns to Coal Hill School and the Totter's Lane junkyard.

2 The Mutants (aka The Daleks)

(seven episodes) by Terry Nation
Exploring the seemingly dead world of Skaro, the travellers encounter the Daleks – hostile, paranoid creatures housed in armoured travel machines. The war that caused their mutation is about to erupt again…

■ **Where and When** The planet Skaro, exact date unknown.
■ **The Baddies** The Daleks – survivors of a nuclear war who've become dependent on radiation. The design of their travel machines is clearly tailored to their city, which has polished metal floors and interfaces that can be operated by their extendable 'arms'.
■ **Introducing…** We also meet the Thals – the Daleks' age-old enemies, whose experience of war has turned them towards peace rather than greater aggression. They will next appear in **68** *Planet of the Daleks*.
■ **Look out for** You don't actually get to see a Dalek mutant in this story, but the scene where the Doctor and Ian remove one from its casing, and leave it under a cloak on the floor, is so powerfully creepy you could convince yourself you saw it.
■ **What they said** On 2 March 1964 *The Scotsman*'s Peggie Phillips flew in the face of public reaction to the serial

Susan and the Doctor meet hostile aliens in *The Mutants* (aka *The Daleks*).

by describing it as "The funniest thing for years with the baddie Daleks – tin boxes with peeping voices – and the ladylike goodies in Greek tunics and golden hair."

■ **Arcs in Space** Much of what this story suggests about the Daleks' origins is revised and expanded in **78** *Genesis of the Daleks*.

3 Inside the Spaceship (aka The Edge of Destruction)

(two episodes) by **David Whitaker**

An explosion occurs inside the TARDIS, and the travellers are knocked unconscious. Afterwards they all act strangely, and the Doctor accuses Ian and Barbara of sabotage...

■ **Where and When** The TARDIS, no date.

■ **The Baddies** With this story's action confined entirely to the ship, should the four travellers fear each other, some unseen intruder – or the TARDIS itself?

■ **Farewell to...** The antagonistic dynamic between the travellers in the first two stories is resolved here, after which they become a more amiable group.

■ **Look out for...** The striped bandage Susan places on the Doctor's head. The stripes gradually disappear as his wound heals.

■ **What they said** Although the story was commissioned for logistical reasons – it

required no guest cast and only existing sets – producer Verity Lambert described another motivation during an interview for vol 1, issue 7 of the fanzine *TARDIS* in June 1976. "We felt it was necessary to show more of the inside of the TARDIS," she said, "and to explain some of the workings that viewers might not normally see."

■ **Arcs in Space** This is the first time we get any sense that the TARDIS might be sentient – a concept fully explored in **216** *The Doctor's Wife*.

4 Marco Polo

(seven episodes) by **John Lucarotti**

The Doctor, Susan, Ian and Barbara travel the Silk Road with the famed explorer Marco Polo, who intends to gift the malfunctioning TARDIS to the mighty emperor Kublai Khan.

Where and When
From the Himalayas to Cathay, 1289.

The Baddies Marco Polo (Mark Eden) and Kublai Khan (Martin Miller) both cause problems for the Doctor and his companions, but the real villain is Mongol warlord Tegana (Derren Nesbitt),

who makes multiple attempts to sabotage Polo's caravan.

■ **Introducing...** This is the Doctor's first on-screen encounter with real historical figures. Such meetings happen regularly in the First Doctor's era, then very rarely until **159** *The Unquiet Dead*.

■ **Look out for...** Susan's charming friendship with Ping-Cho (Zienia Merton) sees her talking more like a 1963 teenager than at any other time. Ping-Cho responds to contemporary slang such as "crazy" and "dig it" by telling Susan, "This language of yours is very strange."

■ **Where else have I seen...** Tutte Lemkow, who plays Kuiju, swiftly returned to *Doctor Who* in two other historical adventures, playing Ibrahim in **14** *The Crusade* and Cyclops in **20** *The Myth Makers*.

■ **Arcs in Space** "I have seen Buddhist monks make cups of wine fly through the air unaided," says Polo. He also says he believes the monks will be able to open and fly the TARDIS. Alien powers are displayed by Buddhist monks in **38** *The Abominable Snowmen* and **74** *Planet of the Spiders*.

5 The Keys of Marinus

(six episodes) by Terry Nation

Five stories in one, as the TARDIS crew cross continents to find microcircuits that will repair the Conscience of Marinus – a telepathic machine that, ironically, eliminates freedom of conscience and stops people doing, or even thinking, evil things.

Arbitan (George Coulouris) shows the Conscience to the travellers in *The Keys of Marinus*.

■ **Where and When** The planet Marinus – an island in an acid sea, its aggressive jungle, its snowy mountains of terror, and the cities of Morphoton and Millennius (exact date unknown).

■ **The Baddies** The Voord – black-helmeted, skinsuit-wearing, knife-wielding cultists. Under their leader Yartek (Stephen Dartnell), they can resist the Conscience, and plan to control it. There are also the hypnotic Brains of Morphoton (voiced by Heron Carvic), the abusive hunter Vasor (Francis De Woolf) and the corrupt, murderous guards of 'civilised' Millennius. The real enemy, everywhere, is authoritarianism.

"I don't believe that man was made to be controlled by machines." THE DOCTOR

■ **Introducing...** For the first time the TARDIS is seen to actually materialise on screen, albeit silently – without the sound heard *inside* the TARDIS since 1 *100,000 BC* (aka *An Unearthly Child*).

■ **Look out for...** The arms of the (fabulous) statue that grabs Barbara in third episode *The Screaming Jungle* are visibly human.

■ **What they said** The *Daily Mail* of 11 April 1964 ran a photoshoot featuring Carole Ann Ford and a Voord, with the latter described as "Bouncing across

BBC screens tonight... with flappers on his feet and a triangle on his head." Yes, they'd noticed a *Doctor Who* monster was rubbery, for the first time... and not the last.

■ **Arcs in Space** This is the first story not to explicitly follow the previous one. The link is made more subtly, with Ian wearing the clothes he was given in 4 *Marco Polo*. Much later, in 275 *World Enough and Time/The Doctor Falls*, the Twelfth Doctor (Peter Capaldi) names Marinus as one of the planets on which the Cybermen evolve.

6 The Aztecs

(four episodes) by John Lucarotti

Mistaken for a goddess, Barbara battles to save an ancient people from their historical fate. Meanwhile, the Doctor romances a widow who may hold the key to open both the tomb that the TARDIS is trapped inside, and his heart.

■ **Where and When** Tenochtitlan, Mesoamerica – the capital of the Aztec empire. About a generation after 1430, and shortly before the genocide of the Aztecs committed by Spanish imperialist Hernándo Cortés in 1521.

■ **The Baddies** Tlotoxol, high priest of sacrifice (John Ringham) – who may understand that his ritual killings don't bring the rains the harvest depends on, but is unwilling to give up his power.

■ **Introducing...** The idea of changing history. Convinced Cortes wouldn't have destroyed the Aztecs had he not been shocked by their human sacrifices, Barbara tries to end the practice. The Doctor insists that changing history is impossible. But if she can't succeed, why does he want to stop her trying?

■ **Look out for...** Just before he re-enters the TARDIS, when no one else can see, the Doctor pockets a brooch given to him by the widow Cameca (Margot van der Burgh), rather than leaving it behind – since he's unwilling to part with it.

Above right
Tlotoxl (John Ringham, centre) practices human sacrifice in *The Aztecs*.

Right
Barbara takes the place of Aztec goddess Yetaxa.

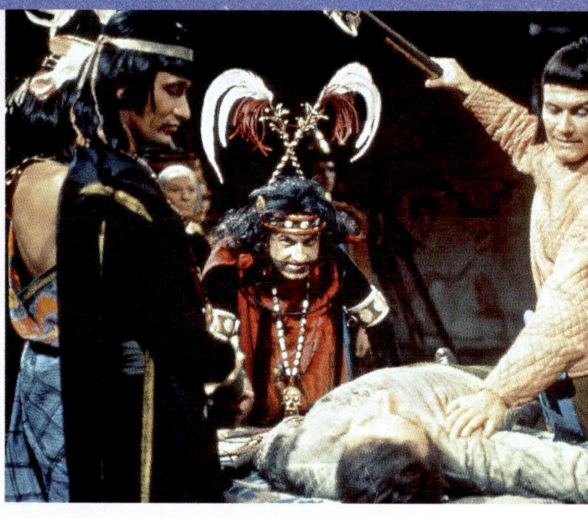

■ **What they said** Despite being founded by the Communist Party of Great Britain, in the 1960s *The Daily Worker* was a mass-market tabloid newspaper, and often reviewed *Doctor Who*. Attracted by the story's anti-imperialism, its 1 June 1964 edition praised the serial's "painstaking attempts [at] historical accuracy".

■ **Arcs in Space** Sometime after leaving Earth the TARDIS materialises, but its instruments say it's still moving – a segue into the next story.

Text by James Cooray Smith

7 The Sensorites

(six episodes) by Peter R Newman

A world afraid of being exploited and ravaged by plague. A spaceship seemingly crewed by the dead. High politics and low cunning amongst a complex alien race. Who are the real monsters this time?

■ **Where and When** The Sense Sphere, planet of the Sensorites, and in its orbit. We're in the 28th century, when human prospectors search the galaxy for minerals.

■ **The Baddies** The Sensorite City Administrator (Peter Glaze) – a rotund, fluffy-haired politician who runs the capital, and who pretends to be everyone's friend, but is secretly a spluttering xenophobe desperate to seize power.

■ **Introducing...** Skaro was said to have been in "the future" in **3** *Inside the Spaceship* (aka *The Edge of Destruction*), but this is the first story to featuring people from Earth's future. Everyone has dog-collared shirts and little rockets on their jackets. Cool.

■ **Look out for...** In the first episode, we follow the TARDIS crew as they cross the threshold of their ship into the control room of the Earth rocket – a remarkable shot that really sells the idea that the TARDIS interior is inside another dimension.

■ **Where else have I seen...** You won't recognise him by sight, but may if you close your eyes and listen: wide-eyed mineralogist and love interest John is played by Stephen Dartnell, who five weeks ago was playing Yartek, leader of the alien Voord.

■ **Arcs in Space** Eventually we'll discover the Sense Sphere is near the Ood Sphere, the eponymous **191** *Planet of the Ood*. A Sensorite is among the notorious criminals pictured in **246** *Time Heist*. More immediately, the Doctor decides to put Ian and Barbara off the ship the very next time it lands, leading into the next story.

8 The Reign of Terror

(six episodes) by Dennis Spooner

Believing they've returned to 1960s England, the TARDIS crew are separated, imprisoned, and try not to lose their heads, as they become involved with those escaping the titular Terror.

■ **Where and When** Paris and its environs. Maximillian Robespierre is arrested in the final episode – something that happened on 26 July 1794. (Or if you prefer, on 8 Thermidor Year II, according to the calendar used in France at the time.)

■ **The Baddies** The Terror has been instigated by the revolutionary government. But the real threats to the Doctor's party come from zealous minions, a drunken, lascivious gaoler (Jack Cunningham), and a traitor in the counter-revolutionary "escape chain" out of Paris.

■ **Look out for...** The Doctor's bombastic impersonation of a revolutionary official in the third episode, wearing massive ribbons and a truly remarkable hat. It's one of William Hartnell's finest moments in the role.

■ **Where else have I seen...** Léon Colbert, who so charms Barbara, is played by Edward Brayshaw – later the War Chief in **50** *The War Games*.

■ **Farewell to...** This was the end of the first 'season' of *Doctor Who*, with the show taking a whole six Saturdays off before its return!

■ **Arcs in Space** We're told that the French Revolution is the period of Earth history the Doctor is most interested in – which might explain Susan's reaction to the book she began to read about it in **1** *100,000 BC* (aka *An Unearthly Child*).

The Daleks were seen at various famous London landmarks in *The Dalek Invasion of Earth*.

"We are the masters of Earth!" DALEK

9 Planet of Giants

(three episodes) by Louis Marks
'Space pressure' shrinks the TARDIS. The now-tiny time-travellers find themselves in the middle of a full-size murder scene, dealing with pesticide perils, among other outsized hazards.

■ **Where and When** England, presumably around 1964 – the Doctor was aiming for "the middle of the 20th century". (Strangely, Ian and Barbara don't seem to realise they've finally arrived home.)
■ **The Baddies** Greedy businessman Mr Forrester (Alan Tilvern), who's untroubled by the deaths of insects – or civil servants – if there's profit to be made.

■ **Introducing...** New TARDIS lore: the most dangerous moment is the point of materialisation. The TARDIS alarm sounds for the first time – a forerunner of the Cloister Bell, which would ring out in 115 *Logopolis*.
■ **Farewell to...** The TARDIS fault locator remained part of the ship's infrastructure for a while, but wouldn't be referenced after this story.
■ **Look out for...** The incredible 'giant-sized' sets and props – including a laboratory sink, a matchbox and a seed packet.
■ **Arcs in Space** This is the first time the TARDIS has been on (presumably) contemporary Earth since 1 *100,000 BC* (aka *An Unearthly Child*). It will next land there in 16 *The Chase*, but not in England before 21 *The Daleks' Master Plan*. Ian's musings on worlds that have giant insects will be answered in 13 *The Web Planet*. The Doctor will be miniaturised again in 93 *The Invisible Enemy*, 103 *The Armageddon Factor*, 115 *Logopolis*, 219 *Let's Kill Hitler* and 243 *Into the Dalek*.

Susan and Ian are shrunk to an inch high in *Planet of Giants*.

10 The Dalek Invasion of Earth

(six episodes) by Terry Nation
The Daleks turn tourists, visiting London landmarks while pursuing an incredible plan to turn the Earth into a spaceship. Meanwhile the TARDIS travellers join the resistance movement, leading to a shock departure...

■ **Where and When** London and Bedfordshire, sometime after 2164.
■ **The Baddies** The Daleks – now sporting rear-mounted power discs and enlarged bases. Their modified human prisoners, the helmeted Robomen. Their pet Slyther, which changes between the fourth and fifth episodes – from a plastic rubbish sack with claws to something resembling a black Krynoid from 85 *The Seeds of Doom*.
■ **Introducing...** The Supreme Controller Dalek, differentiated initially by a black dome and alternated black and silver skirt slats – and later, having popped out for a paint job between episodes, by a fully black skirt. *Doctor Who*'s first quarry appears – but unlike most future appearances, it here represents... a quarry.
■ **Farewell to...** Susan. In the first ever companion departure, the Doctor locks

his granddaughter out of their ship so she can marry freedom fighter David Campbell (Peter Fraser); this isn't a whirlwind romance, it's a full-on cyclone. When grandfather and granddaughter next meet, in **129** *The Five Doctors*, the Doctor doesn't even think to ask how the wedding went!

■ **Look out for...** No one has ever quite worked out why a Dalek is submerged in the Thames, but that doesn't detract from the striking image it makes as it emerges from the river to arrest the Doctor and Ian at the end of the first instalment.

■ **Arcs in Space** We edge closer to the Daleks' cry of "Exterminate!" In **2** *The Mutants* (aka *The Daleks*) we had "They are to be exterminated." Here, we have "Exterminate him!" We won't get the singular command until **16** *The Chase*. Daleks' outer casings are made of Dalekenium – this substance would pop up frequently in later appearances, mostly as a metal, but also as an explosive in **60** *Day of the Daleks*.

11 The Rescue

(two episodes) by David Whitaker
The TARDIS team find two shipwreck survivors on the planet Dido in thrall to a strange and frightening figure. Who is going to rescue young Vicki from the claws of Koquillion?

■ **Where and When** The planet Dido – in, or shortly after, 2493.

■ **The Baddies** Koquillion is absolutely a real monster, and not the human Bennett (Ray Barrett) in a mask. (Oh, OK, it's Bennett in a mask.) Sandy the sand beast is absolutely *not* a baddie, but that doesn't stop Barbara from killing it with a flare gun.

■ **Introducing...** Vicki (Maureen O'Brien) – the first companion to voluntarily join the TARDIS. Arguably, the next person who specifically agrees to become a crewmember is Jamie in **31** *The Highlanders*. This is the Doctor's first acknowledged return to a planet other than Earth, although his earlier visit to Dido happened before he met Ian and Barbara.

■ **Look out for...** At the end of the final episode, the Doctor 'sells' TARDIS travel to Vicki: "If you like adventure, my dear,

I can promise you an abundance of it." Her delight as she enters the ship is the most beautiful, heart-warming moment.

■ **What they said** "The new girl was intended to be something of a waif and stray, someone basically for the Doctor to adopt in place of Susan and to carry on her role," said writer David Whitaker, quoted in **Doctor Who Magazine** issue 98 (March 1985). "I don't think *The Rescue* was a particularly inspired piece of writing, but it was a necessary one."

■ **Arcs in Space** We end on the show's first literal cliffhanger, as the TARDIS tips off the edge of a precipice. We'll discover in **56** *The Mind of Evil* just how much impact Bennett in a mask had on the Doctor, as the Keller Machine attacks the Doctor with his worst nightmares, one of which is Koquillion.

12 The Romans

(four episodes) by Dennis Spooner
Doctor Who carries on into the realm of farce, with the Emperor Nero lusting after Barbara, Vicki getting involved in a poison plot, and the Doctor accidentally inspiring the Great Fire of Rome.

■ **Where and When** Rome and its outskirts, 64 AD.

■ **The Baddies** Any number of Romans could qualify – Nero (Derek Francis) is the obvious headliner, but slave traders Sevcheria (Derek Sydney) and Didius (Nicholas Evans) are particularly repugnant.

■ **Introducing...** This is the first time the TARDIS crew don't get into an adventure immediately upon their arrival at a new location – excluding the time the Doctor and Susan spent in 1963 prior to **1** *100,000 BC* (aka *An Unearthly Child*).

■ **Where else have I seen...** Anne Tirard, playing court poisoner Locusta, came to a sticky end (again) as the genuinely clairvoyant, clown-faced Seeker in **98** *The Ribos Operation*.

■ **Look out for...** When Nero invites the Doctor, who's posing as the lyre player Maximus Pettulian, to perform in an arena full of lions, the Doctor winds him up by promising "Something they can really get their teeth into..."

■ **Arcs in Space** We end with the TARDIS dragged off course towards **13** *The Web Planet*. It won't land in the Roman Empire again until **190** *The Fires of Pompeii*. The Doctor can't play the lyre, and doesn't pick up another musical instrument until he unearths a recorder in **30** *The Power of the Daleks*.

Above inset Vicki (Maureen O'Brien) is threatened by Koquillion in *The Rescue*.

Right A rare moment of relaxation, in *The Romans*.

13 The Web Planet

(six episodes) by Bill Strutton

A strange power draws the TARDIS to a craggy world inhabited by giant insects. But what does their controller want with the Doctor's ship?

■ **Where and When** The planet Vortis, in the Isop galaxy. We're "many light years from Earth" – and sometime in its future, since the evil Animus wants to "take from man his mastery of space."

■ **The Baddies** The Animus (voiced by Catherine Fleming) – a spider-like space parasite that's drained Vortis of life, caused the butterfly-like Menoptra to flutter away to the moon Pictos, and made the chirping, ant-like Zarbi "militant" – menacing all and sundry with their venom-spraying larvae guns.

■ **Introducing...** The Doctor's astral map – seen again in 18 *Galaxy 4* and 276 *Twice Upon a Time*.

■ **Look out for...** Never mind the infamous bit in the third episode, when a Zarbi runs into the camera. There's a shocking scene in the fifth episode in which one of the woodlouse-like Optera sacrifices itself to save Ian, and its allies – by blocking an acid leak with its head!

■ **What they said** "Those Zarbies [sic] are daft. I hate that noise they make. It's enough to drive anyone mad," complained a *Junior Points of View* correspondent on 12 March 1965.

■ **Arcs in Space** The Animus can use gold to manifest its power – so it

The Doctor enjoys an audience with King Richard (Julian Glover) in *The Crusade*.

possesses Barbara via the bracelet that Nero gave her as a love token in 12 *The Romans*. The Isop galaxy is home to more than Menoptra and Zarbi; according to the Anne Droid in 166 *Bad Wolf/ The Parting of the Ways*, its "oldest inhabitant" in 200,100 is the Face of Boe – introduced in 158 *The End of the World*.

14 The Crusade

(four episodes) by David Whitaker

Caught up in a holy war, the Doctor, Ian and Vicki find themselves in Richard

the Lionheart's court, while the mighty Saladin takes Barbara for his story-telling Scheherazade.

■ **Where and When** In and around Jaffa and Lydda, during the Third Crusade of 1189-92 – sometime after the battle of Arsuf, on 7 September 1191.

■ **The Baddies** El Akir (Walter Randall) is undisputably a villain – a kidnapper, murderer and harem-keeper who relishes telling Barbara: "The only pleasure left for you is death..."

■ **Look out for...** The third-episode scene in which the King's sister Joanna (Jean Marsh) rebels against her brother's plan to wed her to Saladin's sibling Saphadin for the sake of expediency crackles unlike any other in 1960s *Doctor Who*: "I am no sack of flour to be given in exchange!"

■ **Where else have I seen...** Richard actor Julian Glover reappears as Count Scarlioni in 105 *City of Death*. Saphadin actor Roger Avon turns up in 21 *The Daleks' Master Plan*, as the treacherous Daxtar – as does Jean Marsh, playing the brave Sara Kingdom. She'll graduate from princess to Queen of the S'rax as Morgaine in 152 *Battlefield*.

■ **What they said** David Whitaker, in an archive interview published in **Doctor Who Magazine** issue 98 (March 1985): "I relished the dialogue that the story allowed me to write, and the period itself was so interesting that it became almost a labour of love to produce a script worthy of the depth of drama that had inspired it..."

A Menoptra, one of several native insectoid species on *The Web Planet*.

■ **Arcs in Space** The Doctor tells Vicki he wished Richard had knighted him, like Ian. A robot double of Richard's brother John will anoint "Sir Doctor" in `128` *The King's Demons*, but he won't be ennobled by a British monarch until `169` *Tooth and Claw*.

`15` The Space Museum

(four episodes) by Glyn Jones
The TARDIS travellers preview themselves as museum exhibits, frozen in display cases… and must find a way to cheat that seemingly pre-ordained fate.

■ **Where and When** The planet Xeros, the future (exact date unknown).
■ **The Baddies** The Moroks – luxuriantly coiffed ex-conquistadors who established a museum to their glorious imperial heyday 300 'mimmians' ago (where one mimmian is 1,000 Xeron days, not that it helps). Strangely, there's no sign of a gift shop.
■ **Introducing…** The TARDIS wardrobe – at this stage, a closet where the travellers' crusading clothes are hung. The Moroks' freezing machine – a hemispherical prop repurposed from the 1963 horror film *Curse of the Fly*, which will make occasional appearances up till `51` *Spearhead from Space*. The Time and Space Visualiser, which the Doctor liberates from the Moroks' museum at the end of the story (although we don't actually *see* it until the next adventure).
■ **Look out for…** Towards the end of the second episode, the Doctor pranks Governor Lobos (Richard Shaw) by using a 'thought selection' chair to project an image of himself as an 'amphibian' – wearing a one-piece bathing suit!
■ **What they said** "The latest adventure seemed enormously contrived… [it] had little more life in it than some of the exhibits in the glass cases of the planet," claimed *The Times Educational Supplement* on 28 May 1965.
■ **Arcs in Space** As the TARDIS departs Xeros, it's being tracked by the Daleks… who've prepared a time machine to follow it into the next story.

`16` The Chase

(six episodes) by Terry Nation
Having built a time and space machine of their own, the Daleks send an assassination squad on the trail of their "greatest enemies" – the crew of the TARDIS!

■ **Where and When** The planet Aridius (date unknown). At the top of the Empire

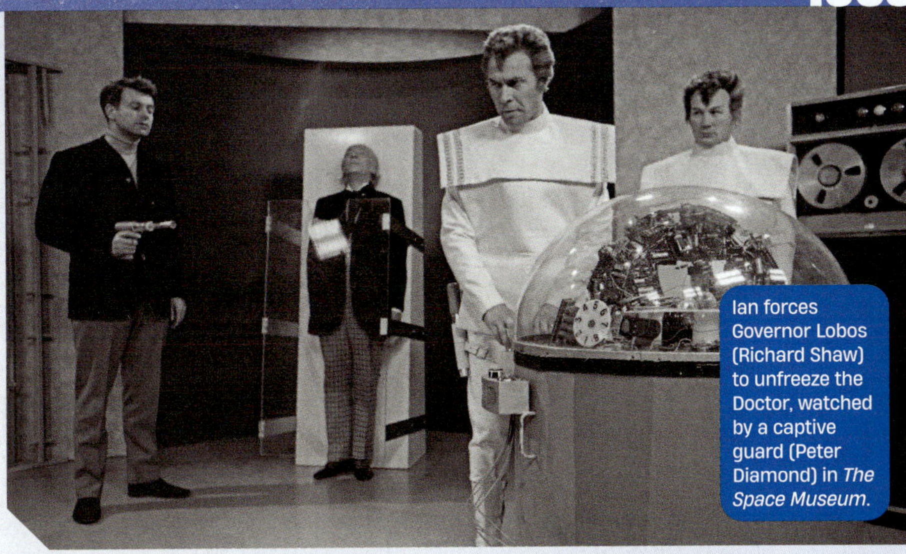

Ian forces Governor Lobos (Richard Shaw) to unfreeze the Doctor, watched by a captive guard (Peter Diamond) in *The Space Museum*.

State Building, New York, 1966. Aboard the *Mary Celeste*, somewhere in the mid-Atlantic, early November 1872. A haunted house exhibit at the Festival of Ghana, 1996. The planet Mechanus (date unknown). London, 1965.
■ **The Baddies** The Daleks, still sore from their defeat in `10` *The Dalek Invasion of Earth*, and their robotic duplicate Doctor (Edmund Warwick). People-collecting, fire-spitting machine creatures called Mechonoids. Plus Dracula and Frankenstein's monster – so far as the Doctor and friends will ever know.
■ **Look out for…** Two of the Daleks in their bigger-on-the-inside time and space machine are recognisable as empty casings borrowed from the set of the 1965 motion picture *Dr. Who and the Daleks*, with their bases removed.
■ **Introducing…** Steven Taylor (Peter Purves), a crashed astronaut who's been stuck in the Mechonoids' human zoo for some two years – and who happens to be the exact double of Morton Dill, an Alabaman tourist who runs into the Daleks at the Empire State.
■ **Farewell to…** Ian and Barbara, who use the Daleks' ship to return home. Ian later became chairman of the Coal Hill School governors, as seen in `240` *The Day of the Doctor*, and was part of an ex-TARDIS support group in `300` *The Power of the Doctor*.
■ **Arcs in Space** The Time and Space Visualiser shows Shakespeare (Hugh Walters), Elizabeth I (Vivienne Bennett) and The Beatles (themselves) ahead of their Doctor encounters in `180` *The Shakespeare Code, The Day of the Doctor* and `306` *The Devil's Chord*. The Daleks create another Doctor double in `133` *Resurrection of the Daleks*, and will later occupy the under-construction Empire State in `182` *Daleks in Manhattan/ Evolution of the Daleks* – perhaps because they knew of it, after their earlier landing?

The Daleks battle the Mechonoids in *The Chase*.

DALEKS

The first hostile aliens the Doctor encountered turned out to be his greatest adversaries. **Eddie Robson** ranks the landmark confrontations in a seemingly never-ending battle.

Outstanding

The first season finale of 21st-century *Doctor Who*, 166 *Bad Wolf/The Parting of the Ways*, is an extraordinary collision of elements – TV game shows, dystopian chaos, a pickup truck. It's also an unbeatably great Dalek story. Russell T Davies runs with themes from the 1980s Dalek stories and gives us quasi-religious Daleks driven mad by their own flesh, touching on a fundamental truth about evil – that it's often driven by self-hatred. The creeping horror as the Daleks tear through the Game Station and despatch their ships to destroy whole *continents* showcases them at their most ruthless, driving up the stakes to the point where the story can only end with a regeneration.

Essential

While *Bad Wolf/Parting* nudges into first place on overall brilliance, 148 *Remembrance of the Daleks* is magnificent and more Dalek-y, using a war between two factions to delve into what defines the creatures. It's an extremely good entry point into 20th-century *Doctor Who*. One of its most memorable elements, the Special Weapons Dalek, returns in the equally Dalek-y 226 *Asylum of the Daleks*, which throws pretty much every Dalek design at the screen. It's a brilliant concept that leans into one of the things that makes Daleks so fun – they're just *insane*. And 2 *The Mutants* (aka *The Daleks*) is an essential, foundational text. The episodes that introduce the Daleks are some of the eeriest and most sinister *Doctor Who* has ever produced.

Excellent

Another foundational story, 78 *Genesis of the Daleks*, rewrites the Daleks' origin by introducing their creator, Davros. 161 *Dalek*, devised to reintroduce the creatures to a new audience, remains a perfect starting point, using the simple but brilliant tactic of establishing what a threat *one* Dalek can be, so an army of them becomes a terrifying prospect. They're at their most implacable in 198 *The Stolen Earth/Journey's End*, with their grandest, most deranged plan of all. Two of the great Dalek epics are sadly incomplete in the archives: 21 *The Daleks' Master Plan* is a high-stakes, brutal battle across time and space, while the alchemical, philosophical 36 *The Evil of the Daleks* would have been a fitting end to the Daleks if, as intended, it had been their final appearance in *Doctor Who*.

The Best of the Rest

Very few civilisations in *Doctor Who* have successfully conquered our home planet, so 10 *The Dalek Invasion of Earth* establishes the Daleks as a cut above the rest. In 60 *Day of the Daleks* they use time travel to restage that invasion; no wonder even the Time Lords saw them as a threat. Time travel is also central to 298 *Eve of the Daleks*, the first Dalek story to also be a romcom. Despite its obtuse title, 254 *The Magician's Apprentice/The Witch's Familiar* is a *Genesis* sequel with many brilliant moments, including Clara's discovery of why the Daleks' speech is so limited. A battle with a group of scheming, seemingly subservient Daleks does a vital job of establishing the new Doctor's credentials after his first regeneration in 30 *The Power of the Daleks*. 142 *Revelation of the Daleks* restores a gruesomeness to the Daleks that largely disappeared after their debut story, while also borrowing from the Cybermen. Indeed, a face-off between Daleks and Cybermen was long overdue, and 177 *Army of Ghosts/Doomsday* finally delivered it.

"Mankind will be harvested because of your weakness."
THE EMPEROR DALEK, *THE PARTING OF THE WAYS*

Right
Vicki, the Doctor and Steven (Peter Purves) in *The Time Meddler*.

Below
The Monk (Peter Butterworth) is a fellow time-traveller.

17 The Time Meddler

(four episodes) by **Dennis Spooner**
On the eve of the battle of Hastings, someone is trying to change the future using anachronistic technology. The TARDIS crew must keep history on the right track.

■ **Where and When** Northumbria, late summer 1066.

■ **The Baddies** Vicious Vikings, bent on invasion. Also a morally ambiguous meddling monk (Peter Butterworth) with a love of 20th century technology.
■ **Introducing…** The first fellow time-traveller from the Doctor's world (other than Susan), and the fact that TARDISes are built to a template, with periodic upgrades – two hugely consequential developments. Perhaps following on from the Daleks' brief boarding of the *Mary Celeste* in 16 *The Chase*, this is the first full adventure to combine history and sci-fi in one.
■ **Look out for…** A Viking helmet that belongs more in a Wagner opera rather than in the 11th century. "What do you think it is?" the Doctor asks the sceptical Steven. "A space helmet for a cow?" Also the Doctor enjoying a drink of mead – although he claims never to touch alcohol by 25 *The Gunfighters*.
■ **Where else have I seen…** Alethea Charlton, who plays the Saxon villager Edith, was the cavewoman Hur in the prehistoric parts of 1 *100,000 BC* (aka *An Unearthly Child*).
■ **Arcs in Space** The Monk will return in the eighth, ninth and tenth episodes of 21 *The Daleks' Master Plan*.

"It's a TARDIS. The Monk's got a TARDIS!"
VICKI

18 Galaxy 4

(four episodes) by **William Emms**
On a doomed world, the TARDIS crew become entangled in a stand-off between two groups of grounded aliens – the humanoid, militaristic Drahvins and the peaceful, batrachian Rills.

■ **Where and When** An unnamed planet in Galaxy 4, date unknown.
■ **The Baddies** The Drahvins, a predominantly female race, ruthless and aggressive, beautiful by contemporary Western European standards. Their leaders are intelligent and enjoy high social status while their lowly, test tube-grown soldiers are a bit dim.
■ **Listen out for…** The distinct Dalek 'heartbeat' effect can be heard throbbing away in the control room of the Rills' spaceship.
■ **What they said** The Rills' robot servants, the Chumblies, got a mixed reception from viewers of children's feedback programme *Junior Points of View*. "The Chumblies are pathetic… like jellies that have been taken out of the mould too soon," said Mairi Stewart. Others wanted them back as soon as possible: "They are so kind and sweet," said Fiona Knight. "I like them better than the Daleks."
■ **Where else have I seen…** In the very final scene, the action shifts to an alien jungle, where Earth astronaut Jeff Garvey snaps his eyes open and vows to kill – a prelude to 19 *Mission to the Unknown*.

Barry Jackson was the incompetent assassin Ascaris in **12** *The Romans*, and will go on to play Time Lord wideboy Drax in **103** *The Armageddon Factor*.
■ **Arcs in Space** The Drahvins are said to be among the alien races hovering over Stonehenge in **212** *The Pandorica Opens*. The ankle that Vicki sprains in the final episode will have consequences at the start of the next-but-one story, **20** *The Myth Makers*.

19 Mission to the Unknown

by **Terry Nation**
On a planet so hostile that no one ever visits, an Earth mission is in dead trouble. Their ship is broken, they're surrounded by killer plants and something even worse is hunting them through the jungle.

■ **Where and When** The planet Kembel, circa 4000 AD.
■ **The Baddies** The Daleks, plotting in secret with several other non-human races, in their latest bid to dominate the universe.
■ **Introducing** The six-strong 'Planetarians' of the Galactic Council – some of whom reappear, albeit in amended form, in **21** *The Daleks' Master Plan*. Astronaut Marc Cory (Edward De Souza) turns out to be an undercover member of the Space Security Service, a military and intelligence organisation dedicated to protecting the Earth and its interests.

Daleks and alien delegates gather on Kembel in *Mission to the Unknown*.

Several other SSS operatives will feature in *Master Plan*, too…
■ **Where else have I seen…** Earthman Gordon Lowery succumbs to Varga plant infection – the same fate suffered by Jeff Garvey in **18** *Galaxy 4*. Jeremy Young was caveman Kal in **1** *100,000 BC* (aka *An Unearthly Child*).
■ **What they said** Young recalled the Varga make-up effect in **Doctor Who Magazine** issue 296 (October 2000): "I remember them covering my hands in rabbit skin and furry pink balls. Then I went mad and Edward de Souza shot me…"
■ **Arcs in Space** The Doctor will stumble across Cory's tape-recorded warning to the Earth authorities in *Master Plan*'s first episode…

20 The Myth Makers

(four episodes) by **Donald Cotton**
The story of the siege and fall of Troy, as told by bards and poets for millennia… only this time, there's a Doctor in the Horse.

■ **Where and When** Troy, circa 1200 BC.
■ **The Baddies** One of the rare occasions when there aren't any real villains – just people pursuing their own agendas while the TARDIS crew get caught in the crossfire. In particular, the wily Greek hero Odysseus (Ivor Salter) remains suspicious of the Doctor, who's been mistaken for the great god Zeus, while Trojan prophetess Cassandra (Frances White) is convinced Vicki is up to no good.
■ **Look out for…** The 'bootstrap paradox' of the Trojan horse. The Doctor knows the story and eventually suggests the ruse to Odysseus. Then it becomes a legend, which is how the Doctor got to hear of it in the first place. So where did the idea originate?
■ **Introducing…** Trojan handmaiden Katarina (Adrienne Hill), who carries the wounded Steven into the TARDIS, and also thinks the Doctor's a god.
■ **Farewell to…** Plucky space orphan Vicki. On meeting the handsome Troilus (James Lynn), she decides to stay with him, to found a new city under a new name: Cressida.
■ **Arcs in Space** Having got away with it once, the Doctor uses the Trojan Horse trick again in **103** *The Armageddon Factor* – albeit miniaturised, inside K9. His attempt at impersonating a god is less successful, and he should know better than to try it again in **256** *The Girl Who Died*.

Left Maaga (Stephanie Bidmead, third left) and her Drahvin clones in *Galaxy 4*.
Right Paris (Barrie Ingham) and Steven battle near Troy in *The Myth Makers*.

Mavic Chen (Kevin Stoney) flanked by delegate Zephon (Julian Sherrier) in *The Daleks' Master Plan*.

21 The Daleks' Master Plan

(twelve episodes) by Terry Nation, Dennis Spooner

Having built a device that can reverse and accelerate time, the Daleks plan to use it to conquer the universe, starting with Earth's solar system. But what if someone were to steal their Time Destructor's power source and run away?

■ **Where and When** From planets Earth, Tigus, Mira, Desperus and Kembel in the year 4000, to ancient Egypt. From 1960s Britain to 1920s Hollywood. With the whole universe in peril, the whole universe is the canvas.

■ **The Baddies** The Daleks – led by a Machiavellian, oleaginously voiced Supreme, capable of pride, paranoia and even cruel humour. Mavic Chen (Kevin Stoney), Guardian of the Solar System – the ultimate traitor, who's sold humanity out to the Daleks for even more power. Compared to him, the Daleks' delegate allies, returning from **19** *Mission to the Unknown*, are small fry.

■ **Farewell to...** The Monk (Peter Butterworth) from **17** *The Time Meddler* makes a welcome, but sadly final, appearance in the eighth, ninth and tenth episodes.

■ **Look out for...** Early on in the surviving tenth episode, *Escape Switch*, Chen gets so theatrical he smacks a Dalek in the eye-stalk with a pointy-nailed finger. The Dalek bristles with rage.

■ **What they said** Writing in *The Observer* on 6 February 1966, eight days after the final instalment aired, Maurice Richardson mourned "the loss of an old friend, Mavick Chen [sic] boss of the Solar System, would-be Emperor of the Universe, victim of his own personality cult, annihilated by the Daleks in a stupendous terminal episode of *Dr Who*."

■ **Arcs in Space** The Daleks began as city-bound despots on the planet Skaro, before becoming world conquerors and then time travellers. *The Daleks' Master Plan* sees them using time itself as a weapon. The road to their role in the Time War – as described in **161** *Dalek* – is now clear.

22 The Massacre of St Bartholomew's Eve

(four episodes) by John Lucarotti, Donald Tosh

Alone in France after the Doctor disappears on a visit to an historical pioneer, Steven is lost in a world as alien to him as any in outer space.

■ **Where and When** Paris, 19-24 August 1572, from the day after the wedding of King Henry of Navarre to Princess Marguerite of France, to the start of a massacre of religious minorities.

■ **The Baddies** Marshall Tavannes (André Morell), Queen Catherine (Joan Young) and the Abbot of Amboise, a clergyman with a remarkable resemblance to the Doctor. Together, they plot to murder a political rival. Ultimately, the ordinary people of Paris assume the roles of villains, as they prepare to slaughter thousands of their fellows with sectarian hatred.

■ **Introducing...** At the end, the TARDIS seemingly guides itself to Dodo Chaplet (Jackie Lane), a 1960s schoolgirl apparently descended from Anne Chaplet (Annette Robertson) – a French girl whom the Doctor left behind in 1572, in case history had plans for her.

■ **Listen out for...** This is a story with overtones of Christian theology. It begins with Steven being turned away from an inn, and ends with the Doctor's seeming resurrection three days after we last saw him.

Space Security Service agent Sara Kingdom (Jean Marsh).

■ **What they said** On 7 February 1966, *The Daily Worker*'s Ann Lawrence wrote: "The programme [is] moving to 16th century Paris... but I fear the Daleks may return yet again. *Doctor Who*, now in its 'third successful year', is definitely showing signs of age and my spies have it that even the youngsters are getting tired of it."

■ **Arcs in Space** An unhappy Doctor ponders returning to "my own planet, but I can't." See **50** *The War Games* and **262** *Hell Bent* for the reasons why.

23 The Ark

(four episodes) by Paul Erickson and Lesley Scott

Dodo brings the common cold to a multi-species civilisation that cured it so long ago they no longer have any immunity. The consequences for its human population are disastrous.

■ **Where and When** A colony ship heading away from the doomed Earth, packed full of its flora and fauna and crewed by both humans and the reptilian Monoids. Halfway through, the TARDIS leaves and immediately returns to the Ark 700 years later, as it approaches its final destination – the planet Refusis II.

■ **The Baddies** The human Guardians take their alien comrades, the Monoids, for granted, and it's hard to blame the latter for revolting, and turning the tables. But after centuries on top, the Monoids are no better than the humans once were. Monoid

Steven befriends Nicholas (David Weston), Anne (Annette Robertson) and Gaston (Eric Thompson) in *The Massacre of St Bartholomew's Eve*.

The Monoids assume control of *The Ark*.

leader 'One' (Edmund Coulter) is explicitly genocidal, even before civil war breaks out.

■ **Look out for...** A real elephant in studio! It looks like it might be stock footage until the Doctor, Steven and Dodo walk over and touch it. Happily for a story about an Ark, the episodes come in two by two.

■ **Where else have I seen...** The Guardian Rhos is played by Michael Sheard, who returned to *Doctor Who* five times – perhaps most memorably in **82** *Pyramids of Mars* and **148** *Remembrance of the Daleks*.

■ **What they said** Producer John Wiles had fond memories of the story when interviewed in *TARDIS* Volume 6, No 1, published in 1981. "I loved the idea of *The Ark*!" he said. "I'm pretty sure this came from me! It's always been one of my joys to imagine the world as a giant spaceship travelling on and on and on."

■ **Arcs in Space** The destruction of the Earth is referred to in **132** *Frontios* and revisited in **158** *The End of the World*. It's possible it's not actually destroyed, just relocated – as seen in **143** *The Trial of a Time Lord*.

24 The Celestial Toymaker

(four episodes) by **Brian Hayles**

The Doctor plays the Trilogic Game against the ruthless Toymaker, while Steven and Dodo face off against his deadly creations in the Celestial Toyroom.

■ **Where and When** "The world of the Celestial Toymaker," says the Doctor. "Nothing is just for fun." This is a mysterious domain outside time and reality, although the Toymaker's knowledge of Victoriana suggests that we are at some point after Earth's 19th century.

■ **The Baddies** The clowns Joey and Clara (Campbell Singer and Carmen Silvera), the King and Queen of Hearts (Campbell Singer and Carmen Silvera), and the Victorian couple Sergeant Rugg and Mrs Wiggs (Campbell Singer and Carmen Silvera). But are they six people or two? And are those people even real?

■ **Look out for...** Dodo's hoop-adorned outfit – so fashionable that pop star Lulu had worn something exactly the same on ITV's *Thank Your Lucky Stars* four months earlier, in January 1966.

■ **Where else have I seen...** The Toymaker was played by Michael Gough, who'd return as Hedin in **123** *Arc of Infinity*. Carmen Silvera (see above) later played Ruth in **71** *Invasion of the Dinosaurs*.

■ **What they said** "Cyril, a bespectacled fat boy whom TV viewers thought looked like Billy Bunter's double has got the BBC into trouble," reported the *Daily Express* on 25 April 1966. They weren't wrong. The murderous Cyril (Peter Stephens) – "known to my friends as Billy" – is wearing a stock costume from *Billy Bunter of Greyfriars School* (1952-61), a series based on the children's books by Frank Richards. The BBC apologised.

■ **Arcs in Space** The Toymaker returned, with a new face, to battle a Doctor with a new/old face in **303** *The Giggle*. Produced 57 years after the original adventure, this belated rematch was another story where the strict rules that bind the Toymaker, and the nature of his own universe, were of vital importance.

Steven and Dodo (Jackie Lane) play the games of the Celestial Toymaker (Michael Gough).

Left
The Doctor, Steven and Dodo encounter Wild West legends Bat Masterson (Richard Beale) and Wyatt Earp (John Alderson) in *The Gunfighters*.

Below inset
Chal (Ewen Solon) in *The Savages*.

25 The Gunfighters

(four episodes) by Donald Cotton
The Doctor has his tooth removed by Doc Holliday and gets caught up in events leading to the legendary gunfight at the OK Corral. Turns out the Wild West isn't quite like it is in the movies…

■ **Where and When** Tombstone, Arizona, USA, 1881.
■ **The Baddies** The Clantons – namely Billy (David Cole), Ike (William Hurndell) and Phineas (Maurice Good) – get the time travellers into deadly trouble as they seek revenge on Doc Holliday (Anthony Jacobs) over the death of their brother Reuben. Holliday isn't a great friend to the Doctor either, hoping a case of mistaken identity means the Clantons will kill the Doctor instead of him.
■ **Farewell to…** This is the final story where each episode has its own individual title until the whole format of *Doctor Who* was rethought with 157 *Rose*.
■ **Look out for…** This is another of the more comedic historical stories, with a song, *The Ballad of the Last Chance Saloon*, used to narrate the action. The highlight, however, is the Doctor calling Tombstone's sheriff, Wyatt Earp (John Alderson), "Mr Wearp", for no apparent reason.
■ **What they said** Bill Norris, writing in *The Stage and Television Today*, 19 May 1966: "I suppose you could say it is a daring experiment… to tell one of the best known legends involving some of the best known characters that have been played by some of Hollywood's greatest actors. I think it was plain foolish."
■ **Arcs in Space** The Doctor visits the Wild West again – this time in Nevada, and 11 years earlier – in 228 *A Town Called Mercy*.

26 The Savages

(four episodes) by Ian Stuart Black
The travellers land on the home planet of an advanced civilisation, the Elders, who have been eagerly awaiting the Doctor's arrival. But is their idyllic existence all it seems?

■ **Where and When** An unknown planet in the far future.
■ **The Baddies** While the seemingly violent Savages wander around outside the city, the Elders are the evil ones here. They've been watching the Doctor's travels from afar – basically they're *Doctor Who* fans. But not nice ones, and when they discover their hero doesn't approve of their way of life, they attempt to drain his life force as they do with the Savages.
■ **Farewell to…** Steven Taylor, who leaves the TARDIS to accept a new role on the planet.
■ **Listen out for…** Frederick Jaeger's wonderful performance as the Elder Jano, after he absorbs the Doctor's life-force and takes on some of his distinctive mannerisms.
■ **Where else have I seen…** Frederick Jaeger and Ewen Solon (playing the 'savage', Chal) both reappear in 81 *Planet of Evil*; Jaeger is also in 92 *The Invisible Enemy*. Claire Jenkins (playing female outsider Nanina) turns up again in 43 *The Wheel in Space*.
■ **Arcs in Space** Does the energy drain suffered by the Doctor contribute to his frail state in 29 *The Tenth Planet*?

27 The War Machines

(four episodes) by Ian Stuart Black
Housed at the top of the Post Office Tower, the new super-computer WOTAN will control all the world's computer systems, for the greater good of humanity. At least, that's the idea…

■ **Where and When** London, 12-20 July 1966.
■ **The Baddies** Will Operating Thought Analogue (WOTAN), created by Professor Brett (John Harvey) with benign intentions, deems humans to be inferior and uses hypnotic powers to covertly control them. It also starts to construct War Machines to take over the world. *Doctor Who* is ahead of the curve here – telephone connections with other computers are the key, 25 years before the World Wide Web opened to the public.
■ **Introducing…** With this story *Doctor Who* returns to contemporary Earth, and with it come cockney sailor Ben Jackson (Michael Craze) and upper-crust secretary Polly (Anneke Wills), epitomising the young, class-fluid world of 1960s London.
■ **Look out for…** The television newsreader reporting on the War Machines' invasion is real-life newsreader Kenneth Kendall – the first person to play themselves in *Doctor Who*.
■ **What they said** "We were still rather overawed by computers back then," said Director Michael Ferguson in **Doctor Who Magazine** issue 185 (April 1992). "They were a daunting concept – something that appeared to have almost human qualities."
■ **Arcs in Space** The TARDIS returns to the exact same time and place in 35 *The Faceless Ones*.

28 The Smugglers

(four episodes) by Brian Hayles
Ben and Polly's first trip in the TARDIS sees them caught between a smuggling ring and pirates searching for hidden treasure. And a dead man has given the Doctor the key to finding that treasure!

The Doctor and Sir Charles (William Mervyn) capture a War Machine.

■ **Where and When** The coast of Cornwall, sometime in the 17th century.
■ **The Baddies** A rum bunch: the bloodthirsty Captain Pike (Michael Godfrey) and his shipmates Cherub (George A Cooper) and Jamaica (Elroy Josephs) once served under the pirate Captain Avery, and are now seeking his gold. Meanwhile local magistrate Squire Edwards (Paul Whitsun-Jones) covertly runs the smuggling operation in the area. As usual in the early historical stories, the Doctor and friends are mostly just trying to get out alive.
■ **Listen out for...** According to Longfoot (Terence de Marney), the names given in a treasure-locating riddle are "Smallwood, Ringwood, Gurney". It should be "Smallbeer" – but later on, the Doctor nevertheless recalls the correct version he hasn't been told. (Somehow.)
■ **Where else have I seen...** John Ringham, playing Josiah Blake, is also in **6** *The Aztecs*, while Paul Whitsun-Jones is in **63** *The Mutants*.
■ **What they said** "We filmed for a week down in Cornwall," Anneke Wills told

Captain Pike (Michael Godfrey) in *The Smugglers*.

DWM issue 322 (October 2002): "It was unusual for *Doctor Who* to leave London, because the programme had such a tiny budget."
■ **Arcs in Space** **215** *The Curse of the Black Spot* is a prequel to this story, outlining what actually happened to Captain Avery...

29 The Tenth Planet

(four episodes) by Kit Pedler and Gerry Davis
A routine space probe is drawn off course. The tracking station monitoring the probe is invaded by cyborg creatures from Earth's long-lost twin planet... creatures who plan to make us like them!

■ **Where and When** The South Pole, 1986.
■ **The Baddies** Mondas developed along parallel lines to Earth, but after the planet drifted away through space, the Mondasians swapped their body parts with artificial replacements and eliminated their emotions – becoming the Cybermen. But Mondas is running out of energy, so they've returned to steal Earth's, and convert its people into Cybermen too.
■ **Introducing...** As well as the Cybermen, this story introduces the concept of regeneration to *Doctor Who*. The Doctor's body is wearing a bit thin, so he gets himself a new one.
■ **Look out for...** The Doctor is a little disengaged from the action in his final story, but he gets one last great moment in Episode 2, when a Cyberman express bafflement at Polly's talk of "feelings". "Emotions,"

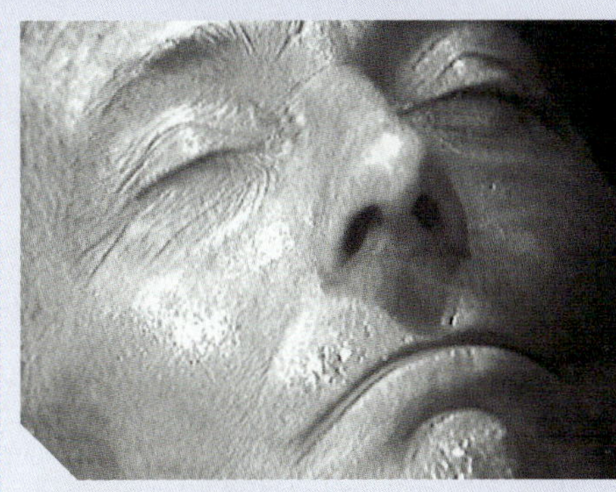

the Doctor clarifies. "Love, pride, hate, fear. Have you no emotions, sir?"
■ **What they said** "It was very exciting to be there at the birth of something new," director Derek Martinus told **DWM** issue 243 (September 1996). "We specifically worked hard on the voice [of the Cybermen], trying to find something a bit different and chilling, getting away from the Dalek sound."
■ **Arcs in Space** Sandra Reid's original Cyberman costume design was dispensed with after this story – but it was gloriously brought back for **275** *World Enough and Time/The Doctor Falls*. Parts of *The Tenth Planet*'s final episode are recreated in **276** *Once Upon a Time*.

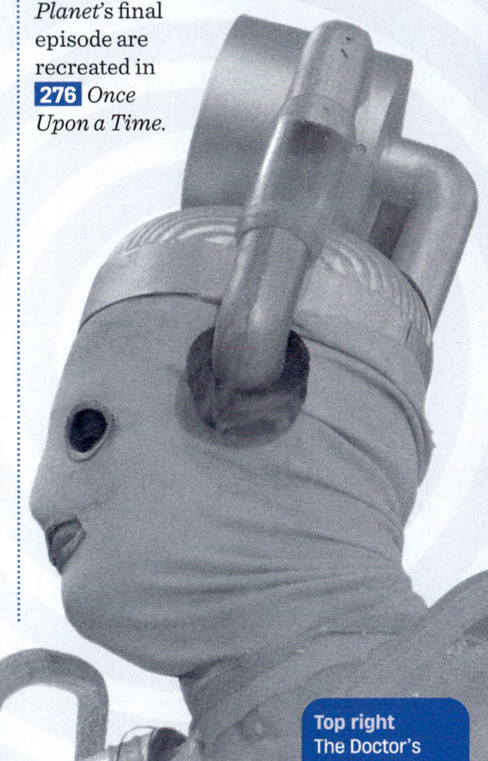

Top right The Doctor's face begins to change, in *The Tenth Planet*.

Above A cloth-masked Mondas Cyberman.

The
SECOND
DOCTOR

Patrick Troughton
Stories 30–50, 1966–69

Worn out by the exertion of his first encounter with the Cybermen, the Doctor was suddenly, shockingly "renewed" – becoming a younger, scruffier, space itinerant, fond of hats and disguises and tootling tunelessly on a school recorder. But his Time Lord past would eventually catch up with him…

The new Doctor (Patrick Troughton) consults his 500 Year Diary in *The Power of the Daleks*.

30 The Power of the Daleks

(six episodes) by David Whitaker
In the the Second Doctor's first adventure, he investigates a murder and uncovers an existential threat to a remote Earth colony.

■ **Where and When** The planet Vulcan, in the future (exact date unspecified).
■ **The Baddies** The Dalek survivors of a crash-landing in a mercury swamp. Cunningly, they feign subservience while constructing a new Dalek race, enabled by power-hungry colonists Bragen (Bernard Archard) and Janley (Pamela Ann Davy).
■ **Introducing...** The Second Doctor (Patrick Troughton), together with his battered felt stovepipe hat, green-tasselled recorder and 500 Year Diary. Rather than describing what has happened to him as 'regeneration', the Doctor simply agrees with Ben's supposition that he's "been renewed."
■ **Look out for...** Although every episode of this serial has been lost, some short clips survive – including parts of the well-remembered 'Dalek production line' sequence in Episode Four, with seven-inch-high push-along Dalek toys (available only at Woolworths, priced 4s 11d each) moving along a conveyor belt.
■ **Farewell to...** The Doctor's signet ring. It falls off his finger after his renewal and Polly picks it up.
■ **Arcs in Space** The Doctor, Ben and Polly travel to another Earth colony in 34 *The Macra Terror*. This early phase of Earth's interplanetary expansionism is also visited in 58 *Colony in Space*, 63 *The Mutants*, 67 *Frontier in Space*, 74 *Planet of the Spiders*, 149 *The Happiness Patrol* and 266 *Smile*.

31 The Highlanders

(four episodes) by Elwyn Jones and Gerry Davis
In the aftermath of the Battle of Culloden, the TARDIS trio fall foul of slave traders... and meet a new friend.

■ **Where and When** Culloden and Inverness, Scotland, April 1746.
■ **The Baddies** Solicitor Grey (David Garth), George III's Commissioner of Prisons – secretly a slave trader operating in collusion with Captain Trask (Dallas Cavell) of the *Annabelle*.
■ **Introducing...** Jacobite piper James Robert McCrimmon (Frazer Hines), who travels in the TARDIS for the next 19 stories. Although he enters the TARDIS at the end of Episode 4, his first sight of the interior appears at the start of 32 *The Underwater Menace*.
■ **Look out for...** Masquerading as a German physician, the Doctor introduces himself to Redcoat Lieutenant Algernon ffinch (Michael Elwyn) as Doctor Von Wer. "Doctor who?" asks ffinch. "That's what I said," the Doctor replies.
■ **Where else have I seen...** Solicitor Grey is portrayed by David Garth, also seen as the Time Lord who comes to Earth to warn of the Master in 55 *Terror of the Autons*. Dallas Cavell, who plays Captain Trask, was previously seen as the criminal Bors in 21 *The Daleks' Master Plan* and later appears as Sir James Quinlan in 53 *The Ambassadors of Death*.

Jamie (Frazer Hines) joins the TARDIS crew in *The Highlanders*.

Text by Chris Bentley

The augmented Fish People of *The Underwater Menace*.

Investigating the source of a plague epidemic at a weather control centre on the Moon, the Doctor and his companions discover it's been infiltrated by the Cybermen.

■ **Where and When** The Moon, 2070.
■ **The Baddies** The Cybermen, now upgraded with silver body suits, solid metal helmets, vacuum tubes and, for some reason, budgie balls. Their earlier sing-song delivery has been replaced with (occasionally unintelligible) monotone electronic speech.
■ **Look out for…** During the Cybermen's takeover of the Gravitron control room, the Doctor thinks through the invaders' actions and we hear both his unspoken thoughts and verbal responses.
■ **Where else have I seen…** Alan Rowe, who plays the unfortunate Dr Evans and provides the voice of Space Control, also appears as Edward of Wessex in **70** *The Time Warrior*, Colonel Skinsale in **92** *Horror of Fang Rock*, and Decider Garif in **111** *Full Circle*.
■ **What they said** "The present futuristic episode of *Dr Who* [sic] is of a much higher quality than we have been used to for some time," wrote Ann Lawrence in *The Morning Star* on 25 January 1967. "The present adventure of the Tardis [sic] has a better-balanced mixture of science and fiction."
■ **Arcs in Space** The Doctor and Jamie return to the Moon to face another monstrous threat to 21st-century Earth's global weather-control systems in **48** *The Seeds of Death*. The Cybermen's tactic of decimating the crew of a space habitat with a 'plague' that attacks the nervous system is repeated on Nerva Beacon in **79** *Revenge of the Cybermen*.

He also has small roles in **8** *The Reign of Terror* and **116** *Castrovalva*.
■ **Arcs in Space** Jamie eventually returns to 18th-century Culloden at the end of **50** *The War Games*. The Doctor visits Scotland again in **80** *Terror of the Zygons*, **169** *Tooth and Claw*, **255** *Under the Lake/ Before the Flood* and **274** *The Eaters of Light*. In *Tooth and Claw*, the Doctor adopts the persona of a Scottish doctor named James McCrimmon.

32 The Underwater Menace

(four episodes) by Geoffrey Orme
A crazed scientist has promised to raise the lost city of Atlantis from the sea, but the Doctor discovers that his plan involves draining the Atlantic through a bore hole in the Earth's crust, thereby destroying the world!

■ **Where and When** Atlantis in the North Atlantic Ocean, 1970 – or at least some time after the 1968 Mexico Olympics. Polly suggests 1970, and we're given no reason to doubt her.
■ **The Baddies** Barking mad Professor Zaroff (Joseph Fürst) – nothing in the world can stop him.
■ **Look out for…** The Atlantis power station set includes a countdown timer with a distinctive misaligned number 2. It previously appeared as a Dalek rel counter in the 1966 movie *Daleks' Invasion Earth 2150 A.D.* An almost identical counter (one with correctly aligned numerals and no 'rel' label) can be seen in **27** *The War Machines*.

■ **Farewell to…** The Doctor's stovepipe hat, seen for the last time when worn by Polly in the TARDIS at the end of the story.
■ **Where else have I seen…** Atlantean surgeon Damon – who tries to give Polly gills – is played by Colin Jeavons, who also appears as Hecate cultist George Tracey in *K9 and Company: A Girl's Best Friend* (1981). Noel Johnson, who portrays King Thous, is later seen as misguided politician Sir Charles Grover in **71** *Invasion of the Dinosaurs*.
■ **Arcs in Space** In **59** *The Dæmons*, Azal claims that his people destroyed Atlantis as a failed experiment. The Doctor also visits another Atlantis that was part of the ancient Minoan civilisation in **64** *The Time Monster*.

33 The Moonbase

(four episodes) by Kit Pedler

34 The Macra Terror

(four episodes) by **Ian Stuart Black**
The Doctor, Polly, Ben and Jamie are welcomed to a colony world that feels more like a holiday camp. But one of the colonists insists he sees horrifying creatures at night…

■ **Where and When** An unnamed colony world in the far future, date unknown.
■ **The Baddies** The Macra, giant crablike beings that feed on poisonous gas. They've brainwashed the human colonists to mine it for them, and no one is allowed to admit they exist. Ben falls victim to their conditioning, and is soon intoning "There are no such things as Macra…"
■ **Introducing…** This was the first time the Doctor's face appeared in the opening title sequence. So it's a shame that these are among the series' 'lost' episodes.
■ **Look out for…** The Second Doctor is more irreverent and anarchic than his predecessor. After calculating a secret formula, he awards himself ten out of ten. Subsequently, when colony boss the Pilot (Peter Jeffrey) says he must have seen a copy of the formula because it's the *exact* computation, the Doctor changes his mark to eleven out of ten.
■ **What they said** Interviewed in **Doctor Who Magazine** issue 170 (February 1991), Ian Stuart Black said: "The Macra needed to live in an atmosphere that was destructive to humanity, and that contrast was a simple idea that interested me as a writer."
■ **Arcs in Space** The Macra don't give up that easily, and can be found infesting another human colony in **181** *Gridlock*.

35 The Faceless Ones

(six episodes) by **David Ellis** and **Malcolm Hulke**
After the TARDIS lands on a runway at Gatwick Airport, the Doctor discovers that young passengers who book flights via Chameleon Tours aren't coming home…

■ **Where and When** Gatwick Airport, 20 July 1966.

An untreated Chameleon in *The Faceless Ones*.

■ **The Baddies** The Chameleons, alien beings who've lost their faces and identities in a gigantic explosion. Being "the most intelligent race in the universe" (in their own opinion), they devised a way of stealing the identities of others – and so naturally they came to 1960s London to take on the identities of the capital's hip youngsters.
■ **Farewell to…** Ben and Polly, who return to London on the day they first stepped into the TARDIS in **27** *The War Machines*.
■ **Look out for…** Towards the end of Episode 4, there's a jaw-dropping moment when Chameleon Tours Flight 419 turns into a rocket… and shoots straight up into space.
■ **Where else have I seen…** Pauline Collins, playing chirpy Scouser Samantha Briggs – one of the greatest 'companions who never were' – reappears as Queen Victoria in **169** *Tooth and Claw*.
■ **Arcs in Space** London is certainly a happening place in July 1966. As well as WOTAN's attempt to take over the world, the Daleks are plotting to steal the TARDIS, setting up the events of the subsequent adventure…

A deadly gas-breathing Macra.

36 The Evil of the Daleks

(seven episodes) by **David Whitaker**
The Doctor and Jamie are drawn through time to Victorian England, where the Daleks have a task for their greatest enemy – he must identify the 'Human Factor' that has always led to their defeat…

■ **Where and When** London, 20 July 1966. A house near Canterbury, 2-3 June 1866. The planet Skaro, date unknown.
■ **The Baddies** The Daleks have made contact with Victorian scientist Edward Waterfield (John Bailey) and his benefactor Theodore Maxtible (Marius Goring) as part of a plot to ensnare the Doctor… one that will ultimately bring him face to face with the Emperor Dalek.
■ **Introducing…** Edward's daughter Victoria (Deborah Watling), who's become a pawn in the Daleks' game – and joins the Doctor and Jamie in the TARDIS at the end.
■ **Look out for…** The Doctor playfully naming three Daleks Alpha, Beta and Omega – a small action that has major consequences.
■ **What they said** Quoted in **DWM** issue 98 (March 1985), David Whitaker said: "Although it was intended to be the final Dalek story, because [their creator] Terry Nation wanted to launch them in America, I didn't really think they'd be gone for good."
■ **Arcs in Space** When the Doctor leads the human survivors on Skaro down a tunnel into the Dalek city, Jamie remarks

Text by Eddie Robson

The Cybermen emerge from their icy tombs.

37 The Tomb of the Cybermen

(four episodes) by Kit Pedler and Gerry Davis

An archaeological survey team from Earth has landed on Telos in search of the last remains of the Cybermen. But as the tomb is uncovered, members of the party start to die…

The Dalek Emperor made its first appearance in *The Evil of the Daleks*.

"How long have you known that's there?" He's known it since **2** *The Mutants* (aka *The Daleks*).

■ **Where and When** Telos, the 26th century.

■ **The Baddies** Kleig (George Pastell) and Kaftan (Shirley Cooklin), members of the Brotherhood of Logicians, have joined the expedition with the secret aim of forging an alliance with the Cybermen and taking over Earth. It would seem they've not researched the Cybermen's modus operandi that well.

■ **Introducing…** The Cybermats – cybernetic rodents used as sneaky servants by the Cybermen. They reappear in **43** *The Wheel in Space*, **79** *Revenge of the Cybermen* and **223** *Closing Time*. A Cyberman Controller (Michael Kilgarriff), whose enlarged head differentiates him from the rank-and-file, also debuts.

■ **Look out for…** A touching scene in the midst of the action sees the Doctor talking to Victoria about his family, comforting her on the loss of hers, and holding out promise for the future: "Our lives are different to anybody else's. That's the exciting thing. There's nobody in the universe can do what we're doing."

■ **What they said** "I think it was really where the Cybermen came into their own," story editor Victor Pemberton told **DWM** in issue 184 (March 1992). "The kids of the day were certainly quite scared of them."

■ **Arcs in Space** The Doctor returns to the ice tombs of Telos in **137** *Attack of the Cybermen* – a sequel to both this story and **29** *The Tenth Planet*.

38 The Abominable Snowmen

(six episodes) by Mervyn Haisman and Henry Lincoln

The Doctor seeks to return a holy relic to the Himalayan monastery where it belongs. But the monks have other concerns – the Yeti that live in the mountains have turned savage!

■ **Where and When** Tibet, 1935.

■ **The Baddies** The Great Intelligence, a formless, powerful being of unknown origin. It has possessed Padmasambhava (Wolfe Morris), the Master of Det-sen monastery, and has constructed robot Yeti to do its bidding.

■ **Introducing…** Professor Travers (Jack Watling), an explorer seeking the Yeti, who is initially antagonistic to the Doctor, believing he's a newspaper reporter. Travers reappears in **41** *The Web of Fear*, where he'll be hostile to an *actual* journalist.

■ **Look out for…** The Doctor's reaction to Jamie having an idea: "Victoria, I think this is one of those instances where discretion is the better part of valour."

■ **What they said** Co-writer Mervyn Haisman told **DWM** in issue 268 (August 1998): "We decided to develop an idea about which people knew, but which had never been proved – a bit like the Loch Ness Monster. 'What about Yeti?' we thought, and it took off from there."

■ **Arcs in Space** The Doctor's familiarity with Tibetan culture comes back to the fore in **74** *Planet of the Spiders*.

A Martian with the sonic cannon used to menace mankind, in *The Ice Warriors*.

39 The Ice Warriors

(six episodes) by **Brian Hayles**

Scientists drilling in a glacier discover Varga, the commander of a buried Martian spaceship. Varga wants the humans to use their heat-focusing Ioniser to set his spaceship free.

■ **Where and When** Britannicus Base – a scientific establishment inside a Georgian mansion, within a protective dome in the frozen wastelands of Europe, over 3,000 years in the future.

■ **The Baddies** The Martians are given the name 'Ice Warriors' by one member of the base. Large humanoid reptilians with shell-like armour and sonic guns, they are led by the determined but rational Commander Varga (Bernard Bresslaw). The rest of the warriors are brutal killers, however.

■ **Introducing…** As well as being the debut of the Ice Warriors, this story has the TARDIS landing on its side for the first time – with the doors opening outwards.

■ **Look out for…** The fabulous futuristic costumes of the Britannicus Base crew members.

■ **What they said** In **Doctor Who Magazine** issue 243 (September 1996), director Derek Martinus described hiring comedy star Bernard Bresslaw to play Varga. "It was the first time that a 'name' actor had gotten into make-up as a monster," he recalled. "He laughed along with the cast and crew, of course, but his patience got a bit tested. He would say, 'You ought to try this bleedin' helmet on, mate! Not very comfortable, I tell you! Bloody hot!'"

■ **Arcs in Space** This is the first of many stories to feature the Ice Warriors – although all of them are explicitly set *before* this adventure takes place, making it a bit of a mystery why nobody recognises them. Jamie's line "I think you've just put us down further up the mountain" refers directly to the preceding story, 38 *The Abominable Snowmen*.

40 The Enemy of the World

(six episodes) by **David Whitaker**

Leader Salamander is one of the most popular people on Earth, having saved the world from starvation. But he has ambitions of becoming a global dictator… and looks exactly like the Doctor.

■ **Where and When** The story begins on a beach in Australia, before moving to the President's Palace in Hungary, then it's back to Australia and the Research Centre in Kenowa. The year is 2018.

■ **The Baddies** The earthquake-generating Salamander (Patrick Troughton) is a swarthy, urbane man originating from Yucatan, Mexico. His charming veneer conceals a ruthless interior. He is aided by the wily sadist Benik (Milton Johns).

■ **Introducing…** This is the first story to be recorded in the higher-definition format of 625 lines (as opposed to 405), although BBC1 wouldn't begin transmitting in 625 until November 1969.

■ **Look out for…** The scene where the Doctor is reunited with Jamie and Victoria in Episode 5, where Patrick Troughton switches from the Doctor pretending to be Salamander back to the Doctor in an instant.

■ **Where else have I seen…** Milton Johns would return as two more craven opportunists – Guy Crayford in 83 *The Android Invasion* and Castellan Kelner in 98 *The Invasion of Time*.

■ **Arcs in Space** The story ends on a cliffhanger, with the TARDIS in flight and

The Doctor's evil double Salamander in *The Enemy of the World*.

The Yeti corner Captain Knight (Ralph Watson), Staff Sgt Arnold (Jack Woolgar), Jamie and Cpl Lane (Rod Beacham) in *The Web of Fear*.

the exterior doors open. Much to his alarm, the Doctor mishears "Disused jetty" as "Disused Yeti" – referring back to **38** *The Abominable Snowmen*.

41 The Web of Fear

(six episodes) by Mervyn Haisman and Henry Lincoln

Londoners flee! Menace spreads! Only a small band of soldiers remain behind to face the monstrous Yeti. Meanwhile, the Great Intelligence sets a trap for the Doctor.

■ **Where and When** The tunnels and stations of the London Underground, including a Second World War 'fortress' based at Goodge Street station. The date is the near future – sometime after 1975.

■ **The Baddies** The Yeti return, now with glowing eyes and larger claws, to enable them to operate their new cobweb-spraying guns. Once again, they're directed by the Great Intelligence, acting through a possessed human but also manifesting as a deadly mist and a pulsating, web-like fungus.

■ **Introducing...** Episode 3 marks the first appearance of Alistair Gordon Lethbridge-Stewart (Nicholas Courtney) – later promoted to Brigadier on attachment to UNIT, but here serving as a Colonel in the regular army.

■ **Where else have I seen...** Nicholas Courtney had previously assisted the Doctor in the guise of Space Security Agent Bret Vyon, in the first four episodes of **21** *The Daleks' Master Plan*.

■ **Look out for...** The most nightmarish moment is Driver Evans (Derek Pollitt) recovering the cobweb-coated corpse of Corporal Lane (Rod Beacham).

■ **Arcs in Space** It's over 40 years since the events of **38** *The Abominable Snowmen*, with Professor Travers (Jack Watling) now an elderly man. The Doctor and his friends attempt to visit the Professor and his daughter Anne (Tina Packer) in **46** *The Invasion*, while the Great Intelligence returns in **231** *The Snowmen* – in which the Eleventh Doctor gives it the idea of invading the London Underground!

42 Fury from the Deep

(six episodes) by Victor Pemberton

Euro Sea Gas fuels the whole of the south of England and Wales – but they're losing contact with their rigs, and there's a strange 'heartbeat' coming from inside the pipes...

■ **Where and When** The high-security Euro Sea Gas refinery, plus its residential block and beach, and the control rig complex in the North Sea. The time is the near future.

■ **The Baddies** A colonial weed-like organism with the ability to possess human beings and give them the power to survive underwater and exhale poison gas. The organism intends to take over the world, beginning with the gas rigs, then the British Isles.

■ **Look out for...** The most chilling moment from the story is, happily, one of the few clips that exist – as the sinister Mr Oak (John Gill) and Mr Quill (Bill Burridge) visit Maggie Harris (June Murphy) at home and knock her out by breathing poison gas.

■ **Introducing...** At the beginning of the story the Doctor uses a new gadget to unscrew an inspection box on a section of pipeline – the sonic screwdriver!

■ **Farewell to...** Although she appears briefly on the TARDIS scanner at the beginning of **42** *The Wheel in Space*, this story marks Victoria Waterfield's departure from the series.

■ **Arcs in Space** Victoria notes that the TARDIS always seems to land on Earth, referring to the previous four stories, while the idea of the TARDIS taking off vertically is reprised in **178** *The Runaway Bride*.

Left inset The terrifying Mr Quill (Bill Burridge) attacks in *Fury from the Deep*.

Left The Doctor and Victoria (Deborah Watling) detect a heartbeat in the gas pipeline.

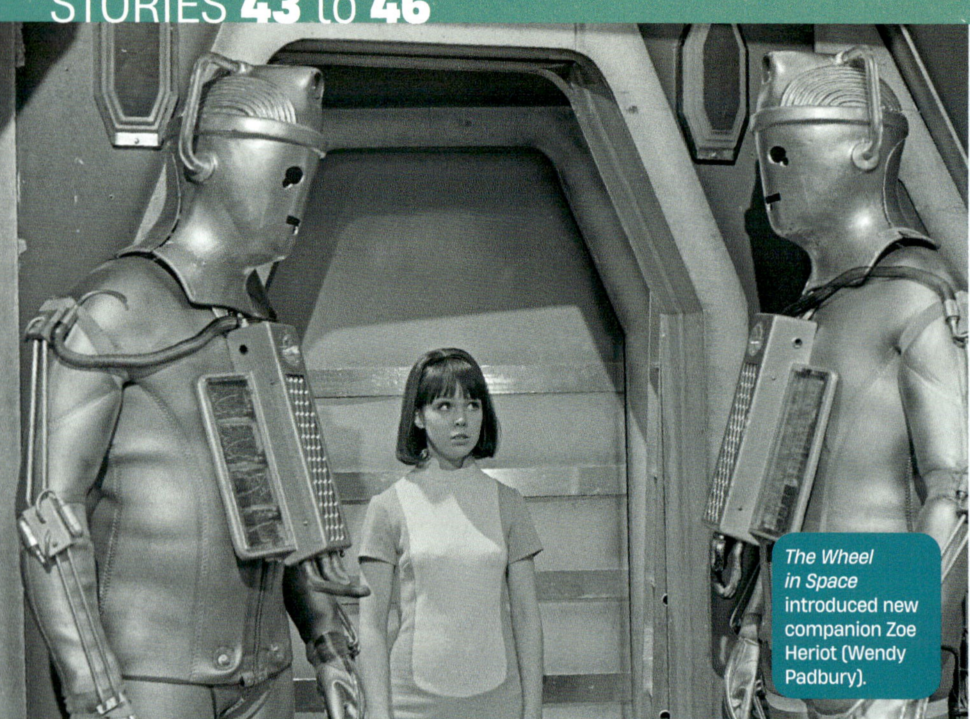

The *Wheel in Space* introduced new companion Zoe Heriot (Wendy Padbury).

43 The Wheel in Space

(six episodes) by David Whitaker
The TARDIS lands on a deserted spaceship. When it drifts close to a space station, the Doctor and Jamie realise this is all part of a plot by the Cybermen…

■ **Where and When** The *Silver Carrier* and Space Station W3, known as the Wheel, in Earth's solar system. It's the 21st century.
■ **The Baddies** The Cybermen are back with another plan to take over the Earth. You'll need to pay attention, though, as this one's rather convoluted. You have to wonder if the Cyber Planner's algorithms have got corrupted somewhere.
■ **Introducing…** Zoe Heriot (Wendy Padbury), a young genius who's been hothoused through her education and assigned to work in the Wheel's parapsychology library.
■ **Look out for…** After a TARDIS mishap leads to scenes reminiscent of **3** *Inside the Spaceship* (aka *The Edge of Destruction*), the Doctor removes the time vector generator – which reduces the interior to the size of an ordinary police box.
■ **Where else have I seen…** Donald Sumpter, playing radio operator Enrico Casali, is promoted to naval commander Ridgeway in **62** *The Sea Devils*, ultimately ascending to the post of Time Lord president Rassilon in **262** *Hell Bent*.
■ **Arcs in Space** At the end, the Doctor decides to show Zoe one of his old adventures on the TARDIS scanner – **36** *The Evil of the Daleks*, which was repeated in *Doctor Who*'s summer break. The Wheel is revisited briefly in **50** *The War Games*, in which Russian 'astrogator' Tanya Lernov (Clare Jenkins) also reappears.

44 The Dominators

(five episodes) by Norman Ashby
The Doctor assures his companions that the peaceful planet of Dulkis is ideal for a holiday – but Dulkis and its passive inhabitants have been targeted by the bloodthirsty Dominators.

■ **Where and When** The planet Dulkis, date unknown.
■ **The Baddies** The humourless, aggressive Dominators, Toba and Rago, are members of a civilisation that proclaims itself "Masters of the Ten Galaxies". Their colonisation kit includes robotic servants known as Quarks.
■ **Introducing…** Jelly babies – we think. The Doctor eats sweets from a crumpled paper bag, and we know from **65** *The Three Doctors* that the Second Doctor carries this confectionery item more typically associated with the Fourth. But we don't get a clear look at the sweets.
■ **Look out for…** The Doctor and Jamie's amazing double-act as they deliberately fail the Dominators' intelligence test. The part where Jamie grabs the Doctor and passes the electric shock onto him is a particular highlight.
■ **What they said** *The Dominators* was written by Yeti creators Mervyn Haisman and Henry Lincoln, who took their names off it following disputes over rewrites. "The idea was influenced by the flower power and 'love conquers everything' philosophy of the time," Haisman said in **Doctor Who Magazine** issue 268 (July 1998). "What would happen if some Attila the Hun appeared on the scene and wiped the whole bloody lot of you out?"
■ **Arcs in Space** The Daleks are fond of creating volcanic eruptions in a similar style to the Dominators – as seen in **10** *The Dalek Invasion of Earth* and **300** *The Power of the Doctor*.

45 The Mind Robber

(five episodes) by Peter Ling
An emergency take-off sends the TARDIS into a place populated by fictional characters and creatures, all controlled by a mysterious Master.

■ **Where and When** "We're nowhere," says the Doctor, "it's as simple as that." A void outside of time and space, and the Land of Fiction.

Text by Eddie Robson

"This world that we've tumbled into is a world of fiction."
THE DOCTOR

■ **The Baddies** The Master (Emrys James), a prolific writer of children's adventure fiction, has been ensnared by the Master Brain, a computer of unknown origin with megalomaniac ambitions.

■ **Introducing…** Zoe's glittery catsuit. It only appears in this story and **46** *The Invasion*, but it's still one of the most iconic outfits in *Doctor Who*, and a cosplay favourite.

■ **Look out for…** The end of Episode 1, in which the TARDIS breaks up and Jamie and Zoe are left clinging to the console as it spins through the void, is a shocking moment for audiences used to the TARDIS being a safe space – and it's brilliantly realised, despite the show's limited resources.

■ **What they said** After **44** *The Dominators* was cut down by one episode, a new opening episode for *The Mind Robber* had to be created. "It came to me to fill this one-episode gap – with no money, no sets other than our stock ones, and no actors," script editor Derrick Sherwin told **DWM** in 1983. "I had to create the whole story from scratch on an empty white set."

Strange White Robots surround Jamie and Zoe in *The Mind Robber*.

■ **Arcs in Space** Blackbeard (Gerry Wain) and D'Artagnan (John Greenwood) were historical figures who were heavily mythologised – which underlines the story's point about how real people can become subsumed by fiction. Similar issues come to the fore in **244** *Robot of Sherwood*.

46 The Invasion

(eight episodes) by Derrick Sherwin
Back on Earth, the Doctor, Jamie and Zoe encounter a sinister global electronics company, and their concerns are shared by a new paramilitary organisation. The Cybermen are seeking to invade again!

■ **Where and When** London and its environs, four years after **41** *The Web of Fear*. (The UNIT stories are set in the very near future at time of broadcast, but the date is never pinned down.)

■ **The Baddies** The Cybermen have forged an alliance with electronics magnate Tobias Vaughan (Kevin Stoney), planting hypnotic circuits in equipment made by his company, International Electromatics. With this, they will take over the world!

■ **Introducing…** UNIT – the United Nations Intelligence Taskforce. Lethbridge-Stewart has been drafted in to run this international military group, tasked with investigating unusual and extraterrestrial threats… and he's been promoted to Brigadier.

■ **Look out for…** We're used to our heroes being menaced by relentless, emotionless Cybermen, so the end of Episode Five, where they encounter a crazed, screaming Cyberman in the sewers, is startling and disturbing.

■ **What they said** Ralph Slater in the *Reading Evening Post* on 9 December 1968: "*Doctor Who* continues a shatteringly high level of inventiveness. Sometimes I think that children can't appreciate all that goes into it."

■ **Arcs in Space** At the end of Episode 6, the Cybermen march down the steps from St Paul's Cathedral – and they'll do so again in **252** *Dark Water/ Death in Heaven*.

Left The cruel Dominators – Rago (Ronald Allen) and Toba (Kenneth Ives).

Opposite page inset One of the Dominators' robotic Quark servants.

A Kroton seeks the TARDIS.

47 The Krotons

(four episodes) by Robert Holmes
Once a year the Gond people send their brightest students to be "companions of the Krotons" – the ostensibly beneficent overlords they've never seen. But where do the "companions" really go?

■ **Where and When** The unnamed planet of the Gonds, date unknown.
■ **The Baddies** The titular Krotons – clawed, crystal-headed robots, who have a nuclear space empire and want to get back to it.
■ **Farewell to…** 1960s *Doctor Who* is noted for its monsters – so it's worth pointing out that the Krotons are the last new monsters of the decade. For the remaining five months of the 1960s, the show will have old monsters, or no monsters at all.
■ **Look out for…** At the end of Episode Three, Beta (James Cairncross) manages to be in two places at once; he's in his house making acid, and simultaneously in the Underhall as its roof comes down.
■ **Where else have I seen…** Philip Madoc, playing the shifty Eelek, will be back in just 20 episodes' time, as the War Lord in **50** *The War Games*. He'll reappear as a mad surgeon in **84** *The Brain of Morbius*, then as a methane refiner in **103** *The Power of Kroll*.
■ **Arcs in Space** The TARDIS activates the Hostile Action Displacement System (HADS) in order to avoid being destroyed by a Kroton. Reset years later, it'll trap the Eleventh Doctor and Clara in a Soviet nuclear submarine, in **234** *Cold War*.

Later still, its accidental activation will trap the Fourteenth Doctor and Donna at the edge of the universe in **302** *Wild Blue Yonder*… with consequences for all of reality.

48 The Seeds of Death

(six episodes) by Brian Hayles
On 21st-century Earth, T-Mat is the ultimate form of travel – it's abolished the motor car and killed off humanity's interest in outer space. But what if outer space is interested in humans?

■ **Where and When** From the Earth to the Moon and back again, via T-Mat and rocket.
■ **The Baddies** The Martian warrior species encountered in **39** *The Ice Warriors*. This time they're planning to take over the Earth and reconfigure its biosphere to their needs.
■ **Introducing…** The Martians are led by Slaar (right) – a slimmer-than-usual, and more talkative, aristocrat. Further members of this 'officer class' will reappear in **61** *The Curse of Peladon* and **73** *The Monster of Peladon* (all of them played by Alan Bennion).

■ **Look out for…** Professor Eldred's museum of space travel contains several props from previous stories, including the TARDIS' astral map from **13** *The Web Planet* and **18** *Galaxy 4*. How did Eldred (Philip Ray) come by that?!
■ **Where else have I seen…** Harry Towb, playing moonbase technician Osgood, will later be smothered to death by a plastic armchair in **55** *Terror of the Autons*. But is this Osgood a descendant of the technically minded 20th-century Osgood clan, seen in **59** *The Dæmons* and **240** *The Day of the Doctor*, among others?
■ **Arcs in Space** The moonbase may be the same one from **33** *The Moonbase*, with a more sophisticated version of its weather-control system.

49 The Space Pirates

(six episodes) by Robert Holmes
Space pirates are roaming the galaxy, exploding navigational beacons and stripping the wreckage for minerals. The Space Corps are desperate to find them.

■ **Where and When** Aboard the orbital beacons targeted by the pirates; on planet Ta, in the fourth galactic quadrant, where the pirates have their base; and on spaceships travelling between the two. We're at some point in humanity's future – far enough ahead that humans can live outside Earth's solar system.
■ **The Baddies** Swaggering murderer Caven (Dudley Foster) leads the pirates, conspiring with industrialist Madeleine Issigri (Lisa Daniely) to fence their booty.

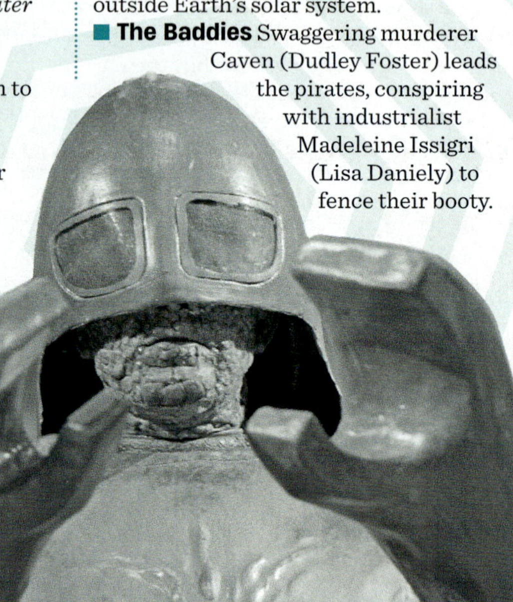

Space pirates Dervish (Brian Peck) and Caven (Dudley Foster).

The Doctor struggles to evade the Time Lords in *The War Games*.

■ **Where else have I seen…** Following his appearance as Space Corps Major Warne in this penultimate Second Doctor story, Donald Gee played the villainous Eckersley in the penultimate Third Doctor story, **52** *The Monster of Peladon*.

■ **Listen out for…** At the end of Episode Three, the TARDIS crew drop into a hole, their screams echoing as they fall a long way down. At the start of Episode Four, we discover it's quite a shallow hole, and their screams are appropriately much shorter!

■ **What they said** Writing in *The Spectator* on 14 February 1969, Stuart Hood was impressed with the story's space-walking sequences: "The effect was so excellently simulated that for a moment or two I was undecided whether what I saw was not perhaps a piece of documentary film fed into the programme."

■ **Arcs in Space** Having been talked down to by Zoe for seven stories straight, Jamie gets his own back when she doesn't recognise candles, and tells her to eat more porridge when she can't open a door.

50 The War Games

(ten episodes) by **Terrance Dicks** and **Malcolm Hulke**

'The War Games' are an alien experiment to recreate historical human conflicts – but ending them will mean an end to the Doctor's time and space travels.

■ **Where and When** Ostensibly the Western Front in 1917, Roman Britain and the American Civil War, among many others – but really, on the unnamed planet selected as the setting for the War Games.

"You have returned to us, Doctor. Your travels are over."

TIME LORD

■ **The Baddies** The War Lord (Philip Madoc), his deputy the War Chief (Edward Brayshaw), his rival the Security Chief (James Bree), plus Generals Smythe (Noel Coleman) and Von Weich (David Garfield) – all of them aliens conducting the War Games.

■ **Introducing…** The Time Lords. First said to be the War Chief's people, they're later revealed to be from the Doctor's home planet as well – which we also travel to, although we won't find out its name until **70** *The Time Warrior*.

■ **Look out for…** Some of the same location footage is used to show two separate Roman attacks, one bridging episodes Two and Three, and another during Episode Seven.

"Isn't this where we were attacked by the Romans?" asks Lieutenant Carstairs (David Savile). Cheeky!

■ **Farewell to…** Jamie and Zoe are returned home by the Time Lords, having had their memories of their travels with the Doctor taken from them. Not a dry eye in the house.

■ **Arcs in Space** *The War Games* is both an end and a beginning – giving answers to questions raised as far back as **1** *100,000 BC* (aka *An Unearthly Child*) and resulting in the Doctor being exiled to 20th-century Earth for the crime of interfering in the affairs of other planets… his new face pending.

The THIRD DOCTOR

Jon Pertwee
Stories 51–74, 1970–74

Exiled to a near-future England, the new, frilly-shirted Doctor ended up scientific adviser to the paramilitary UNIT organisation, defending the world against alien attack. But this was more than a dandified dilettante with a fondness for vintage cars and a line in Venusian karate; he possessed a deep moral sensibility, too.

51 Spearhead from Space

(four episodes) by Robert Holmes

With his appearance changed by the Time Lords, the Doctor is exiled to present-day Earth. He's soon recruited by Brigadier Lethbridge-Stewart to help UNIT fight the Auton invasion.

■ **Where and When** UNIT dating notwithstanding, we're in the south of England, near London, sometime in the 1970s.

■ **The Baddies** The Nestene Consciousness – an extraterrestrial, disembodied gestalt intelligence, although "their basic form is analogous to a cephalopod" (as we'll learn in 55 *Terror of the Autons*.) They can create things that kill from plastic – predominantly, mannequin automatons the Autons.

■ **Introducing…** The Third Doctor (Jon Pertwee) – the action-hero dandy who'll be with us for the next 128 episodes. Also: Dr Liz Shaw (Caroline John), the Doctor's new companion, whose fearsome intellect is matched only by her fabulous dress sense.

"We deal with the odd, the unexplained – anything on Earth, or even beyond."

THE BRIGADIER

■ **Look out for…** The commissionaire in UNIT's underground car park is played by outgoing series producer Derrick Sherwin.

■ **What they said** *Daily Mirror* TV critic Matthew Coady, writing on 26 January 1970: "This *Doctor Who* adventure wins my vote as the best in the lifetime of the series so far. What it did was to suggest an authentic sense of the uncanny."

■ **Arcs in Space** The "two attempts to invade this planet", mentioned by the Brigadier in Episode 1, refer to 41 *The Web of Fear* and 46 *The Invasion*. This story is the first to establish that the Doctor has two hearts. It's also the first occasion the Doctor states he isn't human. The Nestenes/Autons will return in 55 *Terror of the Autons*, later becoming the monsters chosen to launch 21st-century *Doctor Who* in *Rose*.

52 Doctor Who and the Silurians

(seven episodes) by Malcolm Hulke

Lizard people from the dawn of time? Earth's original inhabitants have woken up and want their planet back. The Doctor thinks they have a point.

■ **Where and When** Shortly after the events of 51 *Spearhead from Space*. The majority of the action takes place at Wenley Moor, which, according to 62 *The Sea Devils*, is in Derbyshire.

■ **The Baddies** The Silurians – Earth reptiles who were the dominant species 200 million years ago (so not the actual Silurian era).

■ **Introducing…** Bessie, the Doctor's car! She'll appear regularly until *Robot*, and then make guest appearances in 129 *The Five Doctors* and 152 *Battlefield*.

■ **Look out for…** In Episode 4, the Doctor and Liz encounter the dinosaur on guard – the first use of CSO (Colour Separation Overlay, also known as chromakey) in the series.

■ **Where else have I seen…** Major Baker is Norman Jones, also seen in 38 *The Abominable Snowmen* and 86 *The Masque of Mandragora*. Dr Lawrence actor Peter Miles is in 71 *Invasion of*

Left
A dashing new Doctor (Jon Pertwee) makes his debut in *Spearhead from Space*.

Above inset
An Auton readies its 'wrist gun'.

the Dinosaurs and **78** *Genesis of the Daleks*. This is also the first appearance of Geoffrey Palmer, here playing Masters. He'll turn up again in **63** *The Mutants* and **189** *Voyage of the Damned*. Also look out for Captain Hawkins actor Paul Darrow in **141** *Timelash*.

■ **Arcs in Space** The Silurians will be revived in 50 years, as seen in **209** *The Hungry Earth/Cold Blood*, though they'll next appear in **130** *Warriors of the Deep*. One of their number, Madame Vastra (Neve McIntosh), will become a semi-regular between **218** *A Good Man Goes to War* and **242** *Deep Breath*.

53 The Ambassadors of Death

(seven episodes) by **David Whitaker**
Alien invaders from Mars? Not exactly. The threat is rather closer to home…

■ **Where and When** Space Control and surrounding areas. Seemingly in the south of England, shortly after the events of **52** *Doctor Who and the Silurians*.
■ **The Baddies** The aliens certainly kill (they are, after all, the Ambassadors of Death), but they're not the baddies. That sobriquet goes instead to xenophobic soldier General Carrington (John Abineri) and his suave deputy Reegan (William Dysart).

Bromley (Ian Fairbairn) is infected by the primordial slime released in *Inferno*.

■ **Look out for…** The all-action set-piece hijack of the *Recovery 7* capsule in Episode 2. Amid the mayhem, a UNIT soldier tries to board the baddies' helicopter. He's played by HAVOC stunt agency head Derek Ware – who'd been one of the UNIT men shot point blank in a warehouse in Episode 1!
■ **Introducing** As the story opens, the Doctor has installed the TARDIS console in his (new) lab at UNIT HQ – meaning we see it in its original camera flare-preventing colour scheme for the first time. Who knew it wasn't white, but off-green?
■ **Where else have I seen…** Arch traitor General Carrington is John Abineri, also seen as Van Lutyens in **42** *Fury from the Deep*, Railton in **72** *Death to the Daleks* and Ranquin in **102** *The Power of Kroll*.
■ **Arcs in Space** Corporal Benton (John Levene) from **46** *The Invasion* is now a Sergeant – promoted after the death of Sergeant Hart (Richard Steele) in the preceding adventure, perhaps? The next UK Mars mission we know about is the scheduled landing of the unmanned *Guinevere One* probe on Mars on Christmas Day, two or three decades later (as seen in **167** *The Christmas Invasion*).

54 Inferno

(seven episodes)
by **Don Houghton**
Seeking a new power source, the UK government is behind an experiment to bore deep into the Earth. But it unleashes a mysterious force that could destroy the world twice over…

■ **Where and When** The drill site of Project Inferno. Seemingly England in the 1970s… and the same on an alternative Earth!
■ **The Baddies** People exposed to a green slime brought up by the drilling regress into savage Primords (though they're not named as such on screen) – super-hot, super-strong fanged humanoids. Ruthless project head Professor Stahlman (Olaf Pooley). Worst of all, the Brigadier's alternative-universe counterpart – the eyepatch-wearing Brigade-Leader.
■ **Introducing…** Venusian karate – the alien martial arts technique used by the Doctor against Stahlman in Episode 2. Later, it'll be called 'Venusian aikido' and even "Venusian ooja"!
■ **Where else have I seen…** Derek Newark, oil-rigger Gregg Sutton here, was in **1** *100,000 BC*, which also features lots of primate humans. Sir Keith Gold actor Christopher Benjamin will turn up later as Henry Gordon Jago in **91** *The Talons of Weng-Chiang* and Colonel Hugh in **194** *The Unicorn and the Wasp*.
■ **Farewell to…** Dr Liz Shaw. She doesn't get a departure scene, but in **55** *Terror of the Autons* we'll learn she returned to Cambridge. Also: the original TARDIS console. It'll be a new prop when we next see it in **57** *The Claws of Axos*.
■ **Arcs in Space** The footage of a volcano erupting, used for the title sequence, was also seen in **40** *The Enemy of the World* and **64** *The Time Monster*. The Doctor will also visit a parallel Earth in **172** *Rise of the Cybermen/The Age of Steel*.

> **"That jackanapes! All he ever does is cause trouble."** THE DOCTOR

55 Terror of the Autons

(four episodes) by Robert Holmes
The Nestenes have returned, and this time they have a villainous Time Lord on their side. Expect death from everyday items such as plastic daffodils, toys, telephones and even chairs…

■ **Where and When** Earth, the late 20th century (exact date unknown).

■ **The Baddies** Nehru-suited renegade Time Lord, the Master (Roger Delgado). The Nestene Consciousness, a disembodied entity that materialises in a form not dissimilar to calamari, and its Auton foot soldiers – returning from 51 *Spearhead from Space*.

■ **Look out for…** Searching for the missing Goodge (Andrew Staines), the Doctor locates the scientist's doll-sized body in his sandwich box – the Master's gruesome calling card, which we'll see again in 88 *The Deadly Assassin*.

■ **Introducing…** "Fully qualified agent" Jo Grant (Katy Manning), who barges into the UNIT lab and transforms the Doctor's delicate experiment into mush. Plus: the Master, a jackanapes who only ever causes trouble. Also: Captain Mike Yates (Richard Franklin), the Brigadier's right-hand man.

■ **Where else have I seen…** Andrew Staines was previously a sergeant in 40 *The Enemy of the World*. He'll return (promoted!) as a naval captain in 66 *Carnival of Monsters*, and again as Keaver in 74 *Planet of the Spiders*.

■ **What they said** Interviewed in **Doctor Who Magazine** issue 160 (May 1990), producer Barry Letts reflected on the press controversy inspired by the Autons' murderous doll and fake policemen. "I think we did go over the top," he said, "but when you think of it, the most terrifying things are the ordinary things that can't be trusted."

■ **Arcs in Space** This is the first time we've encountered any members of the Doctor's own race since they were named in 50 *The War Games*.

56 The Mind of Evil

(six episodes) by Don Houghton
The Doctor goes to prison! Accompanied by Jo Grant, he visits HMP Stangmoor to witness a new method for rehabilitating criminals. But inside the machine there's an alien mind parasite controlled by the Master – and it threatens world peace.

■ **Where and When** Earth, the late 20th century (exact date unknown).

■ **The Baddies** The Master, posing as the brilliant scientist Emil Keller. An unnamed alien mind parasite. And a particularly nasty criminal named Harry Mailer (William Marlowe, below left).

■ **Look out for…** Episode Four's blockbusting nerve-missile heist sequence, in which Captain Yates gets to be a proper action hero.

■ **Introducing…** Corporal Bell (Fernanda Marlowe). A welcome female addition to UNIT's ranks, Bell continues into 57 *The Claws of Axos*, before vanishing forever.

■ **Where else have I seen…** Simon Lack, who plays drowned Keller Machine victim Professor Kettering, will return as Zadek in 101 *The Androids of Tara*.

■ **Arcs in Space** Subjected to the Keller Machine, the Doctor recalls various horrors from his past, including a Zarbi from 13 *The Web Planet*, a War Machine from 27 *The War Machines*, a Cyberman from 46 *The Invasion*, an Ice Lord from 48 *The Seeds of Death*, a Dalek, and volcanic fire from 54 *Inferno*.

57 The Claws of Axos

(four episodes) by Bob Baker and Dave Martin
The apparently benevolent golden-skinned Axons offer humanity Axonite, a gift to end world hunger. But the Axons are not what they appear, and deep within the belly of their 'craft' is a familiar prisoner…

■ **Where and When** Earth, the late 20th century (exact date unknown).

■ **The Baddies** The Master, showing he's not too wise in choosing his allies. Axos, a parasitical alien creature that consumes entire worlds (and expands frogs).

■ **Look out for...** The scene in Episode Four where the Doctor throws his lot in with the Master, so they can both escape the doomed Earth together. He *couldn't*, surely...?

■ **Introducing...** The tendril-covered Axon monster costumes, one of which will later be painted green and repurposed as a Krynoid for **85** *The Seeds of Doom*.

■ **Where else have I seen...** Peter Bathurst, who plays the fussy ministry official Chinn, was the fussy Governor Hensell of Vulcan in **30** *The Power of the Daleks*.

■ **What they said** Speaking in **DWM** issue 477 (October 2014), script editor Terrance Dicks admitted that the 1971 season became too formulaic. "If the villain in every story is revealed to be the Master, by about story three, when the Doctor is saying 'I wonder who could be behind this', it becomes less and less convincing."

■ **Arcs in Space** The TARDIS control room is seen for the first time since the Doctor was exiled to Earth in **50** *The War Games* – but now with an all-white console!

The Doctor and the Master form a pact to defeat the Axons in *The Claws of Axos*.

58 Colony in Space

(six episodes) by Malcolm Hulke

It's colonists vs the Interplanetary Mining Corporation on a barren and infertile world. The Doctor and Jo are caught in the conflict, and then the Master arrives...

■ **Where and When** The colony world Uxarieus, in the year 3000.

■ **The Baddies** The Master, now disguised as the Earth Adjudicator. IMC, which values money above human life, and its cruel representative, Dent (Morris Perry).

■ **Look out for...** The tense scene in which the Doctor and Jo break into the Master's TARDIS and the young UNIT agent accidentally breaks the trip-laser. Cue knock-out gas...

■ **Introducing...** This is the first time that the Third Doctor acts as an agent of the Time Lords, and also his first trip away from Earth. Future missions during his exile take place in **61** *The Curse of Peladon* and **63** *The Mutants*. It's also the first time we see the interior of the Master's TARDIS.

■ **Where else have I seen...** John Ringham, who plays the colonists' leader Ashe, previously portrayed Tlotoxl in **6** *The Aztecs* and Josiah Blake in **28** *The Smugglers*.

■ **Arcs in Space** *Colony in Space* begins this era's exploration of the future of humanity. The effects of pollution – seen in **69** *The Green Death* and **71** *Invasion of the Dinosaurs* – eventually force humankind to colonise the stars, forging the empire seen in **63** *The Mutants*.

The Axons in their more pleasing golden form (Bernard Holley, Patricia Gordino).

The doll-like native Guardian of Uxaerius, in *Colony in Space*.

59 The Dæmons

(five episodes) by Guy Leopold

The Doctor tries to halt an archaeological dig near Devil's End, while the Master raises an ancient force poised to make a final judgment on mankind.

■ **Where and When** The village of Devil's End and the barrow known as the Devil's Hump, somewhere in rural England, between 30 April and 1 May.

■ **The Baddies** The Master, posing as a country vicar. He later rocks some crimson robes for a ceremony that resembles a Black Mass. Also: horned beast Azal (Stephen Thorne), a bellicose super-sized alien scientist awakened from suspended animation, and 'Bok' (Stanley Mason) – a stone gargoyle come to life.

■ **Look out for...** A warm and fuzzy final scene, with the captured Master being booed by the assembled villagers as he's driven away by UNIT, and the Doctor and Jo enjoying a dance around a maypole.

■ **Where else have I seen...** Before appearing as snooty broadcaster Alastair Fergus, David Simeon was Private Latimer in 54 *Inferno*. Playing UNIT technician Corporal Osgood, Alec Linstead will reappear as Arthur Stengos in 142 *Revelation of the Daleks*. (Surely Cpl Osgood is some relation to later UNIT scientist Petronella Osgood, introduced in 240 *The Day of the Doctor*?)

■ **What they said** On 2 November 2023, *The Daily Telegraph*'s review panel nominated *The Dæmons* the 11th best *Doctor Who* of all – "a story that was very much a product of its time with references to the Age of Aquarius, as well as black magic covens that brought classic Hammer films to mind."

■ **Arcs in Space** While speaking of the Dæmons' abortive experiments in evolving humanity, Azal says "Remember Atlantis" – suggesting, in retrospect, that his people had a hairy hand in 64 *The Time Monster*.

60 Day of the Daleks

(four episodes) by Louis Marks

A ghost tries to kill the host of a conference crucial to world peace. Investigating, the Doctor and Jo are flung forward to a ruined Earth where the Daleks have enslaved the human race.

■ **Where and When** Auderly House in England, sometime in the late 20th century, and at the Daleks' HQ in a 22nd-century alternative timeline.

■ **The Baddies** The Daleks (making their first full appearance in five years), silver-faced human turncoat the Controller (Aubrey Woods), and – spoiler – misguided freedom fighters from the future.

■ **Introducing...** The hulking and rather stupid Ogrons – "simply guard dogs", according to the Controller.

■ **Look out for...** Episode Three's distinctly 'meta' cliffhanger, in which Dalek technology reads the Doctor's mind. Cue the first-ever returns of past Doctors (albeit in photographs), backed by the closing title patterns and blending seamlessly into the end credits.

■ **What they said** "The present Dr Who, Jon Pertwee, with his frilly shirt and taste for good wine, seems more of a dandy than a scientific inventor," huffed Sylvia Clayton in *The Daily Telegraph* after the first episode went out. "The prospect of imminent ex-ter-min-a-tion at the hands of the Daleks may perhaps stimulate him to more dramatic efforts."

■ **Arcs in Space** We see the Daleks' second successful conquest of our world, a century after 10 *The Dalek Invasion of Earth*. The same hierarchy of a gold leader, grey soldiers and Ogron servants is carried over to their next appearance in 67 *Frontier in Space*. It's another bootstrap paradox, with the freedom fighters' attempt to prevent their dystopian future actually creating it. The Twelfth Doctor elaborates on the concept in 255 *Before the Flood*.

Above
Azal the Dæmon (Stephen Thorne).

Above inset
Azal's servant Bok (Stanley Mason).

Princess Jo, Alpha Centauri (Stuart Fell) and Ixlyr (Alan Bennion) are among the delegates in *The Curse of Peladon*.

61 The Curse of Peladon

(four episodes) by Brian Hayles

Testing the repaired TARDIS, the Doctor and Jo arrive on feudal Peladon, where the ancient beast Aggedor has risen, seemingly to prevent the planet's entry into the Galactic Federation.

■ **Where and When** The citadel of Peladon, in the far future.

■ **The Baddies** High Priest Hepesh (Geoffrey Toone), covertly plotting to derail Peladon's membership of the Galactic Federation. He's working in cahoots with delegate Arcturus (voiced by Terry Bale) – a whingeing green skull suspended in liquid, intent on netting a trade deal for precious minerals.

■ **Introducing...** The Galactic Federation. This interplanetary alliance, including Mars and Earth, riffed on Britain's then-imminent membership of the European Union, and was one of *Doctor Who*'s first concerted attempts at wider world-building. The story also marks the first appearance of hermaphrodite hexapod Alpha Centauri (voiced by Ysanne Churchman).

■ **Look out for...** The closing moments of Episode Four, with the Doctor and Jo scarpering when the real Earth ambassador (Wendy Danvers) arrives. We get a cheeky query of "Doctor who?" and an elegant split-screen effect as onlookers watch the blue box fading away.

■ **Where have I seen...** Before playing glam-rock monarch King Peladon, Patrick Troughton's son David played an uncredited guard in 40 *The Enemy of the World* and Private Moor in 50 *The War Games*. He'll reappear as Professor Hobbes in 196 *Midnight*.

■ **Arcs in Space** After dreams of conquest in 39 *The Ice Warriors* and 48 *The Seeds of Death*, the sibilant Martians have become a more peaceful race. The Doctor placates the royal beast Aggedor (Nick Hobbs) by singing a Venusian lullaby – expanding on the line he used to repel the gargoyle Bok a couple of stories ago, in 59 *The Dæmons*. The Doctor will return to Peladon in 73 *The Monster of Peladon*.

62 The Sea Devils

(six episodes) by Malcolm Hulke

Visiting the imprisoned Master on a remote island, the Doctor investigates reports of mysterious attacks on ships, uncovering a plan to awaken a prehistoric race and supplant humanity.

■ **Where and When** An island prison off the south coast of England, the nearby naval base *HMS Seaspite*, an abandoned sea fort, and the Sea Devils' bunker, deep underwater – again, sometime in the late 20th century.

■ **The Baddies** The Master, sprung from prison, and bipedal amphibian Earth reptiles colloquially known as Sea Devils.

■ **Introducing...** "Reverse the polarity of the neutron flow" – a memorable piece of technobabble synonymous with the Third Doctor. Surprisingly, however, this is the only time it comes up during his original run (near-misses notwithstanding). He reprises it in 129 *The Five Doctors*, as does the Twelfth Doctor in 256 *The Girl Who Died*: "I bet that means something. It sounds great."

■ **Look out for...** A rare pop-culture sidestep for 20th-century *Doctor Who*, when the Master watches the children's animated series *Clangers*, whistling along with the knitted alien mice. "It seems to be a rather interesting extraterrestrial life form."

■ **What they said...** "The relationship between Who and his sparring partner [the Master] is one of the most fascinating aspects of the series," mused James Towler in *The Stage* on 30 March 1972. "There is, I suspect, a mutual respect between them. So much so that there would be a national outcry if the Doctor ever managed to exterminate his enemy."

■ **Arcs in Space** The Sea Devils are marine cousins of the reptiles seen in 52 *Doctor Who and the Silurians*, roused from the same hibernation. Both species teamed up for 130 *Warriors of the Deep*, while the Sea Devils made a solo return in 299 *Legend of the Sea Devils*.

The Doctor gets to grips with a Sea Devil in an abandoned sea fort.

Records of the top-secret Intelligence Taskforce that defends the Earth, compiled by **Mark Wright**.

Outstanding

The best way to experience UNIT is with the whole ensemble at peak performance. **59** *The Dæmons* represents the zenith of the UNIT 'family', during the Earth exile imposed on the Third Doctor (Jon Pertwee). The ultra-modern militia finds itself fighting folk horrors in the village of Devil's End, where the Master (Roger Delgado) is seeking to commune with cloven-hoofed Dæmon, Azal (Stephen Thorne). For once, UNIT seems moderately well-funded, with Captain Yates (Richard Franklin) and Sergeant Benton (John Levene) taking their CO's chopper for a spin; "My helicopter?!" barks Brigadier Lethbridge-Stewart (Nicholas Courtney) in fatherly horror. The Brig himself pitches up with a mobile HQ and an officer called Osgood (Alec Linstead). Confronted with the animated stone familiar Bok (Stanley Mason), Lethbridge-Stewart's phlegmatic order "Chap with the wings there, five rounds rapid" is the perfect UNIT motto.

Essential

80 *Terror of the Zygons* is a last-ish hurrah for the Brig in his pomp – his final deployment for seven years. UNIT proves its effectiveness as a military outfit, taking on the shape-changing Zygons, who would return as antagonists in UNIT's modern era. **240** *The Day of the Doctor* is populated with Zygon doubles, including Kate Lethbridge-Stewart (Jemma Redgrave) and a first appearance for Petronella Osgood (Ingrid Oliver). This 50th anniversary knees-up reaffirms how key UNIT has been, is and will be to the Doctor's lives, going right back to **46** *The Invasion*. The blueprint for every UNIT story to come, this has the newly formed Taskforce facing down a Cybermen assault from the dark side of the moon, with the Brigadier leading from the front.

Excellent

Several UNIT stories incorporate significant ends and beginnings. **51** *Spearhead from Space* commences the Doctor's exile to Earth – successfully applying to become its scientific adviser by defeating the Nestene Consciousness. Its plasticated servitors return in **55** *Terror of the Autons*, a soft reboot that completes the family circle with the debuts of Jo Grant (Katy Manning) and Captain Yates. Multi-Doctor birthday fun ensues in **65** *The Three Doctors*, ending the Third Doctor's enforced Earth residency; UNIT HQ falling through a black hole into an anti-matter universe is as audaciously absurd a *Doctor Who* image as you're likely to find. Perhaps better known as 'the one with the giant maggots',

69 *The Green Death* provides a bitter-sweet departure for Jo Grant, the first of the UNIT family to fly the coop. Decades later, **303** *The Giggle* is not only a farewell to one Doctor and a hello to another, it also drops the UNIT Tower into the 21st-century London skyline – a beacon for an exciting future.

The Best of the Rest

57 *The Claws of Axos* has tentacled vampire blobs from space, the Master, a self-serving civil servant, blown-up jeeps, a power station, and freak weather conditions: what more could you want from a UNIT adventure? The Axons may be a beguiling one-off monster, but the thrill of UNIT versus (three) Daleks in **60** *Day of the Daleks* is the stuff elevator pitches are made of. Similarly, 'UNIT fights dinosaurs in deserted London and the Brigadier holds off a stegosaurus with a flare' would make **71** *Invasion of the Dinosaurs* hard for any script commissioner to ignore. As a fond farewell to Lethbridge-Stewart, **152** *Battlefield* brings UNIT up to state of the (late 1980s) art, introducing Brigadier Winifred Bambera (Angela Bruce). The 1970 season's **53** *The Ambassadors of Death* is an atypical thriller, documenting some of UNIT's most kinetically staged battles, while **54** *Inferno* sidesteps into a parallel universe to see what a dystopian, quasi-Fascist UNIT might look like, led by a Brigade-Leader with duelling scar and eyepatch. **311** *The Legend of Ruby Sunday/Empire of Death* brings the story full circle: Earth is protected.

"Chap with the wings there, five rounds rapid."
BRIGADIER LETHBRIDGE-STEWART, *THE DÆMONS*

The Doctor surrounded by *The Mutants* on the planet Solos.

(exact date unknown). The Time Vortex.

■ **The Baddies** The Master, claiming to be Professor Thascales. As Jo surmises, "Thascales is Greek for Master!"

■ **Introducing (and Farewell to...)** The new walls of the TARDIS control room, with their smooth, shiny, concave roundels. They will never appear again.

■ **Look out for...** In Episode Six, the Doctor tells Jo about his childhood, and a hermit who helped him through his 'blackest day'. We will meet that hermit in **74** *Planet of the Spiders*, and visit the barn where the Doctor slept as a child in **240** *The Day of the Doctor*, **245** *Listen* and **262** *Hell Bent*.

■ **What they said** "Yes, it was complex," reflected director Paul Bernard in **Doctor Who Magazine** issue 168 (December 1990), "but isn't that part of what is required of *Doctor Who*?"

■ **Arcs in Space** *Doctor Who*'s third and (to date) final exploration of the fate of Atlantis, following **32** *The Underwater Menace* and **59** *The Daemons*. In Episode Five the Doctor lands his TARDIS in the Master's control room, while the Master's TARDIS is inside the Doctor's control room. There's a callback to this head-scratching scenario in **115** *Logopolis*.

63 The Mutants

(six episodes) by **Bob Baker** and **Dave Martin**

Solos is to be granted independence from Earth's declining galactic empire, but why are its inhabitants mutating into monsters? The Doctor and Jo take on the Marshal, leader of Skybase One, and his evil scheme to change Solos' climate.

■ **Where and When** The planet Solos and Skybase One in its orbit, in the 30th century.

■ **The Baddies** The Marshal (Paul Whitsun-Jones), a xenophobe, a murderous tyrant... and "quite mad".

■ **Introducing...** The Mutants, one of whom will later make a cameo appearance in **84** *The Brain of Morbius*.

■ **Look out for...** Strap yourselves in for the cliffhanger of Episode Four, as the Marshal blows a hole in the side of Skybase One and explosive decompression threatens to suck Jo and her new friends into the vacuum of space.

■ **What they said** "By the impression the first episode gave me," wrote Keith Miller in *The Doctor Who Fan Club Newsletter* in 1972, "I thought this was going to be one of the biggest failures in the history of the programme. I was soon proved to be wrong."

■ **Arcs in Space** This is the exiled Doctor's last mission for the Time Lords – see **57** *The Claws of Axos* and **61** *The Curse of Peladon*.

64 The Time Monster

(six episodes) by **Robert Sloman**

From the Newton Institute, the Master is seeking to obtain the fabled Crystal of Kronos, so he might control a powerful being that exists outside time. Meanwhile, a V1 flying bomb drops on Captain Yates, and Sergeant Benton reverts to a baby.

■ **Where and When** UNIT HQ, plus the Newton Institute in Wootton and surrounding area, planet Earth, late 20th century (exact date unknown). Atlantis

Above inset Atlantean Queen Galleia (Ingrid Pitt).

Left Kronos (Marc Boyle) – *The Time Monster*.

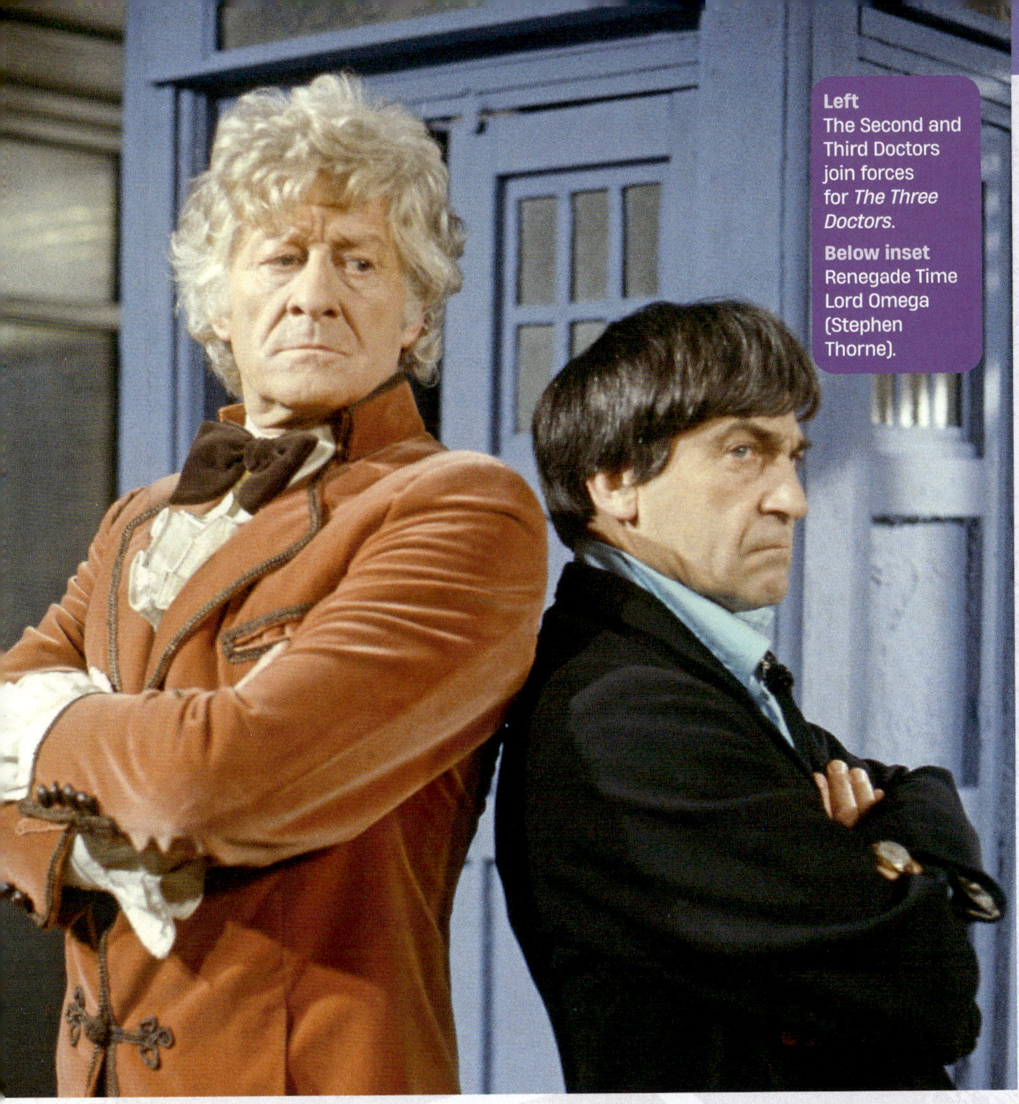

Left The Second and Third Doctors join forces for *The Three Doctors*.
Below inset Renegade Time Lord Omega (Stephen Thorne).

65 The Three Doctors

(four episodes) by **Bob Baker** and **Dave Martin**

The first multi-Doctor story, with the Time Lords sending the Doctor's former selves to help him solve the mystery of a black hole that's draining the universe of its energy.

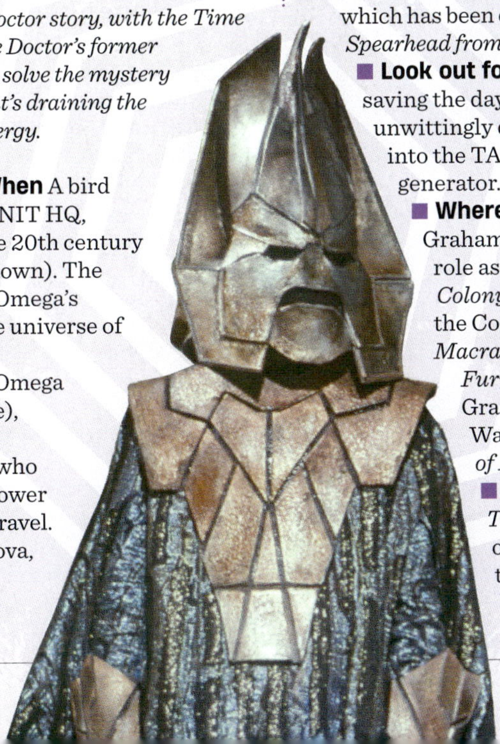

■ **Where and When** A bird sanctuary and UNIT HQ, planet Earth, late 20th century (exact date unknown). The wastelands and Omega's stronghold in the universe of anti-matter.
■ **The Baddies** Omega (Stephen Thorne), the Gallifreyan stellar engineer who discovered the power source for time travel. Lost to a supernova, which became a black hole, all that remained was his will. Also: the Gell Guards, lumbering lumps of anti-matter that shoot fiery death.
■ **Farewell to...** The Doctor's exile to Earth, which has been enforced since **51** *Spearhead from Space*.
■ **Look out for...** The Second Doctor saving the day, marvellously, by unwittingly dropping his recorder into the TARDIS' force-field generator.
■ **Where else have I seen...** Graham Leaman reprises his role as a Time Lord from **58** *Colony in Space*. He was also the Controller in **34** *The Macra Terror*, Price in **42** *Fury from the Deep* and the Grand Marshall of the Ice Warriors in **48** *The Seeds of Death*.
■ **Arcs in Space** *The Three Doctors* provides our first insight into the Time Lords' backstory, which will subsequently be explored further in **88** *The Deadly Assassin*. Proving that he only pops up for landmark anniversaries, Omega will return for a curtain call in **123** *Arc of Infinity*. And in **148** *Remembrance of the Daleks* it's revealed that the First Doctor hid a remote stellar manipulator called the Hand of Omega on Earth in 1963.

66 Carnival of Monsters

(four episodes) by **Robert Holmes**

Roll up and see the monster show! The Doctor and Jo are trapped within a carnival machine in the far future, while, outside it, travelling entertainers Vorg and Shirna take on the dreary bureaucrats of Inter Minor.

■ **Where and When** The worlds and inner workings of a Miniscope and the planet Inter Minor (exact date unknown).
■ **The Baddies** The snide, oh-so-grey Commissioner Kalik (Michael Wisher), who's willing to sabotage the Miniscope and release its deadly alien occupants in order to depose the planet's ruler, Zarb. Drashigs – not evil as such, just omnivores and hungry.
■ **Where else have I seen...** Ian Marter plays Lt John Andrews just two years before his debut as the Fourth Doctor's companion, Harry Sullivan, in **75** *Robot*.
■ **Look out for...** Episode One's gob-smacking cliffhanger, as a giant hand reaches into the hold of the SS *Bernice* and whisks away the TARDIS.
■ **What they said...** Interviewed in **DWM** issue 270 (October 1998), producer-director Barry Letts recalled that "The script was Bob Holmes again. He had a very full imagination, with an odd humour and a horrific side."
■ **Arcs in Space** It's not just humans and Drashigs in the Miniscope, as we also get a glimpse of a Cyberman (the variant seen in **46** *The Invasion*) and an Ogron (from **60** *Day of the Daleks*).

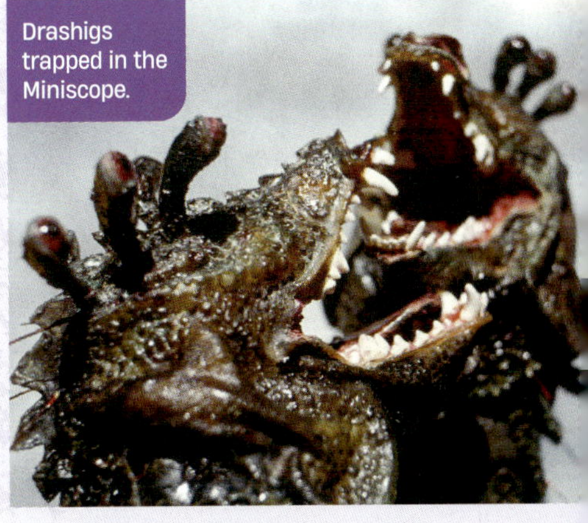

Drashigs trapped in the Miniscope.

67 Frontier in Space

(six episodes) by **Malcolm Hulke**

Twenty years after an interplanetary war, the Milky Way is divided between two empires – Earth and Draconia. At the frontier, ships of both empires have been attacked. But nobody believes the Doctor when he claims a third party is trying to provoke another war.

■ **Where and When** This story, set somewhere in the 26th century, spans the galaxy, taking place in a variety of spaceships, on Earth, on a penal colony on the Moon, on Draconia, and on the planet of the Ogrons.

■ **The Baddies** While the regime on Earth is authoritarian – locking up political prisoners – and the Draconians are proud and bellicose, the real villains are the Ogrons, who in turn are working for the Master, who's formed an alliance with the Daleks.

■ **Farewell to…** This is the final appearance of the Master as played by Roger Delgado. It's rather a low-key send off; prior to the actor's untimely death. the production team had expected to feature the character once more.

■ **Look out for…** The circular design on the Master's Commissioner of Interplanetary Police uniform hints at the identity of his partners.

■ **Where else have I seen…** John Woodnutt, the Draconian Emperor here, also appears as Hibbert in **38** *Spearhead from Space*, as Broton in **80** *Terror of the Zygons* and as Seron in **114** *The Keeper of Traken*.

■ **Arcs in Space** The Master's hypnosound device makes Jo see a Drashig from **66** *Carnival of Monsters*. This story also leads directly into **68** *Planet of the Daleks*. The Doctor is sentenced to a lunar penal colony again in **166** *Bad Wolf/The Parting of the Ways*, and the Draconians are part of the monster alliance in **212** *The Pandorica Opens/The Big Bang*.

68 Planet of the Daleks

(six episodes) by **Terry Nation**

Badly wounded, the Doctor sends a telepathic message to the Time Lords, in order to guide the TARDIS to follow a Dalek spaceship to the planet where their army is hidden. He recovers and allies himself with a native Spiridon and a group of Thal commandos.

■ **Where and When** The planet Spiridon, a world of jungle and ice volcanoes, with a climate that shifts between tropical during the day and below freezing at night. It's directly after **67** *Frontier in Space*, so we're in the 26th century again.

■ **The Baddies** Spiridon has "vegetation that's more like animal life than plant" and "creatures hostile to everything including themselves". But the true villains are the Daleks, led by the gold Dalek Supreme.

■ **What they said** In *The Times* on Monday 9 April, critic Stanley Reynolds wrote that the Daleks still represented "the ultimate bogeyman" and are "the boss of space horrors, something to get the children hiding behind the sofa".

■ **Look out for…** Jo Grant's rather dotty description of being saved by an invisible Spiridon. "It was terrible and then I got rescued by this bowl!"

■ **Where else have I seen…** Bernard Horsfall, playing the Thal leader Taron, had already featured in **45** *The Mind Robber* and **50** *The War Games*; he'll be back in **88** *The Deadly Assassin*. Prentis Hancock, playing Vaber, was in **38** *Spearhead from Space*; he'll be back in **81** *Planet of Evil* and **98** *The Ribos Operation*.

■ **Arcs in Space** This story sees the return of the Thals from **2** *The Mutants* (aka *The Daleks*), who regard the events of that story as a legend. The Doctor later recalls making a jamming device on Spiridon in **148** *Remembrance of the Daleks*, while a Dalek from this story ends up in the **262** *Asylum of the Daleks*.

The Draconians, a noble race on the brink of war in *Frontier in Space*.

A frozen army is hidden on Spiridon, the *Planet of the Daleks*.

69 The Green Death

(six episodes) by Robert Sloman
Global Chemicals promises the former mineworkers in Llanfairfach new jobs and prosperity. But the new 'Stevens process' results in chemical waste – which is lethal to the touch and causes maggots to grow to giant proportions.

■ **Where and When** The Llanfairfach colliery and mine, the nearby Wholeweal Community and the Global Chemicals research complex, including its mysterious top floor. The Doctor also finally gets to visit Metebelis III. We're in the near future, as seen from 1973; the Prime Minister is a man called Jeremy.

■ **The Baddies** As the director of Global Chemicals, Stevens (Jerome Willis) would seem to be responsible for their activities, but he's merely a puppet of the megalomaniac computer BOSS (voiced by John Dearth).

■ **What they said** The story's producer, Barry Letts, expected to receive complaints due to the serial's political content. But the only complaint he received was about Jon Pertwee's pronunciation of the word 'chitinous': "Dear Barry Letts, the reason I'm writin', is how to say 'kitin'."

■ **Look out for…** The Doctor demonstrates that he's a master of disguise, sneaking into the Global Chemicals complex by posing as both an elderly milkman and a cleaning lady.

■ **Farewell to…** Jo Grant, who leaves to get married to Professor Clifford Jones (Stewart Bevan) and to join him on an expedition up the Amazon in search of a high-protein mushroom.

■ **Arcs in Space** The Doctor attempted to visit Metebelis III in **66** *Carnival of Monsters* and will return there in **74** *Planet of the Spiders*, after receiving the Metebelis crystal in the post from Jo Grant. The Doctor utilises another Metebelis crystal in **235** *Hide*.

70 The Time Warrior

(four episodes) by Robert Holmes
Sontaran officer Linx is forced to make an emergency landing on Earth, where he forms an uneasy alliance with the robber baron Irongron. But to repair his spaceship, he needs equipment and skilled technicians – which brings him to the attention of the Doctor and the journalist Sarah Jane Smith.

■ **Where and When** After beginning in the near future in a top-security research centre, the adventure continues in Irongron's castle and the neighbouring Wessex Castle in the 13th century.

■ **The Baddies** Irongron (David Daker) is a ruthless thug with ambitions of becoming King, but he's no match for the cruel, devious and single-minded Linx (Kevin Lindsay).

■ **Introducing…** As well as being the debut for Sarah Jane Smith (Elisabeth Sladen) and the Sontarans, this story also features the first mention of the Rutans. It's also the first time we hear the name of the Doctor's home planet, Gallifrey.

Linx (Kevin Lindsay), the series' original Sontaran, in *The Time Warrior*.

Above
Giant maggots in *The Green Death*.
Below inset
Jo and Cliff Jones (Stewart Bevan).

■ **Where else have I seen…** David Daker will return as Captain Rigg in **107** *Nightmare of Eden*, while Alan Rowe (here playing Sir Edward) appears in other roles in **33** *The Moonbase*, **92** *Horror of Fang Rock* and **111** *Full Circle*.

■ **What they said** Reviewing the story in *The Guardian* on Monday 17 December, critic Nancy Banks-Smith wrote: "*Dr Who* began a new series with a new buddy [who looks] for all the world like a baked potato. I have not lived this long to be frightened of baked potatoes."

■ **Arcs in Space** Sarah refers to this adventure in **77** *The Sontaran Experiment*, while the Doctor deliriously recalls Sontarans "perverting the course of human history!" in **76** *Robot* and **275** *World Enough and Time/The Doctor Falls*.

Sarah Jane Smith (Elisabeth Sladen) and the Doctor in *Invasion of the Dinosaurs*.

71 Invasion of the Dinosaurs

(six episodes) by Malcolm Hulke

As dinosaurs rampage through the streets of an evacuated London, the Doctor, Sarah and UNIT uncover a conspiracy to literally turn back the clock – and a traitor in their ranks.

■ **Where and When** 20th-century London.

■ **The Baddies** Misguided environmentalist group Operation Golden Age, and – gasp – Captain Mike Yates.

■ **Look out for…** In a first for *Doctor Who*, the opening episode was given the foreshortened title *Invasion*, to preserve the surprise of the prehistoric perils. (Unhelpfully, the *Radio Times* illustration for the episode depicted a pterodactyl.)

■ **Introducing…** The Doctor's fab space vehicle – a glam-rock combination of a hovercraft and a Nike trainer sprayed silver, registration number WVO 2M. Known off-screen as the Whomobile, the custom car was commissioned by Jon Pertwee as a canny means of boosting his 'personal appearances' sideline.

■ **Where else have I seen…** Peter Miles returns as Professor Whitaker, bringing with him a vein of seething villainy similar to his Dr Lawrence in **52** *Doctor Who and the Silurians*; he'll turn up later as Nyder in **78** *Genesis of the Daleks*. Martin Jarvis gets to play a human character, Butler, having performed under fur and antennae as Menoptra captain Hilio back in **13** *The Web Planet*. He, too, will reappear – as the Governor in **138** *Vengeance on Varos*.

■ **Arcs in Space** Since being hypnotised in **69** *The Green Death*, Captain Yates has grappled with increasing misgivings about life in the military, making him susceptible to the Operation Golden Age cause. T rex (not the glam rock kind) will again feature in **97** *The Mark of the Rani*, **227** *Dinosaurs on a Spaceship* and **242** *Deep Breath*.

72 Death to the Daleks

(four episodes) by Terry Nation

Trapped on the barren planet Exxilon by an energy-draining force, the Doctor and Sarah dodge the Marine Space Corps, defanged Daleks and a sentient city filled with hidden perils.

■ **Where and When** Exxilon, the future (date unknown).

■ **The Baddies** A Dalek squadron, left sputtering impotently when their weapons are drained of energy.

■ **Look out for…** The adorable miniature TARDIS the Daleks test their new weapons on in Part Two – obviously Skaro standard-issue, to foment anti-Doctor fervour.

■ **Where else have I seen…** John Abineri, previously seen as engineer Van Lutyens in **42** *Fury from the Deep* and traitorous General Carrington in **53** *The Ambassadors of Death*, returns as Marine Corps second-in-command Captain Railton.

■ **What they said** "I can't stand Daleks," a demob-happy Jon Pertwee told the *Daily Mirror* on 9 February 1974, fresh from announcing his departure as the Doctor. "I'm not scared of them, just bored. They have been around too long. I prefer monsters with some life in them, like the Draconians or the Ogrons."

■ **Arcs in Space** All the Daleks are presumed destroyed, but nonetheless the intensive care ward in the **226** *Asylum of the Daleks* contains caged Daleks who survived meeting the Doctor on several planets, including Exxilon. Sarah will later compare the puzzles in the Exxilon city to those she sees on the Red Planet in **82** *Pyramids of Mars*.

73 The Monster of Peladon

(six episodes) by Brian Hayles

Five decades on, the Doctor returns to Peladon, where striking miners, duplicitous Ice Warriors and apparitions of Aggedor threaten to wreck the planet's alliance with the Galactic Federation.

Rebellious Exxilons inflict *Death to the Daleks*.

Text by Stuart Manning

- **Where and When** Peladon, the year 3935.
- **The Baddies** Rogue Ice Warriors, aided by duplicitous mining engineer Eckersley (Donald Gee).
- **Look out for...** A glaring full-face shot of Jon Pertwee's bewigged stunt double Terry Walsh, during the Doctor's fight with Ettis (Ralph Watson) in Part Four.
- **Where else have I seen...** As Azaxyr, Alan Bennion completes his hat-trick of Ice Warrior leaders, following **48** *The Seeds of Death* and **61** *The Curse of Peladon*. Eckersley actor Donald Gee previously played Space Corps officer Major Warne in **49** *The Space Pirates*.
- **What they said** Speaking to broadcaster David Jacobs in 1980, Ysanne Churchman recalled giving voice to the fretful hexapod Alpha Centauri: "Stuart Fell, the stunt man, was in the clothes, of course. We used to have little discussions as to how he [the character] was thinking and feeling."
- **Arcs in Space** In one of *Doctor Who*'s most direct sequels, the Doctor witnesses the consequences of the alliance he helped forge in **61** *The Curse of Peladon*, now aided by the daughter of King Peladon and a returning Alpha Centauri. The hexapod will be back again for a cameo in **273** *Empress of Mars* – with the same voice.

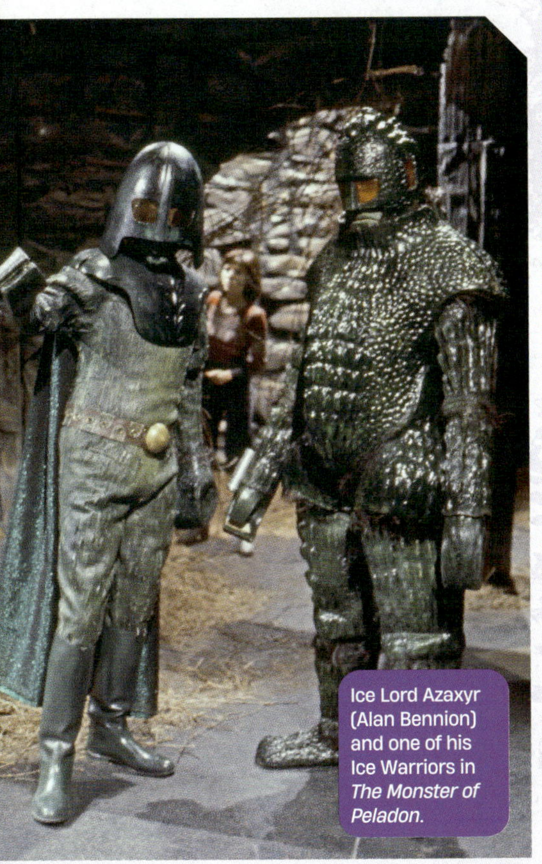

Ice Lord Azaxyr (Alan Bennion) and one of his Ice Warriors in *The Monster of Peladon*.

74 Planet of the Spiders

(six episodes) by Robert Sloman

Meditating Buddhists become unwitting allies to a gaggle of giant spiders intent on ruling the universe. All that stands in the Eight Legs' way is a single blue crystal... and the Doctor.

- **Where and When** 20th-century England, plus Metebelis III (date unknown).
- **The Baddies** The Eight Legs, a race of giant mutated alien spiders, ruled by their goddess, the Great One (voiced by Maureen Morris).
- **Look out for...** The multi-vehicle chase sequence in Part Two, inserted as a sop to Jon Pertwee's James Bond obsessions – involving Bessie, the Doctor's space-age vehicle (which now flies), a gyrocopter, a motorboat and a one-man hovercraft.
- **Farewell to...** Mike Yates, reuniting with his old friends in search of redemption, and the Third Doctor himself, who bows out with panache and pathos. "A tear, Sarah Jane? Where there's life, there's..."
- **Where else have I seen...** *Observer* critic Richard Boston, writing on 26 May 1974 – between Parts Four and Five:

"The present *Doctor Who* story is one of the best, even though the Daleks are not in it. Instead there are some very nasty spiders which are going to take over unless the Doctor proves even more resourceful than usual... His imminent demise will be essential viewing."

- **Arcs in Space** Jo Grant returns the Metebelis crystal given to her as a wedding gift in **69** *The Green Death* – posting it back from the Amazon, since her porters think it's "bad magic".

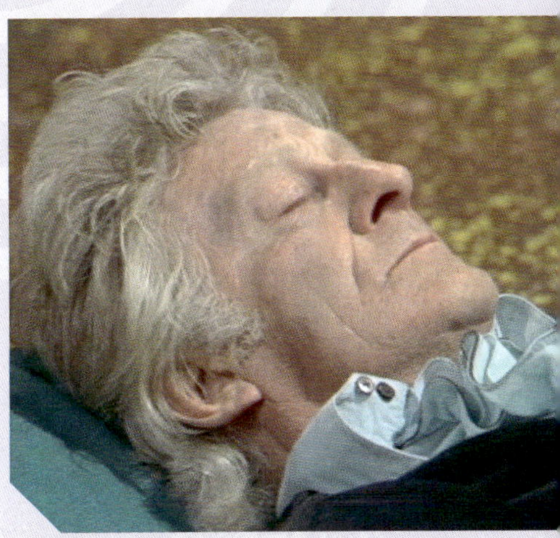

The FOURTH DOCTOR

Tom Baker
Stories 75–115, 1974–81

With the secret of the TARDIS restored to him, the next Doctor was quick to resume his time and space travels – becoming a wild-haired, wide-eyed wanderer, accompanied by an absurdly long scarf, a bag of jelly babies, and sometimes a robot dog.

Left
The new Doctor (Tom Baker) and Sarah Jane Smith hunt a metal menace in *Robot*.

Below
Robot K1.

75 Robot

(four episodes) by **Terrance Dicks**
The Fourth Doctor is soon on the trail of "something more than human" that's stealing the components for a disintegrator gun.

■ **Where and When** Earth, late 20th century (exact date unknown).
■ **The Baddies** Miss Hilda Winters (Patricia Maynard), leader of the Scientific Reform Society, an elite that intends to rule the world by any means necessary. The Experimental Prototype Robot K1 (Michael Kilgarriff), built to serve humanity and never harm it, which is driven mad by violations of its programming.
■ **Introducing…** The Fourth Doctor (Tom Baker), with his immensely long scarf, and his immensely deep pockets. Mentioned in **74** *Planet of the Spiders*, seconded-to-UNIT naval surgeon Harry Sullivan (Ian Marter) appears here for the first time.
■ **Look out for…** The Doctor tries out some unusual options for his new costume, dressing as a Viking warrior, the King of Hearts and a pierrot.
■ **What they said** Writing on 24 January 1975, *New Statesman* reviewer Elizabeth Thomas was unimpressed, noting how "the poor unfortunate robot with the mixed-up principles… went to his doom in a quite appalling imitation of King Kong, trampling tiny buildings and midget men underfoot and even stooping to lift the screaming girl reporter in his huge mailed fist."
■ **Arcs in Space** The Fourth Doctor meets more robots that have been forced to violate their prime directive in **90** *The Robots of Death*. That doesn't end well either.

76 The Ark in Space

(four episodes) by **Robert Holmes**
The Fourth Doctor's first foray into space. He discovers humanity's future, where survivors lie in cryogenic suspension after Earth was destroyed by solar flares. As if that wasn't grim enough, there are giant insects to fight!

■ **Where and When** Space station Nerva, in Earth orbit, sometime over 10,000 years in the future.
■ **The Baddies** The Wirrn: nasty, man-sized insects that lay their eggs in the bodies of human sleepers so that "when the larvae emerge they have a ready-made food supply."
■ **Farewell to…** Harry's shoes, zapped into smouldering ruins by the Autoguard. Thankfully, other footwear is available.
■ **Look out for…** Arriving on Nerva, the Doctor tests the gravity with his yoyo.
■ **What they said** Interviewed in issue 2 of the fanzine *Moonbase* in 1978, Ian Marter said: "I thought *The Ark in Space* was perhaps the best script we got to do, with its very strong idea consistently maintained."
■ **Arcs in space** This story kicks off the Nerva arc that spans stories **76** through **79**. The fate of Earth and humanity had previously been explored in **23** *The Ark*, and the Ninth Doctor and Rose Tyler will witness its demise in **158** *The End of the World*.

Text by David Richardson

Field Major Styre (Kevin Lindsay) conducts *The Sontaran Experiment.*

77 The Sontaran Experiment

(two episodes) by Bob Baker and Dave Martin

The Doctor, Sarah and Harry transmat to the surface of the devastated Earth, where Sontaran Field Major Styre is conducting a G3 military assessment survey – by carrying out cruel experiments on a group of Galsec colonists.

The insectoid Wirrn take over the transport rocket of space station Nerva in *The Ark in Space.*

■ **Where and When** The overgrown site of London, more than 10,000 years in the future.

■ **The Baddies** Even nastier and more brutish than Linx from 70 *The Time Warrior*, Styre tortures the colonists by testing their strength, reaction to fear and dehydration, and resistance to pressure.

■ **Where else have I seen…** Styre is played by Kevin Lindsay, who also portrayed Linx. Additionally, he was Cho-Je, a projection of the Doctor's former mentor, in 74 *Planet of the Spiders*.

■ **Look out for…** Styre deflates like a party balloon when Harry removes the Terrulian Diode Bypass Transformer from his ship.

■ **What they said** Reviewing this story in *The Doctor Who Fan Club Newsletter 23* (March-April 1975), Keith Miller wrote: "It seemed to be a runabout with the Doctor looking for Sarah who was looking for Harry who was looking for the Doctor."

■ **Arcs in Space** At the end of this, the first two-parter since 11 *The Rescue*, the Doctor, Sarah and Harry transmat back to Nerva – only to find themselves arrive somewhere totally different in the next adventure.

78 Genesis of the Daleks

(six episodes) by Terry Nation

The Time Lords send the Doctor, Sarah and Harry to the battle-ravaged world of Skaro to avert or alter the creation of the Daleks.

■ **Where and When** Skaro, exact date unknown, but long before 2 *The Mutants* (aka *The Daleks*).

■ **The Baddies** Davros, the Kaleds' chief scientist (Michael Wisher), plus the Mark III Travel Machines, aka the Daleks.

■ **Introducing** The Time Ring, which also features in 79 *Revenge of the Cybermen*.

■ **Look out for…** The futuristic rifles used by the Thals are actually Drahvin guns from 18 *Galaxy Four*. Plus the freeze-frame cliffhanger to Part Two, with Sarah falling from a gantry – an effect that director David Maloney liked so much, he'd use it again in 81 *Planet of Evil* and 88 *The Deadly Assassin*.

■ **What they said** Interviewed in **Doctor Who Magazine** issue 369 (May 2006), Elisabeth Sladen said: "There's always a moment on *Doctor Who* when you get the

"Just touch these two strands together and the Daleks are finished." THE DOCTOR

'reality shiver'. It's when you forget that it's just pretend. I got it the first time I did a scene with Davros."

■ **Arcs in Space** This story continues directly from 77 *The Sontaran Experiment* and leads into 79 *Revenge of the Cybermen*. The Twelfth Doctor will run into the young Davros amid the thousand-year war that led to the Daleks' creation in 254 *The Magician's Apprentice/ The Witch's Familiar*. *Destination: Skaro*, a mini-episode that featured as part of the 2023 Children in Need telethon, was set in the run-up to *Genesis of the Daleks*, and showed Davros unveiling his travel machine (see pages 112-113).

Davros (Michael Wisher) and fellow kaled scientist Kavell (Tom Georgeson).

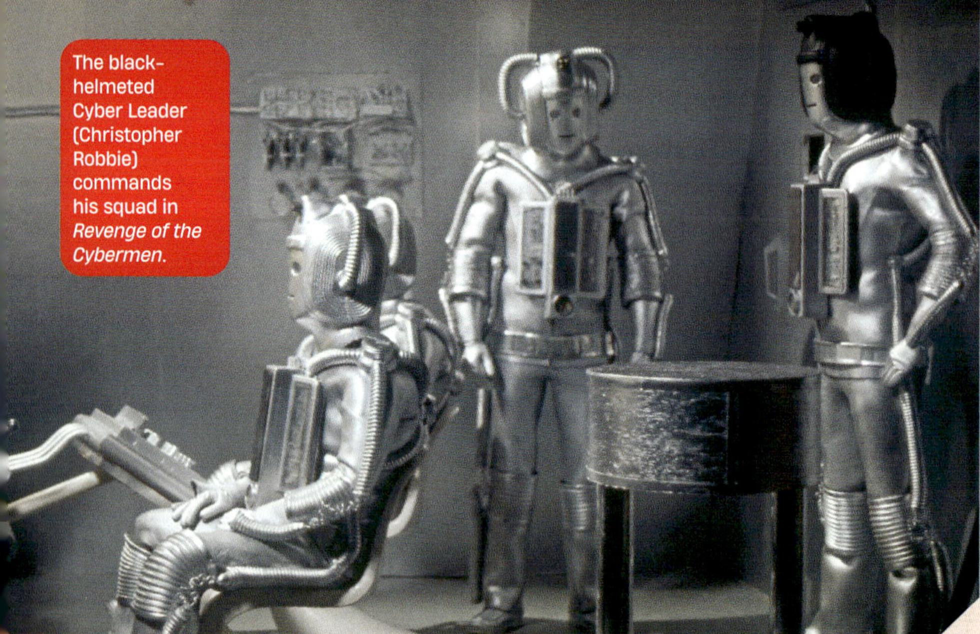

The black-helmeted Cyber Leader (Christopher Robbie) commands his squad in *Revenge of the Cybermen.*

79 Revenge of the Cybermen

(four episodes) by Gerry Davis
A space station stricken by plague tries to warn ships of Jupiter's mysterious new moon – unaware of the civilisation under its surface, and the plans of a watching enemy…

■ **Where and When** Nerva Beacon and the interior of the nearby moon, Voga, where the streets really are paved with gold. We're sometime in the future, but thousands of years before the TARDIS landed in **77** *The Ark in Space.*
■ **The Baddies** The last surviving Cybermen, who plan to destroy Voga – its supply of gold having been key in their defeat in the Cyber Wars, thanks to the invention of the glitter-gun. Also: Vorus (David Collings), leader of the Guardians of Voga, who's paid gold-hungry human surveyor Kellman (Jeremy Wilkin) to lure the Cybermen back to the beacon, in order to destroy them with his Skystriker rocket.
■ **Introducing…** Gold is shown for the first time to be fatal to Cybermen, attacking their breathing systems and suffocating them – an element that will become crucial in **121** *Earthshock.*
■ **Look out for…** The treacherous Kellman uses a radio concealed in a hairbrush in Part One, the same prop having appeared two years earlier in the James Bond film *Live and Let Die.*
■ **Where else have I seen…** Christopher Robbie, who plays the original Cyber Leader, offered a different set of power

stances as the Karkus, comic-strip hero of the *Hourly Telepress*, in **45** *The Mind Robber.*
■ **Arcs in Space** Continuing directly from the previous story, the Doctor, Sarah and Harry arrive on Nerva via Time Ring, while a summons from the Brigadier at the end leads into **80** *Terror of the Zygons.* The Eleventh Doctor will encounter the Cybermats again in **223** *Closing Time.*

80 Terror of the Zygons

(four episodes) by Robert Banks Stewart
Called to the vicinity of Loch Ness to investigate the sinking of oil rigs, the Doctor, Sarah and Harry discover, not just a legendary creature, but a plan for global conquest centuries in the making…

■ **Where and When** The Scottish village of Tulloch and the surrounding countryside, the nearby shores and depths of Loch Ness, and London. The near-present, after the events of **75** *Robot.*
■ **The Baddies** The Zygons, shape-changing beings led by their warlord Broton (John Woodnutt). Able to mimic the form of anyone for whom they have a body print, they plan to take over the world and convert it to their climate, prior to the arrival of their fleet in a few hundred years' time.
■ **Farewell to…** Harry Sullivan decides not to join the Doctor and Sarah on their return trip to London by TARDIS, putting his trust in British Rail instead. But he'll have a brief reunion with his friends in **83** *The Android Invasion.*
■ **Look out for…** On the telephone with the Prime Minister in Part Four, Brigadier Lethbridge-Stewart (Nicholas Courtney) refers to Downing Street's most famous resident as "madam",

Broton (John Woodnutt) in *Terror of the Zygons.*

Left
The Doctor and Sarah on *The Planet of Evil*.

Right inset
The alter-ego of Professor Sorenson (Frederick Jaeger).

befitting the near-future setting of the UNIT stories. Margaret Thatcher, appointed leader of the Conservative Party a month before filming started, would become Britain's first female Prime Minister four years later.

■ **Where else have I seen...** Angus MacRanald, the maybe-psychic landlord of Tulloch's Fox Inn, is played by Angus Lennie, previously the fur-clad science refusenik Storr in **39** *The Ice Warriors*.

Arcs in Space The Tenth, Eleventh and War Doctors, plus UNIT, would face a new generation of Zygons many decades later in **240** *The Day of the Doctor*.

Right
Sutekh (Gabriel Woolf) and his robotic servants in *Pyramids of Mars*.

81 Planet of Evil

(four episodes) by Louis Marks
Sent to rescue a scientific expedition on a planet at the edge of the universe, a Morestran mission finds only a collection of corpses... plus the Doctor and Sarah.

■ **Where and When** Zeta Minor, the single most remote planet on the very limit of the known cosmos; a void between the universes of matter and anti-matter; and in space. By the Morestran calendar, it's the year 37,166. (The Doctor notes that he's overdue at UNIT by 10,000 years.)

■ **The Baddies** Not only the anti-matter creature that emerges from the planet's "black pool" to suck the life from transgressors, but also Professor Sorenson (Frederick Jaeger) – whose exposure to anti-matter causes him to hybridise into "anti-man", the Hyde to his Jekyll.

■ **Look out for...** The Doctor takes a sample of anti-matter to study, but needs a small container. What does he use to carry this mysterious substance of seemingly unlimited destructive power? A toffee tin.

■ **Where else have I seen...** Ponti, the Morestran crewman who falls into the void to his death (if he's lucky), is played by Louis Mahoney, previously seen briefly in **67** *Frontier in Space* as a newsreader, then more substantially as the older Billy Shipton in **186** *Blink*.

■ **What they said** "You can't tell the heroes from the heavies, it's all so sophisticated," quipped Clive James in his *Observer* review column on 11 July 1976, adding: "When Dr Who talks nonsense, it sounds like Science."

■ **Arcs in Space** There's another visit to the edge of the universe, with beings crossing over from the other side, in **302** *Wild Blue Yonder*, while **65** *The Three Doctors* offers another perspective on the realm of anti-matter.

82 Pyramids of Mars

(four episodes) by Stephen Harris
Arriving at UNIT HQ 70 years early, the Doctor and Sarah discover an angry Egyptian,

a prototype radio telescope, mummies building a rocket, and an imprisoned god who threatens all life...

■ **Where and When** Egypt, Mars and a country house in England, all in 1911. Not forgetting a side visit to a possible Earth in 1980, after Sutekh the Destroyer has been set free – rendering the planet blasted and lifeless.

■ **The Baddies** Jackal-headed death god Sutekh (Gabriel Woolf), who destroyed his own planet, Phaester Osiris, and who was finally cornered on Earth by Horus and 739 of his fellow Osirans, who imprisoned him under a pyramid. Assisting him is the possessed corpse of crotchety Egyptologist Marcus Scarman (Bernard Archard).

■ **Introducing...** Sutekh, one of the most dangerous and powerful beings the Doctor has ever encountered, who will wait patiently for his revenge in **311** *The Legend of Ruby Sunday/Empire of Death*.

■ **Look out for...** When they catch up to the undead Scarman and his robot mummies in the Martian pyramid, the Doctor and Sarah's sudden about-face and retreat is a rare bit of physical comedy, beautifully timed.

■ **Where else have I seen...** Bernard Archard, who plays Scarman in modes both living and otherwise, portrays another two-faced authority figure in **30** *The Power of the Daleks*.

■ **Arcs in Space** Another devilishly powerful entity (also voiced by Gabriel Woolf) is found imprisoned in **174** *The Impossible Planet/The Satan Pit*. And the Osirans weren't the only aliens around in ancient Egypt – see **21** *The Daleks' Master Plan* and **105** *City of Death*.

83 The Android Invasion

(four episodes) by Terry Nation

The Doctor and Sarah return to Earth – or do they? The village of Devesham is eerily deserted, save for strange figures in hazard suits, and the calendar in the pub says that every day is the 6th of July.

■ **Where and When** A simulation of Devesham and its space centre on the planet Oseidon, plus the real Devesham and its space centre, at some point in the near future.

■ **The Baddies** There are many sinister androids, including duplicates of the Doctor and Sarah, but they're merely tools in a plan formulated by Styggron (Martin Friend), merciless chief scientist of the Kraals, based on information supplied by craven astronaut Guy Crayford (Milton Johns).

■ **Farewell to...** RSM Benton and Harry Sullivan, neither of whom gets a great send-off. If it wasn't for a reference to him in **125** *Mawdryn Undead*, you could be forgiven for thinking that Benton is killed in this story.

■ **Look out for...** One of the android villagers seems to have a box-like chest section, almost certainly because the actor in question was keeping his packed-lunch container under his jumper.

■ **What they said** Writing in his diary on Saturday 29 November 1975, the actor Kenneth Williams was unimpressed: "'Dr Who' gets more & more silly."

■ **Arcs in Space** Writer Terry Nation first used the idea of an android duplicate in **17** *The Chase*. Similar duplicates appear in **101** *The Androids of Tara*, **117** *Four to Doomsday*, **135** *The Caves of Androzani* and **205** *Victory of the Daleks*.

84 The Brain of Morbius

(four episodes) by Robin Bland

A fanatical surgeon has been recovering body parts from crashed spacecraft to build a new body for his master, Morbius. But then a better receptacle for Morbius' brain turns up: the Doctor!

■ **Where and When** The storm-ravaged planet Karn, a few billion miles from Gallifrey. Date unknown.

■ **The Baddies** Morbius (voiced by Michael Spice), a ruthless Time Lord war criminal reduced to just a brain. Crazed neurosurgeon Mehendri Solon (Philip Madoc). And the Sisterhood of Karn, who are suspicious of all Time Lords and very keen on ritual sacrifice.

■ **Farewell to...** This is the last time the Time Lords send the Doctor on a mission – at least until **137** *Attack of the Cybermen*.

■ **Look out for...** During the Doctor's mind-bending contest with Morbius, we see images of the first three Doctors... and a succession of previously unknown earlier incarnations.

■ **What they said** This story drew considerable criticism from Mary Whitehouse of the National Viewers' and Listeners' Association. "The latest *Dr Who* series contained some of the sickest and most horrific material ever seen on children's television," she told the *Daily Express* on Monday 26 April 1976.

■ **Arcs in Space** The Eighth Doctor regenerates on Karn in the mini-episode *The Night of the Doctor* (see pages 112-113) and returns there in **254** *The Magician's Apprentice/The Witch's Familiar*, before meeting Ohila of the Sisterhood again in **262** *Hell Bent*. The idea of the Doctor having mysterious, earlier incarnations is explored further in **295** *Ascension of the Cybermen/The Timeless Child* and **297** *Flux*.

Solon (Philip Madoc) is attacked by his own creature (Stuart Fell) in *The Brain of Morbius*.

Kraals Styggron (Martin Friend) and Chedaki (Roy Skelton) in *The Android Invasion*.

85 The Seeds of Doom

(six episodes) by Robert Banks Stewart

A scientific expedition discovers a strange pod buried in Antarctic ice. Thawed out, it infects one of the scientists, who begins to transform into a vegetable-based life form…

■ **Where and When** Camp Five base in the Antarctic, the World Ecology Bureau, and a mansion belonging to a millionaire plant-collector (plus its extensive gardens). The time is the near future.

■ **The Baddies** The Krynoid not only has the capacity to infect, possess and transform humans into monsters, but it can see and hear through plants and channel its power into them. This is a source of delight to the debonair Harrison Chase (Tony Beckley), who envisages the extinction of all animal life on Earth, to be replaced by "A harmony of root, stem, leaf, flower."

■ **Look out for…** The Fourth Doctor at his most action-packed, getting into fist fights and jumping through a skylight. "What do you do for an encore, Doctor?" asks Chase. "I win!" he replies.

■ **Farewell to…** The original police-box prop used for the TARDIS is seen here for the last time; it collapsed on the heads of actors Tom Baker and Elisabeth Sladen during recording of the final scene. This is also the last story to feature UNIT in the heat of action until **152** *Battlefield*.

■ **What they said** This was another serial that upset Mary Whitehouse. Her claim that "strangulation – by hand, by claw, by obscene vegetable matter – is the latest gimmick" made it into *The Sun* on Tuesday 6 April 1976.

■ **Arcs in Space** The Doctor has only visited Antarctica on two other occasions – in **29** *The Tenth Planet* and **276** *Twice Upon a Time*, although the TARDIS accidentally ends up there again in **234** *Cold War*.

86 The Masque of Mandragora

(four episodes) by Louis Marks

The TARDIS accidentally brings energy from the mysterious Mandragora Helix to Renaissance Italy – where the cult of Demnos have been preparing for its arrival.

■ **Where and When** The picturesque town of San Martino, somewhere in Italy towards the end of the 15th century. (The Doctor makes a historically inaccurate reference to Galileo inventing the telescope in 50 years' time.)

■ **The Baddies** The Mandragora Helix is a form of "astral energy" that exploits and possesses humans, abetted by the high priest of Demnos (Robert James) and the arrogant astrologer Hieronymous (Norman Jones). The ruthless Count Federico (Jon Laurimore) has his own ambitions.

■ **Introducing…** The Doctor shows Sarah the TARDIS' second control room, with dark wood walls and a console that resembles a small writing desk, with the controls hidden within.

■ **Look out for…** The end of the second episode has no fewer than *three* cliffhangers – the Doctor is attacked by the Helix, Giuliano (Gareth Armstrong) is ambushed by Federico's men, and Sarah is grabbed by members of the cult.

■ **Where else have I seen…** Robert James has a more substantial role as the scientist Lesterson in **30** *The Power of the Daleks*.

■ **Arcs in Space** This story introduces the idea that being able to understand foreign languages is a "Time Lord gift". This is clarified as involving the TARDIS in **158** *The End of the World*, and is also a plot point in **167** *The Christmas Invasion* and **302** *Wild Blue Yonder*.

Hieronymous (Norman Jones) in *The Masque of Mandragora*.

SCARY STORIES

Sixteen reasons why *Doctor Who* will forever be associated with watching from behind the sofa, tabulated by **Alan Barnes**.

Outstanding

The Weeping Angels are quantum-locked beings that literally turn to stone when they're observed... but which return, snarling, to life whenever their prey turns away, or simply blinks. They established themselves as the true stuff of nightmares right from their first appearance, in the 2007 season – but when they reappeared in **206** *The Time of Angels/Flesh and Stone*, it was with an added twist: *That which holds the image of an angel becomes itself an angel*. Cue an extraordinary sequence in which a grainy, flickering Angel emerges from security-camera footage to menace Amy Pond (Karen Gillan) – not unlike the vengeful spirit that comes out of a TV in the infamous 1998 'J-horror', *Ring*. Not even watching them at home is safe...

Essential

But the worst horrors always emerge from the most mundane things – as the Angels' creator,

Steven Moffat, proved in **245** *Listen*, an episode devoted entirely to whether or not something's hiding under your bed... and which makes a red crocheted bedspread scarier than 98.5 per cent of all *Doctor Who* monsters. In the 21st century, *Doctor Who* first signalled its commitment to chill with **159** *The Unquiet Dead*, which began – startlingly for just 7.00pm – with an old woman's corpse coming back to life in an undertaker's parlour. It turned out to be a zombie filled with gas, as distinct from the 'gas-mask zombies' that rose before Rose a few episodes later, in Moffat's debut, **164** *The Empty Child/The Doctor Dances*.

Excellent

Everyone knows what Daleks are now, but once upon a time, they were something new – croak-voiced and uncanny. All *Doctor Who* horror descends from **2** *The Mutants* (aka *The Daleks*) – not just in the creatures themselves, but in Susan's flight through the petrified forest and the ghastly 'whatever' in the Lake of Mutations. **42** *Fury from the Deep* was designed purely for the purpose of pumping fear directly into the home; the only reason we have the extraordinary footage of open-mouthed gas engineers Mr Oak and Mr Quill (John Gill, Bill Burridge) is because it was cut out of foreign prints, judged too disturbing to show. The programme went through another horror phase in the mid-1970s, with Sarah Jane Smith (Elisabeth Sladen) central – struggling through the Wirrn-infested conduits of **76**

The Ark in Space, stalked by robot mummies in **82** *Pyramids of Mars*, and temporarily blinded in **84** *The Brain of Morbius*, unaware of the headless assemblage behind her.

The Best of the Rest

Steven Moffat may have established himself as *Doctor Who*'s dark prince, but fellow showrunner Russell T Davies gave him a run for his money with **196** *Midnight*, which had a bizarre, maddening alien presence manifesting itself by repeating your speech back at you. He did it again with **302** *Wild Blue Yonder*, which has the Fourteenth Doctor (David Tennant) and Donna (Catherine Tate) encountering a pair of literally twisted doppelgängers. Those suffering from one of the most common fears will run screaming from both **280** *Arachnids in the UK* and **74** *Planet of the Spiders* – the second of which was widely reported, in 1975, to have "caused an epidemic of spider-phobia among young children". **268** *Knock Knock* sets itself up as the *Doctor Who* version of a slasher movie, with a succession of student housemates getting offed one by one. **214** *The Impossible Astronaut/Day of the Moon* introduced Moffat's second-most horrible creations, the Silence – with the 'spooky orphanage' sequence in the second half proving unforgettable (ironically). Finally, **252** *Dark Water/Death in Heaven* contains probably the most disturbing scene in the entire series, when Dr Chang (Andrew Leung) isolates the voices of the dead. You won't rest easy, that's for sure.

"A Weeping Angel...
is the deadliest,
most powerful, most
malevolent life form
evolution has ever
produced."

THE DOCTOR,
THE TIME OF ANGELS

87 The Hand of Fear

(four episodes) by **Bob Baker** and **Dave Martin**

Exposed to radiation, a stone hand found in a quarry regenerates into Eldrad, who was sentenced to obliteration by his fellow Kastrians millennia before. Returned home by the Doctor, Eldrad is set upon revenge.

■ **Where and When** Earth in the near future, and the frozen planet Kastria.

■ **The Baddies** Eldrad, the Kastrian engineer who designed the barriers protecting his people from solar winds and then destroyed them in an attempt to gain power. Partly regenerated, Eldrad takes a female form (Judith Paris) and, when fully regenerated, a male one (Stephen Thorne). Eldrad uses a jewelled ring to control the minds of those who wear it, leading to them exclaiming: "Eldrad must live!"

■ **Where else have I seen…** Rex Robinson, playing Dr Carter, was also Dr Tyler in **65** *The Three Doctors* and Gebek in **73** *The Monster of Peladon*.

■ **Farewell to…** This is the last regular appearance of Sarah Jane Smith. Tired of the stresses of travelling with the Doctor, she packs her bags and threatens to leave, expecting him to persuade her to stay. What she doesn't know is that the Doctor has had the call from Gallifrey and he can't take her with him

■ **Look out for** Sarah's stuffed owl toy and pot plant, among the belongings she's packed. She didn't keep much on board the TARDIS, but these were clearly essentials!

■ **Arcs in Space** The Doctor drops Sarah off in Aberdeen instead of Croydon (but he doesn't know this until **170** *School Reunion*). Responding to the call from Gallifrey, the Doctor sets the controls for home, leading him straight into **88** *The Deadly Assassin*.

88 The Deadly Assassin

(four episodes) by **Robert Holmes**

Returning to Gallifrey to prevent the assassination of the President, the Doctor is framed for the crime instead. He must battle the Master's agent in the Matrix, the repository of all Time Lord knowledge.

■ **Where and When** Gallifrey, date unknown.

■ **The Baddies** The Master (Peter Pratt) in his 'final', decomposing incarnation. He plans to use the energy from the Eye of Harmony, deep underneath the Panopticon, to regenerate his emaciated body.

■ **Look out for…** Surreal nightmarish sequences set in the Matrix, as the Master replaces the computational background with scenes from his own deranged imagination, including a speeding steam train and an operating table in the desert.

■ **Introducing…** The legend of Rassilon, founder of the Time Lords, who captured the power of a black hole and placed it within the Eye of Harmony, deep beneath Gallifrey's central Capitol. Gallifrey's system of Chapters, its 'staser'-toting Chancellery Guards, and its secretive Celestial Intervention Agency (CIA). Cardinal Borusa (Angus Mackay) – the Doctor's former tutor at the Time Lords' Academy. The APC net, better known as the Matrix – a repository for the brain

impulses of dead Time Lords, which can be used to predict the future. The Matrix will be pivotal in later stories, including **123** *Arc of Infinity*, **143** *The Trial of a Time Lord* and **262** *Hell Bent*.

■ **What they said** Writing in the *Doctor Who* Appreciation Society magazine *TARDIS* (volume 2, issue 1, 1977), Society president Jan Vincent-Rudzki was famously outraged by the story's revisionism, claiming: "I've spoken to many people, many of whom were not members, and they all said how this story shattered their illusions of the Time Lords, and lowered them to ordinary people."

■ **Arcs in Space** The Doctor becomes Lord President of Gallifrey by default when his only opponent Chancellor Goth (Bernard Horsfall) – the assassin of the title – dies. He uses the title in **97** *The Invasion of Time* (but only as part of his cover), escapes his duties again in **129** *The Five Doctors*, hears in **143** *The Trial of a Time Lord* that he was deposed, and assumes the role briefly in **262** *Hell Bent*.

89 The Face of Evil

(four episodes) by Chris Boucher
On a jungle planet, two violently opposed tribes worship a god named Xoanon. But Xoanon is a computer with a split personality, experimenting with eugenics – and it's all the Doctor's fault.

■ **Where and When** An unnamed planet, date unknown.

■ **The Baddies** The Tesh and the Sevateem perceive each other as the enemy, but the Doctor is known as 'the Evil One', which makes him the baddie. Xoanon wants to destroy the Doctor, so he's a baddie, too. It's complicated.

■ **Introducing…** Leela (Louise Jameson), warrior of the Sevateem, who becomes the Doctor's companion. Fiercely loyal, brave, curious, and handy in a fight, she slips into the TARDIS even though the Doctor has said no to taking her with him.

■ **Look out for…** Leela recognises the Doctor as the Evil One because the image of his face is carved into the hillside. She's wary of him, so he tries to put her at ease by offering her a jelly baby. In horror, she gasps: "It is true, then! They say the Evil One eats babies!" A great example of how fact can be distorted as myth.

■ **Where else have I seen…** Two actors in this story also appeared in **50** *The War Games*. David Garfield, who plays the Sevateem's shaman, Neeva, appeared as Von Weich, one of the aliens, and Leslie Schofield, who plays the devious Calib, was Leroy, a soldier in the Confederate Army.

■ **Arcs in Space** The Doctor arrives alone and talks out loud to himself – still missing Sarah following her departure in **87** *The Hand of Fear*, perhaps. Crazed computers are also seen in **27** *The War Machines*, **69** *The Green Death* and **96** *Underworld*.

90 The Robots of Death

(four episodes) by Chris Boucher
Someone has been breaking the programming

of the robots that staff an isolated Sandminer – turning them into homicidal killers, as the prelude to a robot revolution.

■ **Where and When** Aboard Storm Mine Four – a mineral-chasing machine in the deserts far beyond Kaldor City, date unknown.

■ **The Baddies** Robotics expert Taren Capel (David Bailie) has inveigled his way on board the Sandminer using a stolen identity. Raised by robots, he wants to free them from slavery. He even wants to look like them, styling his hair and make-up to match theirs, and wearing a robot's clothes. Creepy.

■ **Look out for…** When the Doctor and Leela are assumed to be the killers and are questioned by the crew, the Doctor responds to Borg's comments by saying, "You know, you're a classic example of the inverse ratio between the size of the mouth and the size of the brain." One of the best put-downs of all time!

■ **Where else have I seen…** Pamela Salem (Toos) also plays Professor Rachel Jensen in **148** *Remembrance of the Daleks*, while David Collings (Poul) plays Vorus in **79** *Revenge of the Cybermen* and Mawdryn in **125** *Mawdryn Undead*.

■ **What they said** In his obituary for Chris Boucher (*The Guardian*, 21 December 2022), Toby Hadoke described the story as "a fusion of Agatha Christie, Isaac Asimov and Frank Herbert" that becomes "more than a sum of its parts thanks to Boucher's sardonic exchanges… well-drawn characters, world-building through dialogue and hard sci-fi concepts."

■ **Arcs in Space** The Doctor will find himself aboard another vast vessel in which the blank-faced robot staff are being made murderous by a hidden malefactor in **188** *Voyage of the Damned*.

A speaking Voc-class robot, in *The Robots of Death*.

91 The Talons of Weng-Chiang

(six episodes) by Robert Holmes

The Doctor decides to show Leela how her ancestors lived – and becomes embroiled in a complex plot involving a homicidal ventriloquist's dummy, giant rats, a secret cult and an ancient Chinese god.

■ **Where and When** The foggy streets of London in the late 19th century – particularly the Palace Theatre, the sewers beneath it, and a 'fortress' called the House of the Dragon.

■ **The Baddies** Girls are being kidnapped by stage hypnotist Li H'sen Chang (John Bennett), a devotee of Weng-Chiang – who is in fact Magnus Greel (Michael Spice), a time-travelling fugitive accompanied by a pig-brained cyborg, the Peking Homunculus, aka 'Mr Sin' (Deep Roy).

■ **Look out for...** This story draws on a myriad of literary sources, from *The Phantom of the Opera* and *The Mystery of Dr Fu Manchu* to the works of Arthur Conan Doyle – which is why the Doctor is cosplaying Sherlock Holmes, and police pathologist Professor Litefoot (Trevor Baxter) has a housekeeper called Mrs Hudson.

■ **Where else have I seen...** Throughout, the Doctor is assisted not just by Litefoot, but also by theatre proprietor Henry Gordon Jago (Christopher Benjamin). Previously Sir Keith Gold in **54** *Inferno*, Benjamin will return as Colonel Hugh in **194** *The Unicorn and the Wasp*.

■ **What they said** Writing in *The Times* on Monday 28 February 1977, Stanley Reynolds observed that "the period charm of Victorian London is caught well enough. Also the prejudices of the time."

■ **Arcs in Space** The idea of 'time agents' from the 51st century is explored further in **164** *The Empty Child/The Doctor Dances*.

92 Horror of Fang Rock

(four episodes) by Terrance Dicks

The isolated lighthouse at Fang Rock has a number of visitors one foggy night – the survivors of a shipwreck, the Doctor and Leela, and a Rutan scout trained in new metamorphosis techniques.

Lighthouse keeper Reuben (Colin Douglas) and the Doctor in *Horror of Fang Rock*.

Mr Sin (Deep Roy), the Peking Homunculus, in *The Talons of Weng-Chiang*.

■ **Where and When** The lighthouse is on a small island somewhere in the English Channel; the shipwrecked yacht was heading for Southampton. A reference to King Edward suggests we're in the 1900s.

■ **The Baddies** Lord Palmerdale (Sean Caffrey), intent on making a killing on the stock market, has obtained some confidential information from parliamentarian Henry Skinsale (Alan Rowe). The Rutan scout (voiced by Colin Douglas) is intent on using Earth to make a killing in the war against the Sontarans.

■ **Look out for...** Leela at her most no-nonsense – smashing a door down with a sledgehammer and giving the hysterical Adelaide (Annette Woollett) a slap to stop her screaming.

■ **Farewell to...** Looking at the explosion of the Rutan mothership causes Leela's eyes to change colour to blue. (Actress Louise Jameson had previously been wearing brown-tinted contact lenses, which she disliked.)

■ **What they said** Writer Terrance Dicks had started writing a vampire story (later to become **112** *State of Decay*) when he was asked to write a serial about a lighthouse instead. "I didn't know anything about lighthouses," he admitted, "so Bob [script editor Robert Holmes] directed me to go and find a *Boys' Book of Lighthouses* and bone up on them."

■ **Arcs in Space** The interminable war between the Rutans and the Sontarans was introduced in **70** *The Time Warrior*. Leela says she isn't a "teshnician" – referring to the Tesh in **84** *The Face of Evil*.

Text by Jonathan Morris

93 The Invisible Enemy

(four episodes) by **Bob Baker** and **Dave Martin**

The Nucleus of the Swarm takes up residence in the Doctor's mind. The only way to fight it is for a clone of the Doctor to enter his own brain…

■ **Where and When** The Titan shuttle, the refuelling base on Titan itself, and the Bi-Al Foundation (also known as the Centre for Alien Morphology, built into asteroid K4067), around the year 5000.

■ **The Baddies** The possessed humans have no control over their actions, being telepathically directed by the Nucleus, a sentient virus that manifests itself in the macrocosm in the form of a large crustacean.

■ **Introducing…** K9, the mobile computer with offensive capabilities built in the shape of a squared-off dog, voiced for most of his appearances by John Leeson (who also voiced the Nucleus in this serial).

■ **What they said** The introduction of K9 received a great deal of newspaper coverage. According to the *Sunday Mirror*'s Colin Wills on 9 April 1977: "No pictures of him have been released yet but I'm told all-metal K-Nine has a tail that wags, eyes that glow red, ears that flap and a nose that sniffs. Instead of woof-woofs, computer tape comes out of his mouth."

■ **Look out for…** While some of the physical effects don't quite make the grade, this story boasts some highly ambitious model-work and electronic effects, featured in one way or another in nearly every scene.

■ **Arcs in Space** The idea of the Doctor being miniaturised to go on a medical mission recurs in 243 *Into the Dalek*.

94 Image of the Fendahl

(four episodes) by **Chris Boucher**

At Fetch Priory, scientists are engaged in a strange experiment involving a 12-million-year-old human skull and a sonic time scanner. But might they be working to a pre-ordained plan?

■ **Where and When** Fetch Priory, a secluded mansion with woods nearby, and the Tyler residence in the village of Fetchborough. The present day.

■ **The Baddies** The fanatical Maximillian

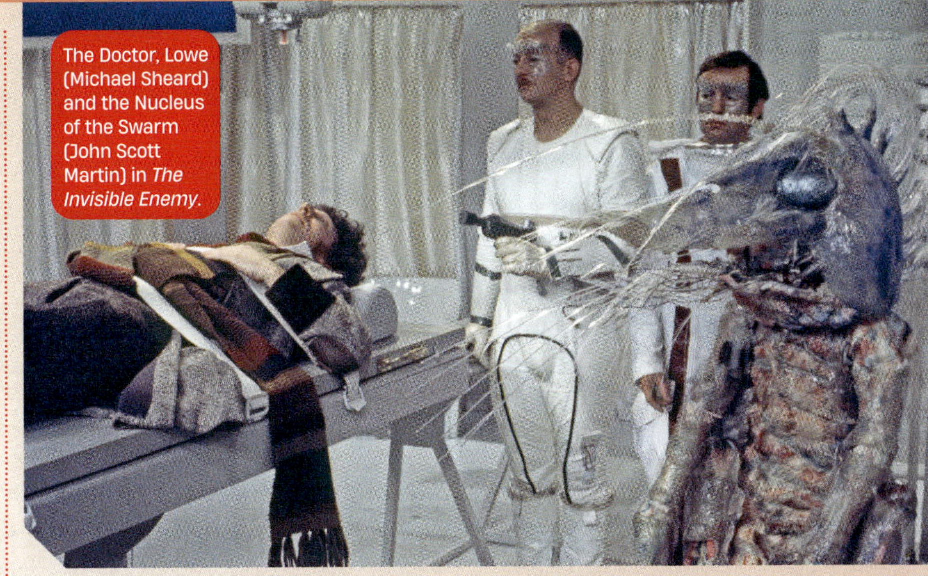

The Doctor, Lowe (Michael Sheard) and the Nucleus of the Swarm (John Scott Martin) in *The Invisible Enemy*.

Stael (Scott Fredericks) intends to invoke the Fendahl, a creature from Time Lord mythology that feeds on life itself – and has assembled a coven to aid him. The millionaire scientist Dr Fendelman (Denis Lill) is an unwitting pawn in Stael's scheme.

■ **Look out for…** The extraordinary moment when Thea Ransome (Wanda Ventham) transforms into the golden Fendahl Core and rises from the floor, as though lifted by an invisible force.

■ **Where else have I seen…** The security guard, David Mitchell, is played by future *EastEnders* star Derek Martin, who previously appeared as an uncredited extra in 12 *The Romans*, 22 *The Massacre of St Bartholomew's Eve*, 31 *The Highlanders*, 41 *The Web of Fear*, 53 *The Ambassadors of Death*, 54 *Inferno*, 56 *The Mind of Evil* and 57 *The Claws of Axos*.

■ **What they said** "That was my attempt at a ghost story," said writer Chris Boucher, interviewed for the 1986 **Doctor Who Magazine** Winter Special. "They did allow me night filming, which is tremendously expensive and is usually cut out straight away. I'd only put it in because I was so green, but they left it in and it looked good."

■ **Arcs in Space** The idea that growing up near a time fissure gives you the power of precognition is revisited in 159 *The Unquiet Dead*. In 287 *Resolution*, the Doctor will dispense of a Dalek in the same way as the Fendahl, by dropping it in a supernova.

The transformed Thea Ransome (Wanda Ventham) and the Doctor in *Image of the Fendahl*.

The Usurian Collector (Henry Woolf) in *The Sun Makers*.

95 The Sun Makers

(four episodes) by Robert Holmes
The TARDIS lands on Pluto, which is now habitable and populated by the human race. They're being subjugated by the Usurians, who are "taxing the life out of them".

■ **Where and When** A terraformed Pluto, which has six artificial suns. It's the distant future, exact date unknown.

■ **The Baddies** Gatherer Hade (Richard Leech) and his turncoat assistant Marn (Jonina Scott). And the Usurians, represented by the Collector (Henry Woolf). In their natural form, the Usurians "look like sea kale with eyes".

■ **Look out for...** The delicious duality of the Doctor insulting the Gatherer while offering him a sweet: "Humbug."

■ **Where else have I seen...** Tom Kelly, who plays a guard, was a different guard in **89** *The Face of Evil*. His biggest role in *Doctor Who* would come in just two stories' time, as one of the Vardans in **97** *The Invasion of Time*.

■ **What they said** Interviewed in **Doctor Who Magazine** 215 (July 1994), Louise Jameson said, "I liked *The Sun Makers* because it had political content. I think it's very important that kids' TV does hold a moral alongside the story."

■ **Arcs in Space** Other stories exploring our solar system include **201** *The Waters of Mars* (Mars), **93** *The Invisible Enemy* (Titan, one of the moons of Saturn), and **33** *The Moonbase*, **48** *The Seeds of Death* and **248** *Kill the Moon* (Earth's Moon).

96 Underworld

(four episodes) by Bob Baker and Dave Martin
At the edge of creation, the Doctor, Leela and K9 encounter an exhausted Minyan crew who are searching for their lost race bank. They discover that the descendants of the lost P7E have become slaves to its computer, which has gone insane...

■ **Where and When** The edge of known space, and on a planet that has formed around the spaceship *P7E*, date unknown.

■ **The Baddies** The Oracle (voiced by Christine Pollon) – "just another machine with megalomania" – and its helmeted servants, the Seers.

■ **Look out for...** The headphones on the torture device used to interrogate Herrick were previously an interface to the BOSS in **69** *The Green Death* and part of the IRIS machine in **74** *Planet of the Spiders* – and later a link to the navigation mechanism of Rorvik's ship in **113** *Warriors' Gate*.

■ **Where else have I seen...** Sacrificial goat Idmon is played by Jimmy Gardner, who'd previously been Chenchu in **4** *Marco Polo*.

■ **What they said** In the April 1978 issue of the fanzine *TARDIS*, Neil Blomley called this "One of the best stories of the season".

■ **Arcs in Space** **81** *Planet of Evil* is also set at "the very edge of the known universe" – and the TARDIS crash-lands on a spaceship at the edge of the universe in **302** *Wild Blue Yonder*.

97 The Invasion of Time

(six episodes) by David Agnew
The Doctor returns to Gallifrey to assume the role of President, but he appears to be in league with a force of invading Vardans.

■ **Where and When** The Citadel and wastelands of Gallifrey, and aboard the TARDIS – time unknown.

■ **The Baddies** The Vardans: first seen as shimmering shapes before taking their real and "disappointing" form of humanoid soldiers. Meanwhile, waiting in the wings... Commander Stor (Derek Deadman) and a squad of Sontaran troopers.

■ **Introducing...** A female Time Lord! Space Traffic Controller Rodan (Hilary Ryan) paves the way for Romana in the following season.

■ **Look out for...** A Sontaran being consumed by a man-eating plant that the Doctor just happens to keep aboard the TARDIS.

■ **What they said** Speaking in 1984 – in an interview published in **Doctor Who Magazine** issue 248 (February 1997) – producer Graham Williams said, re the Sontarans: "I always liked the 'potato

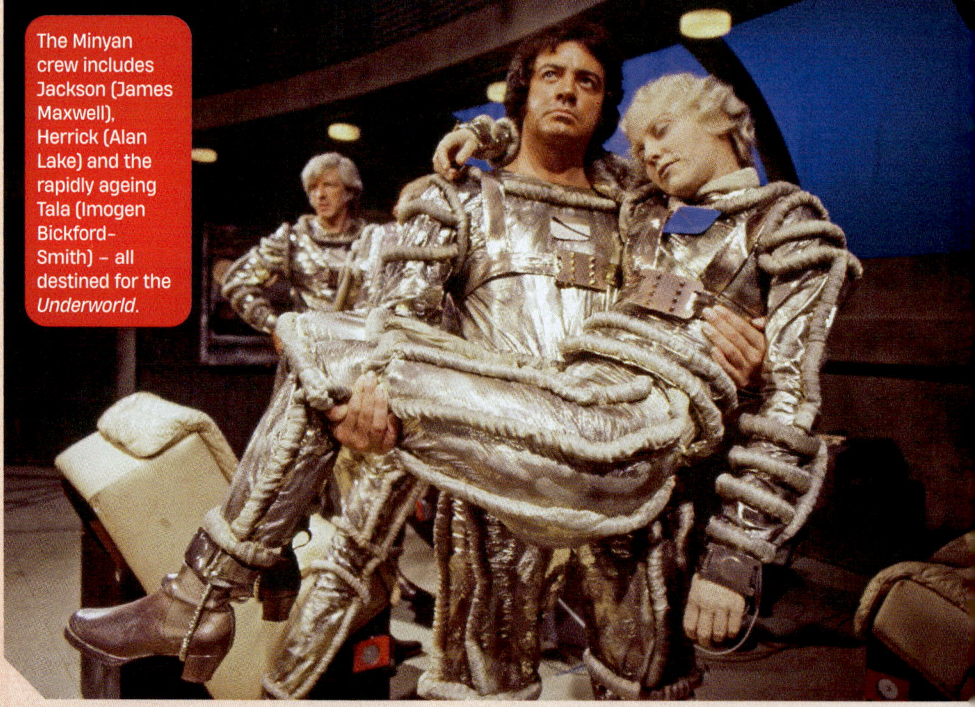

The Minyan crew includes Jackson (James Maxwell), Herrick (Alan Lake) and the rapidly ageing Tala (Imogen Bickford-Smith) – all destined for the *Underworld*.

Left
The oily Castellan Kelner (Milton Johns) aids the Sontaran attack on Gallifrey in *The Invasion of Time*.

Right
The Doctor disguised as one of the Graff Vynda K's guards in *The Ribos Operation*.

heads', as we called them. I thought they were rather more interesting than the Daleks, and posed a bit more of a threat."

■ **Arcs in Space** A regenerated Borusa (John Arnatt) has been elevated from Cardinal to Chancellor, following Goth's demise in **88** *The Deadly Assassin*. Leela and Rodan fall in with the Outsiders in the wilderness – plausibly the same Shobogans mentioned in *The Deadly Assassin*, later described as Gallifrey's indigenous people in **295** *The Timeless Children*. K9 decides to stay on Gallifrey with Leela, who's decided to build a new life with Commander Andred (Christopher Tranchell) – but the Doctor will have made K9 Mark II by the time of the next adventure!

98 The Ribos Operation

(four episodes) by **Robert Holmes**
The Doctor is tasked by the White Guardian to seek out the six disguised segments of the Key to Time, which, once assembled, can prevent the universe plunging into eternal chaos. The TARDIS' first destination is Ribos, a planet that a conman called Garron is trying to sell to the deposed tyrant, the Graff Vynda-K.

■ **Where and When** The planet Ribos within the Greater Cyrrhenic Empire during Ice Time (its orbit around the sun is elliptical, so it's either really parky or a proper scorcher), time unknown.
■ **The Baddies** The Graff Vynda-K (Paul Seed), who's planning a campaign to win back the Levithian crown, plus his trusty general Sholakh (Robert Keegan).
■ **Introducing…** The White Guardian (Cyril Luckham), who supplies the

Doctor with a segment-locating tracer, and a new assistant – the first imposed upon the Doctor since Jo in **55** *Terror of the Autons*. Romanadvoratrelundar (Mary Tamm) – Romana for short – is a 125-year-old graduate from the Time Lords' Academy (and believes she's been sent by the President).
■ **Look out for…** As they bid farewell, Garron (Iain Cuthbertson) slyly switches the first segment for a lump of rock, not noticing that the Doctor has then switched it back again.
■ **What they said** David Farkil, writing in the December 1978 issue of *TARDIS*, pointed out that "A few years ago I asked if there was any magic left in *Doctor Who*, and *Ribos* answered that with a resounding 'Yes!'"
■ **Arcs in Space** The White Guardian will return in **127** *Enlightenment*. The Black Guardian is also mentioned; he'll

The Polyphase Avatron sits on the shoulder of the Captain (Bruce Purchase) in *The Pirate Planet*.

finally appear in **103** *The Armageddon Factor*. The quest for the parts of the Key continues in the next adventure…

99 The Pirate Planet

(four episodes) by **Douglas Adams**
The second segment of the Key to Time is on Calufrax, but where is Calufrax? The search leads the Doctor, Romana and K9 to Zanak, which is entering a new Golden Age of Prosperity…

■ **Where and When** Zanak, date unknown.
■ **The Baddies** The cybernetic Pirate Captain (Bruce Purchase) and his nervy assistant Mr Fibuli (Andrew Robertson). These destroyers of worlds appear to be the main baddies, until a rug-pull reveals that the Captain's nurse (Rosalind Lloyd) is a projection of the evil and ancient Queen Xanxia, who's kept alive within Time Dams.
■ **Look out for…** In a story that's mainly a really inventive and frothy romp, there's a distinct change in tone when the Doctor fiercely admonishes the Captain in his trophy room of plundered planets.
■ **Where else have I seen…** David Warwick, who plays citizen Kimus, returned 28 years later as the Police Commissioner in **177** *Army of Ghosts*.
■ **What they said** Interviewed in 1978 (and finally published in **DWM**'s 1995 Summer Special), Douglas Adams said, "I wanted something really silly in it – 'how about a robot parrot'? I came back and thought 'Good God, don't be so stupid.' And then I thought, 'Why not, I can't think of anything else to put in this scene.'"
■ **Arcs in Space** Calufrax is named among the Sutekh-devastated planets restored to life in **311** *Empire of Death*.

HOW TO WATCH...

COMEDY

Wit and relative dimensions in farce, selected by **Eddie Robson**.

Below
The First Doctor spars with the Meddling Monk (Peter Butterworth) in *The Time Meddler*.

Outstanding

No one did more to establish comedy as a key element of *Doctor Who* than Dennis Spooner, who wrote **17** *The Time Meddler* at the end of his year story-editing the show. The premise: what if there was a version of the Doctor who mucked around with history for larks? The Monk (Peter Butterworth) is written and played as a bumbler, but one who's nevertheless capable of entirely unpicking the world we know. William Hartnell's comic sparring with Butterworth is the highlight, but companions Peter Purves and Maureen O'Brien forge a neat combo of their own. Even the Monk's final defeat is funny.

Essential

Many of the funniest stories are historicals, especially those that parody how other texts depict the past. **310** *Rogue* does this to a tee, with a witty examination of Regency fantasies and lots of nicely antagonistic flirting. **105** *City of Death*, co-written by Douglas Adams under a pseudonym, brings *joie de vivre* to a tale of art theft in Paris. It has many quotable lines, but the "I like concise answers" exchange between Tom Baker's Doctor and Julian Glover's Count Scarlioni in the secret cellar is just a perfect piece of comic writing. Many of the Christmas episodes lean into comedy, and the funniest is **263** *The Husbands of River Song*. Far less plotty than most Steven Moffat-authored episodes, this focuses on Peter Capaldi's Doctor and Alex Kingston's River as a romantic double-act, with delightful results.

Excellent

Russell T Davies' scripts always have great jokes, and perhaps his funniest moment comes in **189** *Partners in Crime*, as the Doctor and Donna communicate silently from behind two windows. Another Dennis Spooner script, **12** *The Romans*, is a glorious piece of farce that splits up the time travellers for comic (and sometimes brutal) effect. Jon Pertwee tended to play it straight in his early performances as the Doctor, but his background was in comedy – and this really comes out in later stories like **70** *The Time Warrior*. The interplay between the deadpan Sontaran Linx (Kevin Lindsay) and the brilliantly OTT Irongron (David Daker) is also excellent. The Sontarans' comic potential is played to the max after the introduction of Dan Starkey's Strax, who gets plenty of screen time in **237** *The Crimson Horror*. And Michelle Gomez's Missy is one of the great comic performances in *Doctor Who*; even a gruelling story like **275** *World Enough and Time/The Doctor Falls* gives her some of her best material.

The Best of the Rest

Sacha Dhawan's take on the Master is also hilarious, and **300** *The Power of the Doctor* offers his extraordinary Rasputin dance number *and* his Doctor mash-up cosplay – perhaps the funniest outfit in *Doctor Who*. The Western parody of **25** *The Gunfighters* has some dodgy accents but many excellent gags. **168** *New Earth* lets Billie Piper off the leash when the evil facelift Lady Cassandra takes over Rose's body. **101** *The Androids of Tara* is a pleasingly low-stakes swashbuckler with Tom Baker clearly having a ball. Similarly sunny vibes come from the 1950s holiday-camp-set **146** *Delta and the Bannermen*, which has one of *Doctor Who*'s most colourful casts (including Ken Dodd as the Tollmaster). If you like your comedy blacker, try **142** *Revelation of the Daleks*, a cynical piece about death and how we deal with it. And a final word for **270** *Extremis*: it may be one of the bleakest episodes ever, but the scene where Bill (Pearl Mackie) brings her date home is a masterpiece, and a gag you could only do in *Doctor Who*.

"Doctor, it's more fun my way. I can make things happen ahead of their time."
THE MONK, *THE TIME MEDDLER*

Ancient Celtic goddess the Cailleach (Susan Engel) in *The Stones of Blood*.

100 The Stones of Blood

(four episodes) by **David Fisher**
The hunt for the third segment of the Key to Time begins with blood-drenched sacrifice… and culminates in a courtroom drama aboard a ship stranded in hyperspace.

■ **Where and When** The Nine Travellers, a stone circle in England, in the late 20th century. And the equivalent position in the alternative dimension of hyperspace.

■ **The Baddies** Cessair of Diplos (Susan Engel), a silver-skinned criminal from a G-class planet in Tau Ceti, who for more than 4,000 years has adopted a number of Earthly aliases. She's acting in cahoots with a trio of Ogri – silicon-based, globulin-deficient natives of the amino-acid swamps on the planet Ogros – and local cultist Leonard de Vries (Nicholas McArdle).

■ **Look out for…** Wielding a policeman's truncheon against a killer stone weighing more than three-and-a-half tons, Professor Emilia Rumford (Beatrix Lehmann) assures the astonished Doctor that "In the cause of science I think it our duty to capture that creature."

■ **Where else have I seen…** Shirin Taylor makes a brief but memorable appearance as Pat, one of a pair of campers who fall victim to an Ogri. In **147** *Dragonfire*, she's a complaining customer in Iceworld, who gets a milkshake tipped over her by Ace.

■ **What they said** Writing in the **Doctor Who Magazine** Special #5 (2004), showrunner Russell T Davies described the 'campers' scene as one of his favourites in the whole of the series: "Pat and her man… play no part in the story. This scene could be cut, without changing any aspect of the plot… But someone persisted, because someone understood exactly what makes this show tick. That death can happen, anywhere, any time. The universe isn't safe. We need the Doctor."

■ **Arcs in Space** Other silicon-based life forms include the Kastrians from **87** *The Hand of Fear* and the animated gargoyle Bok from **59** *The Dæmons*. The Weeping Angels, introduced in **186** *Blink*, are able to turn to stone.

101 The Androids of Tara

(four episodes) by **David Fisher**
On the feudal planet Tara, the Doctor uncovers a sophisticated plot to crown a robot duplicate as king – and Romana comes face to face with her identical double.

■ **Where and When** The Earth-type planet Tara (apparently ten parsecs from Earth), 400 years from the present day that the Doctor and Romana have just left.

■ **The Baddies** Count Grendel (Peter Jeffrey), Knight of Gracht, Master of the Sword. This charming, ambitious, servant-flogging power-monger plans to ascend the throne of Tara. To that end, he uses androids constructed by peasant underlings – and takes members of the Royal House of Tara captive.

■ **Look out for…** Even with the lure of 10,000 gold pieces to whichever bowman can loose an electronic bolt at the fleeing Doctor, the Count's men fail to hit their target, allowing their quarry to be scooped up onto Grendel's favourite charger, as ridden by novice Romana. No wonder the exasperated Count face-palms…

■ **What they said** In **DWM** issue 288 (March 2000), Peter Jeffrey – who'd been the Pilot of the Colony in **34** *The Macra Terror* – recalled: "I was glad [Grendel] wasn't killed off at the end – it was always left open. I would have considered coming back if I'd been asked!"

■ **Where else have I seen…** The hunched figure of Till, bodyservant to the Count, is played by Declan Mullholland – previously Clark, the workman driven mad by an attack from **62** *The Sea Devils*.

Will Prince Reynart (Neville Jason) be crowned King in *The Androids of Tara*?

The Doctor visits the swamplands of Delta Magna in *The Power of Kroll*.

■ **Arcs in Space** The Doctor demonstrates his fondness for fishing in Part One – a hobby he returns to in **140** *The Two Doctors*.

102 The Power of Kroll

(four episodes) by Robert Holmes
The Doctor is mistaken for a gun-runner plying his trade to the giant-squid-worshipping natives of Delta Magna, whose swamplands are being used by an Earth company for a methane-catalysing refinery.

■ **Where and When** The swamps on the third moon of Delta Magna at an unspecified date, during Earth's future colonisation of other planets.
■ **The Baddies** Thawn (Neil McCarthy), director of the refinery, who's engaged gun-runner Rohm-Dutt (Glyn Owen) to supply gas-operated Stelsons to the displaced natives of Delta Magna – supposedly on behalf of the anti-colonial Sons of Earth group. Further danger comes from Kroll – a 140-foot high, mile-wide giant squid that's awoken from its two-century slumber beneath the lakes.
■ **Look out for…** Some quirky behaviour from the Doctor in Part One. When the servile 'Swampie', Mensch (Terry Walsh), hands round drinks to the refinery technicians, the Doctor accepts his metal tumbler, casts an unimpressed glance at the contents, and then – unnoticed – cups his hand round it and slips it into his coat pocket.

■ **Where else have I seen…** Refinery technician Dugeen is played by John Leeson, who's generally heard rather than seen as the voice of K9 (here confined to the TARDIS).
■ **What they said** Producer Graham Williams "didn't much care for" the story – as he recalled in an interview published in **DWM** issue 249 (March 1997): "the monster in the swamp was one of the worst effects shots that we ever had…"
■ **Arcs in Space** The Doctor performs *Badinerie*, the seventh movement of JS Bach's *Suite No 2 in B minor*, on his reed flute. Later, he'll pick out the opening notes of the same composer's *Toccata and Fugue in D minor* on an organ keyboard (actually the disguised TARDIS), in **137** *Attack of the Cybermen*.

103 The Armageddon Factor

(six episodes) by Bob Baker and Dave Martin
At the climax of their quest to restore universal balance, the Doctor and Romana are faced with the prospect of a nuclear war – and a 'one life against millions' moral dilemma.

■ **Where and When** The twin planets of Atrios and Zeos, engaged in nuclear bombardment on the edge of the helical galaxy, plus a mysterious third planet – presumably in Earth's far future.

■ **The Baddies** The skeletal, black-robed Shadow (William Squire), an evil alien spectator presiding over a vast arena with his towering, mouthless, similarly clad mutes. He glories in destruction, rehearsing for the moment when the two halves of the cosmos go to war. He is, however, merely a servant of…
■ **Introducing…** The Black Guardian (Valentine Dyall), the chaos-loving, shape-changing opposite of the White Guardian. He walks in darkness.
■ **Farewell to…** Romana – at least in this form. In **104** *Destiny of the Daleks*, she'll adopt the appearance of Princess Astra of the Royal House of Atrios (Lalla Ward).
■ **Look out for…** Drax (Barry Jackson), a geezer who, 450 years ago, was in the class of '93 tech course with the Doctor back on Gallifrey, but failed in temporal theory. He went into repairs across the galaxy until his transport broke down in London – and while "investigating replacements" he got done. Result? Ten years in Brixton nick, where he had to learn the lingo.
■ **Arcs in Space** The encounter with the Black Guardian necessitates the fitting of a randomiser to the TARDIS' guidance system, applying the complex scientific principle of pot-luck to the vessel's travels right through to **109** *The Leisure Hive*. The Guardian finally catches up with the Doctor in **125** *Mawdryn Undead*.

Above inset
The Shadow, (William Squire) in *The Armageddon Factor*.

Right
Princess Astra (Lalla Ward) is chained by the Shadow's Mutes.

104 Destiny of the Daleks

(four episodes) by Terry Nation

Locked into an unwinnable conflict with the Movellans and their battle computer, the Daleks attempt to disinter their long-dead creator, hoping that Davros can give them an unbeatable edge. Enslaved humanoids pay the price of the brutal conflict between machine races.

■ **Where and When** Skaro, several hundred years after Davros was seemingly exterminated by his ungrateful creations.
■ **The Baddies** The Daleks, described here (unusually) as a "robot race", plus Davros (David Gooderson), their megalomaniac originator. Also, while the silver-braided Movellan android race don't share the Daleks' hatred for all other species, their implacable determination to win by any means necessary makes them every bit as ruthless as Skaro's finest.
■ **Look out for...** The moment in Episode Two where the Doctor climbs up a shaft and taunts the Daleks about their inability to follow him.
■ **Introducing...** Romana II (Lalla Ward). Regenerating with ease and style, the Time Lady tries on a number of bodies before settling on the appearance of recent acquaintance Princess Astra, much to the Doctor's disapproval. The Movellans, sworn enemies of the Daleks, also make their debut.
■ **Where else have I seen...** Skaro's surface is identical to the route to Atlantis in **32** *The Underwater Menace* (since they share the same Winspit Quarry location).

■ **Arcs in Space** A direct sequel to **78** *Genesis of the Daleks,* in which the Doctor changed the course of Dalek history forever, *Destiny* reunites Davros with his all-grown-up, genocidal "children", initiating a toxic dynamic of co-dependence and eventually triggering major schisms between Davros loyalists and Dalek supremacy factions. Follow the story of the ultimate dysfunctional 'family' in **133** *Resurrection of the Daleks,* **142** *Revelation of the Daleks,* **148** *Remembrance of the Daleks,* **198** *The Stolen Earth/Journey's End,* **254** *The Magician's Apprentice/The Witch's Familiar.*

Right
The Doctor and Romana (Lalla Ward) visit Paris in *City of Death.*
Below inset
The true face of Scaroth, last of the Jagaroth (Julian Glover).

105 City of Death

(four episodes) by David Agnew

A Parisian holiday evolves into fabulous French farce, with the Doctor and Romana defending the birth of humanity from the meddling of a time-splintered alien, helped by a hardboiled detective and seven completely authentic Mona Lisas.

■ **Where and When** Paris, 1979; Florence, 1505; primordial Earth, circa 400 million BC.
■ **The Baddies** Scaroth, last of the Jagaroth, an "infinitely old race" who, according to the Doctor, were "not nice to know". Leaving aside his utter disregard for human life, Scaroth's motives are sympathetic – he just wants to save his people by correcting his own ancient mistake. Unfortunately, he can only do so by erasing humankind from history.
■ **Introducing...** Overseas location filming. Yes, that's really Paris. *City of Death* was the first ever *Doctor Who* story shot outside the UK.
■ **Look out for...** John Cleese and Eleanor Bron cameo as pretentious art critics who are dazzled by the "absolutely exquisite" dematerialisation of the TARDIS.

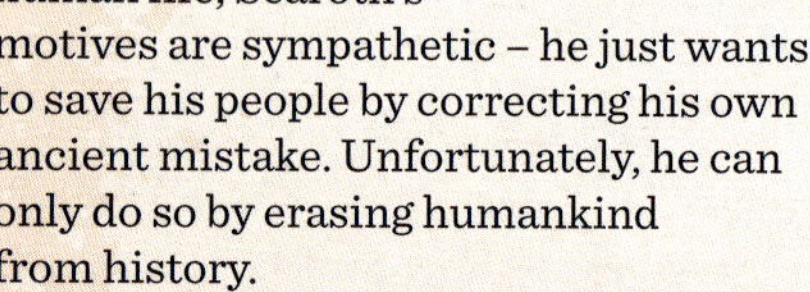

Davros (David Gooderson) is rescued by his errant creations in *Destiny of the Daleks.*

The Huntsman (David Telfer), Romana, the Doctor and Lady Adrasta (Myra Frances) meet Erato – aka *The Creature from the Pit*.

- **Where else have I seen…** Julian Glover (Count Scarlioni) played Richard the Lionheart in **14** *The Crusade*. Eleanor Bron returned, in a much more substantial role, as the villainous Kara in **142** *Revelation of the Daleks*.
- **Arcs in Space** The catastrophic explosion of his spaceship shatters Scaroth into 12 fragments, which are dispersed throughout Earth's history. Clara Oswald experiences a similar, much more extreme effect when she enters the Doctor's timeline, becoming splintered throughout space and time in **239** *The Name of the Doctor*.

106 The Creature from the Pit

(four episodes) by **David Fisher**

The Doctor, Romana and K9 answer a distress call from Chloris, a matriarchal dictatorship where metal is scarce but vegetation abundant (if often deadly). The oppressed population live in fear of the entity known as the Creature, a hundred-foot-long living brain that lives in the Place of Death and is reputed to eat people alive…

- **Where and When** The planet Chloris, date unknown.
- **The Baddies** Lady Adrasta (Myra Frances), a metal-loving monster who'll go to any lengths to preserve her mining monopoly. Her formidable forces encompass both fauna (human henchpeople) and flora (deadly Wolfweeds). There are also some local bandits, but they, in Romana's words, are "a pretty duff bunch".
- **Look out for…** Physical evidence of the Doctor's encounters with figures from Greek mythology (a ball of string, a souvenir from

Theseus and Ariadne) and the Bible (the jawbone of an ass, as used by Samson against the Philistines in the Book of Judges).
- **Where else have I seen…** Terry Walsh (Engineer Doran) was one of *Doctor Who*'s most prolific stunt doubles and fight directors, first appearing (uncredited) in **28** *The Smugglers*. *The Creature from the Pit* was his final appearance in *Doctor Who*.
- **What they said** In November 1979, *NME* writer Stuart Johnston said that the humour "seldom reaches a standard higher than childish but it's *good* childish, not *Crackerjack* childish."
- **Arcs in Space** The Doctor unplugged the emergency transceiver because he kept getting "nuisance" requests from Gallifrey. The Fourth Doctor helped out his fellow Time Lords in **78** *Genesis of the Daleks*, **84** *The Brain of Morbius*, **88** *The Deadly Assassin* and **97** *The Invasion of Time*. Furthermore, he, K9 and Romana recently completed a six-story mission on behalf of the Guardians (from **98** *The Ribos Operation* to **103** *The Armageddon Factor*). So it's unsurprising that he fancies some time off.

107 Nightmare of Eden

(four episodes) by **Bob Baker**

A seeming accident in space reveals a devious plot to smuggle Vraxoin, a banned substance. The Doctor and Romana must prove their innocence, avoid the rampaging beasts known as Mandrels, and identify the true source of the deadly, addictive 'Vrax'.

- **Where and When** The site of a crash between two spaceships – the *Empress* cruise liner and the trade ship *Hecate* – in space near the planet Azure, circa 2116.
- **The Baddies** Drugs, and drug smugglers. Minor spoilers – humans are the only villains in this story. The furry, feral Mandrels may inspire fear, but they're entirely innocent victims of human greed, selfishness and entitlement.
- **Look out for…** The Doctor's cold response when a drug trafficker attempts to justify his actions; he invests the simple line "Go away" with a world of contempt.
- **Introducing…** The Mandrels, seemingly sentient creatures who turn into recreational drugs at the moment of their death.
- **Where else have I seen…** Peter Craze (here playing Waterguard Fisk) also appeared in **15** *The Space Museum* and **50** *The War Games*. His brother, Michael Craze, played companion Ben Jackson from 1966-67.
- **Arcs in Space** The collateral damage of drug wars is further explored in **135** *The Caves of Androzani*. The Doctor's dislike of addictive substances, and disdain for those who peddle them, can also be seen in his treatment of the Pharmacytown dealers in **181** *Gridlock*.

Mandrels on the loose in *Nightmare of Eden*.

The Doctor tries to prevent a scheme to bleed the planet Skonnos dry in *The Horns of Nimon*.

108 The Horns of Nimon

(four episodes) by **Anthony Read**
The TARDIS collides with a spaceship bound for the planet Skonnos. The Doctor and Romana are horrified to learn that the ship is carrying human sacrifices for a being called the Nimon.

■ **Where and When** A spaceship, plus planets Skonnos and Crinoth (date unknown).
■ **The Baddies** The glorious Skonnon Empire has long since declined, but the mysterious Nimon, a creature with a head like a bull, has arrived on Skonnos promising to bring back the glory days. It lives in a maze called the Power Complex, and demands sacrifices and hymetusite crystals – willingly provided by Skonnos' leader, Soldeed (Graham Crowden).
■ **Introducing...** The TARDIS' defence shield – which creates a breathable atmosphere in the immediate vicinity of the ship, even in space – is a function used regularly by later Doctors, like the Twelfth in 245 *Listen* and the Thirteenth in 300 *The Power of the Doctor*.
■ **Look out for...** The Doctor's attempt to land the TARDIS "somewhere unobtrusive".
■ **Where else have I seen...** Malcolm Terris (playing the co-pilot here) was Etnin in 44 *The Dominators*. John Bailey (Sezom here) plays the Commander in 7 *The Sensorites* and Edward Waterfield in 36 *The Evil of the Daleks*.
■ **Arcs in Space** This story draws on the myth of the Minotaur – as do 45 *The Mind Robber*, 64 *The Time Monster* and 222 *The God Complex*.

109 The Leisure Hive

(four episodes) by **David Fisher**
The Doctor and Romana visit the Leisure Hive of Argolis, founded after a brief but devastating war with the Foamasi. But someone wants to use the Hive's recreation generator for sinister purposes.

■ **Where and When** Brighton circa 1980; and Argolis in 2290.
■ **The Baddies** Pangol (David Haig) is outraged by the proposal from an Earth consortium representing the Argolins' old enemies the Foamasi – they want to buy the near-bankrupt Hive. He has plans for a new Argolis.

■ **Introducing...** A totally new version of the theme tune. Delia Derbyshire's original was revamped a couple of times, debuting in Episode 2 of 35 *The Faceless Ones* and Episode 1 of 51 *Spearhead from Space* – but this is a completely new arrangement by Peter Howell.
■ **Look out for...** The Part One cliffhanger, with the Doctor's scream blending into the new music, is highly effective.
■ **What they said** "The elements of stylish production" in this story convinced Jeremy Bentham, writing in *Doctor Who Monthly* issue 46 (November 1980), that "*Dr Who* has regained its crown for the most inventive science-fiction series ever undertaken."
■ **Arcs in Space** The cliffhanger of the Doctor suffering accelerated ageing is echoed in the cliffhanger of 187b *The Sound of Drums/Last of the Time Lords*.

110 Meglos

(four episodes) by **John Flanagan** and **Andrew McCulloch**
Two factions on Tigella are grappling for possession of the planet's power source – the Dodecahedron. But someone else is plotting to steal it from them both and take over the galaxy...

■ **Where and When** The planets Zolfa-Thura and Tigella; roughly 1980, judging from the appearance of the Earthling (Christopher Owen).
■ **The Baddies** Meglos (Crawford Logan) is an intelligent, shape-shifting cactus from the planet Zolfa-Thura, and he's made an alliance with a group of Gaztaks – space pirates. The Tigellans know and trust the Doctor, so Meglos plans to exploit this by impersonating him.
■ **Farewell to...** Jacqueline Hill, who was part of the original regular cast, here playing the entirely different character of Lexa.

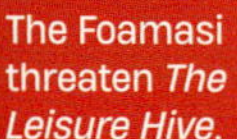

The Foamasi threaten *The Leisure Hive*.

■ **Look out for...** A lovely description of the Doctor by Zastor (Edward Underdown): "I knew a man who solved the insoluble by the strangest means. He sees the threads that join the universe together and mends them when they break."

■ **What they said** Jacqueline Hill remarked in **Doctor Who Magazine** issue 105 (October 1985) that *Meglos* was "almost totally different" from the show she'd worked on in the 1960s. "The special effects were a lot more dominant, it was recorded entirely out of order... It was a happy reunion with a show that was really only the same by name only."

■ **Arcs in Space** Meglos tries to trap the TARDIS in a chronic hysteresis, or time loop – which is what the Doctor did to Axos in **57** *The Claws of Axos*.

111 Full Circle

(four episodes) by Andrew Smith

The TARDIS accidentally slips into a pocket universe known as E-Space, where a group of marooned space travellers are trying to repair their crashed starliner in between attacks from the Marshmen.

■ **Where and When** Alzarius, date unknown.
■ **The Baddies** The Marshmen, creatures who emerge at Mistfall, are the main threat – but there's more going on than meets the eye...
■ **Introducing...** Adric (Matthew Waterhouse), a young mathematical genius whose loyalties are torn between the Deciders, who rule the starliner and promise to get everyone home to Terradon, and the rebellious Outlers led by Adric's brother Varsh (Richard Willis).
■ **Look out for...** The Doctor's righteous anger when Dexeter (Tony Calvin) starts to dissect a live Marsh-child.
■ **What they said** "Part of my quest to restore sanity to *Doctor Who* was to implement an overarching story to escape the arbitrariness of it," script editor Christopher H Bidmead told **DWM** in issue 257 (October 1997). "I wanted the sense that we have a continuity here, although you didn't always see it."
■ **Arcs in Space** This kicks off a trilogy of stories revolving around the travellers being stuck in E-Space, completed by **112** *State of Decay* and **113** *Warriors' Gate*.

Shada

(six episodes) by Douglas Adams

The Doctor takes Romana to Cambridge University to visit his old friend Professor Chronotis. But the trip is disrupted by someone searching for Shada – the Time Lords' prison planet.

■ **Where and When** Cambridge and Shada. It's October, probably 1979 or 1980.
■ **The Baddies** Skagra (Christopher Neame), a Dronnidian scientist who intends to create a merged universal mind, which will give him control of the universe. To complete his plan he needs the skills of the renegade Time Lord Salyavin.
■ **Farewell to...** Six-part stories. For many years the most typical story length, it would never be revived while *Doctor Who* continued to be made in 25-minute episodes.
■ **Look out for...** The revelation of what Chronotis has done with his old TARDIS.
■ **What they said** "I thought it was rather thin – at most a mediocre four-parter stretched over six parts," Douglas Adams said in an interview published posthumously in **DWM** issue 313 (February 2002). The serial's mid-production cancellation (caused by industrial action) was therefore a relief to him – "because it wasn't very good, and now at least I'm spared anybody seeing it." Ironically, there have since been numerous reconstructions of *Shada*. The most recent, a 2017 production that uses animation to fill the gaps between the completed footage, has been made available on iPlayer.
■ **Arcs in Space** Footage from *Shada* was used to cover for Tom Baker's absence from **129** *The Five Doctors*.

The Three Who Rule: Zargo (William Lindsay), Aukon (Emrys James) and Camilla (Rachel Davies), watched over by Adric (Matthew Waterhouse) in *State of Decay*.

112 State of Decay

(four episodes) by Terrance Dicks
On an isolated planet in the pocket universe of E-Space, society has been deliberately regressed to a medieval feudal state presided over by the Three Who Rule, vampiric acolytes of the Time Lords' ancient enemy…

■ **Where and When** An unnamed planet in E-Space, circa the 30th century.
■ **The Baddies** The Three Who Rule, Earth astronauts who were turned into vampires by the Great One (a giant vampire).
■ **Look out for…** References to the works of Shakespeare. Camilla (Rachel Davies) channels Lady Macbeth, washing her hands while exhorting Zargo (William Lindsay) to have courage, and the Doctor borrows from the St Crispin's Day speech in *Henry V*.
■ **Introducing…** The Great Vampires, a race of enormous bloodsuckers, who fought the Time Lords at the dawn of Time Lord history "when even Rassilon was young". According to the Record of Rassilon, only one of these creatures – the King Vampire – survived.
■ **What they said** *The Fourth Doctor Handbook* (published in 1992) described this as: "A very moody and effective story, in which great use is made of music and sound effects, combined with some very effective sets."

■ **Arcs in Space** Initially, the Doctor theorises that the Three Who Rule descended from the crew of the exploration ship *Hydrax* – just as Leela's tribe, the Sevateem, descended from planetary explorers in **89** *The Face of Evil*. Other blood-craving, vampire-like species encountered by the Doctor include the Ogri in **100** *The Stones of Blood*, the Haemovores in **154** *The Curse of Fenric*, the Plasmavores in **179** *Smith and Jones*, and the Saturnyns in **207** *The Vampires of Venice*.

113 Warriors' Gate

(four episodes) by Steve Gallagher
A mysterious stone gateway stands alone in a surreal void in time and space. Here, the enslaved Tharils fight to escape their brutal captors – and confront their own legacy of slavery, looting and conquest.

■ **Where and When** A white void between N-Space and E-Space with null co-ordinates. The time period fluctuates between the halcyon days of the Tharil empire and the devastation after its fall.
■ **The Baddies** Rorvik (Clifford Rose), the captain of the slave ship, is a suitably detestable piece of work, but none of his colleagues are much better. From the bonus-focused Packard (Kenneth Cope) to the nominal comic relief of grunts Aldo (Freddie Earlle) and Royce (Harry Waters), they all exhibit chilling indifference to the lives of their Tharil "cargo".
■ **Look out for…** K9 Mark II gets unusual prominence in his swansong – which also showcases the limitations of the prop, as he has to be carried around a lot. He seems surprisingly lightweight, rather like the piece of "dwarf star alloy" Romana picks up.
■ **Introducing…** The Tharils, a leonine, time-sensitive race who built an empire on their ability to navigate the Time Vortex. A slave rebellion reversed the situation, and the Tharils were enslaved in their turn.
■ **Farewell to…** Romana and K9 both decide to stay behind, to help the Tharils free the rest of their people.
■ **Arcs in Space** The metal dog who stays with Romana is K9 Mark II. Mark I stayed on Gallifrey with Leela (in **97** *The Invasion of Time*). K9 Mark III (sent by the Doctor as a gift to Sarah Jane Smith in the spin-off *K9 and Company*) appears in **129** *The Five Doctors* and in **170** *School Reunion*; the latter also introduces K9 Mark IV.

114 The Keeper of Traken

(four episodes) by Johnny Byrne
In the utopian Traken Union, the benign power of the Source, channeled through its humanoid Keeper, neutralises any entities with malign intentions upon arrival. But the Keeper's life force is waning, and a particularly cunning enemy has waited many years for his chance to take over the Source…

Biroc (David Weston), a time-sensitive Tharil in *Warriors' Gate*.

- **Where and When** Traken, Metulla Orionsis, at the end of the Keeper's 1,000-year reign.
- **The Baddies** Another desperate throw of the dice for the dying, decaying Master, this time with his TARDIS disguised as the Melkur, a creature of pure evil.
- **Introducing…** Anthony Ainley is delightful as the twinkly grey-haired elder, Consul Tremas – who seemingly sheds decades along with his morals when he transforms into the Master.
- **Farewell to…** The rotting, charred, living corpse that fans affectionately refer to as the 'Crispy Master'.
- **Introducing…** Nyssa of Traken (Sarah Sutton), the Doctor's new companion, is the daughter of Tremas, the former owner of the Master's new body. Did the Master target him for his unfortunately anagrammatic name? Anyway, adding insult to injury for poor Nyssa, the Master will sport the Tremas look throughout the 1980s.
- **Arcs in Space** In **88** *The Deadly Assassin,* we learned that the Master had used up all his regenerations and needed to steal a body to survive. He body-snatches again in **156** the 1996 TV movie *Doctor Who*, and in **288** *Spyfall* it's heavily implied that he pulled the same trick on MI6 agent 'O'. He varies the procedure in **300** *The Power of the Doctor*, taking over the Doctor's body and clothes but retaining his 'O' appearance.

Right
The latest incarnation of the Master (Anthony Ainley) and the Doctor in *Logopolis*.
Below inset
The Fourth Doctor's dying moments.

115 Logopolis

(four episodes)
by **Christopher H Bidmead**

The genii of Logopolis can manipulate the physical universe using pure mathematics. Such power is catnip to the Master, who flexes his newly stolen muscles by attempting to take over Logopolis and blackmail the entire universe. The Fourth Doctor can only stop him at the cost of his own life.

- **Where and When** Earth in 1981, and the planet Logopolis.
- **The Baddies** The Master, initially posing as Nyssa's father Tremas. The Pirate Captain, a Dalek, a Cyberman, Davros, a Sontaran, a Zygon and the Black Guardian all pop up briefly to taunt the dying Doctor.
- **Look out for…** The mysterious Watcher (Adrian Gibbs), who merges with the Fourth Doctor to create the Fifth. Did the Doctor create the Watcher, consciously or unconsciously? Certainly, a sense of unease, even doom, hangs over the Fourth Doctor throughout; he first appears pacing the TARDIS' Cloister Room, and, soon enough, the Cloister Bell rings to warn of "wild catastrophe".
- **Farewell to…** The Fourth Doctor, after seven full series – still an unbeaten record. His scarf and curls remain iconic symbols of a golden era.
- **Introducing…** The seemingly mild-mannered, "open-faced" Fifth Doctor (Peter Davison). Plus: Tegan Jovanka (Janet Fielding), an airline stewardess who, like Adric and Nyssa, joins the TARDIS team after suffering a tragic personal loss.
- **Arcs in Space** Tegan isn't always a happy traveller, but she's gutted when she gets left behind in **122** *Time-Flight*, rejoining at the first opportunity (in **123** *Arc of Infinity*). Sadly, the violence of **133** *Resurrection of the Daleks* is the last straw for Tegan; she realises that travelling with the Doctor has stopped being fun. She's eventually reunited with the Doctor in **300** *The Power of the Doctor*.

The FIFTH DOCTOR

Peter Davison
Stories 116–135, 1982–84

The fresh-faced but old-fashioned innocence
of the Fifth Doctor would be increasingly
tested by his ever-more-grim adventures,
which seemed often to end in the slaughter of
baddies and goodies alike. And when one of his
youthful companions lost their life battling
the Cybermen – well, it just wasn't cricket.

Post-regeneration angst for the new Doctor (Peter Davison) in *Castrovalva*.

116 Castrovalva

(four episodes)
by Christopher H Bidmead
To care for the Doctor while he recovers from his regeneration, Nyssa and Tegan take him to a peaceful clifftop town. But Castrovalva turns out to be the very definition of malevolent creativity...

■ **Where and When** The Pharos Project, Earth, on 28 February 1981. An unnamed planet in the Andromeda Galaxy (date unknown).

■ **The Baddies** The Master, who kidnaps Adric and exploits the boy's expertise with block transfer mathematics to create a space-time trap. He also dresses up as an old man in a silly hat.

■ **Introducing...** The Fifth Doctor's Edwardian cricketing outfit, panama hat and spectacles. Also, the stick of celery that somehow adheres so easily to his lapel.

■ **Look out for...** The TARDIS presents its database access in a semblance of the 1981 BBC Microcomputer operating system designed to promote computer literacy in schools – presumably to make it user-friendly for Tegan.

■ **Farewell to...** The Fourth Doctor's burgundy ensemble, introduced in **109** *The Leisure Hive*. The Fifth Doctor discards it, piece by piece, as he makes his way through the TARDIS in search of the Zero Room. He tears the waistcoat in half and completely unravels the scarf, leaving a trail back to the ship's console.

■ **Arcs in Space** The events of this story continue directly from the Doctor's regeneration at the end of **115** *Logopolis* (reprised in a pre-titles sequence). The Master continues his vendetta against the Fifth Doctor, with even more absurd disguises, in **122** *Time-Flight* and **128** *The King's Demons*.

117 Four to Doomsday

(four episodes) by Terence Dudley
On a spaceship due to arrive on Earth in four days' time, the Doctor finds representatives of ancient human civilisations, together with three billion aliens seeking a new home.

■ **Where and When** An Urbankan spaceship, 28 February 1981.

■ **The Baddies** Monarch (Stratford Johns), supreme leader of the people of Urbanka, who plans to invade Earth and kill everyone with a deadly poison. He's assisted by his Ministers of Enlightenment (Annie Lambert) and Persuasion (Paul Shelley), androids with fully integrated personalities.

■ **Look out for...** The distinctive white lights perched on columns in the ship's Mobiliary. They're Italian-made Sorella desk lamps, commercially available from 1972 to 1980. They also formed part of the furnishings of the Bi-Al Foundation in **93** *The Invisible Enemy*.

■ **Where else have I seen...** Bruce Callender, who plays one of the four Aborigine botanists and dancers, previously appeared both as a Movellan and an enslaved miner in **104** *Destiny of the Daleks*, and as one of General Grugger's Gaztaks in **110** *Meglos*.

■ **What they said** In *Doctor Who Monthly* issue 64 (May 1982), this story was received with moderate enthusiasm: "From beginning to end, it is a good, solid, but standard *Doctor Who* which has the nice bonus of being well-made."

■ **Arcs in Space** To recover his TARDIS, the Doctor takes a spacewalk, using a cricket ball from his pocket to provide the momentum to reach his ship. The Fourth Doctor produced a cricket ball from his pocket to get himself out of an equally sticky wicket in **76** *The Ark in Space*. Nyssa's sudden collapse at the end is accounted for at the start of the next adventure...

Enlightenment (Annie Lambert), Monarch (Stratford Johns) and Persuasion (Paul Shelley) in *Four to Doomsday*.

Text by Chris Bentley

Karuna (Sarah Prince) and wise woman Panna (Mary Morris) in *Kinda*.

118 Kinda

(four episodes) by **Christopher Bailey**
On a paradise planet inhabited by peaceful mute telepaths, Tegan unwittingly unleashes a malignant force that threatens a colonial survey team.

■ **Where and When** The planet Deva Loka (aka S14), the future (date unknown).
■ **The Baddies** The Mara, an evil serpentine entity that inhabits "the dark places of the Inside". It seeks to cross over into reality by exploiting the dreaming of an unshared mind. In the Wherever, the Mara's dreamworld, it manifests itself to Tegan as a peculiar young man named Dukkha (Jeffrey Stewart). On arrival in the real world, it possesses Aris (Adrian Mills), a Kinda man whose brother has been taken hostage by the survey team.
■ **Look out for...** Tegan's visit to the Wherever. This is arguably the strangest sequence you'll see in 1980s *Doctor Who*.
■ **Where else have I seen...** Graham Cole, who would later become the longest-serving cast member of police drama *The Bill*, plays one of the Kinda men in the group scenes. Masked, he was Melkur in **114** *The Keeper of Traken* and **122** *Time-Flight*, a Marshman in **111** *Full Circle,* and Cybermen in both **121** *Earthshock* and **129** *The Five Doctors*. He had further small roles in **109** *The Leisure Hive,*

133 *Resurrection of the Daleks* and **136** *The Twin Dilemma*.
■ **What they said** This story was described in the 1995 book *The Discontinuity Guide* as "One of the best *Doctor Who* stories ever, astonishingly directed and written as a theatrical piece brimming with allusions and parallels."
■ **Arcs in Space** Tegan's uncertainty about whether the Mara has truly gone from her mind foreshadows its return in **124** *Snakedance*. She's still disturbed by her experience on Deva Loka at the start of **118** *The Visitation*.

119 The Visitation

(four episodes) by **Eric Saward**
In plague-stricken 17th-century England, the TARDIS crew find villagers in thrall to alien convicts who plan the extinction of human life on Earth.

■ **Where and When** Heathrow village and London, Earth. September 1666.
■ **The Baddies** A trio of Terileptils, fugitives from the tinclavic mines of Raaga. Their disfigured leader (Michael Melia) is assisted by a bejewelled android (Peter van Dissel), dressed as the Grim Reaper to frighten the locals.
■ **Look out for...** The device used by the Terileptil Leader to manufacture his lethal toxin is connected to a large blue crystal

sealed inside a transparent globe – identical to the radioactive hymetusite crystals, taken to Skonnos by the bearers of Aneth's tribute to the Nimon, in **108** *The Horns of Nimon*.
■ **Farewell to...** The Fourth Doctor's sonic screwdriver is irreparably damaged by the Terileptil Leader. The Doctor doesn't use a sonic screwdriver again until **156** the 1996 TV movie *Doctor Who*.
■ **Where else have I seen...** James Charlton, who plays the local miller, previously appeared as one of the Mentiads in **99** *The Pirate Planet* and the artist in the Parisian café in **105** *City of Death*.
■ **Arcs in Space** The Doctor also visits 17th-century England in **28** *The Smugglers*, **150** *Silver Nemesis*, **214** *The Impossible Astronaut/Day of the Moon*, **215** *The Curse of the Black Spot*, **257** *The Woman Who Lived* and **284** *The Witchfinders*. Terileptils can be seen again, albeit briefly, in **122** *Time-Flight* and **246** *Time Heist*. Off-screen, they also respond to the Stonehenge transmission in **212** *The Pandorica Opens/The Big Bang* and the message from Trenzalore in **241** *The Time of the Doctor*.

The Terileptil leader (Michael Melia) in *The Visitation*.

120 Black Orchid

(two episodes) by **Terence Dudley**
A jolly jaunt in the Roaring Twenties comes to a crashing halt when the Doctor is accused of murder during a country-house costume party.

■ **Where and When** The TARDIS lands at Cranleigh Halt – a small English railway station – at precisely 3.00pm on 11 June 1925.

■ **The Baddies** While the story opens with George Cranleigh (Gareth Milne) strangling a servant, the traumatised, unbalanced George can't really be held fully accountable for his actions. Lord Charles Cranleigh (Michael Cochrane) and his mother, Lady Cranleigh (Barbara Murray), are the real villains here – for deciding to lock George, the eldest son, in the attic, after an expedition up the Orinoco left him horribly mutilated.

■ **Look out for…** During the cricket match sequence in Part One, the camera manages to capture Peter Davison showing some genuine sporting prowess. As he proudly explains on the DVD commentary: "Look at this. I want you to watch this very carefully. This is where I bowl the guy out in shot – there's no trick photography involved here!"

The Cyber Leader (David Banks, left) and his Lieutenant (Mark Hardy) in *Earthshock*.

The grieving Ann Talbot (Sarah Sutton), George Cranleigh (Michael Cochrane) and Lady Cranleigh (Barbara Murray) in *Black Orchid*.

■ **Where else have I seen…** Michael Cochrane will return for another period piece set in a sprawling mansion, albeit this time as the crazed former explorer Redvers Fenn-Cooper in **153** *Ghost Light*.

■ **What they said** "Nyssa's denial that Traken was anywhere near Esher was almost as funny as Cranleigh's speculation that Adric was a Scandinavian," enthused Jeremy Bentham in *Doctor Who Monthly* issue 65 (June 1982).

■ **Arcs in Space** At the start of the first 'pure' historical adventure since **31** *The Highlanders*, Tegan tells the Doctor he can stop trying to get her back to Heathrow Airport – putting a cap on her efforts to get back, ever since **115** *Logopolis*. After Romana ran into Princess Strella in **101** *The Androids of Tara*, Nyssa becomes the second companion to meet their identical double – namely George's former fiancée, Ann Talbot.

121 Earthshock

(four episodes) by **Eric Saward**
The unexpected return of the Cybermen leads to devastating consequences for the TARDIS crew… and for prehistoric Earth!

■ **Where and When** A cave system on Earth, and aboard a deep-space freighter, both in 2526. Adric takes an unscheduled trip back to circa 65 million years BC.

■ **The Baddies** After seven years, the Cybermen make a dramatic return, sporting a slick new look that would continue to be used, albeit with minor modifications, throughout the 1980s.

■ **Farewell to…** Poor Adric meets a final end on board the freighter as it crashes into late Cretaceous Earth, destroying himself and the dinosaurs. He's the first companion to bite the dust since Sara Kingdom aged to death at the end of **21** *The Daleks' Master Plan*.

■ **What they said** "It was very odd to end the life of a character one had lived with for two years," reflected Adric actor Matthew Waterhouse in **Doctor Who Magazine** issue 202 (July 1993). "For the children of the time, it's one of the moments of television that will live with them forever."

■ **Look out for…** Uniquely, the end credits to Part Four scroll up the screen in sombre silence, superimposed over an image of Adric's shattered badge for mathematical excellence.

■ **Arcs in Space** In Part Two, the Cybermen view clips from their previous clashes with the Doctors – in **29** *The Tenth Planet*, **43** *The Wheel in Space* and **79** *Revenge of the Cybermen*.

122 Time-Flight

(four episodes) by **Peter Grimwade**
Stranded on prehistoric Earth, the Master drags Concorde back in time from Heathrow Airport in a complex bid to find a new power source for his TARDIS.

■ **Where and When** Heathrow Airport, June 1982, and a corresponding region of prehistoric Earth – presumably long before the dinosaurs (and Adric).

■ **The Baddies** The villain of the piece at first appears to be an eccentric magician by the name of Kalid. At the end of Part Two, however, Kalid is revealed to be the Master (Anthony Ainley) in disguise. No good reason for this elaborate charade is ever given.

■ **Farewell to...** In his haste to avoid having to make explanations to the authorities, the Doctor leaves Tegan behind at Heathrow Airport – much to her dismay.

■ **Look out for...** In Part Two, Tegan and Nyssa appear to encounter Adric, who died at the end of the previous adventure. He turns out to be a psychic projection intended to hinder their progress – confirmed when Nyssa points out that the apparition is wearing Adric's badge, which was seen to be destroyed in 121 *Earthshock*.

■ **Where else have I seen...** John Flint – previously William des Preaux, one of Richard the Lionheart's knights in 14 *The Crusade* – returns here as Captain Urquhart.

■ **Arcs in Space** "So, you escaped from Castrovalva," observes the Doctor when the Master sheds his disguise – referring to their last encounter.

The mysterious magician Kalid (Anthony Ainley) in *Time-Flight*.

Borusa (Leonard Sachs) and the Doctor held at gunpoint by Councillor Hedin (Michael Gough) in *Arc of Infinity*.

123 Arc of Infinity

(four episodes) by **Johnny Byrne**
What are the chances of Tegan blundering into an Amsterdam crypt and running into a renegade Time Lord who plans to escape the universe of anti-matter by bonding with the Doctor?

■ **Where and When** Amsterdam in 1983, and the planet Gallifrey.

■ **The Baddies** The pioneering stellar engineer Omega (here played by Ian Collier) makes a surprise return after 65 *The Three Doctors* – in which he was seemingly destroyed, along with his anti-matter realm.

■ **Farewell to...** This is Omega's final appearance in the TV series. We will, however, encounter his 'hand' – actually a highly advanced stellar manipulator – in 148 *Remembrance of the Daleks*.

■ **Look out for...** Future Doctor Colin Baker plays Commander Maxil of the Chancellery Guard on Gallifrey. Apparently gunning for the job, he even gets to shoot the current incumbent – Peter Davison. (Davison will eventually regenerate into Baker at the end of 135 *The Caves of Androzani*.)

■ **Where else have I seen...** Michael Gough, here portraying the traitorous Councillor Hedin, previously played the Toymaker in 24 *The Celestial Toymaker*.

■ **Arcs in Space** Having been abandoned at Heathrow Airport at the end of 122 *Time-Flight*, it's a remarkable coincidence that Tegan happens to be in Amsterdam to visit her cousin, Colin Frazer (Alistair Cumming) – who has, equally remarkably, been possessed by Omega. On Gallifrey, the Doctor asks about his former companion Leela, who stayed behind after 97 *The Invasion of Time* to marry Commander Andred; he says he's sorry he missed the wedding. President Borusa (Leonard Sachs) is now on his third regeneration since 88 *The Deadly Assassin*.

A renegade returns: Omega (Ian Collier) threatens the Doctor once more.

HOW TO WATCH...

CYBERMEN

You belong to them. You shall be like them. Highlights of the half-man/half-machine monsters, by **Jamie Lenman**.

Outstanding

The Cybermen's third outing – **37** *The Tomb of the Cybermen* – is undoubtedly their quintessential story. Missing, presumed wiped for a quarter of a century, its sudden reappearance in 1992 only added to its legend, confirming what older fans had known since 1967: that this was indeed a classic. Essentially an old Mummy movie in space, *Tomb* introduced the dome-headed Controller (Michael Kilgarriff), the rat-like Cybermats and the creatures' adopted home planet, Telos. But more than that – it's simply a cracking good story, packed with thrills, chills, action set-pieces and some lovely comedy. And those booming timpani all over the place – fantastic!

Essential

The Cybermen as we first meet them in **25** *The Tenth Planet* are markedly different to those that followed – weirder, scarier and more human than the metal monsters who would lumber in their wake, but instantly appealing nonetheless. After 13 years' long service, they were given a 1980s upgrade in the slick *Alien*-inspired **121** *Earthshock*, re-establishing them as a credible threat whilst also hinting at a rather more emotional existence than had previously been seen. When tasked with introducing the sons of Mondas to a new generation, writer Tom MacRae went back to the start and wrote their previously unexplored origin story – albeit set on a parallel Earth – and with **172** *Rise of the Cybermen/The Age of Steel* initiated a countrywide Cyber-craze: "Delete!"

Excellent

In **275** *World Enough and Time/The Doctor Falls*, writer Steven Moffat revisited the original 'cloth-face' versions to underscore their inherent horror, whilst also tidying up the continuity quibbles of the previous era by firmly establishing that Cybermen develop "wherever there are people." In **295** *Ascension of the Cybermen/The Timeless Children* we followed the crusade of Ashad (Patrick O'Kane), the 'Lone Cyberman' who reawoke a deadly warrior class of the species (duly one-upped by the Master's outrageous 'Cyber-Masters', converted from Time Lords). Elsewhere, the spare-parts squad put on a great show in **129** *The Five Doctors*, despite this anniversary adventure not really being about them, and their face-off with the Daleks in **177** *Army of Ghosts/Doomsday* is legendary. And who could forget the adorable disembodied 'Handles' from **241** *The Time of the Doctor*?

The Best of the Rest

33 *The Moonbase* painted the Cybermen as desperate survivors with a penchant for chemical warfare – themes revisited in **79** *Revenge of the Cybermen*. This story also made much of their aversion to gold, a thread that reached its nadir in the otherwise joyful **150** *Silver Nemesis* and was then, thankfully, forgotten. **238** *Nightmare in Silver* introduced a natty redesign for both the Cybermen and the Cybermats, as well as the insectoid Cybermites, capable of small-scale conversions. Meanwhile, the gigantic Cyber King trampled Victorian London in **199** *The Next Doctor* as the shaggy Cybershades ran amok, and **223** *Closing Time* proved how troublesome a single Cybermat could be. Perhaps most horribly of all, **252** *Dark Water/Death in Heaven* suggested that any given Cyberman could well be your dear departed relative. Eek!

"We will use
the power of
cybernetics."
THE CYBERMAN
CONTROLLER, *THE TOMB
OF THE CYBERMEN*

The aged Dojjen (Preston Lockwood) has a vital insight for the Doctor, Chela (Johnathon Morris) and Nyssa in *Snakedance*.

124 Snakedance

(four episodes) by Christopher Bailey

The TARDIS lands on Manussa, where preparations are being made to celebrate the banishment of the Mara, five centuries earlier. But the Mara lives on in Tegan's dreams – and she soon falls back under the creature's control.

■ **Where and When** Manussa – aka Planet G139901KB in the Scrampus system, third planet in the Federation system, former home world of the Manussan Empire (destroyed), former home world of the Sumaran Empire (destroyed).

■ **The Baddies** Snake like dream-invader the Mara, returning from **118** *Kinda*.

■ **Introducing…** With Tegan having finally shed her airline stewardess' uniform in **123** *Arc of Infinity*, Nyssa at last exchanges her Trakenite togs for a colour- and pattern-clashing blouse, skirt and shorts combo.

■ **Look out for…** The Part Two scenes with Tegan meeting the Mara in the Hall of Mirrors, where the creature takes over foppish Federator's son Lon (Martin Clunes), are remarkably creepy.

■ **Farewell to…** After the completion of the titular dance – a rite of purification involving crystals – the Mara returns to the dark places of the inside, and has yet to re-emerge (thankfully). Likewise Nyssa's new costume (again, thankfully).

■ **Arcs in Space** Both Mara stories are heavily rooted in Buddhism – the source for **74** *Planet of the Spiders*, where the power of crystals is also prominent. Tegan briefly regresses mentally to the age of six; in the next story, **125** *Mawdryn Undead*, she'll physically regress to a young age (alongside Nyssa). In **310** *The Legend of Ruby Sunday*, Harriet Arbinger names the Mara as "the god of Beasts" – one of the pantheon presided over by Sutekh.

125 Mawdryn Undead

(four episodes) by Peter Grimwade

Former UNIT Brigadier Lethbridge-Stewart now teaches maths at an English public school. But when the Black Guardian offers one of the school's pupils the opportunity to escape Earth if he'll destroy the Doctor, the stage is set for a reunion…

■ **Where and When** Brendon School, in 1977 and 1983; and in an opulent spaceship trapped in a warp ellipse for over 3,000 years.

■ **The Baddies** The Black Guardian, returning after **103** *The Armageddon Factor* – with the Doctor having given away the Guardian-evading Randomiser in **109** *The Leisure Hive*. Mawdryn (David Collings) – one of a group of scientists who became horribly mutated after seeking the Time Lords' regenerative process, and who impersonates a newly regenerated Doctor. Plus Turlough (Mark Strickson) – will he or won't he murder the Doctor?

■ **Introducing…** Shifty schoolboy Turlough – whose unearthly back-story won't be fully disclosed until **134** *Planet of Fire*.

■ **Look out for…** A trip through the Brigadier's past in Part Two, incorporating flashbacks to Yeti in **41** *The Web of Fear*, Cybermen in **46** *The Invasion*, Axons in **57** *The Claws of Axos*, Daleks in **60** *Day of the Daleks*, Robot K1 in **75** *Robot* and Zygons in **80** *Terror of the Zygons*.

Mawdryn (David Collings) wants the Doctor to sacrifice his lives in *Mawdryn Undead*.

Text by Jacqueline Rayner

■ **Where else have I seen…** Angus Mackay, playing the Headmaster, was previously the Doctor's teacher Borusa in **88** *The Deadly Assassin*. David Collings appears with more make-up than in his last role, as Poul in **90** *The Robots of Death*, but considerably less than in his first role, as Vorus in **79** *Revenge of the Cybermen*.

■ **Arcs in Space** The Blinovitch Limitation Effect – a catastrophic shorting-out of the time differential when one person encounters their younger self, as with the 1983 and 1977 Brigadiers – was first mentioned in **60** *Day of the Daleks*. The Brigadier having retired from UNIT in 1977 contradicts the idea that the UNIT stories between **46** *The Invasion* and **85** *The Seeds of Doom* were set a few years into the near future, circa 1979-80 – hence the Tenth Doctor telling Donna in **192** *The Sontaran Stratagem* that he used to work for UNIT "Back in the 70s. Or was it the 80s?" This is the first in a trilogy of adventures, all with Turlough under the Black Guardian's control…

126 Terminus

(four episodes) by **Steve Gallagher**
In a broken-down ship at the precise heart of the known universe, a plague-ridden Nyssa reaches her journey's end.

■ **Where and When** The exact centre of the known universe, billions of years after the Big Bang.
■ **The Baddies** The Black Guardian is still out for the Doctor's blood. Vanir chief Eirak (Martin Potter) is particularly unpleasant, but his employers Terminus Inc are the real bad guys here.
■ **Introducing…** New TARDIS lore: removing the "heart of the TARDIS", aka the space-time element under the console (previously seen in **123** *Arc of Infinity*), causes dimensional instability. The TARDIS fail-safe means that, on impending break-up, it seeks out and locks on to the nearest spacecraft.
■ **Farewell to…** Nyssa decides to stay on Terminus to help the people infected by Lazar's Disease – although she'll pop up as a vision in **135** *The Caves of Androzani*.
■ **Look out for…** The dreaded Garm (RJ Bell) turns out to be a giant Scottie dog in armour, or so it appears.
■ **Arcs in Space** Turlough is still under the influence of the Black Guardian. He's given Adric's room, last seen in **121** *Earthshock*, and is unimpressed by props from **115** *Logopolis*, **118** *Kinda* and **119** *The Visitation*. Kari (Liza Goddard) and Olvir (Dominic Guard) prove that, whenever space pirates are involved, amazing hairstyles must follow – see Madeleine Issigri in **49** *The Space Pirates*. The Big Bang, which nearly destroyed the TARDIS in **116** *Castrovalva*, was caused by the Terminus pilot ejecting unstable fuel into the void.

127 Enlightenment

(four episodes) by **Barbara Clegg**
All-powerful Eternals are engaged in a literal space race, with planets as marker buoys: winner takes all! But Turlough's soul is at stake too…

■ **Where and When** The solar system, date unknown.
■ **The Baddies** The Eternals, immortals who regard humans as mere 'ephemerals', include the larger-than-life Captain Wrack (Lynda Baron), murderous mistress of the *Buccaneer*, and her henchman Mansell (Leee John).
■ **Look out for…** In a story filled with elegance and insight, the first glimpse of the sailing ships in space at the end of Part One is hard to beat.
■ **Where else have I seen…** Tony Caunter, playing the sailor Jackson, was the murderous Morgan in **58** *Colony in Space* and the thieving Thatcher way back in **14** *The Crusade*.
■ **Farewell to…** Evil Turlough, who becomes (more or less) Good from now on. Neither the Black nor the White Guardian is seen again. In **303** *The Giggle*, the Toymaker will claim that he "played against the Guardians of Time and Space and shrank them into voodoo dolls."
■ **Arcs in Space** The Eternals aren't the first aliens to abduct humans from historical time zones for their amusement: see **50** *The War Games*.

Captain Striker (Keith Barron) takes the wheel of the SS *Shadow* in *Enlightenment*.

Space pirate Kari (Liza Goddard) and the Doctor discover the dead pilot of *Terminus*.

128 The King's Demons

(two episodes) by **Terence Dudley**

The TARDIS gatecrashes a joust, with the crew taken for 'demons' by the locals and even King John himself. But the King isn't quite himself, and there's something sinister about his champion…

■ **Where and When** England, Castle Fitzwilliam, 4 March 1215. Around dinner time.

■ **The Baddies** The Master turns time meddler, posing as king's champion 'Sir Gilles Estram' (the best swordsman in France, apparently) to prevent King John (Gerald Flood) from signing the reform charter, Magna Carta.

■ **Introducing…** Bad King John turns out to be a shape-changing robot named Kamelion, recovered by the Master on ancient Xeriphas after 122 *Time-Flight*. Subsequently, Kamelion joins the TARDIS crew – but isn't seen again until 134 *Planet of Fire*, when his story comes to a tragic end.

■ **Look out for…** The cliffhanging swordfight, when the Doctor battles the Master in his Sir Gilles guise. The Doctor previously bested his former bestie in a duel in 62 *The Sea Devils*, and puts on further displays of swordsmanship in 70 *The Time Warrior*, 86 *The Masque of Mandragora*, 101 *The Androids of Tara* and 167 *The Christmas Invasion*.

■ **Where else have I seen…** Financially embarrassed nobleman Sir Ranulf Fitzwilliam is played by Frank Windsor, who will return as ill-fated copper Inspector Mackenzie in 153 *Ghost Light*.

■ **Arcs in Space** The First Doctor met the real King John's elder siblings, Richard and Joanna, in 14 *The Crusade*. On leaving 1215, the Doctor promises a trip to the Eye of Orion – and for once he delivers, as seen in the next story.

129 The Five Doctors

by **Terrance Dicks**

Past Doctors, several companions and a horde of old monsters play the Game of Rassilon, where to lose is to win and he who wins shall lose. (In other words, immortality just isn't worth it.)

■ **Where and When** A rose garden, the Eye of Orion, UNIT HQ, a random country road, Ealing (probably), Cambridge, Gallifrey's Capitol, the Death Zone (nowhere, no time), and the Tomb of Rassilon. Phew!

■ **The Baddies** President Borusa (Philip Latham) has an itch for immortality, timescooping various Doctors into the deadly Game of Rassilon to get his hands on the original Time Lord's eternal monopoly. Throw in the Master, Cybermen, a lone Dalek, a random Yeti, and let the games commence.

■ **Introducing…** A shiny new TARDIS console, looking rather splendid. It'll

The First Doctor (Richard Hurndall) meets three of his later selves in Rassilon's Tower in *The Five Doctors*.

> ## "A man is the sum of his memories, you know. A Time Lord even more so." THE DOCTOR

work, too, once everything's run in.

■ **Look out for…** The Second Doctor's discussion with the Brigadier about the hitherto unseen "Terrible Zodin". Oblique references to creatures – "covered in hair, they used to hop like kangaroos" – raise eyebrows as well as questions.

■ **What they said** In Australia, the 14 December 1983 edition of *The Age* included some of Brian Courtis' supposed highlights: "A Dalek rattled around blaring 'exterminate' before blowing its own head off, the rather stupid Cybermen marched up and down the hill trying to zap anything that moved and there was a Yeti chasing Patrick Troughton through a tunnel."

■ **Arcs in Space** "Why not? After all, that's how it all started." This is the Fifth Doctor's response to the idea of going on the run from his own people in a rickety old TARDIS, tracing things right back to 1 *100,000 BC* (aka *An Unearthly Child*). He's avoiding political duty after his snap election as Gallifrey's President – an office previously held in 62 *The Invasion of Time*, lost by 143 *The Trial of a Time Lord*, regained by 148 *Remembrance of the Daleks*, and taken again (from Rassilon) in 262 *Hell Bent*.

The Doctor meets the Master's robotic servant Kamelion in *The King's Demons*.

Text by Mark Wright

Left
The Silurians in their undersea base in *Warriors of the Deep.*

Below inset
The Sea Devils assist.

130 Warriors of the Deep

(four episodes) by Johnny Byrne
On an Earth boiling with geopolitical tensions, opposing power blocks face mutually assured destruction. The planet's original tenants want to help humanity push the button…

■ **Where and When**
Sea Base 4, a nuclear deployment facility near a Sea Devil hibernation shelter – on Earth in 2084.
■ **The Baddies** A cabal of Earth reptiles led by Ichtar (Norman Comer), sole survivor of the Silurian Triad, and his companions Tarpok (Vincent Brimble) and Scibus (Stuart Blake). Also, the leather-clad warriors of Sea Devil Elite Group One, commanded by Sauvix (Christopher Farries). Elsewhere, Sea Base 4 traitors Solow (Ingrid Pitt) and Nilson (Ian McCulloch) prove that humans can often be relied upon to more dangerous than aliens.
■ **Farewell to…** The Doctor's original cricket ensemble bowls a final over, lost in some random Sea Base airlock after his tumble into the reactor pool.
■ **Look out for…** The Sea Devils' sea monster the Myrka is quite something to behold – as is Solow's attempt to fight it off with the best martial arts since the Third Doctor "Hai'd!" his way through a Venusian aikido routine.
■ **Where else have I seen…** If you could see through Tarpok's reptilian carapace, you might recognise Vincent Brimble, who sheds Silurian skin for a suit and hat in **297** *Flux*, playing the unpleasant Gerald.
■ **Arcs in Space** A direct sequel to **52** *Doctor Who and the Silurians* and **62** *The Sea Devils* – although it's unclear whether the Doctor and Ichtar's previous encounter took place during the former story. The Silurians' aquatic cousins will be seen to command another underwater behemoth, the Hua-Shen, in **299** *Legend of the Sea Devils.*

131 The Awakening

(two episodes) by Eric Pringle
Tegan books a visit to her grandfather, whose village is in the middle of a Civil War reenactment. Past and present collide, treason is spoken fluently, and Tegan becomes the toast of Little Hodcombe.

■ **Where and When** Chocolate-box village Little Hodcombe, England. Earth, circa 1984.
■ **The Baddies** The Malus – a giant, devilish, smoke-belching head – re-engineered on the planet Hakol into an instrument of war. Fomenting violence through psychic projection, the Malus lay dormant for centuries, until awakened by Little Hodcombe's power-hungry magistrate, Sir George Hutchinson (Dennis Lill).
■ **Introducing…** Only a dedicated follower of fashion might notice, but it's a first innings for the Doctor's new togs – green-lined cricket shirt, natty new jumper with maroon and black stripes, and some subtly different striping on the trousers.
■ **Look out for…** Three mounted soldiers in full Civil War regalia, with a telegraph pole and red phone-box in the background, make a charmingly absurd image in Part One.
■ **Where else have I seen…** Peel away the luxuriant wig and beard of Sir George and you'll find Dennis Lill, previously Dr Fendelman in **94** *Image of the Fendahl.* Playing Colonel Wolsey, Glyn Houston previously popped up as Professor Watson in **87** *The Hand of Fear.*
■ **Arcs in Space** Sir George's stress ball of tinclavic (mined for the exclusive use of the people of Hakol) refers back to **119** *The Visitation*, where the Terileptil leader sustained facial injuries in the tinclavic mines of Raaga. The family relationship of Andrew Verney (Frederick Hall) to Tegan's Aunt Vanessa is unclear, so one wonders at the awkward conversation to be had about Vanessa's grisly fate at the hands of the Master in **115** *Logopolis*, and just where on Earth Tegan has been ever since…

The Malus is uncovered inside a church in *The Awakening.*

The Doctor and Tegan (Janet Fielding) face the Gravis (John Gillett) and his Tractators deep beneath *Frontios*.

132 Frontios

(four episodes)
by Christopher H Bidmead

Sci-fi meets body horror when hardy human refugees battle meteor bombardments and corpse-snatching alien grubs on the edge of the known universe.

■ **Where and When** Frontios, an Earth colony in the distant Veruna system – "too far" into the future, even for the TARDIS.

■ **The Baddies** The Tractators – giant woodlice who are stealing the bodies of Frontios' human colonists for use in their gruesome excavating machines.

■ **Look out for...** The Part One cliffhanger, in which the actual TARDIS is actually destroyed, leaving only the Doctor's hat stand (and he hasn't even brought his hat).

■ **Where else have I seen...** Lesley Dunlop, playing Norna, will return as another Earth colonist, Susan Q, in 149 *The Happiness Patrol*. Jeff Rawle, cast here as Plantagenet, plays museum curator Lionel Harding in the *Sarah Jane Adventures* story *Mona Lisa's Revenge*, plus *Doctor Who*'s original associate producer, Mervyn Pinfield, in the 50th anniversary docudrama *An Adventure in Space and Time*.

■ **What they said** In **Doctor Who Magazine** 106 (November 1985), Peter Davison declared that "*Frontios* was excellent – an extremely well-rounded script, which got hold of the way that I saw the Doctor."

■ **Arcs in Space** The TARDIS lurching out of control in the final scene leads directly into 133 *Resurrection of the Daleks*. Turlough has a race memory of the Tractators infesting his home planet – the name and history of which will be revealed in 134 *Planet of Fire*. For Earth's "catastrophic collision with the sun" (as Turlough puts it with some relish), take your pick from 23 *The Ark* or 158 *The End of the World*.

133 Resurrection of the Daleks

(two episodes) by Eric Saward

The Daleks get the Earthshock *treatment in a gritty – and gruesome – militaristic action-adventure in which the Doctor's arch-enemies embark on a fiddly plot to assassinate the High Council of Time Lords.*

■ **Where and When** London docklands, 1984, and a prison space station, 4590.

■ **The Baddies** The Daleks, who have returned to defrost their creator Davros from cryogenic suspension, and Lytton (Maurice Colbourne), a mercenary leading a squad of Dalek troopers.

■ **Introducing...** A Davros not merely defrosted but also re-cast. Terry Molloy – taking over from Michael Wisher in 78 *Genesis of the Daleks* and David Gooderson in 104 *Destiny of the Daleks* – would reprise the role in 142 *Revelation of the Daleks* and 148 *Remembrance of the Daleks*.

■ **Farewell to...** Tegan Jovanka. Sickened by all the slaughter, the Doctor's companion departs after three years, telling him "It's stopped being fun." Sob.

■ **Look out for...** As the Doctor is wired up to the duplication machine, memories are extracted of all his former selves and companions – except, for some reason, Leela (and Kamelion, if he counts).

■ **What they said** "In many ways," claimed script editor Eric Saward in **DWM** issue 347 (August 2004), "it's probably the worst script ever written for *Doctor Who*."

■ **Arcs in Space** The opening TARDIS scene carries on directly from 132 *Frontios*. Davros has been in the freezer for 90 years, since the events of 104 *Destiny of the Daleks*. The Doctor will face a quick rematch with Lytton and his henchmen in 137 *Attack of the Cybermen*.

Kiston (Leslie Grantham), Davros (Terry Molloy) and a hesitant Doctor in *Resurrection of the Daleks*.

134 Planet of Fire

(four episodes) by Peter Grimwade
The Doctor and Turlough travel from the Canary Islands to an alien world where a miniature Master is trying to harness the power of a volcano to get himself out of an embarrassing fix.

■ **Where and When** Lanzarote, 1984, and the equally volcanic planet of Sarn.
■ **The Baddies** The Master, who's gone and got himself shrunk down to the size of an action figure.
■ **Introducing...** Miss Perpugilliam Brown, aka Peri (Nicola Bryant), a botany student who becomes the Doctor's first American companion.
■ **Farewell to...** Turlough, revealed to be a political prisoner who's now free to return to his home world of Trion. Farewell also to Kamelion (if he counts).
■ **Look out for...** As the Doctor condemns the Master to burn in the flames of Sarn, his nemesis begs him: "Please – won't you show mercy to your own...?" Your own what? Brother? Family? Or does he just mean his own kind?
■ **Arcs in Space** The Doctor is still brooding over the events of 133 *Resurrection of the Daleks*. We finally learn why Turlough was sent to the English public school where the Doctor met him in 125 *Mawdryn Undead*.

The Master is cut to down to size in *Planet of Fire*.

135 The Caves of Androzani

(four episodes) by Robert Holmes
Caught up in a grubby little war on a desolate backwater planet, the dying Fifth Doctor makes his heroic last stand, racing against time to save his companion's life.

■ **Where and When** The planets of Androzani Minor and Major, date unknown.
■ **The Baddies** Sharaz Jek (Christopher Gable), a disfigured criminal genius who skulks in the subterranean caves like the Phantom of the Opera, is the headline antagonist – but corporate profiteer Morgus (John Normington) is the real boo-hiss villain of the piece.
■ **Look out for...** The cliffhanger to Part Three, in which a desperate, dying Doctor crashes a spaceship into the planet's surface with a defiant cry of "I owe it to my friend, because I got her into this, so you see I'm not going to let you stop me now!"
■ **Farewell to...** The Fifth Doctor, who regenerates after coming down with a dose of deadly spectrox toxaemia. And hello to the Sixth Doctor (Colin Baker), making his debut in the story's final moments – "and it seems not a moment too soon."
■ **Where have I seen...** John Normington, playing the duplicitous Morgus, will return as census-taking bureaucrat Trevor Sigma in 149 *The Happiness Patrol*.
■ **What they said** Reacting to this bleak but brilliant revenge tragedy being voted the greatest *Doctor Who* story of all time in **DWM** issue 413 (September 2009), Peter Davison recalled that "It was really great to finish on a story where *everything* came together."
■ **Arcs in Space** The Doctor finally reveals why he's worn a stick of celery on his lapel since 116 *Castrovalva* – it turns purple in the presence of certain gases in the praxis range to which he's allergic. All the Fifth Doctor's companions briefly return during his regeneration, which leads directly into 136 *The Twin Dilemma*.

The SIXTH DOCTOR

Colin Baker
Stories 136–143, 1984–86

The Sixth Doctor started out as he meant to continue – choosing a lurid patchwork coat to wear, seemingly as an expression of some wilful desire to offend all sense of good taste. Waspishly witty, he seemed on occasion to almost revel in the carnage around him – and ended up back in the Time Lords' dock.

Left
The new Doctor (Colin Baker).

Below left
Gastropod leader Mestor (Edwin Richfield) in *The Twin Dilemma*.

136 The Twin Dilemma

(four episodes) by **Anthony Steven**
The newly regenerated Doctor exhibits some alarming behaviour, while a bloated alien makes an elderly Time Lord kidnap some twins so he can abuse their genius and distribute his eggs throughout the universe.

- **Where and When** Mainly Titan III and Jaconda, sometime in the future.
- **The Baddies** Mestor the Gastropod (Edwin Richfield). The Sylvest twins, Romulus and Remus (Gavin and Andrew Conrad), aren't actually baddies, but they're *very* rude to their parents.
- **Look out for...** The Doctor's moments of psychosis are genuinely disturbing; his brief hysteria in the TARDIS about "the grinding engines of the universe" is particularly unsettling.
- **Introducing...** The cat badge! The first example of the Sixth Doctor's celery-substitute is a predominantly white, seated cat in 3D. We also learn that Time Lords can force-regenerate, even if it kills them.
- **Where else have I seen...** Edwin Richfield was thankfully not required to wear a slug suit as Captain Hart in 62 *The Sea Devils*. Seymour Green (Chamberlain) was Hargreaves in 85 *The Seeds of Doom*. Kevin McNally (Lang) will return as almost-companion Professor Jericho in 297 *Flux*. Dennis Chinnery (Sylvest) was briefly in 16 *The Chase* as Richardson, and more lengthily in 78 *Genesis of the Daleks* as Gharman.
- **Arcs in Space** The Doctor was apparently in his fourth incarnation when he last met Azmael (Maurice Denham), his "old friend and mentor". The Doctor mentions taking Peri to the Eye of Orion, as seen in 129 *The Five Doctors*. The Doctor echoes the First Doctor's words: "And kindly refrain from addressing me as Doc" (also from 129) and says "Brave heart, Tegan," as established in 121 *Earthshock*. The TARDIS wardrobe includes the Second Doctor's fur coat and the Third Doctor's velvet jacket.

137 Attack of the Cybermen

(two episodes) by **Paula Moore**
The Cybermen want to crash Halley's Comet into the Earth in 1986 – thereby changing their own history, by preventing the destruction of their home planet.

- **Where and When** Earth in the present day, and the Cyberman tombs of Telos.
- **The Baddies** The Cybermen, under the control of the Cyber Controller (Michael Kilgarriff) and Cyber Leader (David Banks). Keep an eye out, also, for the one-and-only appearance of an all-black Cyberman, lurking creepily in the background.
- **Look out for...** Lytton's cyber-conversion in Part Two really underlines the fact that the horror of the Cybermen is not them stomping around shooting people but their theft of humanity and individuality.
- **Farewell to...** Mercenary and stone-cold killer Lytton dies, with the Doctor for some reason thinking he misjudged the man. This story also represents the first and last time the TARDIS appears as anything other than a police box.
- **Where else have I seen...** Undercover cop Russell is played by Terry Molloy, the actor who wore a mask to play Davros from 133 *Resurrection of the Daleks* to 148 *Remembrance of the Daleks*.
- **Arcs in Space** The Cybermen – who, we learn, have an inbuilt distress call – intend to use time travel to prevent

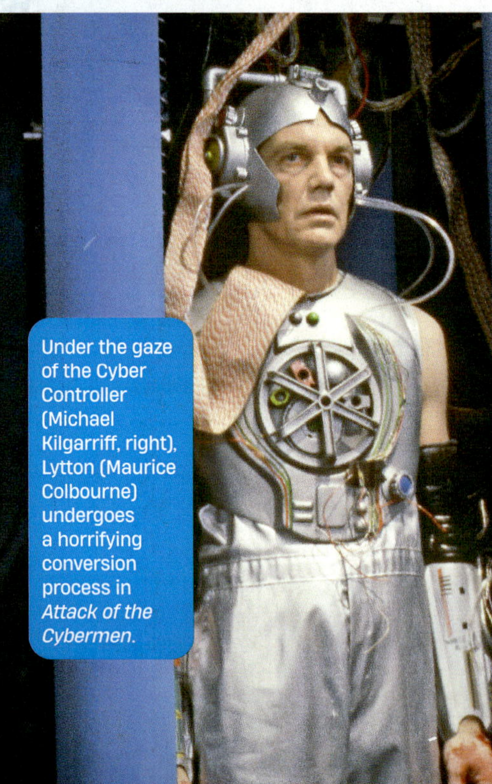

Under the gaze of the Cyber Controller (Michael Kilgarriff, right), Lytton (Maurice Colbourne) undergoes a horrifying conversion process in *Attack of the Cybermen*.

Galatron Mining Corporation envoy Sil (Nabil Shaban) in *Vengeance on Varos*.

Mondas from being destroyed, as happened in **29** *The Tenth Planet*. The Doctor won't tell Earth about it as he can't interfere "to that extent" and "the Time Lords would have him destroyed". The Cyber Controller wasn't dispatched in **37** *The Tomb of the Cybermen*, merely damaged. (He retains a domed head in his redesign here.) It's clarified that the Cybermen originated on Mondas (which had a propulsion unit to move it through space), then colonised the Cryons' planet, Telos. The Doctor revisits IM Foreman's yard in Totter's Lane, as seen in **1** *100,000 BC* (aka *An Unearthly Child*). The Doctor has called Peri such names as Tegan, Zoe, Susan, Jamie and Zodin, as referenced in **129** *The Five Doctors*.

138 Vengeance on Varos

(two episodes) by Philip Martin

On the planet Varos, where televised torture is offered as entertainment, the Doctor and Peri become embroiled in a power struggle between the beleaguered Governor and an acquisitive, slug-like alien.

■ **Where and When** Varos, nearly three centuries after Peri was born.
■ **The Baddies** Sil (Nabil Shaban), the marshminnow-eating capitalist who represents the Galatron Mining Corporation. Varos' technical director, Quillam (Nicolas Chagrin), is in charge of the sadistic 'entertainment' broadcast from the Punishment Dome.
■ **Look out for...** The knowing final scene, with viewers Arak and Etta wondering what to do now that there'll be no more executions or torture to watch.
■ **Farewell to...** The TARDIS Manual. The Eleventh Doctor later reveals, in **208** *Amy's Choice*, that he threw it in a supernova because he disagreed with it.
■ **Where else have I seen...** The Governor, Martin Jarvis, was previously Butler in **71** *Invasion of the Dinosaurs* and haughty butterfly Hilio in **13** *The Web Planet*. Stephen Yardley (Arak) was the Muto Sevrin in **78** *Genesis of the Daleks*. Sheila Reid (Etta) will return as Clara Oswald's paternal grandmother in **241** *The Time of the Doctor* and **252** *Dark Water/ Death in Heaven*. The priest, Hugh Martin, was the short-lived Munro in **80** *Terror of the Zygons*.
■ **Arcs in Space** Zeiton-7 is needed to reline the TARDIS' transpower system. Sil's race, the Mentors, won't be named until his next appearance, in **143** *The Trial of a Time Lord*.

139 The Mark of the Rani

(two episodes) by Pip and Jane Baker

The TARDIS lands in a Northern mining town, where the Rani is draining brain fluid from the locals under cover of the Luddite riots.

■ **Where and When** Killingworth, early in the 19th century.
■ **The Baddies** The amoral Rani (Kate O'Mara) and the immoral Master bond over their shared love of fancy dress.

Above The Master and the Rani (Kate O'Mara) in *The Mark of the Rani*.

Below inset Neurochemist the Rani experiments on the people of the mining town Killingworth.

■ **Introducing...** This is the first appearance of the Rani, who'll next pop up in **144** *Time and the Rani*. And the Doctor has a new cat badge: a 2D black cat with arched black-and-white eyes.
■ **Look out for...** The tragedy of Luke Ward (Gary Cady), George Sephenson's assistant. In the second episode he suffers the surprising fate of stepping on a mine that transforms him into a tree.
■ **Where else have I seen...** Richard Steele, playing a guard, had been in a couple of episodes of **52** *Doctor Who and the Silurians*, as Hart, and an episode of **50** *The War Games*, as Commandant Gorton.
■ **Arcs in Space** The Doctor says that, unlike George Stephenson, he's never changed the course of history. Best not to examine that claim too closely. The Master once more assumes a disguise (a scarecrow), for nefarious reasons not immediately obvious to mere mortals; he also uses his hypnotic abilities yet again. Peri remembers that she's a botanist! (See **134** *Planet of Fire*.) The Doctor thought the Master had been burned to a crisp in their previous meeting – in, again, **134** *Planet of Fire*.

The hybrid Borad (Robert Ashby) in *Timelash*.

Left
The Second Doctor gets the point from his successor in *The Two Doctors*.

Below left
Statuesque Sontarans in Seville!

140 The Two Doctors

(three episodes) by Robert Holmes
We're off to sunny Spain as the Sixth Doctor runs into his second self, together with Jamie and some suspiciously tall Sontarans.

■ **Where and When** Seville, 1985 – and a research space station in the Third Zone.
■ **The Baddies** Group Marshal Stike (Clinton Greyn) and Major Varl (Tim Raynham) of the Ninth Sontaran Battle Group, who've kidnapped the Second Doctor to aid their time-travel experiments. Androgums Shockeye (John Stratton) and Chessene (Jacqueline Pearce) – naturally warty barbarian gluttons with a taste for human flesh.
■ **Look out for...** From the opening scene, the Second Doctor and Jamie openly discuss the Time Lords, leading to countless theories that this somehow takes place *after* **50** *The War Games*. But there are also a ton of reasons why it can't, so probably best not to think too hard about it.

■ **Farewell to...** The Second Doctor and Jamie McCrimmon, taking their final bow after 19 years in time and space.
■ **Where else have I seen...** Laurence Payne (here playing the deeply misguided scientist, Dastari) was outlaw Johnny Ringo in **25** *The Gunfighters* and the Argolian Morix in **109** *The Leisure Hive*.
■ **Arcs in Space** As well as including the Second Doctor, Jamie and an unseen Victoria, there are numerous references here to the Sontarans' mortal enemies the Rutans (first mentioned in **70** *The Time Warrior* and first seen in **92** *Horror of Fang Rock*). Seeing Space Station J7 on the TARDIS scanner, Jamie tells the Doctor, "Look at the size of that thing" – echoing his reaction to the Emperor Dalek in **36** *The Evil of the Daleks*. Peri refers to the restorative effects of celery, which she learned about in **135** *The Caves of Androzani*.

141 Timelash

(two episodes) by Glen McCoy
On the planet Karfel, the Doctor and Peri try to avoid a terrible fate in a tinselly time tunnel, with help from Herbert George Wells.

■ **Where and When** The Citadel of Karfel in the Mutter's Spiral, plus Scotland, 1885.
■ **The Baddies** The Borad (Robert Ashby) – Karfel's despotic ruler, whose unethical scientific experiments have caused him to become fused with one of the planet's reptilian Morlox creatures – and his scheming stooge, Maylin Tekker (Paul Darrow).
■ **Look out for...** An unexpected appearance – of sorts – from the Third Doctor and Jo Grant.
■ **Where else have I seen...** *Blake's 7* legend Paul Darrow (Tekker) was Captain Sam Hawkins in **52** *Doctor Who and the Silurians*.
■ **What they said** According to Colin Baker in **Doctor Who Magazine** issue 322 (October 2002): "It wasn't one of my favourites; not one of anybody's favourites."
■ **Arcs in Space** The Third Doctor and Jo Grant previously visited Karfel during an unseen adventure. The suggestion that

Text by Paul Kirkley

Left
What remains of Arthur Stengos (Alec Linstead) in *Revelation of the Daleks*.

Right
Peri and the Doctor inside the Great Healer's domain.

the Borad becomes the Loch Ness Monster directly contradicts **80** *Terror of the Zygons*. HG Wells (played here by David Chandler) is referenced in **67** *Frontier in Space*, **82** *Pyramids of Mars*, **92** *Horror of Fang Rock*, **120** *Black Orchid* and **156** the 1996 TV movie *Doctor Who*.

The scheming Maylin Tekker (Paul Darrow) in *Timelash*.

142 Revelation of the Daleks

(two episodes) by Eric Saward
Evelyn Waugh meets Soylent Green in Doctor Who's most pitch-black comedy, as Davros lays a trap for the Doctor in a funeral parlour with a macabre secret...

■ **Where and When** Tranquil Repose, a luxury funeral home on the snowy planet of Necros.
■ **The Baddies** The Great Healer, aka Davros – who has solved the galaxy's famine problem by producing food from recycled human corpses, while harvesting their organs to create a new race of Daleks.
■ **Look out for...** The scene in which the horribly mutated agronomist Arthur Stengos (Alec Linstead) is placed inside a glass Dalek casing is a twist on an idea first mooted two decades earlier, in David Whitaker's novelisation of **2** *The Mutants* (aka *The Daleks*).
■ **Where else have I seen...** Clive Swift, aka peacocking embalmer Mr Jobel, will play Mr Copper in **188** *Voyage of the Damned*. Eleanor Bron (playing Davros' treacherous business associate, Kara) had previously made a cameo appearance alongside John Cleese in **105** *City of Death*. Colin Spaull (here playing mortician Lilt) is Mr Crane in **172** *Rise of the Cybermen/The Age of Steel*.

"Davros has finally done it. Daleks that can reproduce anywhere." THE DOCTOR

■ **What they said** "My scripts certainly got darker and more violent as the years went by," said Eric Saward in **DWM** issue 348 (October 2004). "*Revelation of the Daleks* is almost cannibalistic!"
■ **Arcs in Space** Davros explains how he used a handy escape pod to survive the exploding prison ship in **133** *Resurrection of the Daleks*.

The Great Healer is revealed as Davros (Terry Molloy).

143
The Trial of a Time Lord
Parts One to Four

by Robert Holmes

The Doctor is brought aboard a Time Lord space station to face an enquiry into his meddling. Prosecuting, the apparently biased Valeyard offers scenes from a previously unseen adventure as (unreliable) evidence…

■ **Where and When** A Time Lord space station, date unknown, and the planet Ravolox, two million years or more after the 20th century.

■ **The Baddies** The sneering, black-clad Valeyard (Michael Jayston), whose title the Doctor delights in mispronouncing as "Graveyard", "Farmyard" and "Scrapyard".

■ **Introducing…** Sabalom Glitz (Tony Selby) – a ducker and diver from the planet Salostopus. The presiding Inquisitor (Lynda Bellingham). And, of course, the Valeyard himself (Michael Jayston). Plus, the Doctor's costume gains two new cat badges: one black, one grey and white.

■ **Look out for…** The stunning visual effects shot of the space station that opens the first episode of this season-long story.

■ **Where else have I seen…** Tom Chadbon (Merdeen) was the pugnacious private detective Duggan in **105** *City of Death*. Roger Brierley, who voices the towering Ravolox robot Drathro, had briefly appeared in **21** *The Daleks' Master Plan* as cricket commentator Trevor – although, sadly, there's no surviving visual evidence of him in the role.

■ **Arcs in Space** Having been made Lord President of Gallifrey in **129** *The Five Doctors*, the Doctor has been deposed in his absence. He produces jelly babies for the first time since his fourth incarnation. An ancient London underground station will once again help to solve a mystery in **289** *Orphan 55*. The Valeyard thinks the Time Lords were "too lenient" in the Doctor's previous trial, which occurred at the end of **50** *The War Games*.

The Trial of a Time Lord
Parts Five to Eight

by Philip Martin

As the trial continues, more evidence from the Matrix features the Doctor's old adversary Sil. Peri meets the warlord King Yrcanos, before her travels in the TARDIS come to a seemingly tragic end.

■ **Where and When** The Time Lord space station, and the planet Thoros-Beta in the last quarter of the 24th century – specifically the third day in the seventh month of the fourth year.

■ **The Baddies** Sil (Nabil Shaban), Kiv (Christopher Ryan) and the ruthless surgeon Crozier (Patrick Ryecart) are obvious villains. A surprise addition to this category, though, is… the Doctor. Of course, he might have been affected by Crozier's brain-altering tech. Or he might just have been pretending to have turned evil. Or his actions might have been fabricated by the Matrix.

■ **Farewell to…** This is not quite Peri's final appearance, but it's the last time we see Sil.

■ **Look out for…** Peri's apparent fate at the end of Part Eight is one of the series' most shocking moments to date.

■ **Where else have I seen…** Christopher Ryan will later play two Sontarans – General Staal in **192** *The Sontaran Stratagem/The Poison Sky* and Commander Stark in **212** *The Pandorica Opens*. Trevor Laird (Frax) will feature as Martha's father Clive in **179** *Smith and Jones*, and **187b** *The Sound of Drums/*

The Doctor encounters the Drathro L3 maintenance robot on the planet Ravalox.

The ailing Mentor Kiv (Christopher Ryan).

Last of the Time Lords. The suspiciously Terileptil-like face of Kiv's business partner from Possicar is a mask hiding Deep Roy, previously hidden behind the mask of Mr Sin in **91** *The Talons of Weng-Chiang.*

■ **Arcs in Space** Peri mentions Sil trying to turn her into a bird woman, referencing the events of **138** *Vengeance on Varos.*

The Trial of a Time Lord
Parts Nine to Twelve

by Pip and Jane Baker
The next round of evidence sees the Doctor and a future companion, Mel, embroiled in a mystery aboard a space liner with a very sinister cargo…

■ **Where and When** The Time Lord space station and the *Hyperion III*, in 2986.

■ **The Baddies** Homicidal human Doland (Malcolm Tierney) and homicidal vegetables called Vervoids.

■ **Introducing…** Bubbly, keep-fit fan Melanie, known as Mel (Bonnie Langford). Mel is already travelling with the Doctor when we first meet her, and we're still waiting for an explanation of how they met. The Doctor adds a new, ginger-cat badge to his collection.

■ **Look out for…** The reveal of the face of the horribly transformed Ruth (Barbara Ward) at the end of Part Ten is a make-up triumph.

■ **Where else have I seen…** As Bruchner, David Allister comes to a sticky end, as he had done previously as Stimson in **109** *The Leisure Hive.* Arthur Hewlett (Kimber) was Kalmar in **112** *State of Decay.*

■ **Arcs in Space** Professor Lasky (Honor Blackman) reads *Murder on the Orient Express* while the Doctor talks of exercising his "grey cells" (à la Hercule Poirot); the Doctor will later meet the story's author, Agatha Christie, in **194** *The Unicorn and the Wasp*, and will travel on a spacebound version of the famous train in **249** *Mummy on the Orient Express.* Ruth's fate recalls that of Winlett and Keeler in **85** *The Seeds of Doom.* Article Seven of Gallifreyan law prohibits genocide, despite the Time Lords' instructions to the Fourth Doctor **78** *Genesis of the Daleks.*

The Trial of a Time Lord
Parts Thirteen to Fourteen

by Robert Holmes, Pip and Jane Baker
The Doctor's trial reaches its shattering conclusion with the arrival of a familiar nemesis, and a revelation about the Valeyard's true identity.

■ **Where and When** The Time Lord space station and inside the Matrix, date unknown.

■ **The Baddies** The Master and the Valeyard, who turns out to be an amalgamation of the darker sides of the Doctor's nature, somewhere between his Twelfth and final incarnations.

■ **Farewell to…** The Valeyard. But he takes over the role of Keeper of the Matrix at the end, so he lives to fight another day. We also get our final glimpse of Peri in her newfound happiness with King Yrcanos (Brian Blessed).

One of the plant-like Vervoids.

■ **Look out for…** "Daleks, Sontarans, Cybermen – they're still in the nursery compared to us!" The Sixth Doctor's impassioned attack on Time Lord hypocrisy is his standout moment.

■ **Where else have I seen…** James Bree, Keeper of the Matrix, was the Security Chief in **50** *The War Games* and Nefred in **111** *Full Circle.*

■ **Arcs in Space** The Doctor's adventures in the Matrix recall his ordeal in **88** *The Deadly Assassin.* The Key of Rassilon allows qualified people to enter the Matrix; the Great Key of Rassilon, in **97** *The Invasion of Time*, appears to be a different artefact. At the end of the story, the High Council is deposed and insurrectionists run amok on Gallifrey – but we won't see the High Council or any part of Gallifrey again until **202** *The End of Time.*

Above inset New companion Mel (Bonnie Langford).

Right Inside the Matrix with Mr Popplewick (Geoffrey Hughes)

The SEVENTH DOCTOR

Sylvester McCoy
Stories 144–155, 1987–89

When he wasn't playing the clown, he was playing the spoons – but there was more to this Doctor than met the eye. A cosmic schemer on the sly, he was forever pulling the puppet strings of his 80s-streetwise companion Ace – and hinting at unknowable secrets from his long, dark past.

Right
The new Doctor (Sylvester McCoy) on the planet Lakertya in *Time and the Rani*.

Below left
One of the Rani's Tetrap slaves.

144 Time and the Rani

(four episodes)
by **Pip** and **Jane Baker**

A giant brain in an attic and an inspiration of geniuses gathered against their will… including the Doctor himself. But the process of kidnapping him has prompted a change of appearance.

■ **Where and When** The planet Lakertya, where the indigenous people are oppressed by the Rani – whom we last saw in **139** *The Mark of the Rani*. The time is unknown, but the Rani intends to rewind Earth's timeline "back to the Cretaceous" – so it must be significantly later than the time of the dinosaurs.

■ **The Baddies** The Rani, whom we now discover is 953 – the same age as her university classmate, the Doctor. She's assisted by four-eyed, bipedal, bat-like hench-beings called Tetraps, led by the slavering Urak (Richard Gauntlett).

■ **Introducing…** The new Doctor (Sylvester McCoy) – a ball of energy right from the start, seemingly untroubled by post-regenerative trauma until the Rani injects him with an amnesia drug. He's prone to malapropisms and, although seeming jolly, he's also quick to melancholy and anger.

■ **Look out for…** For the first and only time, this Doctor wears a tartan scarf and tucks his jumper into his trousers, with braces on top. He'll switch to a paisley scarf, an untucked jumper and hidden braces before the next adventure.

■ **Where else have I seen…** Donald Pickering (reluctant Lakertyan collaborator Beyus) and Wanda Ventham (his wife Faroon) previously appeared together in **35** *The Faceless Ones*. Ventham is also in **94** *Image of the Fendahl*.

■ **Arcs in Space** The Doctor retains an enthusiasm for The Beatles, as previously demonstrated in **16** *The Chase*, citing the potential loss of their music as a tragedy for the universe – something that actually comes about in **306** *The Devil's Chord*!

145 Paradise Towers

(four episodes) by **Stephen Wyatt**
In a dilapidated luxury tower block, people are disappearing… because something in the basement is hungry.

■ **Where and When** Paradise Towers, an award-winning housing estate on a planet that may or may not be Earth, sometime after the 21st century.

■ **The Baddies** The Chief Caretaker (Richard Briers), who isn't terribly interested in taking care of people. Or Paradise Towers. Or anything but his hungry 'pet'. Cannibalistic old ladies lurk in the towers' seemingly more salubrious areas, and the late great architect Kroagnon, appalled by what's been done to his masterpiece, is waiting in the wings.

■ **Look out for…** Some may perceive a political subtext in how the Kangs are divided into red, blue and yellow subgroups. This being the 1980s, the blues win the game.

■ **Where else have I seen…** Deputy Chief Caretaker Clive Merrison previously played rocket man Jim Callum, one of the few survivors of **37** *The Tomb of the Cybermen*.

■ **What they said** Jonathan Powell, the then Controller of BBC1 – a man not known for his enthusiasm for *Doctor Who* – sent a memo to the production office, commending this story as "absolutely first rate".

A cleaner robot apprehends the Doctor in *Paradise Towers*.

A holiday in 1950s Wales for the Doctor and Mel in *Delta and the Bannermen*.

■ **Arcs in Space** The Doctor has jettisoned the TARDIS swimming pool seen in **97** *The Invasion of Time,* because it was leaking. This is a problem, because Mel fancies a swim.

146 Delta and the Bannermen

(four episodes) by **Malcolm Kohll**
The Doctor and Mel take a nostalgic trip back to the rock and roll years, but their holiday camp break is interrupted by a refugee alien queen on the run. Oh, why do fools fall in love?

■ **Where and When** The planet of the Chimerons. Toll port G715, somewhere in space in the distant future. But mostly South Wales, 1959.
■ **The Baddies** Raw-meat gobbling Gavrok (Don Henderson) and his genocidal Bannermen mercenaries.
■ **Introducing…** The new Doctor's trademark question-mark umbrella makes its debut. In **144** *Time and the Rani,* he carried a multi-coloured model, as used by his predecessor on Ravalox in **143** *The Trial of a Time Lord,* and in **145** *Paradise Towers* a simpler, cane-handled model was on show.
■ **Look out for…** "Love never has been known for its rationality," mutters the Doctor sadly, hugging a guitar. This was later quoted by McCoy as a favourite moment, and a line that helped him grasp the emotional depths of the part he was playing.

■ **Where else have I seen…** Morgan Deare, playing satellite-hunting CIA man Hawk, returned to *Doctor Who* 31 years later, playing Arthur in **279** *Rosa.* That's longer than the 28-year gap between *Delta and the Bannermen*'s 1959 setting and its 1987 production.
■ **Arcs in Space** Extraordinarily, this is the first *Doctor Who* story to contain no overt references to an earlier one since **107** *Nightmare of Eden.*

147 Dragonfire

(three episodes) by **Ian Briggs**
When shopping for mercenaries, please remember that revenge is a dish best served cold. Especially if you have a body temperature of minus 193 celsius.

■ **Where and When** Iceworld, a freezer centre and supermarket on the dark side of the planet Svartos, which has secrets of its own.
■ **The Baddies** Kane (Edward Peel), a "heat vampire" and exiled criminal, originally from Proamon. He wants to revenge himself on his own people, not only for his banishment to Svartos, but for the death of his lover and co-gang leader Xana during his capture.
■ **Introducing…** Ace (Sophie Aldred), a 20th-century teenager who's ended up on Iceworld in the far future thanks to a time storm she conjured up with her school chemistry set. Her chemistry with the Doctor sees her leave with him in the TARDIS.
■ **Farewell to…** Melanie, at least until **300** *The Power of the Doctor.* She departs in the company of grotzit-seeking conman Sabalom Glitz, last seen in **143** *The Trial of a Time Lord* – and who'll be mentioned fondly in **303** *The Giggle.*
■ **Look out for…** "This is the real McCoy, this is!" insists Glitz, when it's implied his treasure map may be fake – with the Doctor's expression acknowledging the in-joke.
■ **Arcs in Space** "Strange business, time." As Mel leaves, she and the Doctor have a conversation about time that seems to reference the paradoxical nature of their friendship. At the end of **143** *The Trial of a Time Lord,* she left the space courtroom with a version of the Doctor who hadn't actually met her yet. The real cause of the time storm that ensnared Ace will be revealed in **154** *The Curse of Fenric.*

The biomechanoid creature (Leslie Meadows), Mel, Glitz (Tony Selby), Ace (Sophie Aldred) and the Doctor seek treasure in *Dragonfire*.

Ace and the Doctor at Coal Hill School, with some familiar enemies, in *Remembrance of the Daleks*.

148 Remembrance of the Daleks

(four episodes) by Ben Aaronovitch
We go back to the Swinging Sixties as the Doctor returns to the scene of his first TV adventure – to settle a bit of unfinished business with his mortal enemies.

■ **Where and When** Shoreditch, London, November 1963.
■ **The Baddies** Imperial and Renegade Daleks – rival factions hunting the Hand of Omega, a powerful Gallifreyan stellar manipulator.
■ **Look out for...** The Part One cliffhanger, where a Dalek chases the Doctor *up the stairs* – to the dismay of second-rate comedians and newspaper cartoonists everywhere.
■ **Where else have I seen...** Pamela Salem (playing Rachel here) was Toos in 65 *The Robots of Death*. William Thomas (Martin) will play Mr Cleaver in 165 *Boom Town*. Peter Halliday (the vicar) had previously appeared as Packer in 46 *The Invasion*, Pletrac in 66 *Carnival of Monsters*, and a soldier plus second Jagaroth in 105 *City of Death*. Michael Sheard (the headmaster) was another seasoned *Doctor Who* veteran, having played Rhos in 23 *The Ark*, Dr Summers in 56 *The Mind of Evil*, Laurence Scarman in 82 *Pyramids of Mars*, Lowe in 93 *The Invisible Enemy* and Mergrave in 116 *Castrovalva*.

■ **What they said** "Whatever your taste in *Doctor Who*, this story probably satisfied it," wrote Justin Richards in issue 60 of *Doctor Who Bulletin*. "[Producer] John Nathan-Turner and [script editor] Andrew Cartmel have got right back on track with the spirit of *Who*."
■ **Arcs in Space** The action is set concurrently with the events of 1 *100,000 BC* (aka *An Unearthly Child*). There's much talk of Omega, from 65 *The Three Doctors* and 85 *Arc of Infinity*, and of Rassilon, from 129 *The Five Doctors*, 202 *The End of Time* and 262 *Hell Bent*.

149 The Happiness Patrol

(three episodes) by Graeme Curry
On a world where misery is punishable by death, the Doctor sets out to topple an empire in one night – and to remind its citizens that there are no other colours without the blues...

■ **Where and When** Terra Alpha, an Earth colony planet "some centuries" in Ace's future.
■ **The Baddies** The Happiness Patrol – a female execution squad who eliminate 'killjoys' at the behest of Terra Alpha's despotic

ruler, Helen A (Sheila Hancock). And the Kandy Man (David John Pope), a sadistic android executioner who's not as sweet as he looks...
■ **Look out for...** The scene where our hero uses existential philosophy to persuade a pair of snipers to throw away their guns is peak Seventh Doctor.
■ **Where have I seen...** Lesley Dunlop (here playing Susan Q) was another Earth colonist in 132 *Frontios*, while John Normington (Trevor Sigma) was the treacherous Morgus in 135 *The Caves of Androzani*.
■ **What they said** "It's sort of Kafka meets the Marx Brothers," said script editor Andrew Cartmel in **Doctor Who Magazine** issue 225 (May 1995).
■ **Arcs in Space** In 152 *Battlefield*, the warrior Mordred turns the tables on the Doctor with the same line – "Look me in the eye, end my life" – that our hero uses here to disarm the snipers.

150 Silver Nemesis

(three episodes) by Kevin Clarke
It's Doctor Who's silver jubilee – so the Cybermen have had a shiny chrome glow-up, just in time to fall into the increasingly Machiavellian Time Lord's latest trap.

■ **Where and When** Windsor, Berkshire, 23 November 1988 and 1638.
■ **The Baddies** The Cybermen, time-travelling Jacobean sorceress Lady

The Kandy Man (David John Pope) in *The Happiness Patrol*.

Peinforte (Fiona Walker) and Herr De Flores (Anton Diffring), who's looking to establish the Fourth Reich with a ragtag army of neo-Nazis who can comfortably fit inside a Ford Transit.

■ **Look out for...** Lady Peinforte's hints that she knows the Doctor's "secrets" from Gallifrey in "the old time, the time of chaos" – a deliberate move to introduce a new element of mystery around the Time Lord's origins.

■ **Where have I seen...** Fiona Walker made her TV debut as Kala, *Doctor Who*'s first ever villainess, in **5** *The Keys of Marinus*.

■ **What they said** "The jubilee story finds the series in splendid form," said Mark Lawson in *The Listener* (1 December 1988), "with Sylvester McCoy the best actor in years."

■ **Arcs in Space** 23 November 1988 is, of course, the 25th anniversary of **1** *100,000 BC* (aka *An Unearthly Child*) – also of the date when **148** *Remembrance of the Daleks* is set. The Cybermen claim the Earth will be "the new Mondas" – the twin planet first featured in **29** *The Tenth Planet*. More is revealed about the Doctor's origins in **295** *Ascension of the Cybermen/The Timeless Children*.

Right
The Doctor and Ace visit the Psychic Circus on Segonax in *The Greatest Show in the Galaxy*.

Below inset
The Circus' Chief Clown (Ian Reddington).

151 The Greatest Show in the Galaxy

(four episodes) by Stephen Wyatt
The Doctor and Ace run away to join the circus – where they discover that keeping the audience entertained is a matter of life and death...

The black-handled Cyber Leader (David Banks) flanks Ace and the Doctor in *Silver Nemesis*.

"I have fought the Gods of Ragnarok all through time."

THE DOCTOR

■ **Where and When** The desert planet of Segonax, current location of the once celebrated, now rather tatty Psychic Circus.

■ **The Baddies** The Gods of Ragnarok, powerful elemental beings who pass eternity by forcing mere mortals to entertain them, and the Chief Clown (Ian Reddington), sinister head pierrot of the Psychic Circus.

■ **Look out for...** The sequence in Part One where the Chief Clown, dressed in undertaker's garb, glides through the dunes in a silent black hearse – a deliciously creepy moment of surrealist fantasy.

■ **Farewell to...** The classic TARDIS control room (if you don't count the hastily assembled flats in **152** *Battlefield*, which we absolutely don't).

■ **What they said** *"The Greatest Show in the Galaxy* was the most aptly named script for years," wrote Gary Russell in **DWM** issue 147 (April 1989), adding: "it was sheer brilliance."

■ **Arcs in Space** Ace models the Fourth Doctor's scarf, plus Mel's costume from **145** *Paradise Towers*. The Fifteenth Doctor will recall fighting the Gods of Ragnarok in **303** *The Giggle*.

152 Battlefield

(four episodes) by **Ben Aaronovitch**
While UNIT is transporting a nuclear missile, figures from Arthurian legend appear in near-future England – and the Doctor is repeatedly mistaken for Merlin.

■ **Where and When** Carbury in the near future.
■ **The Baddies** The Arthurian characters are apparently from another universe, the Doctor theorising that the Earth is about to become the centre of a war that "doesn't even belong to this dimension". Morgaine (Jean Marsh) has a pet demon, the Destroyer (Marek Anton), whose exact nature is shrouded in mystery – but he's apparently capable of devouring whole worlds.
■ **Farewell to...** This is the last time we see the Doctor's yellow roadster, Bessie, in the main series; it first featured in **52** *Doctor Who and the Silurians*. This is also our final glimpse of the 1980s TARDIS console, in play since **129** *The Five Doctors*. And it's a lap of honour for Brigadier Lethbridge-Stewart; though not seen in the main series again, he'll reappear many years later in *The Sarah Jane Adventures*.

The mysterious Light (John Hallam) in *Ghost Light*.

The sorceress Morgaine (Jean Marsh) in *Battlefield*.

■ **Look out for...** During studio recording, a glass tank containing Sophie Aldred shattered; the cracks are clearly visible on screen. It was Sylvester McCoy who realised what was happening and urgently instructed that she be pulled out.
■ **Where else have I seen...** Jean Marsh was short-lived companion Sara Kingdom in **21** *The Daleks' Master Plan*, preceded by Joanna in **14** *The Crusade*.
■ **Arcs in Space** The Brig, previously seen in **129** *The Five Doctors*, and his wife Doris (Angela Douglas), who was briefly mentioned in **74** *Planet of the Spiders*, refer reminiscently to Sergeant Benton, who was last sighted in **83** *The Android Invasion*. The Doctor gives Ace the UNIT pass that belonged to Elizabeth Shaw (gone since **54** *Inferno*).

153 Ghost Light

(three episodes) by **Marc Platt**
The Doctor takes Ace back to the Victorian past of a 'haunted' house she burnt down when she was 13, to discover why the place so unsettled her.

■ **Where and When** A house called Gabriel Chase in Perivale, 1883.
■ **The Baddies** Light (John Hallam), an alien who came to Earth to catalogue all the different forms of life, unaware that evolution would make this a Sisyphean task. He's accompanied by a creature that takes on the form of Josiah Samuel Smith (Ian Hogg), as well as a 'Control' specimen (Sharon Duce).
■ **Look out for...** The energy escaping from Light's ship causes Ace to have a funny turn, during which she recalls burning down Gabriel Chase in the future. We'll discover more about her life in 1980s Perivale in **155** *Survival*.
■ **Where else have I seen...** Frank Windsor, playing Inspector Mackenzie, previously played Sir Ranulf Fitzwilliam in **128** *The King's Demons*.
■ **What they said** "Part One of *Ghost Light* was the most baffling and intriguing piece of television I have seen for a long time," said David Ryan in a letter published in **Doctor Who Magazine** issue 156 (January 1990). "The flatmates that I watched it with were as puzzled as I was, but I assured them that everything would be explained in the final episode. When Part Three finished we still didn't understand the story (and we're at university so we're not thick, you know)."
Arcs in Space Josiah's grand plan is to assassinate Queen Victoria, whom the Doctor will eventually meet in **169** *Tooth and Claw*.

154 The Curse of Fenric

(four episodes) by **Ian Briggs**
An ancient evil awakens during the Second World War, summoning its pawns for a final battle with its old enemy – the Doctor.

■ **Where and When** A British army base and the surrounding costal area, near Maiden's Point, 1943.

■ **The Baddies** Fenric ("evil since the dawn of time," the Doctor tells us) has an army mainly comprised of Haemovores – bloodsucking creatures that appear to be animated corpses in differing states of decomposition. We also meet 'The Ancient One', who, perhaps confusingly, is from the far future. Arguably, he could be related to the Dregs in **289** *Orphan 55* – also creatures from a possible future Earth that's suffered environmental catastrophe.

■ **Farewell to...** Ace using Nitro-9, the homemade explosive she's carried ever since we met her in **147** *Dragonfire*.

■ **Look out for...** In Part Three, realising he needs to have faith in order to repel the Haemovores, the Doctor mutters the names of various former companions under his breath, including Susan, Barbara, Steven, Vicki... But not Ian, for some reason.

■ **Where else have I seen...** Anne Reid (ill-fated Nurse Crane here) will return for another vampiric vignette, as sinister Florence Finnigan in **179** *Smith and Jones*.

■ **Arcs in Space** At the climax it's revealed that Fenric has been manipulating Ace's life since before she encountered the Doctor. References are made to Lafy Peinforte's chess set (**150** *Silver Nemesis*) and Iceworld, where the Doctor and Ace first met (**147** *Dragonfire*).

A vampiric Haemovore attacks in *The Curse of Fenric*.

Left
The Cheetah People in *Survival*.

Below inset
The Master succumbs to the planet's malign influence.

Bottom
The final, poignant scene of *Doctor Who*'s original run.

155 Survival

(three episodes) by Rona Munro
The Doctor takes Ace back to Perivale, where several of her friends have gone missing and mysterious black cats are stalking the streets...

■ **Where and When** Perivale 1989, and the unnamed planet of the Cheetah People.

■ **The Baddies** The Cheetah People and the Kitlings are mere components of the natural world; the real villain is the Master, who's manipulating them for his own ends.

■ **Farewell to...** *Doctor Who* – for a while. Goodbye, too, to Sophie Aldred's Ace (until **211** *The Power of the Doctor*). This is also the last we see of Anthony Ainley as the Master. And a final farewell to the fibreglass TARDIS police-box prop constructed for **109** *The Leisure Hive*.

■ **Look out for...** When it was realised the show was unlikely to be coming back, a final Doctor voiceover (building up to "Come on, Ace, we've got work to do") was hastily written by script editor Andrew Cartmel to give the series some sense of a tangible end.

■ **What they said** "The concept of unusual events taking place in mundane every-day situations is not new to *Doctor Who*," claimed Vanessa Scott in **DWM** issue 160 (May 1990), "but it is in this area that the show is most consistently successful. Thus, with this in mind, present day Perivale proved to be a superb setting for disappearing milk-men, dimension-hopping cats and Cheetah people on horseback."

■ **Arcs in Space** Sergeant Patterson (Julian Holloway) tells Ace that "The police let you off with a warning" – possibly referring to the burning of Gabriel Chase, as recounted in **153** *Ghost Light*.

The EIGHTH DOCTOR

Paul McGann
Story 156, 1996

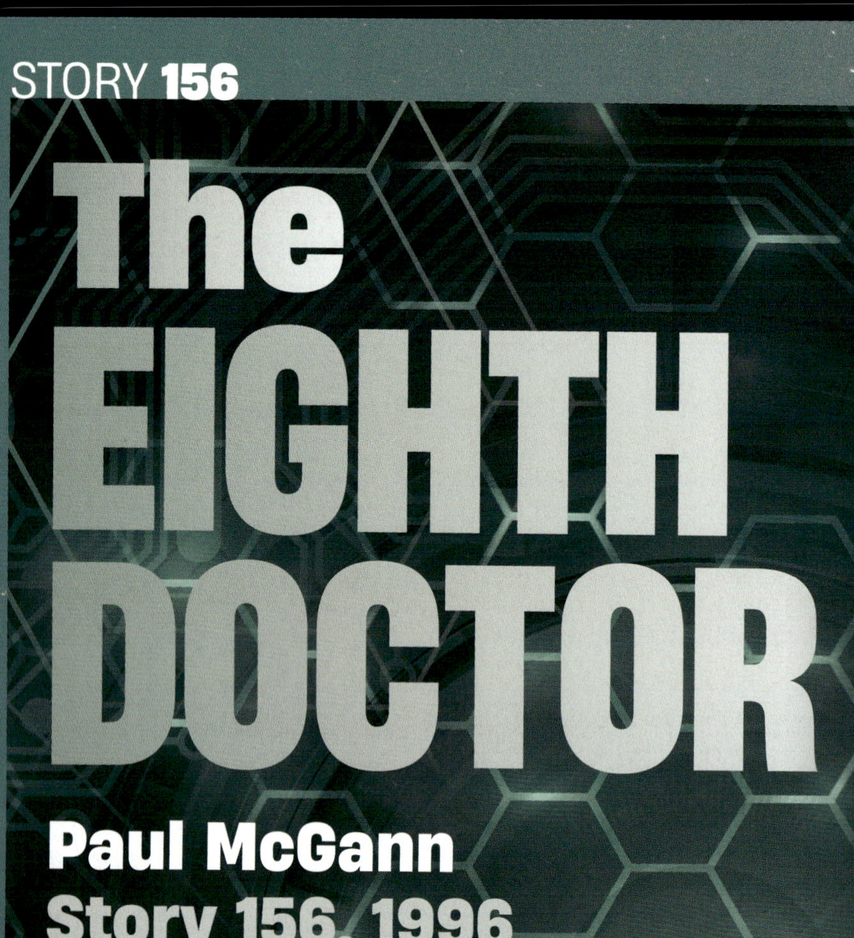

All flowing locks, and kitted out in 19th-century Western fancy dress, this "half-human" Doctor cut a retro, 'romantic hero' dash – a representation perhaps pre-empted by his TARDIS, which resembled something out of a Jules Verne fantasy. Breathless and breathy, no wonder he set hearts a-flutter.

156 Doctor Who

by **Matthew Jacobs**

A mystery man with an alien physiology dies on surgeon Grace Holloway's operating table, only to be reborn in a new body. But the Master's machinations threaten to turn the world inside-out.

■ **Where and When** San Francisco, 1999.

■ **The Baddies** The Master (Eric Roberts), in a newly acquired and rapidly decaying body, plus an off-screen cameo from some strangely squeaky Daleks.

■ **Introducing…** As the first canonical television adventure in seven years, there's a lot to squeeze in – including the Eighth Doctor (Paul McGann), his temporary associates Dr Grace Holloway (Daphne Ashbrook) and Chang Lee (Yee Jee Tso), a new Master and a radically redesigned TARDIS set, which the previously Gallifrey-bound Eye of Harmony is now somehow *inside…*

■ **Look out for…** The brief return of Seventh Doctor Sylvester McCoy in a new costume, all ready for the regeneration sequence he'd sworn to film as a promise to the fans.

■ **What they said** According to Stephen Pile, writing in *The Daily Telegraph* on 1 June 1996: "the car chases and the morgue scenes and the master's [sic] spirit turning into a green *X Files* type plasma were a tour of genre clichés that made this programme no different to any other. Only the excellence of Paul McGann in the title role made it recognisable."

■ **Arcs in Space** The Doctor has a sonic screwdriver again, for the first time since **119** *The Visitation*. The sight of a Leonardo da Vinci sketch on Grace's wall prompts the Doctor to recall "He had a cold when he drew that" – their prior acquaintance having been hinted at in **105** *City of Death*. The shocking (but plot-crucial) revelation that the Doctor is half-human ("on my mother's side") was quietly ignored until it was hinted at again in **262** *Hell Bent*. The equally shocking revelation that he enjoys snogging people at any given opportunity has been much more readily accepted.

Above
The Doctor (Paul McGann) and Grace Holloway (Daphne Ashbrook).

Right
The Master (Eric Roberts) and Chang Lee (Yee Jee Tso).

1996

MINI-EPISODES

From charity skits to continuity keystones, **Jamie Lenman** looks between the cracks in the main series to uncover a hoard of tiny gems.

Outstanding

Pandemonium ensued when *The Night of the Doctor* was suddenly added – in the middle of the day, with barely an hour's notice – to the BBC iPlayer on 14 November 2013. Work stopped, trains were missed and appointments were skipped (probably) as *Doctor Who* fandom scrambled to watch the surprise return of Eighth Doctor Paul McGann in a 50th-anniversary special of his own. Making good on the potential he'd shown in **156** the 1996 TV movie *Doctor Who* in just under seven minutes, *Night* also presented fans with the longed-for regeneration of the character, but probably – to coin the Doctor's irresistible new catchphrase – not the one they were expecting. Either way, birthday surprises don't get much better than this.

Essential

It's perhaps no coincidence that these three 'essentials' all feature David Tennant's Doctor(s). *Attack of the Graske* – an interactive adventure initially made available on the BBC's Red Button service on Christmas Day 2005, immediately after he'd made his TV debut – helped cement him in our affections, as he addressed the viewer directly. By November 2007, when *Time Crash* aired as part of the BBC's Children in Need telethon, he was in his pomp – eminently capable of standing toe-to-toe with Peter Davison's Fifth Doctor. Tennant's oddly familiar Fourteenth Doctor featured in 2023's Children in Need fundraiser *Destination: Skaro* – which drummed up excitement for the programme's 60th-anniversary specials by offering a cheeky insight into the Daleks' development, and a new look for Julian Bleach's Davros.

Excellent

Known as *Born Again*, 2005's Children in Need scene bridged the gap between the Tenth's regenerative appearance, new teeth and all, between **166** *Bad Wolf/ The Parting of the Ways* and his debut proper in **167** *The Christmas Invasion*. Both written by teams of children as part of competitions run by BBC Learning and *Blue Peter* respectively, 2011's *Death is the Only Answer* (featuring Nickolas Grace as Albert Einstein) and 2012's Olympics-themed *Good as Gold* (with a Flame-thieving Weeping Angel) fitted surprisingly well with the overall tone of the Eleventh Doctor's era. *The Last Day* – the other 50th-anniversary mini-ep – gave us a glimpse of the fabled Gallifreyan city of Arcadia, bracing itself against the Time War. *The Defence Drones* – a 30-second webcast released in 2020, to promote **296** *Revolution of the Daleks* – was a great example of the in-universe advertising used by the show to demonstrate how thin the wall between reality and fiction can sometimes become.

The Best of the Rest

The so-called 'wilderness' period between 1989 and 2005 delivered the deepest cuts, when a minute or two of anything even remotely resembling *Doctor Who* would quicken our hearts – which is why 1990's educational children's show *Search Out Science* and 1993's two-part *EastEnders* crossover *Dimensions in Time* – made for Children in Need – are still dearly cherished by some. Any one of 2006's innovative but short-lived 'Tardisodes' could have made this list, but the second – a prelude to **169** *Tooth and Claw* – remains perhaps the most effective. Two short episodes relayed into successive *Doctor Who* Proms at the Royal Albert Hall – 2008's *Music of the Spheres* (in which the Tenth Doctor again encountered the Graske) and its untitled 2009 follow-up (featuring Julian Bleach as Davros, with the Daleks ordering the orchestra to play Dalek music) demonstrated how pre-recorded footage could be incorporated into live performances. Finally, the specially shot mini-films produced to promote *The Collection* Blu-ray sets have grown ever more ambitious, with 2023's Season 20 trailer *The Passenger* and 2024's post-Season 15 'Leela in the Time War' piece *The Final Battle* proving particularly impressive.

"I'm a doctor. But probably not the one you're expecting."
THE DOCTOR, *THE NIGHT OF THE DOCTOR*

The NINTH DOCTOR

Christopher Eccleston
Stories 157 to 166, 2005

Dressed in a leather jacket and jeans, the Ninth was an Everyman Doctor, with a Northern accent – but then again: "Lots of planets have a North." Haunted by his experiences at the heart of an unseen Time War, this was a Doctor in recovery – healed by his connection with young shopworker Rose Tyler, from London's Powell Estate.

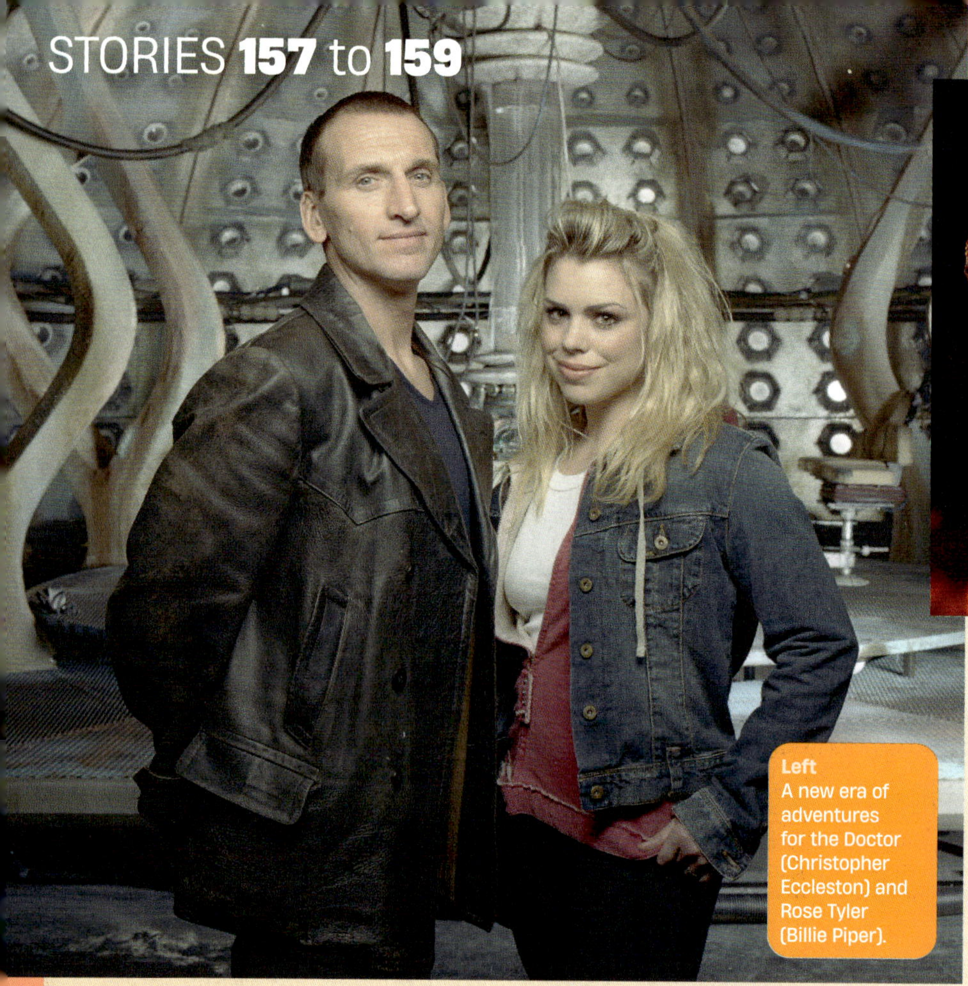

Left
A new era of adventures for the Doctor (Christopher Eccleston) and Rose Tyler (Billie Piper).

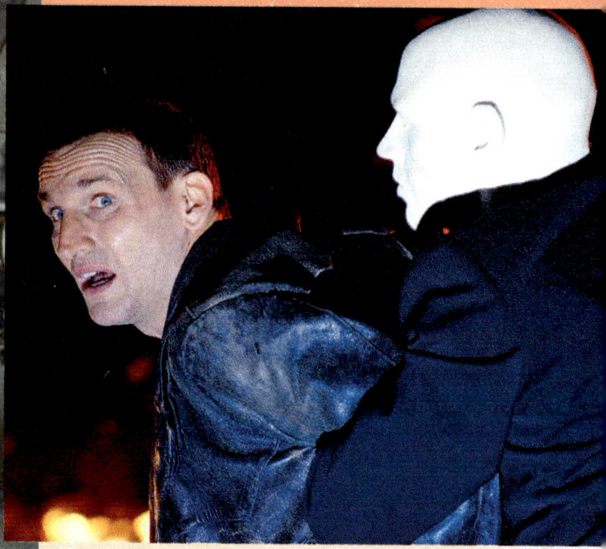

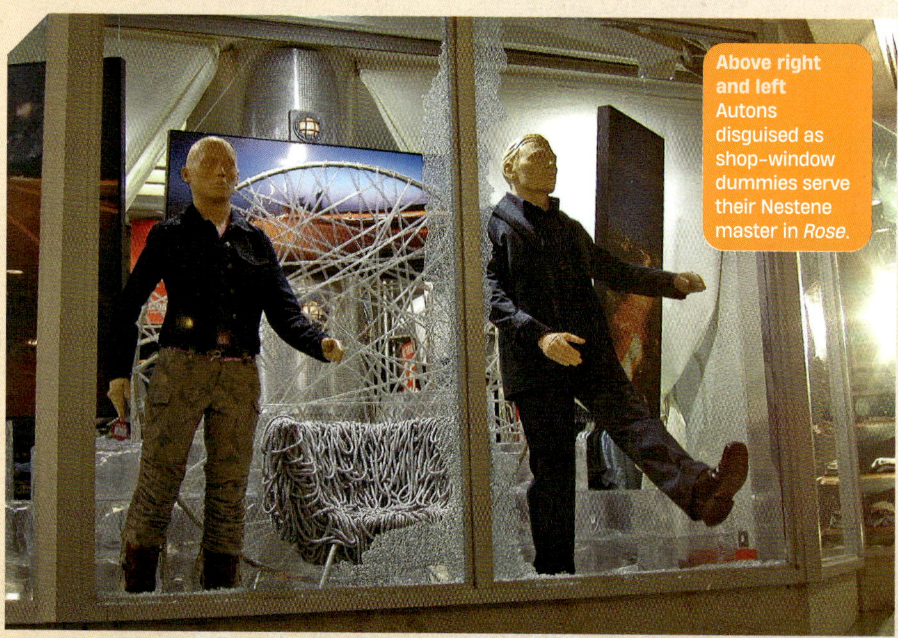

157 Rose

by Russell T Davies

A young woman loses her job after a strange man blows up the department store where she works, to help save the world. The two strangers end up becoming firm friends...

■ **Where and When** London, England, in the year 2005.
■ **The Baddies** The plasticated Autons – living shop-window dummies controlled by the Nestene Consciousness, a shapeless entity that's come to Earth to feed. The Third Doctor previously faced them in **51** *Spearhead from Space* and **55** *Terror of the Autons*.
■ **Introducing...** A roll call of entirely new characters – not just the leather-jacketed, Northern-accented Ninth Doctor (Christopher Eccleston), but also Rose Tyler (Billie Piper), her mother Jackie (Camille Coduri) and her boyfriend Mickey Smith (Noel Clarke). An expansive but distinctly lived-in TARDIS interior, with battered seats and coral-like formations surrounding the console, and a new sonic screwdriver.
■ **Look out for...** Clive (Mark Benton) showing Rose a photo of the Doctor at the assassination of President Kennedy in 1963 – an event associated by many with the start of *Doctor Who*, which began the following day.
■ **What they said** Playwright Bonnie Greer, expressing her bewilderment at *Rose* on BBC Two's *Newsnight Review* on 18 March 2005, inadvertently summed up the broad appeal of *Doctor Who*: "Who is this for? Is it for my generation? Is it for forty-somethings? Is it for babies? What is it for? They haven't made up their mind who they're talking to."
■ **Arcs in Space** "I fought in the War. It wasn't my fault. I couldn't save your world! I couldn't save any of them!" the Doctor tells the Consciousness in the first allusion to the Time War – a major part of the show's mythology from here onwards. The Doctor also refers to "Convention 15 of the Shadow Proclamation" – whom we'll meet in **198** *The Stolen Earth/ Journey's End*. Rose's unwitting first encounter with the Doctor, albeit in his next incarnation, took place just after midnight on the previous New Year's Day – as seen in **202** *The End of Time*.

Above right and left
Autons disguised as shop-window dummies serve their Nestene master in *Rose*.

Text by Paul Hayes

A plethora of alien races gather for *The End of the World*.

158 The End of the World

by **Russell T Davies**

Orbiting above the Earth in the far future, an array of esteemed representatives gathers to watch the death throes of the planet below.

■ **Where and When** Aboard the space station Platform One in the year 5.5/Apple/26 – five billion years in the future.

■ **The Baddies** The self-styled 'Last Human', Lady Cassandra O'Brien Dot Delta Seventeen (voiced by Zoë Wanamaker) – reduced by numerous plastic surgeries to a single, flat piece of skin stretched out onto a frame, with a brain in a jar below. Cassandra will battle the Doctor again in **168** *New Earth*.

■ **Introducing…** The Doctor's blank pass, printed on psychic paper, which enables him to access the hospitality zone. The Face of Boe, a giant head in an even more giant jar from the Silver Devastation – who'll be seen again in **168** *New Earth* and **181** *Gridlock*. The Head's possible origin will be given in **198** *The Stolen Earth/ Journey's End*.

■ **Look out for…** Rose's penchant for chips at the end of the story – something Mickey will warn her against in **170** *School Reunion*.

■ **What they said** On 1 April 2005, *Evening Standard* previewer Imogen Ridgway pointed out that: "The BBC model-making department has clearly been working overtime. There are no *Blake's 7*-style thinly disguised washing-up-liquid bottles in evidence."

■ **Arcs in Space** The First Doctor, Steven and Dodo watched a live scan of the Earth's final end in **23** *The Ark* – simultaneously, perhaps, with the Ninth Doctor and Rose? "Indubitably, this is the Bad Wolf Scenario," you can just overhear the Moxx of Balhoon (Jimmy Vee) say in passing to the Face of Boe. 'Bad Wolf' will be a recurring motif throughout the 2005 season…

159 The Unquiet Dead

by **Mark Gatiss**

Gaseous creatures fleeing the destruction of an all-consuming war seek sanctuary on 19th-century Earth by inhabiting the bodies of the dead.

■ **Where and When** Cardiff, Wales, Christmas Eve 1869.

■ **The Baddies** The Gelth – blue, elemental, shapeless life forms who were ravaged by the Time War. They initially convince the Doctor that they seek a peaceful co-existence with humanity in order to find a new home on Earth, but they soon reveal that they have conquest in mind.

■ **Introducing…** The Cardiff space-time rift, which the TARDIS will tap as a power source in **165** *Boom Town* and **187a** *Utopia*, and which Torchwood will establish a Hub beneath – as seen in *The Stolen Earth/Journey's End*. Charles Dickens, one of the greatest writers in the history of English literature, played here by Dickens expert Simon Callow – who'll return for a cameo as a time-displaced Dickens in **224** *The Wedding of River Song*.

■ **Look out for…** "What the Shakespeare…?" The expression "What the dickens?" doesn't actually relate to the writer, but having Dickens utter an equivalent was clearly irresistible.

■ **What they said** Mark Gatiss, interviewed in *The Daily Telegraph* on 19 March 2005, reflected how: "It is quite unusual for a Saturday evening family show to feature Victorian zombies."

■ **Arcs in Space** Rose hears the expression 'Bad Wolf' for the first time when fearful maidservant Gwyneth (Eve Myles) says it to her after looking into her thoughts. Like Martha Tyler (no relation) in **94** *Image of the Fendahl*, living on top of a space-time fissure has turned Gwyneth psychic. Communicating with 21st-century Torchwood operative Gwen Cooper (Eve Myles) in *The Stolen Earth*, the Doctor wonders if she's from "an old Cardiff family…"

The Doctor shares a stage with Charles Dickens (Simon Callow) in *The Unquiet Dead*.

160 Aliens of London/ World War Three

(two episodes) by **Russell T Davies**

A pig pilots a spaceship into Big Ben and flatulent monsters disguise themselves as politicians. What on earth is going on in Downing Street?

■ **Where and When** London, 2006.

■ **The Baddies** The Slitheen – a family of (large) calcium-based aliens from the planet Raxacoricofallapatorius.

■ **Look out for...** Could any other show come up with something like the 'space pig' scene? Unexpected, touching, enraging, and perfectly realised.

■ **Introducing...** This is the first time we see the Doctor hit by someone's irate mum. We meet Harriet Jones (Penelope Wilton), MP for Flydale North, and the as-yet unnamed newsreader Trinity Wells (Lachele Carl). The TARDIS key now glows when the TARDIS is about to appear. The appearance of 'Dr Sato' (Naoko Mori) functions, retroactively, as the first appearance of Torchwood.

■ **Where else have I seen...** 'Space pig' Jimmy Vee can be found inside many diminutive monsters, including the Moxx of Balhoon in **158** *The End of the*

Above
Slitheen at the heart of power in *Aliens of London/ World War Three.*

Right inset
A human disguise for Margaret Slitheen (Annette Badland).

World, Banakaffalata in **188** *Voyage of the Damned* and the Graske in **202** *The End of Time*.

■ **Arcs in Space** A boy graffitis 'Bad Wolf' onto the TARDIS – these mysterious words will take on greater significance. Rose Tyler has been missing from her home on the Powell Estate since 6 March 2005 – a year ago, when the TARDIS departed at the end of **157** *Rose*. The government brings in UNIT, but the Doctor says they won't recognise him – so what happened between **152** *Battlefield* and now? Albion Hospital will reappear in **164** *The Empty Child/The Doctor Dances*. 'Margaret Blaine' Slitheen (Annette Badland) will return in **165** *Boom Town*, and Harriet Jones in **167** *The Christmas Invasion*. We saw a cabinet meeting, presumably inside 10 Downing Street, in **69** *The Green Death*; the rebuilt Downing Street will feature in **187b** *The Sound of Drums/Last of the Time Lords* and **296** *Revolution of the Daleks*.

161 Dalek

by **Robert Shearman**

The last of the Time Lords faces the last of the Daleks.

■ **Where and When** Utah, 2012.

■ **The Baddies** The 'Metaltron' – a battered, metallic alien instantly

Rose shows sympathy towards the 'Metaltron' in *Dalek*.

recognisable to those in the know as a Dalek. The last of its kind, since the entire species was wiped out in the Time War – ten million ships burned in one second, alongside the Time Lords. This single Dalek fell through time, landing in the Ascension Islands over 50 years earlier.

■ **Look out for...** The scene where the Doctor is told "You would make a good Dalek." Is it time for him to take a good hard look at himself?

■ **Introducing...** New companion Adam Mitchell (Bruno Langley). It's been a while since we had a male companion, so let's hope he sticks around for a bit! (Oh dear. See **162** *The Long Game*.) This is the first time we've seen a Dalek sucker someone to death, or self-destruct using its skirt-spheres – and the first time anyone interacts with an unhoused Dalek mutant.

■ **What they said** On 2 May 2005, *The Times*' Ian Johns described *Dalek* as "A surprisingly poignant story".

■ **Arcs in Space** The museum maintained by Henry Van Statten (Corey Johnson) contains a Slitheen arm and a Cyberman head, of the type seen in **79** *Revenge of the Cybermen*. His helicopter is code-named 'Bad Wolf One'. The Dalek's mutation after contact with Rose's DNA echoes the 'Human Factor' Daleks in **36** *The Evil of the Daleks*.

The Editor of Satellite 5 (Simon Pegg) in *The Long Game*.

162 The Long Game

by **Russell T Davies**

A futuristic but slightly grotty space station isn't what it seems. And neither is its 'Editor', who is controlled by an alien with the hardest name to remember since Raxacoricofallapatorius.

■ **Where and When** Satellite 5, circa 200,000 AD, during the Fourth Great and Bountiful Human Empire.

■ **The Baddies** The Editor (Simon Pegg) and the Editor-in-Chief – the Mighty Jagrafess of the Holy Hadrojassic Maxarodenfoe.

■ **Look out for…** The vomitomatic – a convenient vomit-freezer that's simultaneously gross and a really good idea.

■ **Introducing…** When it comes to travelling companions, the Doctor now says he "only takes the best" – rather than just anyone who accidentally wanders in off the street, or stows away, or has been trying to murder him (as hitherto). We also get our first look at Satellite 5, and this is the first time the Doctor uses his sonic screwdriver on an ATM.

■ **Farewell to…** Adam Mitchell – dropped off home in disgrace, never to be spoken of again.

■ **Arcs in Space** Satellite 5 will be revisited in **166** *Bad Wolf*. Speaking of which: the Bad Wolf TV channel is showing news about the Face of Boe, introduced in **158** *The End of the World*.

163 Father's Day

by **Paul Cornell**

Being a TARDIS traveller gives Rose the opportunity to witness her dad's last day. But can she resist the opportunity to change the laws of time and avert his death?

■ **Where and When** London, 7 November 1987.

■ **The Baddies** The Reapers (unnamed on screen) – dragon-like creatures that repair wounds in time by consuming everything inside.

■ **Look out for…** The simultaneously devastating and heart-warming final scene – an inversion of the opening one, in which we learn that time has been changed in ways that are small for the universe but unbelievably huge to the individuals involved.

■ **Introducing…** For the first time, the Doctor is genuinely erased from existence. (It gets undone, of course, but it still counts…)

■ **What they said** "The emotional heft of the story is similar to Audrey Niffenegger's 2003 novel *The Time Traveller's Wife*," observed the *Times Higher Education* critic.

■ **Arcs in Space** The Doctor thinks Rose only went with him once he told her the TARDIS could travel in time as well as space – as he did at the end of **157** *Rose*. Rose making physical contact with her younger self causes a paradox, unleashing the Reapers. "There used to be laws stopping this kind of thing from happening. My people would have stopped this," says the Doctor – perhaps thinking of the Blinovitch Limitation Effect, first mentioned in **60** *Day of the Daleks*. We will meet a Pete Tyler again, in **171** *Rise of the Cybermen* – but knowing that doesn't lessen the impact of Pete's sacrifice here.

Rose meets her late father, Pete Tyler (Shaun Dingwall), in *Father's Day*.

A new horror descends on Blitz-ravaged London in *The Empty Child/The Doctor Dances.*

164 The Empty Child/ The Doctor Dances

(two episodes) by Steven Moffat

In the Blitz, the Doctor and Rose meet a handsome time-traveller hoping to make a quick buck, and a lost little boy who keeps repeating the same, spine-chilling question.

■ **Where and When** London, 1941.

■ **The Baddies** There's no clear baddie here. The gas-mask zombies are the main threat, but it's a little more complicated than that.

■ **Introducing…** Captain Jack Harkness (John Barrowman), who'll go on to have many more adventures in the TARDIS and will become the star of four seasons of *Torchwood*. When we meet him here, he's an ex-Time Agent who's turned to a life of crime.

■ **Look out for…** Jack's sonic blaster, which Rose dubs the "squareness gun". The next time we see a sonic blaster is in the hands of River Song, in 195 *Silence in the Library/Forest of the Dead.*

■ **What they said** The May 2005 issue of *SFX* magazine pointed out that "No previous story has packed in the scares like this one: the hideous transformations into Gas Mask People [and] the moment the tape runs out in room 802… This chilling two-parter must have caused wet sheets all around the nation."

■ **Arcs in Space** The Doctor strongly implies that he destroyed the Weapons Factories of Villengard, telling Jack that "There's a banana grove there now." We'll finally see the ruins of the factories in 276 *Twice Upon a Time* – then in 307 *Boom* we get to see the impact of the Villengard Corporation, which is profiting from a war on the devastated planet Kastarion 3.

165 Boom Town

by Russell T Davies

After thwarting Margaret Slitheen's plan to build a deadly nuclear power station in the Welsh capital, the TARDIS team have to decide what to do with her.

■ **Where and When** Cardiff, 2006.

■ **The Baddies** Flatulent capitalist Blon Fel-Fotch Passameer-Day Slitheen, aka Margaret Blaine – last seen "shaking her booty" in 160 *Aliens of London/World War Three.*

■ **Look out for…** Margaret's fresh-faced and out-of-his-depth PA, Idris Hopper (Aled Pedrick), who can be heard pleading "Leave the Mayor alone!" as she's pursued by the TARDIS team.

■ **Where else have I seen…** Mr Cleaver, the ill-fated adviser to the Blaidd Dwrg (Bad Wolf) nuclear power project, is played by William Thomas, previously the incredulous undertaker Martin in 148 *Remembrance of the Daleks* (making him the first actor to appear in both the original run of *Doctor Who*, and its 21st-century revival).

■ **What they said** "*Doctor Who* came off the rails this week, with a character-based episode that really didn't work," lamented Dek Hogan for Digital Spy on 4 June 2005. "Bringing back farting alien Margaret Slitheen was a poor idea."

■ **Arcs in Space** The tribophysical waveform macro-kinetic extrapolator (Margaret's space surfboard) is used by Jack in 166 *Bad Wolf/The Parting of the Ways* to create force-fields around the TARDIS and the upper floors of the Game Station. The heart of the TARDIS will play an even more significant role in the same series finale…

Margaret Slitheen returns to threaten Rose in *Boom Town.*

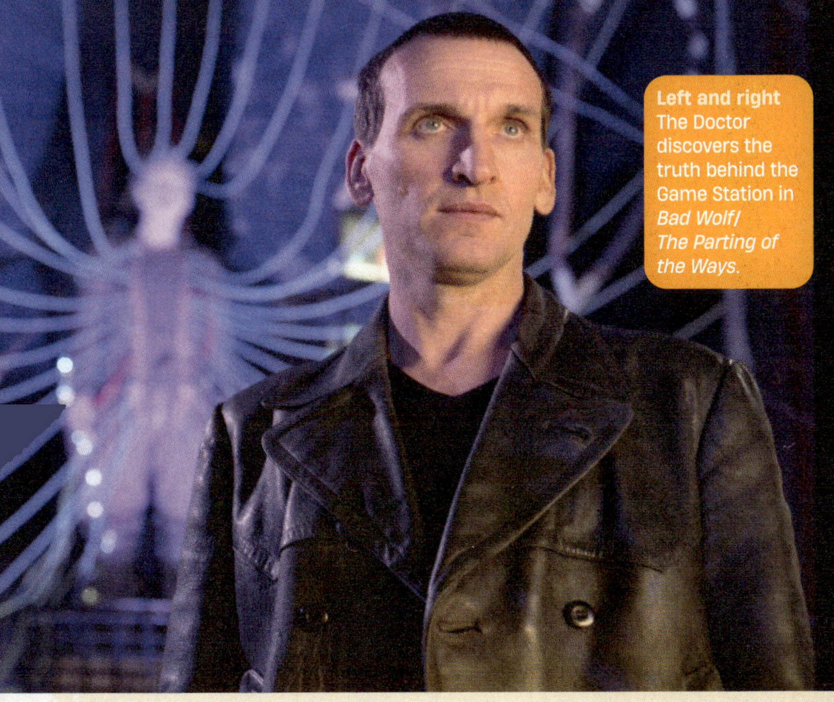

166 Bad Wolf/ The Parting of the Ways

(two episodes) by Russell T Davies

Light-entertainment spoof meets intergalactic reckoning in a momentous confrontation that brings the Ninth Doctor's life to an end.

■ **Where and When** The Game Station in 200,100. London in 2006.

■ **The Baddies** The Daleks – this time regrown from human remains, led by a gigantic Emperor and hiding behind a crew of killer droids modelled after 21st-century TV celebrities Davina McCall, Anne Robinson, and Trinny and Susannah.

"I am the god of all Daleks!" EMPEROR DALEK

■ **Introducing...** We've only ever seen him transform on his back before, but this time the Doctor regenerates standing upright. Every regeneration since has happened this way, with variations on the same orange light show we get here.

■ **Look out for...** When Lynda Moss (Jo Joyner) asks the Doctor how the public feels about her, he reassures her that she's "dead sweet". 'Dead' as an intensifier generally used by people from Manchester, suggesting that when the Doctor inherits a new accent, he takes on its associated dialect too.

■ **Where else have I seen...** The Davina Droid is voiced by its real-life counterpart Davina McCall, who hosted *Big Brother* on Channel 4 from 2000 to 2010. In 304 *The Church on Ruby Road*, she once again plays herself – this time actually appearing on screen.

The Tenth Doctor (David Tennant) arrives.

■ **Arcs in Space**

During the *Weakest Link* sequence, the Torchwood Institute receives its first mention, after Broff (Sebastian Armesto) incorrectly calls it the Touchdown Institute. Rose will be present at the institute's founding in 169 *Tooth and Claw*.

The TENTH DOCTOR

David Tennant
Stories 167–202, 2005–10

A cheeky, Estuary-accented gabbler, the next Doctor shared doomed romances with Rose Tyler, young widow Joan Redfern and Madame de Pompadour. But there was a dark and dangerous streak in his nature, too – one that found its ultimate expression in the persona of the history-defying 'Time Lord Victorious'.

Above
The new Doctor returns to Earth with Rose in *The Christmas Invasion*.

Below
The Sycorax Leader (Sean Gilder).

167 The Christmas Invasion

by Russell T Davies

A pioneering Mars probe draws the attention of aliens scouring space for prey, bringing them to Earth at Christmas to demand the spoils of conquest.

■ **Where and When** London on Christmas Eve and Christmas Day, 2006.
■ **The Baddies** The Sycorax – a warrior race with strict codes regarding honour and combat, travelling the galaxy in what appears to be a sculpted and hollowed-out asteroid, drawn to Earth by a chance encounter with the *Guinevere One* space probe.
■ **Introducing...** The Tenth Doctor (David Tennant) – although, as with the Third Doctor in **51** *Spearhead from Space* and the Fifth Doctor in **116** *Castrovalva*, he spends much of the adventure out of action, suffering from the after-effects of his regeneration, before recovering to help save the day.
■ **Look out for...** The Doctor briefly donning one of the Fourth Doctor's scarves while choosing his new outfit from the TARDIS wardrobe.
■ **What they said** In January 2006, the *Off The Telly* website, in its annual Christmas TV review, called this "Probably the best, most welcome sight on Christmas Night for years."
■ **Arcs in Space** The British had sent probes to Mars long before *Guinevere One* – as seen in **53** *The Ambassadors of Death*. The still mysterious Torchwood organisation shoots down the Sycorax vessel at the behest of Prime Minister Harriet Jones – an action that causes the Doctor to set in motion Jones' eventual downfall. Harold Saxon becomes PM in **187b** *The Sound of Drums/Last of the Time Lords*, but Jones redeems herself in **198** *The Stolen Earth*.

Text by Paul Hayes

168 New Earth

by Russell T Davies

After receiving a request to visit an acquaintance in hospital, the Doctor takes Rose to New New York in the far far future... where they encounter an old old adversary.

■ **Where and When** The city of New New York on the planet New Earth in the galaxy M87, in the year five billion and 23.
■ **The Baddies** Initially Lady Cassandra, the 'Last Human', whom the Doctor and Rose previously met in **158** *The End of the World*. But the main antagonists turn out to be the cat-nuns running New New York's hospital – who'll do anything to maintain their reputation for healing the sick, while Cassandra will go just as far to prolong her own life.
■ **Farewell to...** Zoë Wanamaker makes her second and final appearance as Cassandra, briefly playing the character in person rather than purely as a voiceover.
■ **Look out for...** Cassandra mentioning early on that she modelled the body of her custom-grown manservant Chip (Sean Gallagher) on her "favourite pattern". We find out at the end why she was so fond of this particular body pattern, seeing her encounter it for the first time earlier in her life – creating a time paradox that otherwise goes unmentioned.
■ **What they said** "*Doctor Who* remains a clever mix of old-fashioned sci-fi and modern knowingness," said James Walton in *The Independent* on 17 April 2006. "Once again, the gags keep coming, and the references pile up faster than on the average page of *Ulysses*."

Rose is possessed by Cassandra in *New Earth*.

The Doctor and Rose are honoured by Queen Victoria (Pauline Collins) in *Tooth and Claw*.

■ **Arcs in Space** Feline humanoids previously featured in **155** *Survival*. Novice Hame (Anna Hope) tells the Doctor the legend of the Face of Boe's final message, and the Doctor will query this with the Face (voiced by Struan Rodger) at the end of the story. Boe, as the Doctor puts it, is "textbook enigmatic" – but the message will finally be revealed in **181** *Gridlock*.

169 Tooth and Claw

by **Russell T Davies**
A cult of monks seeks to gain control of the British throne by forcing Queen Victoria to fall victim to an alien werewolf virus.

■ **Where and When** Torchwood House in the north of Scotland, 1879.
■ **The Baddies** The monks of the Glen of St Catherine, led by Father Angelo (Ian Hanmore). Also, the werewolf they've raised ever since abducting its human host as a child, turning it into what the Doctor calls a "lupine wavelength haemovariform". Having tricked Queen Victoria into Torchwood House on the night of the full moon, they mean to use the creature's bite to infect her and create the Empire of the Wolf.
■ **Look out for...** The Doctor initially identifying himself as "Dr James McCrimmon" – Jamie McCrimmon having been a companion of the Second Doctor from **31** *The Highlanders* to **50** *The War Games*.
■ **Where else have I seen...** As Queen Victoria, Pauline Collins made her second major guest appearance after a gap of 39

years – having previously appeared as Samantha Briggs, who aided the Second Doctor in **35** *The Faceless Ones*.
■ **What they said** "Supremely silly, superbly sinister and sensationally spooky – this is a blistering history mystery." So ran the *Daily Record*'s preview on 22 April 2006.
■ **Arcs in Space** This is the second alien werewolf encountered by the Doctor, after allying himself with a specimen from the planet Vulpana in **151** *The Greatest Show in the Galaxy*. Queen Victoria creates the Torchwood Institute to combat otherworldly threats. Around two years after these events, a British mission will take Her Majesty's portrait to the Red Planet, in **273** *Empress of Mars*. And around two years after that, the Seventh Doctor will help foil Josiah Smith's plan to assassinate Victoria – as seen in **153** *Ghost Light*.

170 School Reunion

by **Toby Whithouse**
At a school where some of the children are demonstrating intelligence well beyond their experience, events are being manipulated by the Krillitanes. An old friend of the Doctor's is already on the case...

■ **Where and When** Deffry Vale Secondary School, somewhere in the south of England, in the early 2000s – almost certainly 2007.
■ **The Baddies** The Krillitanes – a constantly evolving species that takes on the characteristics of those they conquer and consume. While initially appearing in human guise, at this stage in their development they are, in fact, bat-like creatures.
■ **Look out for...** A hint that the Doctor has provided someone with a winning lottery ticket – something he'll do again in **202** *The End of Time*.
■ **Where else have I seen...** Elisabeth Sladen returns as the Doctor's friend Sarah Jane Smith for the first time since **129** *The Five Doctors*, again with computer dog K9, again voiced by John Leeson.
■ **What they said** "I was only one year old when Sarah Jane originally left *Doctor Who*," said Caitlin Moran in *The Times* on 1 May 2006, "so I didn't have a danny [La Rue – clue] who she was, really, but even I was blubbing by the end."
■ **Arcs in Space** Sarah reveals where the Fourth Doctor actually deposited her at the end of **87** *The Hand of Fear* – and it wasn't South Croydon! She and the rebuilt K9 will return in **198** *The Stolen Earth/ Journey's End*, with Sarah making a further appearance in **202** *The End of Time*. Mickey finally joins the TARDIS crew, on the grounds that "You need a Smith on board."

The Doctor with old friends Sarah Jane Smith (Elisabeth Sladen) and K9 in *School Reunion*.

Left
Reinette (Sophia Myles) falls for the Doctor in *The Girl in the Fireplace*.

Below left
One of the clockwork androids.

171 The Girl in the Fireplace

by Steven Moffat

A spaceship is full of portals, all leading to points in the life of the legendary French courtesan Madame de Pompadour. What do the sinister clockwork androids want with her?

■ **Where and When** A spaceship in the 51st century, plus Paris and Versailles at various dates between 1727 and 1764.
■ **The Baddies** The clockwork androids, created as repair drones. They're clockwork so they're not reliant on the ship's own power. Also, they're just cool. "Space age clockwork, I love it," the Doctor says. "I've got chills!"
■ **Introducing...** Time windows are the means of accessing the life of Reinette (Sophia Myles), aka Madame de Pompadour. UNIT have developed a version of the technology, seen later in 311 *The Legend of Ruby Sunday/Empire of Death*.
■ **Look out for...** Reinette immediately understanding the situation on the spaceship from Rose's hesitant explanation: "There is a vessel in your world where the days of my life are pressed together like the chapters of a book..."
■ **What they said** Caitlin Moran wrote in *The Times* on 6 May 2006 that this was "another thrillingly good episode, with a twist at the end that will put a narratively satisfied smirk on your face for days."
■ **Arcs in Space** The fate of another group of clockwork androids from a sister vessel is central to 242 *Deep Breath*.

172 Rise of the Cybermen/The Age of Steel

(two episodes) by Tom MacRae

The TARDIS accidentally crash-lands in a parallel universe where Rose's father is still alive, and she was never born. In this version of Earth, technology is taking a different and more dangerous path.

■ **Where and When** London in a parallel universe, 1 February 2007.
■ **The Baddies** Tech mogul John Lumic (Roger Lloyd Pack) has created wearable devices to feed information directly into the user's brain, but he wants to go one step further and transplant people's brains into metal exoskeletons.
■ **Introducing...** A new strain of Cybermen, with a new design. An exchange between the Doctor and Rose acknowledges that these are different from the ones encountered by previous Doctors.
■ **Look out for...** Who, or rather what, ended up being called 'Rose' in the parallel universe.
■ **What they said** "It was hard getting the Cybermen to key into current technology," showrunner Russell T Davies said in **Doctor Who Magazine** issue 370 (June 2006). "Once we hit upon the idea that only the brain was being transplanted – like moving a SIM card to an upgraded phone – then the idea started to click."

Right inset
John Lumic (Roger Lloyd Pack) in *Rise of the Cybermen/The Age of Steel*.

Right
Lumic's ultimate, cybernetic form.

Text by Eddie Robson

Right
Rose and the Doctor liven up austerity London in *The Idiot's Lantern*.

Right inset
The Wire (Maureen Lipman) hides behind the new technology of television.

■ **Arcs in Space** Before now, the Doctor has visited parallel Earths in **54** *Inferno* and **82** *Pyramids of Mars*. The existence of contradictory origins for the Cybermen is addressed in **275** *World Enough and Time/The Doctor Falls*. The Cybus Industries Cybermen return in **177** *Army of Ghosts/Doomsday*, along with Mickey (who stays behind on the alt-world), the parallel Pete, and 'Preacher' Jake Simmonds (Andrew Hayden-Smith).

173 The Idiot's Lantern

by **Mark Gatiss**

Sales of television sets are soaring as the coronation of Queen Elizabeth II approaches. But something sinister is lurking in a Muswell Hill electricals shop…

■ **Where and When** London on 1 and 2 June 1953.
■ **The Baddies** The Wire (Maureen Lipman) is an energy being that takes on the form of a BBC continuity announcer – and has the ability to use the TV network to feed on the essence of other creatures.
■ **Introducing…** Magpie Electricals, which evidently didn't perish after the events of this episode; their brand can be seen in **187b** *The Sound of Drums/Last of the Time Lords*, **188** *Voyage of the Damned*, **254** *The Magician's Apprentice/The Witch's Familiar* and more. A Magpie shop can be seen aboard *Starship UK* in **204** *The Beast Below*.
■ **Look out for…** The shocked reaction from Det-Insp Bishop (Sam Cox) when the Wire turns the TV to colour. Sorry, fella, you'll have to wait until 1967 to get that in the UK.
■ **What they said** In **DWM** issue 372 (August 2006), Matt Michael described this episode as "quietly innovative, taking the TARDIS into the kind of 'real history' of ordinary people, and away from kings and queens."
■ **Arcs in Space** "It's never too late, as a wise person once said. Kylie, I think." This line establishes that Kylie Minogue exists in the *Doctor Who* universe – but the Doctor will meet someone who looks remarkably like her in **189** *Voyage of the Damned*. Elvis Presley certainly does exist, since the Doctor and Rose are hoping to see him perform live on American TV. It's implied that the next Doctor is hoping to take his companion to see Las Vegas-era Elvis in **234** *Cold War*; and in **279** *Rosa*, the Thirteenth Doctor reveals that 1955 Elvis has a mobile phone she (or an earlier incarnation) gave him!

174 The Impossible Planet/The Satan Pit

(two episodes) by **Matt Jones**

After landing on a deep-space expedition's base, the Doctor and Rose are stranded when the TARDIS falls down a chasm – and the base comes under attack from a being claiming to be Satan himself!

■ **Where and When** Sanctuary Base 6, on the planet Krop Tor – which is somehow in geostationary orbit around a black hole. The date is given as 43K2.1.
■ **The Baddies** The Beast (voiced by Gabriel Woolf), a giant red-horned creature with telepathic powers, which claims to be from before our universe existed.
■ **Introducing…** The Ood, who appear here as a servant class for humanity – but their backstory is further explored in **191** *Planet of the Ood*.
■ **Look out for…** One of the Doctor's best speeches as he descends into the chasm: "If that thing had said it came from beyond the universe, I'd believe it, but before the universe? Impossible. Doesn't fit my rule. Still, that's why I keep travelling. To be proved wrong."
■ **What they said** "The Doctor's a hard man to scare," Russell T Davies mused in **DWM** issue 370 (June 2006), "so I wanted something with a scale and impact that would really challenge him."
■ **Arcs in Space** "You get representations of the Horned Beast right across the universe," the Doctor notes, before mentioning Dæmos. Azal in **59** *The Dæmons* was previously suggested as similar influence on humanity's belief in the Devil. The Beast describes Rose as "The valiant child who will die in battle so very soon" – a prophecy that will come true, sort of, after the Battle of Canary Wharf in **177** *Army of Ghosts/Doomsday*.

A spacesuited Doctor in *The Impossible Planet/The Satan Pit*.

175 Love & Monsters

by **Russell T Davies**

A Doctor Who story without the Doctor. In his place we have everyman Elton Pope and his band of like-minded misfits, a lonely woman with a broken washing machine, and a creature from the planet Clom...

■ **Where and When**
London, 2007.

■ **The Baddies** The Abzorbaloff (Peter Kay) – a green monstrosity straight out of the mind of a child. As his name suggests, if you're unlucky he'll absorb you, feeding on your hopes and dreams in the process and wearing your face on his behind.

■ **Introducing...** The gruesome monster the Doctor and Rose are attempting to capture at the start is a Hoix. We'll see one again as part of the Alliance in 212 *The Pandorica Opens/The Big Bang*. Yet another shows up in Cardiff in *Torchwood: Exit Wounds* (2008). Or perhaps it's all the same Hoix?

■ **Look out for...** The Abzorbaloff's Bolton accent, which emerges only once he's shed his Victor Kennedy disguise. Maybe he thought that Elton Pope's LINDA agency would be more likely to trust somebody southern.

■ **What they said** Only nine years old when he created the Abzorbaloff as an entry to a *Blue Peter* competition, William Grantham commented, many years later, on the Doctor's relative absence from this story. "I can understand why not everyone is willing to overlook that," he said on the *Bigger on the Inside* podcast on 24 February 2021, "but personally I love the episode."

■ **Arcs in Space** Victor Kennedy mentions he's retrieved photos of Rose from the Torchwood files, which have been corrupted by "something called Bad Wolf virus". This is the first Bad Wolf mention since 166 *Bad Wolf/The Parting of the Ways*.

176 Fear Her

by **Matthew Graham**

As London hosts the Olympics, we meet Chloe Webber – a child whose drawings are a bit more than just something to stick on the fridge.

■ **Where and When** Dame Kelly Holmes Close in London, 2012.

■ **The Baddies** The late, abusive father of Chloe Webber (Abisola Agbaje) – whom she's resurrected with the power of pencils, thanks to the alien Isolus.

■ **Farewell to...** Though we say our final farewells in the next story, this is the last time we get a business-as-usual adventure with Rose Tyler. And the Doctor seems to know it when he tells her, "There's something in the air. Something coming."

■ **Look out for...** In a future-set story that's since become a historical, one of the story's less accurate predictions for the year 2012 comes when the TARDIS parks next to a poster for a 'Greatest Hits' album by 2005 *X Factor* winner Shayne Ward.

■ **What they said** According to Dave Bradley of *SFX* magazine: "The spookiness is cranked up for kids because of the it-could-be-your-street mentality... It's clear this wasn't an expensive episode, but that doesn't mean the scenes are insipid."

■ **Arcs in Space** The Doctor tells Rose that "I was a dad once" – a claim he repeats to Donna in 193 *The Doctor's Daughter*, and makes again in 307 *Boom*, when he speaks to Vater "dad to dad".

177 Army of Ghosts/Doomsday

(two episodes) by **Russell T Davies**

It's Cybermen vs Daleks in the Battle of Canary Wharf. The pay-off is some of the most heartbreaking human drama in Doctor Who.

■ **Where and When** The Torchwood Institute, Canary Wharf, 2007.

■ **The Baddies** The Cybermen *and* the Daleks. The steel stompers have jumped over from Pete's World, and the Cult of Skaro have followed them through the void. Four Daleks doesn't sound too bad, until we discover they have a Genesis Ark ready to go, full of millions more.

Chloe Webber (Abisola Agbaje) in *Fear Her*.

Above inset
Victor Kennedy (Peter Kay) in *Love & Monsters*.

Right
Ursula Blake (Shirley Henderson) confronts Kennedy in his true, Abzorbaloff form.

Text by Molly Marsh

A parting of the ways for the Doctor and Rose in *Army of Ghosts/ Doomsday*.

The Daleks' Genesis Ark, at Torchwood's Canary Wharf HQ.

■ **Look out for...** The members of the Cult of Skaro are truly unique, each bearing their own 'recognition code' underneath their eyestalk. Yet when they reappear in **182** *Daleks in Manhattan/Evolution of the Daleks*, their recognition codes appear to have switched. Curious!

■ **Farewell to...** Agonisingly, Rose makes her final goodbye to a projection of the Doctor on the beach at Dårlig Ulv Stranden, about 50 miles from Bergen, in Norway – its name roughly translating as 'Bad Wolf Bay'. Also bidding their what they think are their last adieux to the Time Lord: Mickey, Jackie and the alt-Pete Tyler –but the only one who's gone for good is Pete. The Doctor returns to the bay – for real, this time – in **198** *The Stolen Earth/ Journey's End*.

■ **What they said** "Forget Italy versus France in the World Cup Final," advised Harry Venning in *The Stage* on 17 July 2006, "the only contest worth watching last weekend was Daleks versus the Cybermen on *Doctor Who*... Funny and fantastic, scary and sad, *Doctor Who* has everything."

■ **Arcs in Space** Converted Torchwood employee Adeola (Freema Agyeman) may remind you of future companion Martha Jones. In **179** *Smith and Jones,* we find out that they're cousins. But first: one Donna Noble (Catherine Tate) has appeared inside the TARDIS...

178 The Runaway Bride

by **Russell T Davies**

Donna Noble is an unwilling arrival in the TARDIS, kitted out in a white dress and ready to marry a man secretly in cahoots with a prehistoric alien.

■ **Where and When** London, Christmas Eve, 2007.

■ **The Baddies** The Empress of the Racnoss (Sarah Parish), leader of a long-dormant spider-like race that's been waiting under the Earth for millennia. And the Robot Santas from **167** *The Christmas Invasion* are back!

■ **Introducing...** Donna's mother Sylvia (Jacqueline King) and her supposed best friend Nerys (Krystal Archer). Sadly, we won't see Donna's father Geoffrey Noble (Howard Attfield) again; he's passed away by the time the Doctor runs into Donna again in **189** *Partners in Crime*. In **202** *The End of Time*, the Doctor will reveal that he's been back in time to borrow a quid from Geoffrey, in order to buy a significant lottery ticket.

■ **Look out for...** The Doctor tells Donna his pockets are bigger on the inside, which could explain the origin of the cup of tea in **254** *The Magician's Apprentice/ The Witch's Familiar*.

■ **What they said** "The Tardis [sic] chasing the taxi was a great scene but it all seemed to peter out a bit after that," said Dek Hogan of the website Digital Spy on 31 December 2006.

■ **Arcs in Space** When the military destroy the Racnoss Webstar above London, they do so on "orders from Mr Saxon" – whose true identity is revealed in **187a** *Utopia*. These events are revisited in **197** *Turn Left*, when the Doctor dies confronting the Empress beneath the Thames Barrier.

The Doctor introduces Donna Noble (Catherine Tate) to the wonders of the TARDIS in *The Runaway Bride*.

TORCHWOOD

Outside the government, beyond the police, Captain Jack Harkness leads a motley crew of alien-hunters based in Cardiff. **Richard Unwin** accesses the secret files of this *Doctor Who* spin-off.

Outstanding

Broadcast over five consecutive nights in 2009, the multi-episode *Children of Earth* was 'event' television that stands proudly as the pinnacle of *Torchwood*. Children across the globe begin reciting sinister messages in unison, triggering events that lead to a horrifying encounter with mysterious alien species the 456. With regulars Toshiko Sato (Naoko Mori) and Owen Harper (Burn Gorman) having both been killed off at the end of the preceding series, team Torchwood is already seriously depleted at the start of this epic adventure. But that doesn't prevent everyone's favourite coffee boy, Ianto Jones (Gareth David-Lloyd), from also being dramatically dispensed with partway through. The darkest moment of all is saved for the climax – when Captain Jack Harkness (John Barrowman) is forced to make the agonising decision to sacrifice his own grandson for the greater good. Everything about this excellent serial is both shocking and sublime.

Essential

The show's fixation on bumping off its regular cast members can be traced back to its first episode *Everything Changes*, in which Suzie Costello (Indira Varma) dramatically shoots herself dead at the climax. (But not before she puts a bullet in Jack – who proceeds to defy death for the first of many times in the series.) Thanks to a 'resurrection gauntlet', Suzie herself will be temporarily brought back to life later in the first series for *They Keep Killing Suzie* – a richly dark and moody meditation on life and death. (Is there a theme developing here?) Another highlight of the inaugural season is *Out of Time*. The dimensional rift that runs through Cardiff – and generates a lot of the early plots – ejects an aeroplane from 1953, carrying three people, into the modern world of 2006. Each of the displaced travellers forms a bond with a different member of the Torchwood team, and the various attempts to acclimatise them to a different century, successful or otherwise, make for compelling drama.

Excellent

For those interested in the backstories of the regular characters, *Fragments* is an insight-stuffed anthology episode mainly comprised of flashbacks delving into how the regular team members ended up working at Torchwood. And to find out more about the man our lead protagonist took his name from, *Captain Jack Harkness* is well worth a watch. *A Day in the Death* is the high point of an arc dealing with the fallout of Owen Harper being (you guessed it) killed, then resurrected with that pesky gauntlet. Ways in which living on top of a space-time rift affects the local population are powerfully explored in the devastating *Adrift*. And for an instalment that's a little lighter in tone, the comic escapades of Gwen Cooper's wedding, as seen in *Something Borrowed*, are not to be missed.

The Best of the Rest

While not as highly regarded as *Children of Earth*, the ten-part *Miracle Day* epic, in which death itself takes a holiday, still has plenty to enjoy. The first two series both have rewarding and action-packed climaxes in *End of Days* and *Exit Wounds*, while the gruesome *Countrycide* is distinguished as the only episode without any science-fiction elements. *Greeks Bearing Gifts* is a bitter-sweet character exploration of the sometimes-misunderstood Toshiko Sato, and *Adam* allows us to delve into the psychology of the whole team by having them infiltrated by an alien impostor. The most *Torchwood*-y episode of *Torchwood*, however, is probably *Day One* – alien sex-gas shenanigans and all.

"Sometimes the Doctor must look at this planet and turn away in shame."
GWEN COOPER, *CHILDREN OF EARTH*

Left
Martha (Freema Agyeman) joins the Doctor in *Smith and Jones.*

Below inset
A Judoon trooper.

The Bard himself (Dean Lennox Kelly) in *The Shakespeare Code.*

By the 26th century, the Moon is a penal colony in **67** *Frontier in Space*, and let's not forget its origins as a giant space egg in **248** *Kill the Moon.* Martha's cousin Adeola – also played by Freema Agyeman – was killed in the battle of Canary Wharf, as depicted in **177** *Army of Ghosts/Doomsday.*

180 The Shakespeare Code

by **Gareth Roberts**
Science meets magic, smashing into the power of genius and words. In the hurly-burly of a celebrity historical, Martha experiences history up close and meets the Bard himself. Author! Author!

■ **Where and When** London, the Globe Theatre, 1599.
■ **The Baddies** Carrionites – Lilith (Christina Cole), Bloodtide (Linda Clarke), Doomfinger (Amanda Lawrence) – legendary shape-changing beings with the power to alter reality through words – in this case, the grief-stricken genius of Shakespeare (Dean Lennox Kelly) himself, focused through the Globe Theatre to "lead the universe back into the old ways of blood and magic."
■ **Introducing…** A crystal ball imprisoning the swarm of Carrionites, and dumped in a nice attic somewhere in the TARDIS. It's seen again, briefly, when the Doctor searches for an Agatha Christie novel in **194** *The Unicorn and the Wasp.*
■ **Look out for…** The Doctor explaining the "infinite temporal flux" via the plot of *Back to the Future* (film, not novelisation). It's certainly a contrast to the First Doctor's "Not one line!" approach in **6** *The Aztecs.*
■ **What they said** "It's somehow appropriate," wrote Scott Matthewman

179 Smith and Jones

by **Russell T Davies**
Medical drama meets police procedural on the Moon, as only Doctor Who *can do. Doctor Jones, meet Doctor Smith…*

■ **Where and When** Royal Hope Hospital, London, mid-2000s. The Moon. With a Judoon platoon.
■ **The Baddies** Fugitive Plasmavore Florence Finnegan (Anne Reid) – a vampire in the body of a dotty senior citizen – and her Slab henchthings. The Judoon: "great big space rhinos with guns", a colourful but accurate description of these leather-clad coppers.
■ **Introducing…** Medical student Martha Jones (Freema Agyeman) gets a crash course in interplanetary adventure when Royal Hope Hospital is transported to the Moon during ward rounds. Her fractious family also make their debuts – mum Francine (Adjoa Andoh), dad Clive (Trevor Laird) and siblings Tish (Gugu Mbatha-Raw) and Leo (Reggie Yates).

■ **Look out for…** When the Doctor invites Martha for a trip in the TARDIS, pay attention to the 'Vote Saxon' posters on the alley wall. This will be important… (in **187a** *Utopia* and **187b** *The Sound of Drums/Last of the Time Lords*).
■ **What they said** According to Jim Shelley in *The Sun* (3 April 2007): "Russell T Davies came out all guns blazing… blitzing the audience with an opening as fast and smart and slick as an advert for Pepsi."
■ **Arcs in Space** The Doctor uses the alias John Smith, first tagged to the Time Lord by Jamie in **43** *The Wheel in Space.* The Second Doctor had lunar layovers in **33** *The Moonbase* and **48** *The Seeds of Death.*

Brannigan
(Ardal O'Hanlon)
in *Gridlock*.

in *The Stage* (8 April 2007), "that it's David Tennant's Tenth Doctor who becomes the first to meet William Shakespeare (at least on screen). More than any other, this incarnation of *Doctor Who* revels in wordplay."

■ **Arcs in Space** Queen Elizabeth I (Angela Pleasance) pitches up to confront the "pernicious Doctor"... but why? The Doctor mentions in **202** *The End of Time* that he married "Good Queen Bess", while **240** *The Day of the Doctor* explains why she wants a word with her sworn enemy; he jilted her and did a bunk in the TARDIS. (He only proposed because he thought Her Maj was a Zygon double!)

181 Gridlock

by **Russell T Davies**

The Doctor dreams of the burnt orange skies of home, Martha gets stuck in traffic, the Face of Boe has the last word, and there's something lurking beneath the motorway. You take care now, and drive safely...

■ **Where and When** New Earth, New New York in the year five billion and fifty three.
■ **The Baddies** There's such a thing as Macra; once the scourge of the galaxy, these giant crabs were at the height of their empire in **34** *The Macra Terror*. Billions of years later, they've devolved into savage beasts, welcoming careful drivers into their claws beneath New Earth's fast lane.
■ **Where else have I seen...** Struan Rodger – 'voice' of the Face of Boe – shuffles through **257** *The Woman Who Lived* as Clayton, faithful retainer to Me (Maisie Williams), before returning to voice duties as Kasaavin **288** in *Spyfall*.

■ **Look out for...** The Doctor being introduced to the family Brannigan, a litter of the cutest kittens ever fussed by a Time Lord.
■ **Farewell to...** A final appearance (bar flashbacks) for that mysterious big old boat race, the Face of Boe, the oldest being in the Isop Galaxy.
■ **Arcs in Space** The Face of Boe makes good on his promise in **168** *New Earth*, that "We shall meet again, Doctor, for the third time, for the last time, and the truth shall be told," telling the Time Lord "You are not alone." An acronym of 'Yana', this points neatly forward to the reappearance of the Master, in **187a/b** *Utopia*, *The Sound of Drums/Last of the Time Lords*, as the kindly Professor Yana (Derek Jacobi). The Doctor's memory of Gallifrey's burnt orange skies echoes Susan's description in **7** *The Sensorites*.

182 Daleks in Manhattan/ Evolution of the Daleks

(two episodes) by Helen Raynor

In a concrete jungle that (Dalek) dreams are made of, the last of the Time Lords finds the last of the Daleks, battling for survival – whatever the cost.

■ **Where and When** Manhattan, New York City, 1930 – taking in a show, the Statue of Liberty, a tour of Central Park and a trip up the Empire State Building.
■ **The Baddies** Daleks, specifically the Cult of Skaro – Sec, Caan, Thay, Jast – and their pig slaves, following their temporal Manhattan transfer in **177** *Army of Ghosts/ Doomsday*. Fighting for their future from a lab beneath the Empire State Building, Dalek Sec assimilates the human Mr Diagoras (Eric Loren), becoming something... other.
■ **Where else have I seen...** Behind the porcine mask of 'Hero Pig' is Paul Kasey, whose numerous monster guises have included an Auton in **157** *Rose*, Slitheen in **160** *Aliens of London/World War Three*, Cyber-Leader in both **172** *Rise of the Cybermen/The Age of Steel* and *Army of Ghosts/Doomsday*, and Judoon Captain in **179** *Smith and Jones*.
■ **Look out for...** Pig slaves crammed impatiently into a rising lift – just another day at the office for Dalek henchmen.
■ **What they said** "There are only four Daleks left in the whole universe," said Russell T Davies (*Radio Times*, 21 April 2007), "but they're so powerful, you have to find ways of robbing them of their power, and then they become fascinating."
■ **Arcs in Space** A direct sequel to *Army of Ghosts/Doomsday*, this isn't the Daleks' first trip to New York, or indeed the Empire State Building. Their time ship briefly landed on the observation deck while pursuing the TARDIS in **16** *The Chase*, perhaps lodging this architectural achievement in Dalek subconscious for future use...

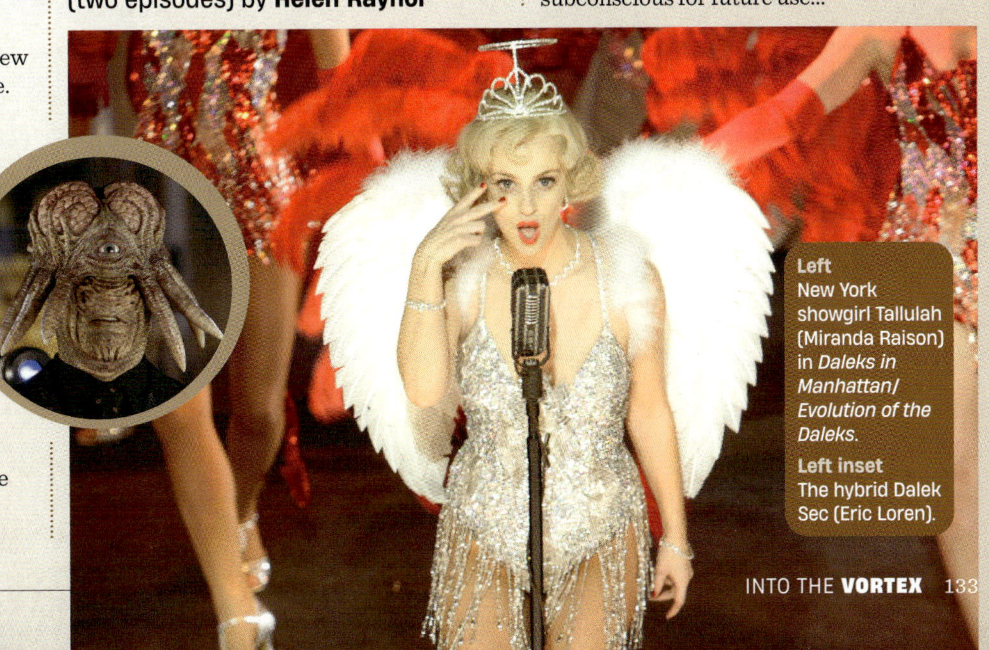

Left
New York showgirl Tallulah (Miranda Raison) in *Daleks in Manhattan/ Evolution of the Daleks*.

Left inset
The hybrid Dalek Sec (Eric Loren).

Right
The aged Professor Lazarus (Mark Gatiss) in *The Lazarus Experiment*.

Below inset Lazarus mutates into a hideous creature.

183 The Lazarus Experiment

by Stephen Greenhorn

The 76-year-old Professor Lazarus says he's perfected a machine that will rejuvenate his physical body – a claim in which the Doctor takes an understandably personal interest. At first glance, the experiment looks to have been a complete success, but things are rarely that simple…

■ **Where and When** London, Earth, 2007.

■ **The Baddies** Richard Lazarus (Mark Gatiss) seems lovely until he reveals a nasty streak after his rejuvenation, and an even nastier one later on. There's also a certain Mr Saxon pulling various strings off screen…

■ **Where else have I seen…** Lazarus' hypersonic soundwave manipulator is the same prop as the descent capsule from 174 *The Impossible Planet/The Satan Pit*, redressed and repainted. The Doctor's tuxedo is also a holdover from the previous year, having first appeared in 172 *Rise of the Cybermen/The Age of Steel*.

■ **Look out for…** Martha's slinky black dress. She's been wearing that same old jeans and jacket for the past four episodes!

■ **What they said…** On the *Radio Times* website on 5 May 2007, Patrick Mulkern called this story "an almost perfect slice of *Doctor Who* hokum. Decent villain. Huge, shonky monster. No hanging about and lots of dashing around. Quick simple hook at the start and a grand denouement in a sacred building."

■ **Arcs in Space** The rumblings about Harold Saxon will come to a head in 187b *The Sound of Drums/Last of the Time Lords*, which also features a last hurrah for the Jones family. On the bright side, The Doctor will at least get one more wear out of that tux in 189 *Voyage of the Damned*.

184 42

by Chris Chibnall

The crew of the SS Pentallian *have only 42 minutes to stop it plunging into a nearby star, battling through 30 locked security doors to reach the controls. To make matters worse, the captain's husband appears to be wandering through the ship and murdering people…*

■ **Where and When** The Torajii System in the 42nd century.

■ **The Baddies** Ostensibly Hal Korwin (Matthew Chambers), but really he's been possessed by the living sun Torajii – which, technically, is only defending itself against the *actual* baddie, namely the *Pentallian*.

■ **Look out for…** Director Graeme Harper's on-screen 'signature' – a view through a distorted lens of some sort, in this case a shot of Martha looking through a bulkhead porthole.

■ **Where else have I seen…** The Doctor's space suit bears a striking similarity to the one he nicked from Sanctuary Base 6 in 174 *The Impossible Planet/The Satan Pit*, although it's been dyed red. The orange version would later be worn (with and without the SB6 patch) by several future Doctors, companions and supporting characters in 201 *The Waters of Mars*, 235 *Hide*, 248 *Kill the Moon*, 256 *The Girl Who Died* and 300 *The Power of the Doctor*.

■ **What they said…** Kate Bevan, writing for *The Guardian*'s TV and Radio blog on 21 May 2007, declared it "a triumph: a pacy, tense episode where even though you know that the Doctor isn't due for regeneration any time soon, you (well, at least, I) genuinely thought he was in real peril."

■ **Arcs in Space** The Doctor uses his sonic screwdriver to 'upgrade' Martha's phone so she can call home from wherever she is. He'd previously done the same for Rose in 158 *The End of the World* and will do it again for Ruby in 305 *Space Babies*.

185 Human Nature/ The Family of Blood

(two episodes) by Paul Cornell

In order to evade a gang of galactic hunters, the Doctor erases his identity and assumes the role of an Edwardian schoolteacher, with Martha as his housemaid. Inevitably, the insatiable predators catch up with him, but not before he's fallen deeply in love…

■ **Where and When** Farringham, Earth, 1913.

■ **The Baddies** Father of Mine (Gerard Horan), Mother of Mine (Rebekah Staton), Son of Mine (Harry Lloyd) and Daughter of Mine (Lor Wilson) – the titular family, of unknown origin.

Kath McDonnell (Michelle Collins) in *42*.

'Dr John Smith' and Joan Redfern (Jessica Hynes) in *Human Nature/ The Family of Blood.*

Father of Mine (Gerard Horan), Son of Mine (Harry Lloyd) and Mother of Mine (Rebekah Staton).

■ **Introducing...** The chameleon arch, a piece of Gallifreyan technology that (apparently painfully) replaces a Time Lord's unique essence with a false personality and memories, whilst storing the originals safely in a suitably small and inconspicuous biodata module – in this instance, a fob watch. The technology was highlighted again in `187a` *Utopia,* `199` *The Next Doctor* and `291` *Fugitive of the Judoon,* though the second instance turned out to be a false alarm.

■ **Look out for...** The drawings in John Smith's journal, illustrated by Kellyanne Pugh, detailing events from the Doctor's recent adventures and, for the first time since 2005, images of his past incarnations.

■ **Where else have I seen...** The plot was adapted wholesale (with minor alterations) from Paul Cornell's 1995 novel *Human Nature,* originally featuring the Seventh Doctor. Similarly, elements of both `161` *Dalek* and `172` *Rise of the Cybermen/The Age of Steel* were borrowed from the *Doctor Who* audio plays *Jubilee* and *Spare Parts,* respectively.

■ **Arcs in Space** The Doctor later visits Verity Newman, great-granddaughter of Joan Redfern, on his extended pre-regeneration lap of victory in `202` *The End of Time.* Both characters were played by Jessica Hynes.

`186` Blink

by **Steven Moffat**

Young photographer Sally Sparrow is spooked by a cryptic message on the wall of an abandoned house. Simultaneously, her friend Larry is spooked by a series of equally cryptic Easter eggs on some very specific DVDs. Then people start disappearing, and statues start moving...

■ **Where and When** London, Earth, 2007.
■ **The Baddies** The Weeping Angels – quantum-locked humanoids who feed on the time energy of temporally displaced persons (or sometimes just snap their necks, if they're in a hurry).
■ **Look out for...** The first ever use of the catch-all phrase 'timey-wimey,' soon to become a genre all in itself, as well as the infamous Timey-Wimey Detector, a device cobbled together by the Doctor to... well, the clue's in the name.
■ **Where else have I seen...** For the third week in a row, *Doctor Who* borrowed a plot from a previously existing spin-off – in this case, Steven Moffat's short story *What I Did on My Holidays by Sally Sparrow,* first published in the 2006 *Doctor Who Annual.* The original tale featured the Ninth Doctor, a much younger Sally and no Weeping Angels.
■ **What they said...** "*Doctor Who* this week dispensed with the Doctor entirely in a story about weeping statues sucking the life out of people," noted Tim Teeman in *The Times* on 11 June 2007. "It was really, really scary."
■ **Arcs in Space** The Weeping Angels went on to become the most successful new monsters of the show's 21st-century era, rivalling even the Daleks for popularity, returning in `206` *The Time of the Angels/ Flesh and Stone,* `222` *The God Complex,* `230` *The Angels Take Manhattan,* `241` *The Time of the Doctor,* `262` *Hell Bent,* `272` *The Lie of the Land,* `296` *Revolution of the Daleks* and several chapters of `297` *Flux.*

Above inset Sally Sparrow (Carey Mulligan) in *Blink.*

Left One of the Weeping Angels strikes.

187a Utopia

by **Russell T Davies**

At the end of the universe, the last community of humans prepares to travel to Utopia. The Doctor helps Professor Yana repair their rocket for launch, but Yana is not all he seems…

■ **Where and When** Cardiff (briefly), around 2007 – then the planet Malcassairo, 100 trillion years in the future.

■ **The Baddies** The last humans are terrorised by the Futurekind – humans who've evolved into cannibals and are desperate for food. But there's even worse…

■ **Look out for…** The moment when Martha prompts the benevolent Professor Yana (Derek Jacobi) to open his fob watch… which, via chamelon arch technology, restores the personality of the Master, seen for the first time since **156** the 1996 TV movie *Doctor Who*.

■ **Introducing…** Not one, but two incarnations of the Master. Shot by Yana's dying companion Chan'tho (Chipo Chung), the Master regenerates into a maniac vibrating with energy (John Simm) – who promptly steals the TARDIS, leading straight into the next, two-part story.

■ **Arcs in Space** We're reintroduced here to Captain Jack (last seen in **166** *Bad Wolf/The Parting of the Ways*). Having heard the TARDIS materialise in Cardiff at the end of the first series of *Torchwood*, he clings to its outside, all the way to Malcassairo.

Text by Alison Lawson

187b The Sound of Drums/Last of the Time Lords

(two episodes) by **Russell T Davies**

The Master is the UK Prime Minister, initiating the world's first contact with the Toclafane, which decimate the population. With the Doctor aged to infirmity and Jack and Martha's family held prisoner on the Valiant, it's left to Martha to save the world.

■ **Where and When** London and the *Valiant*, a ship in geostationary orbit above Earth, date unspecified but around 2007 – just after a general election.

■ **The Baddies** The Master in his new incarnation, Harold Saxon, aided by his wife Lucy (Alexandra Moen), who "made her choice" to follow him. The Toclafane are the final form of the humans who escaped from Utopia, vestiges of their flesh encased in metallic airborne globes armed with all manner of weapons.

■ **Look out for…** The Master's first (and only) meeting as Prime Minister with his Cabinet, in which he gasses them all. One MP shouts "You're mad!" The gas-masked Master responds with a gleeful double thumbs-up.

■ **Farewell to…** Martha Jones, who decides she's put her family through enough by travelling with the Doctor. But she will return in **192** *The Sontaran Stratagem/The Poison Sky*.

■ **Where else have I seen…** Trevor Laird (Clive Jones, Martha's dad) played guard commander Frax in **143** *The Trial of a Time Lord*. The American newsreader, Trinity Wells (Lachele Carl), also appears in **160** *Aliens of London/World War Three*, **167** *The Christmas Invasion*, **192** *The Sontaran Stratagem/The Poison Sky*, **197** *Turn Left*, **198** *The Stolen Earth* and **202** *The End of Time*.

■ **Arcs in Space** The origin of the constant 'double-heartbeat' drumming in the Master's head, which began after he looked into the Untempered Schism as a boy, is explained in **202** *The End of Time*. At the end of the story, the TARDIS collides with the *Titanic* – but not the one you were expecting!

Bannakaffalatta (Jimmy Vee), Astrid Peth (Kylie Minogue) and the Doctor aboard the doomed starship *Titanic* in *Voyage of the Damned*.

188 Voyage of the Damned

by **Russell T Davies**
On a luxury space cruiser damaged by meteors and falling towards Earth, the Doctor battles to save the crew and passengers, plus billions of people on the planet below.

■ **Where and When** The starship *Titanic*, a cruise liner from the planet Sto, which is passing Earth on Christmas Day – two years after **167** *The Christmas Invasion* and one year after **178** *The Runaway Bride*.

■ **The Baddies** Max Capricorn (George Costigan) – president of Max Capricorn Cruiselines, a cyborg in a mobile life-support system who plans to destroy the ship in a meteor shower. The Heavenly Hosts – golden robot servants (reminiscent of those in **90** *The Robots of Death*) are programmed to kill survivors after the impact.

■ **Introducing...** The newspaper seller unafraid to stay in London at Christmas (Bernard Cribbins) will be revealed in **189** *Partners in Crime* as Donna's grandfather, Wilfred Mott.

■ **Look out for...** A wonderful potted history of the UK from Mr Copper (Clive Swift), in which Good King Wenceslas rules and the people worship the great god Santa and his wife Mary. With his first-class degree in Earthonomics from a dubious university, Mr Copper is a scream.

■ **Where else have I seen...** Geoffrey Palmer (Captain Hardaker) played Masters in **52** *Doctor Who and the Silurians*, while Clive Swift played Jobel in **142** *Revelation of the Daleks*.

■ **What they said** On Boxing Day 2007, Den of Geek's Simon Brew described the story as "bursting with ambition" and a "rollicking old-fashioned adventure".

■ **Arcs in Space** This story follows directly from **187b** *The Sound of Drums/Last of the Time Lords*. Wilfred Mott, meanwhile, mentions the events of **167** *The Christmas Invasion* and **178** *The Runaway Bride*.

189 Partners in Crime

by **Russell T Davies**
The Doctor and Donna are reunited when battling Adipose Industries, a company selling weight-loss pills that turn body fat into baby Adipose. If needed, though, whole bodies can be converted, alive...

■ **Where and When** Donna's family home and the Adipose Industries offices, London. Date unspecified, but presumably around 2008.

■ **The Baddies** Miss Foster (Sarah Lancashire), foster mother to the baby Adipose. A smart, organised professional, she was employed by the Adiposian First Family after the loss of their breeding planet.

■ **Introducing...** Catherine Tate's Donna Noble as a regular companion. First seen in **178** *The Runaway Bride*, feisty and fun Donna has been looking for the Doctor ever since and is overjoyed to find him. But is it a coincidence that their paths have crossed again?

■ **Look out for...** Donna drops her car keys in a bin and asks a random woman in the crowd to look out for her mother, who will pick them up. The woman turns round... and it's Rose Tyler! As she walks away, she fades from existence.

■ **What they said** Among many good reviews, on 6 April 2008 *The Daily Telegraph*'s John Preston declared this story "as close to 50 minutes of pure pleasure as you're likely to get on television... simultaneously absurd and thoroughly topical... an undiluted triumph."

■ **Arcs in Space** The Doctor met Donna's grandfather, Wilfred Mott, in **188** *Voyage of the Damned* but didn't know of the family connection. Rose will appear in several stories in the 2008 season, finally being reunited with the Doctor in **198** *The Stolen Earth*.

Far left Miss Foster (Sarah Lancashire) in *Partners in Crime*.

Left The Doctor and Donna investigate Adipose Industries.

Lobus Caecilius (Peter Capaldi) and his wife Metella (Tracey Childs) face *The Fires of Pompeii.*

190 The Fires of Pompeii

by James Moran

If the inhabitants of Pompeii are all acquiring powers of prophecy by breathing in particles of rock from Vesuvius, how come none of them have foreseen its cataclysmic eruption?

■ **Where and When** The city of Pompeii in the brand new Roman Empire, with the TARDIS landing on 23 August 79 AD – the eve of Volcano Day (as Captain Jack called it, in **164** *The Doctor Dances*).

■ **The Baddies** The Pyroviles – fire-breathing alien carapaces of stone, whose energy converter will harness the volcanic eruption. Their acolytes in Pompeii include Lucius Petrus Dextrus (Phil Davis) and the High Priestess of the Sibylline Sisterhood (Victoria Wicks).

■ **Where else have I seen...** The Sisterhood Soothsayer and the upwardly mobile Lobus Caecilius are played by Karen Gillan and Peter Capaldi, both of them destined to travel aboard the TARDIS on a regular basis. The Twelfth Doctor will recall Caecilius' face in **256** *The Girl Who Died*.

■ **Look out for...** Donna Noble, moving brilliantly from comedic Latin banter, through livid fury against Time Lord superiority, to the tearful, heart-rending plea: "Not the whole town. Just save someone."

■ **What they said** "As the Doctor and Donna race through the ash-strewn city, [Catherine] Tate perfectly portrayed Donna's anguish as she forlornly appealed for people not to run to the beaches and certain death," wrote *The Stage and TV Today* blogger Scott Matthewman on 13 April 2008.

■ **Arcs in Space** As in **6** *The Aztecs*, the Doctor finds himself in opposition to his travelling companion, who wants to change history for the better. The Doctor found himself in the vicinity of volcanic eruptions in **10** *The Dalek Invasion of Earth*, **21** *The Daleks' Master Plan*, **44** *The Dominators*, **54** *Inferno* and **134** *Planet of Fire*, and was said to have been by Krakatoa in 1883 in **157** *Rose*.

191 Planet of the Ood

by Keith Temple

Ood Operations boasts about the quality of its workforce, but increased instances of the disease 'red-eye' suggest that the once servile aliens are becoming impossible to manage...

■ **Where and When** The premises of Ood Operations in the year 4126 of the Second Great and Bountiful Human Empire.

■ **The Baddies** Mr Halpen (Tim McInnerny), owner of a family-run business that has for two centuries exploited (and lobotomised) defenceless natural Ood. Helping him are sadistic, whip-cracking security officer Mr Kess (Roger Griffiths) and Head of Marketing Solana Mercurio (Ayesha Dharker).

■ **Introducing...** The song of the Ood. They know the Doctor's song will end soon, in **145** *The End of Time*.

■ **Look out for...** Effects house The Mill offers spectacular CGI vistas of the Ood-Sphere. "Look at that view!"

■ **What they said** "The programme is rich in contemporary and historical references – indeed, it is perhaps a little too rich and rather too earnest," wrote *The Financial Times'* Karl French on 19 April 2008.

■ **Arcs in Space** The Doctor realises that he was in this solar system many years ago when he visited the Sense-Sphere, home of **7** *The Sensorites*.

192 The Sontaran Stratagem/The Poison Sky

(two episodes) by Helen Raynor

When 52 people across the globe simultaneously die in cars fitted with ATMOS (Atmospheric Omission System), UNIT's Dr Martha Jones co-ordinates a raid on the factory where the device is manufactured.

■ **Where and When** London, England – notably Chiswick and Richmond – in 2008.

■ **The Baddies** The Sontarans, led by General Staal (Christopher Ryan) and Commander Skorr (Dan Starkey). Also, 18-year-old millionaire genius Luke Rattigan (Ryan Sampson), whose 400 million ATMOS devices will help convert Earth into a Sontaran hatchery.

■ **Introducing...** The Sontarans' haka-like chant: "Sontar-ha!"

■ **Look out for...** Donna telling the Doctor, as he departs for the Rattigan Academy: "I'm not coming with you." The Time Lord is terribly upset but suddenly realises: "You're.... just popping home for a visit, that's what you mean."

Above inset The cruel Mr Halpen (Tim McInnerny) in *Planet of the Ood.*

Right The Ood imprisoned.

Left
The Earth falls victim to *The Sontaran Stratagem*/*The Poison Sky.*

Right
Jenny (Georgia Moffett), *The Doctor's Daughter.*

Below
Agatha Christie (Fenella Woolgar) in *The Unicorn and the Wasp.*

■ **Where else have I seen…** Christopher Ryan, playing General Staal, was previously the Mentor Kiv in Parts Five to Eight of **143** *The Trial of a Time Lord.*

■ **Arcs in Space** "What, have you met before?" asks the startled Donna when her Gramps (Bernard Cribbins) realises that his granddaughter's mysterious new friend is the man who vanished in front of him in **188** *Voyage of the Damned.* Flying UNIT aircraft carrier *Valiant* previously appeared in **187b** *The Sound of Drums/Last of the Time Lords.* Martha returns, taking a TARDIS trip into…

193 The Doctor's Daughter

by Stephen Greenhorn

Arriving in the middle of a war between species, the Doctor is sampled by a Progenation Machine. Moments later he's confronted with a newly born Generation 5000 soldier – his daughter, 'Jenny'!

■ **Where and When** Messaline, a planet co-colonised by a Human/Hath first wave – which the TARDIS is drawn to on the space date 60120724.

■ **The Baddies** General Cobb (Nigel Terry), leader of the humans, now generations into a bitter war involving the deployment of Progenation Machines to fuel soldiers, such as Jenny (Georgia Moffett).

■ **Introducing…** The half-fish, half-humanoid Hath – a species that can be glimpsed in the background of scenes in **202** *The End of Time,* **233** *The Rings of Akhaten* and **254** *The Magician's Apprentice/The Witch's Familiar.*

■ **Look out for…** Donna summing up the appeal of being with the Doctor on his adventures: "Never a dull moment. Can be terrifying, brilliant and funny – sometimes all at the same time."

■ **What they said** On 12 May 2008, *The Times'* David Chater called this a "minor classic of *Doctor Who* writing, with a strong humanistic moral, a decent balance between action and dialogue, and a satisfying sci-fi twist."

■ **Arcs in Space** "It got cut off – he grew a new one," Martha tells Donna, referring to a bubbling jar containing the Doctor's hand, severed from his arm in **167** *The Christmas Invasion* and brought on board the TARDIS by Captain Jack in **187a** *Utopia.*

194 The Unicorn and the Wasp

by Gareth Roberts

Professor Peach is murdered in the library with the lead piping… while the house-party guests assembling outside include the celebrated mystery writer, Agatha Christie.

■ **Where and When** The country home of Lady Clemency Eddison (Felicity Kendal), with the Doctor and Donna arriving just in time for cocktails at 4.30pm, one afternoon in 1926.

■ **The Baddies** The Vespiform – an eight-foot wasp from the Silfrax galaxy, born as a human hybrid and committing murders inspired by the work of Agatha Christie. Also on the prowl is the Unicorn, a jewel thief whose true identity nobody knows.

■ **Look out for…** "So, is she the murderer?" asks Donna, scoffing food as if she's watching an episode of *Poirot,* while the Doctor and Agatha Christie (Fenella Woolgar) reveal the killer's identity in the sitting room.

■ **Where else have I seen…** Colonel Hugh Curbishley? It's Christopher Benjamin, previously Sir Keith Gold in **54** *Inferno* and Henry Gordon Jago in **91** *The Talons of Weng-Chiang.*

■ **What they said** *Daily Telegraph* blogger Shaun Richmond, on 18 May 2008: "Comedy writing needs a light touch, something that has seldom been in evidence in the revived *Doctor Who* and, as the smugness of the show reaches epic proportions, something that's not likely to appear in the near future."

■ **Arcs in Space** When Donna declares that Agatha Christie being surrounded by murders is like Charles Dickens being surrounded by ghosts at Christmas, the Doctor is reminded of the events of **159** *The Unquiet Dead.*

CELEBRITY HISTORICALS

Mark Wright rubs shoulders with the great, the good and the bad of Earth history.

Right
Marco Polo (Mark Eden), Susan (Carole Ann Ford) and Tegana (Derren Nesbitt) in *Marco Polo*.

Outstanding

The 'celebrity historical' was part of the *Doctor Who* format right from the start. **4** *Marco Polo* remains the first and highest of benchmarks for the form, an epic Silk Road movie for the now-bonded regulars in the company of 13th-century Venetian explorer Marco Polo (Mark Eden). With Polo a familiar figure in 1960s classrooms, this seven-week adventure – now missing, sadly, although the audio remains – adhered to the show's semi-educational remit by transporting the Doctor and friends through Himalayan passes and across desert plains to the court of the Chinese emperor Kublai Khan (Martin Miller). Eden's Polo is a heroic but conflicted presence, while warlord Tegana (Derren Nesbitt) brings the villainy.

Essential

159 *The Unquiet Dead* is a triumphant fanfare for the celebrity historical in *Doctor Who*'s modern era. In his twilight years, Charles Dickens (Simon Callow) helps the Doctor and Rose battle the ghostly Gelth in a story tinged with sadness. The Doctor's glee at meeting a hero of his – not to mention Dickens' begrudging "He can stay," when faced with a gushing Time Lord – is a mischievous nod to fan culture. The tragedy of greatness is amplified in **210** *Vincent and the Doctor*, the true enemy being the mental health struggles of artist Vincent Van Gogh (Tony Curran), not the invisible Krafaysis. **279** *Rosa* honours how the tiniest acts of resistance and the most-unassuming individuals like Rosa Parks (Vinette Robinson) can change not just a world, but a whole universe.

Excellent

Adventures into history inevitably lead to royal audiences, and the Doctors have encountered their fair share of monarchs. Queen Elizabeth I (Joanna Page) bags her "dearest love" in **240** *The Day of the Doctor*, just because he thinks she's a Zygon double. Elizabeth's cousin and successor James I (Alan Cumming) is confirmed to be strutting, vain and conceited in **284** *The Witchfinders*. **14** *The Crusade* casts Richard the Lionheart (Julian Glover) as a quick-to-anger egotist, happy to marry his sister Joanna (Jean Marsh) off to Saphadin (Roger Avon) to end a war. Queen Victoria (Pauline Collins) was so unamused by the Doctor and Rose's actions in **169** *Tooth and Claw* that she founded Torchwood; and the mystery behind the disappearance from history of the Egyptian Queen Nefertiti (Riann Steele) is solved in **227** *Dinosaurs on a Spaceship*.

The Best of the Rest

Trips into Earth's past often examine historical A-listers through modern eyes. **180** *The Shakespeare Code* depicts William Shakespeare (Dean Lennox Kelly) as a boorish rock star, while crime novelist Agatha Christie is shown to be as insightful and brilliant as her literary sleuths in **194** *The Unicorn and the Wasp*. Vicki is beside herself to meet Emperor Nero (Derek Francis) in **12** *The Romans* – but it turns out to be a lesson in not meeting your heroes. "There's some good stuff, too," the Doctor sums up controversial US President Richard Nixon (Stuart Milligan) in **214** *The Impossible Astronaut/Day of the Moon*. "Not enough," counters River Song, before arriving in the Oval Office to meet the man himself. Chilling parallels between the Cybermen and Frankenstein's monster are examined when the TARDIS 'fam' arrive for **294** *The Haunting of Villa Diodati*, getting a ringside seat on the night Mary Wollstonecraft Godwin (aka Shelley; Lili Miller) found her terrifying Gothic muse. In **25** *The Gunfighters*, while Dodo and Steven tickle the ivories in the Tombstone saloon, the Doctor styles it out when mistaken for celebrity cowboy dentist Doc Holliday (Anthony Jacobs). And while it may be a long and winding road from 13th-century China to EMI Studios in 1963, The Beatles' turn in **306** *The Devil's Chord* demonstrates the celebrity historical lives on. There's always a twist at the end...

"A flying caravan –
there's something
for you to tell your
friends in Venice."
KUBLAI KHAN,
MARCO POLO

Right
The chilling result of a Vashta Nerada attack in *Silence in the Library/Forest of the Dead*.

Below
The enigmatic River Song (Alex Kingston) makes her first appearance.

Sky Silvestry (Lesley Sharp) in *Midnight*.

195 Silence in the Library/Forest of the Dead

(two episodes) by Steven Moffat

In the biggest library in the universe, the Doctor meets a total stranger who somehow knows him intimately. Just who is Professor River Song? (Spoilers!)

■ **Where and When** The Library is an entire planet, filled with newly-printed editions of every book ever written. At its core is the index computer and a moon is in orbit. The library was opened in the 51st century – but that was a hundred years ago.

■ **The Baddies** The library has been infested by a swarm of Vashta Nerada, minute creatures capable of stripping the flesh from their victims in seconds. They manifest as shadows but can also control spacesuits and communicate using the suits' neural relays.

■ **Introducing…** The first appearance by the enigmatic River Song (Alex Kingston) is also her last, chronologically (at least until **239** *The Name of the Doctor*).

■ **Look out for…** The opening minutes of both episodes are flash-forwards set in virtual reality, which are later reprised from the perspective of genuine reality.

■ **What they said** *Zoinks! It is Dr Scooby-Who* ran a headline in *The Sun* on Saturday 31 May 2008, noting the similarity between the marauding skeleton-in-a-spacesuit and a villain from the Hannna-Barbera cartoon series *Scooby Doo, Where Are You!*

■ **Arcs in Space** River Song refers to the crash of the *Byzantium* (as will be seen in **206** *The Time of Angels/Flesh and Stone*). The last time she met the Doctor in her personal chronology was when he took her to see the singing towers of Darillium (as will be seen in **263** *The Husbands of River Song*).

196 Midnight

by Russell T Davies

On a tourist trip on planet Midnight, the Doctor encounters an entity that repeats everything. On a tourist trip on planet Midnight, the Doctor encounters an entity that repeats everything.

■ **Where and When** Mostly inside the Crusader 50 shuttle, travelling on the surface of the diamond planet Midnight which is bombarded with lethal galvanic radiation. The date is uncertain, but it's the future and during the academic holidays.

■ **The Baddies** The nature of the monster is deliberately ambiguous – we never see it and it has no name. It controls its victims through their voices, echoing them, matching them, and then draining them.

■ **Look out for…** The moment where the Doctor convinces Driver Joe (Tony Bluto) to raise the shields and we are teased with a glimpse of Midnight – and left desperately searching for any sight of the monster.

■ **Where else have I seen…** David Troughton, who plays Professor Hobbs, previously appeared with his father Patrick in small roles in **40** *The Enemy of the World* and **50** *The War Games*, before playing King Peladon in **61** *The Curse of Peladon*.

■ **What they said** Russell T Davies wrote *Midnight* over the space of a weekend. "If I can convince myself by Sunday night that there's a story in this Space Bus – and a story that I can complete in time – then I'll keep going." he confided to Benjamin Cook in *The Writer's Tale* in 2008.

■ **Arcs in Space** Rose makes a brief appearance on the monitor, and there is talk of the mysterious lost moon of Poosh, which will turn up in **198** *The Stolen Earth/Journey's End*.

197 Turn Left

by Russell T Davies

Enticed into a fortune teller's booth, Donna is thrown into her own past – and experiences an alternative history where she never met the Doctor.

■ **Where and When** The fortune teller's tent is on the planet of Shan Shen, while Donna's alternative history takes her from London to a hotel in the country to Leeds and a UNIT warehouse.

■ **The Baddies** The beetle on Donna's back is "one of the Trickster's brigade" (from *The Sarah Jane Adventures*) – a creature that feeds off time by changing one small event that has large consequences. The result is a world where Donna sees humanity at its worst.

■ **Introducing…** Captain Magambo of UNIT (Noma Dumezweni) – who we'll be seeing again, in another life, in **200** *Planet of the Dead*.

■ **Look out for…** Wilf actor Bernard Cribbins was given a choice of reindeer antlers to wear for the Christmas scene; he decided to wear both. Later, he is simply incredible in the moment where the Colasanto family are taken away to a "labour camp".

■ **Where else have I seen…** Here, Joseph Long plays Rocco Colasanto; in the reality seen in **270** *Extremis*, he plays the Pope. Or maybe they are the same person, and Rocco became the Pope?

■ **Arcs in Space** This episode incorporates all the contemporary Earth stories from **178** *The Runaway Bride* onwards, as well as mentioning Sarah Jane, Captain Jack, Henrik's from **157** *Rose* and the Guinevere project from **167** *The Christmas Invasion*. The circle of mirrors recalls the end of **118** *Kinda*, the stars going out happens again in **239** *The Name of the Doctor*, and the TARDIS lettering changes again in **300** *The Power of the Doctor*.

Davros (Julian Bleach) and the strangely disturbed Dalek Caan in *The Stolen Earth/Journey's End*.

198 The Stolen Earth/Journey's End

(two episodes) by Russell T Davies

When the Doctor and Donna find the Earth missing, they seek help from the Shadow Proclamation. In fact, the entire planet has been hidden in the Medusa Cascade… where an old enemy is waiting.

■ **Where and When** Chiswick, Ealing, Cardiff, New York, Germany (60 miles from Nuremberg), the Shadow Proclamation and inside the Dalek mothership, the Crucible. The year is 2009.

■ **The Baddies** Davros (Julian Bleach) is back, having been saved during the Time War by Dalek Caan (voiced by Nicholas Briggs). The Daleks are led by the Supreme Dalek, who has a distinctive red casing.

■ **Farewell to…** While this reunites many companions and characters from the past, it marks the last appearances in *Doctor Who* for K9 and former PM Harriet Jones (Penelope Wilton).

■ **Look out for…** When the Daleks order humanity to leave their homes – "The males, the females, the descendants" – they are repeating a similar broadcast from **10** *The Dalek Invasion of Earth*.

■ **What they said…** The events of *Journey's End* were a closely-guarded secret. "There are probably about 10 of us who have seen it", Russell T Davies told the *Daily Mirror* on Saturday 5 July 2008. "The controller of BBC One hasn't seen it, or the head of drama, because it's been locked away. But I have seen it about 15 times."

■ **Arcs in Space** This story draws together numerous plot strands from as far back as **157** *Rose* (the Shadow Proclamation) while Davros and Sarah Jane recognise each other from **78** *Genesis of the Daleks*. The idea of another Doctor being created during the course of a regeneration anticipates **303** *The Giggle*.

An alternative future for Donna in *Turn Left*.

The Doctor and his friends are reunited for an epic battle with the Daleks.

199 The Next Doctor

by **Russell T Davies**

In Victorian London, the Doctor investigates a series of mysterious deaths, aided by his faithful companion Rosita. And then the real Doctor turns up...

■ **Where and When** London, 24-25 December 1851. What should be a perfect, classically Dickensian Christmas, were it not for...

■ **The Baddies** The Cybermen, having been cast from the Void and now intent on conquering 19th-century Earth, assisted by their Cybershades – conversions with the brains of animals – and Miss Mercy Hartigan (Dervla Kirwan), the matron of a workhouse who, after a lifetime of poverty and abuse, plans revenge on the patriarchal world.

■ **Look out for...** The first clue that the 'next Doctor' (David Morrissey) might not be who he thinks he is comes when the actual Doctor notes that his sonic screwdriver is... a normal screwdriver. That makes a noise when it hits things.

■ **Introducing...** Flashbacks to earlier Doctors are seen for the first time since the series was revived, with William Hartnell's First Doctor making his first on-screen appearance since **133** *Resurrection of the Daleks*.

■ **What they said** Writing in *The Times* on Boxing Day 2008, Tim Teeman was unimpressed by the episode, wondering if it was "ever so slightly self-satisfied" and suggesting the series had gone from "feeling fresh and witty" to "smug – even if you were face down in the brandy butter."

The Doctor and Lady Christina (Michelle Ryan) crashland on San Helios in *Planet of the Dead*.

■ **Arcs in Space** The climactic appearance of the colossal Cyber King is anticipated by the alternative-universe Mickey Smith in **177** *Army of Ghosts/ Doomsday*, when he speculated that the mysterious sphere found by Torchwood might contain a "Cyber Leader, CyberKing, Emperor of the Cybermen..." Why no one remembers the King stomping over London will be explained in **206** *The Time of the Angels/Flesh and Stone*.

200 Planet of the Dead

by **Russell T Davies** and **Gareth Roberts**

A number 200 bus whose passengers include a Time Lord and an aristocratic cat burglar falls through a wormhole to a planet threatened by rapacious flying horrors.

■ **Where and When** Present-day London and the planet of San Helios. An evening in April, and specifically Easter, cheerily noted by the Doctor as he munches on a chocolate egg.

■ **The Baddies** A swarm of semi-metallic creatures not unlike flying stingrays that can generate wormholes to new feeding grounds. They turned the teeming world of San Helios and its 100 million inhabitants to desert in less than a year – and Earth is next.

■ **Introducing...** UNIT scientific adviser Malcolm Taylor (Lee Evans) explicitly namechecks 'Bernard Quatermass' – previously alluded to in **148** *Remembrance of the Daleks* – whose adventures on BBC Television in the 1950s were a major influence on *Doctor Who*.

■ **Farewell to...** Captain Magambo (Noma Dumezweni) of UNIT makes her second and final appearance after the alternative timeline of **197** *Turn Left*.

■ **Look out for...** The stunning first shot of the Doctor stepping out of the bus onto the ravaged surface of San Helios, revealing an endless vista of dunes (actually Dubai).

■ **Arcs in Space** Clairvoyant passenger Carmen (Ellen Thomas) warns the Doctor that "something is returning through the dark" and that "he will knock four times", foreshadowing **202** *The End of Time*, while the Doctor mentions the events of **75** *Robot* and **196** *Midnight*.

201 The Waters of Mars

by **Russell T Davies** and **Phil Ford**

The first colony on Mars comes under attack from the elements at a turning point in Earth's history – and the Doctor must choose between admitting defeat or turning towards darkness...

The Cyber Leader (Paul Kasey), the Doctor, Jackson Lake (David Morrissey) and Mercy Hartigan (Dervla Kirwan) in *The Next Doctor*.

- **Where and When** Bowie Base One, in the Gusev crater on Mars, and in the street outside mission commander Adelaide Brooke's house, both on 21 November 2059 (with a flashback to Adelaide's family home 50 years earlier – ie, in 2009).
- **The Baddies** The Flood exists via water, trapped in a glacier under the Mars base. It takes over the base's crew with the objective of travelling to and spreading across the Earth.
- **Introducing...** Despite visiting the **82** *Pyramids of Mars* with Sarah, this is the first time the Doctor has actually set foot on the Red Planet's surface, using the borrowed spacesuit from **174** *The Impossible Planet/The Satan Pit*.
- **What they said** According to Sam Wollaston, writing in *The Guardian* the day after transmission, David Tennant's Doctor was "looking and behaving like someone who knows his demise isn't far off. There's a new madness about him; he's being erratic and indecisive, and his eyes are open even wider than they normally are – whites visible all the way round the irises, sucking it in, maybe, before it all goes dark."
- **Look out for...** The Doctor realising that they face the most implacable enemy possible: "Water just waits. It wears down the clifftops, the mountains, the whole of the world. Water always wins."
- **Arcs in Space** The Doctor's vision of Ood Sigma signals to him his impending death in **202** *The End of Time*. Adelaide recalls the events of **198** *The Stolen Earth/Journey's End*, and the Doctor mentions the Ice Warriors and alludes to K9, who first appeared in **39** *The Ice Warriors* and **93** *The Invisible Enemy* respectively.

The Doctor begins to regenerate in *The End of Time*.

The Doctor and Adelaide Brooke (Lindsay Duncan), under siege in *The Waters of Mars*.

202 The End of Time

(two episodes) by Russell T Davies
In the last days of the human race, the Doctor and the Master do battle one final time, while a monstrous power reaches out from the dark...

- **Where and When** The Ood Sphere, a century after the events of **191** *Planet of the Ood*, and on and above Earth between 23-26 December in the present day – plus stops at an industrial wasteland, in an alien bar and Ealing. The Doctor drops in on Donna's wedding the following spring, and pays a final visit to an unwitting Rose in the early hours of New Year's Day 2005.
- **The Baddies** The Master (John Simm), subject of a botched resurrection. The Time Lords, led by the Lord President (Timothy Dalton); twisted by the horrors of the Time War, the Doctor's people are seeking to end time itself and ascend into higher beings.
- **Farewell to...** The Tenth Doctor's final adventure, chronologically speaking, incorporates final appearances to date for Martha Jones (Freema Agyeman), Mickey

Above Rassilon (Timothy Dalton) and Wilf (Bernard Cribbins).

Smith (Noel Clarke), Jackie (Camille Coduri) and Rose Tyler (Billie Piper). It's also Elisabeth Sladen's last appearance as Sarah Jane Smith in *Doctor Who* itself.

- **Look out for...** The Tenth Doctor's heartbreaking final words: "I don't want to go."
- **Introducing...** Matt Smith makes his first appearance as the Eleventh Doctor in the concluding scene, thrilled to have a full set of limbs but disappointed to once again not have ginger hair.
- **Arcs in Space** The President is explicitly named Rassilon by the Doctor, making this only the second appearance of this legendary figure (previously played by Richard Mathews in **129** *The Five Doctors*). The Doctor remains traumatised after **201** *The Waters of Mars*, and recounts the events of **187b** *The Sound of Drums/Last of the Time Lords* to Wilf, who returns with Donna, Sylvia (Jacqueline King) and Shaun (Karl Collins) in **303** *The Giggle*. The crashing TARDIS, however, leads directly into **204** *The Eleventh Hour*.

The ELEVENTH DOCTOR

Matt Smith
Stories 203–241, 2010–13

The Doctor's floppy-fringed Eleventh incarnation had something of the newborn calf about him, all big eyes and unco-ordinated limbs. Wholly unworldly, he thought that fish fingers and custard went together, and that bow ties, fezzes and Stetsons were cool.

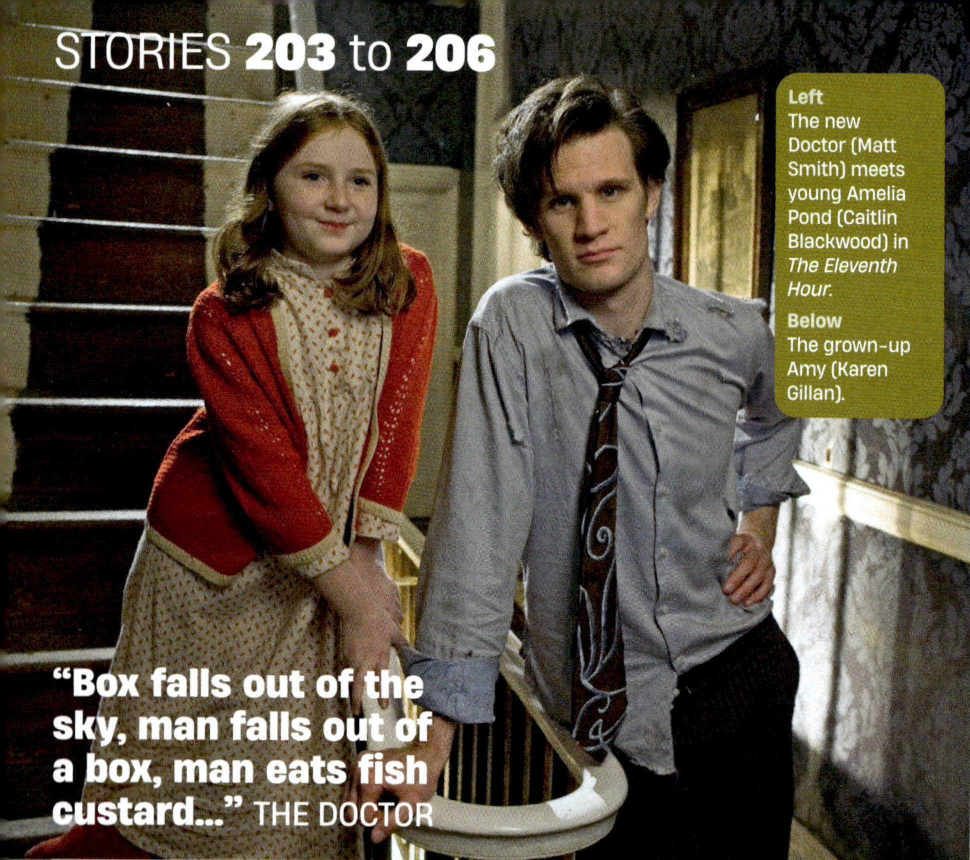

"Box falls out of the sky, man falls out of a box, man eats fish custard..." THE DOCTOR

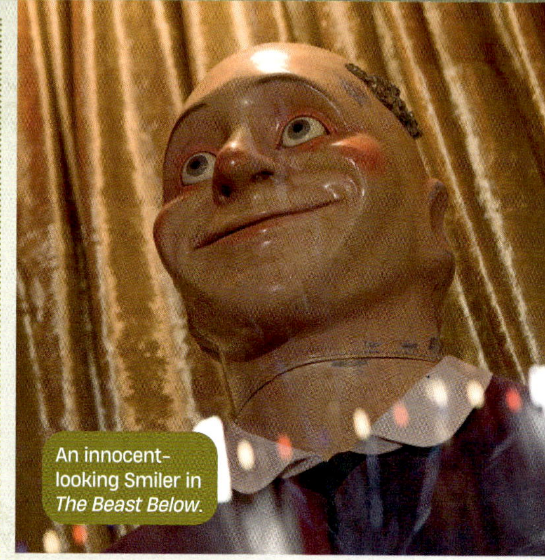

An innocent-looking Smiler in *The Beast Below*.

203 The Eleventh Hour

by Steven Moffat

There's a scary crack in young Amelia Pond's bedroom wall. But then a burning police box dumps a raggedy man at the bottom of her garden...

■ **Where and When** Leadworth, a village in Gloucestershire, England, in the years 1996, 2008 and 2010.

■ **The Baddies** Prisoner Zero – a shapeshifter on the run from the Atraxi, an alien police force able to remotely activate and control electronic media.

■ **Introducing...** The Eleventh Doctor (Matt Smith) who hates apples, yoghurt and beans, but loves fish fingers and custard. Amelia Pond (Caitlin Blackwood) – a little Scottish girl who grows up to be fake police-outfit wearing kissogram Amy Pond (Karen Gillan). And Amy's boyfriend Rory Williams (Arthur Darvill) – a real nurse, not a kissogram.

■ **Look out for...** Famous TV astronomer Sir Patrick Moore as himself, on a conference call.

■ **What they said** "I thought it would be fun if, while he was still regenerating, he had to run around and save the world," incoming showrunner Steven Moffat told *The Daily Telegraph* on 11 March 2010. "He's barely out of the box when he realises: I haven't changed my shirt yet and I've got 20 minutes to save the world. It's like trying to save the world with flu. And he does it with two minutes to spare."

■ **Where else have I seen...?** The hapless Mr Henderson is played by Arthur Cox, previously Dulcian tour guide Cully in 44 *The Dominators*.

■ **Arcs in Space** The Doctor refers the Atraxi to Article 57 of the Shadow Proclamation – first encountered in 198 *The Stolen Earth/Journey's End*. This is the beginning of the 'crack in the universe' arc that runs throughout the 2010 series.

204 The Beast Below

by Steven Moffat

A spaceship with no power. A vast creature lurking in the dark. There are monsters down below, but maybe not the ones you think. This is one story you won't want to forget...

■ **Where and When** *Starship UK* (minus Scotland), 33rd century.

■ **The Baddies** Most obviously, the Smilers – automata mounted in booths, which act as information points and schoolteachers. But their smiling faces can quickly turn to become a grimace, then a fateful snarl...

■ **Look out for...** The moment Amy pieces together what's going on and takes matters into her own hands. Even the Doctor is shocked.

■ **What they said** "Moffat is masterful at exploiting simple things that unsettle children," noted Patrick Mulkern in *Radio Times* on 11 April 2010. "In previous scripts, he's scored with gas masks, clockwork toys, statues, shadows... and now it's a take on those heads with disconcerting rictus [sic] you find in booths at funfairs."

■ **Introducing...** Sophie Okonedo as Liz Ten, who rules, basically – and will reappear in 212 *The Pandorica Opens*. In the final TARDIS scene, the Doctor takes a call from Winston Churchill, played by Ian McNeice – calling for his assistance with a "tricky situation" in 205 *Victory of the Daleks*. He, too, will reappear in *The Pandorica Opens*, plus 224 *The Wedding of River Song*.

■ **Arcs in Space** The events of this story follow on directly from the end of 203 *The Eleventh Hour*. The evacuation of Earth to due to solar flares is detailed in

Text by Jon Dear

An 'Ironside', with Bracewell (Bill Paterson), Winston Churchill (Ian McNeice), and the Doctor and Amy, in *Victory of the Daleks*.

76 *The Ark in Space*. The Doctor nearly ran into Liz Two in **150** *Silver Nemesis*, and was engaged to Liz One in **240** *The Day of the Doctor* – but had become her "sworn enemy" by the time of **180** *The Shakespeare Code*.

205 Victory of the Daleks

by Mark Gatiss

Winston Churchill summons the Doctor to inspect the new weapon he thinks will win the war – the Daleks!

■ **Where and When** Bunkers under Whitehall, in London during the Blitz of 1940.
■ **The Baddies** The Ironsides – sorry, the Daleks. But Daleks so removed from their original purity their own technology wouldn't even recognise them. They need the Doctor to act as referee and unwittingly birth...
■ **Introducing...** The New Dalek Paradigm. Purer. Larger. More powerful. More colourful. And rather short-lived.
■ **Look out for...** The Doctor holding off the Daleks armed only with a Jammie Dodger.
■ **What they said** "I loved writing this episode," Mark Gatiss recalled in August 2024, "and immersing myself in Churchill lore and his 'Paisley Pinnochio' [Prof Bracewell, played by Bill Paterson]. And I'm very proud of the Jammie Dodger scene. It was actually made of plastic so it could be handled repeatedly."
■ **Where else have I seen...** Colin Prockter, playing the ARP Warden, was previously seen doling out 'kronkburgers' in **162** *The Long Game*.

■ **Arcs in Space** The New Dalek Paradigm will be seen again in **212** *The Pandorica Opens/The Big Bang* and **226** *Asylum of the Daleks*. The Ironsides' refrain – "I am your soldier" – echoes the "I am your servant" line trotted out by the equally duplicitous Daleks in **30** *Power of the Daleks*.

206 The Time of Angels/Flesh and Stone

(two episodes) by Steven Moffat
It's space priests versus the Weeping Angels, in the Aliens *to* Blink's Alien...

■ **Where and When** The Delerium Archive. Aboard the spaceship *Byzantium*. And Alfava Metraxis, the seventh planet of the Dundra system, in the 51st century.
■ **The Baddies** The Weeping Angels – seen in far greater numbers than in **186** *Blink*. Initially mistaken for statues of Aplans, they're now being revived by leaking radiation from the *Byzantium*'s engine. Rather than displace victims in time, as before, here the Angels snap the necks of several clerics, stripping the cerebral cortex from one and reanimating a copy of his consciousness in order to speak to the Doctor. It's also revealed that just the image of an Angel can become an Angel.
■ **Look out for...** River Song shoots back into the Doctor's life – from an airlock, albeit before **195** *Silence in the Library/Forest of the Dead* (in which she mentioned "the crash of the *Byzantium*"). She promptly reveals that the TARDIS only makes its famous wheezing, groaning sound because the Doctor leaves the brakes on...
■ **What they said** Daniel Martin, writing in *The Guardian*'s post-transmission blog, said that *Flesh and Stone* "can lay credible claim to being the greatest episode of *Doctor Who* there has ever been... [with] an iconic sequence every couple of seconds."
■ **Where else have I seen...?** If the geology of the *Byzantium* crash site looks familiar, that's because it was shot on Southerndown Beach, near Bridgend – more recognisable as Bad Wolf Bay, first seen in **177** *Army of Ghosts/Doomsday*.
■ **Arcs in Space** The Doctor and Amy visit the Delerium Archive, the final resting place of the Headless Monks, whom we'll meet in **218** *A Good Man Goes to War*, where he reads graffiti written in Old High Gallifreyan, recalling **129** *The Five Doctors*. The crack reappears, and we learn why Amy has no knowledge of the Dalek invasions in *Army of Ghosts/Doomsday* and **198** *The Stolen Earth/Journey's End* – and why no-one remembers the Cyber-King in Victorian London in **199** *The Next Doctor*.

Above inset
An Angel in the forest, in *The Time of Angels/Flesh and Stone*.

Left
Amy, Father Octavian (Iain Glen), the Doctor and River Song in the Maze of the Dead.

207 The Vampires of Venice

by **Toby Whithouse**

The Doctor takes Amy and Rory somewhere romantic: a quarantine city where 10,000 vampiric aliens lurk beneath the surface of the canals.

■ **Where and When** Venice, Italy, in 1580.
■ **The Baddies** Aliens from the planet Saturnyne – not so much vampires as shape-changing "fish from space", led by Rosanna Calvierri (Helen McCrory).
■ **Look out for...** Some knowing dialogue throughout. "I like the bit where someone says, 'It's bigger on the inside.' I always look forward to that," the Doctor tells Rory, as he enters the TARDIS for the first time. "I'm kind of done with running down corridors," says Amy. "Tell me the whole plan! One day that will work," rues the Doctor, facing a horde of hissing vampire girls.
■ **Introducing...** Rory in his new role as one of the Doctor's travelling companions. The suggestion that the Silence is something tangible – something that the Saturnynes lost children to.
■ **What they said** Writing on 7 May 2010, *The Daily Telegraph*'s Gavin Fuller was disappointed by the "very cheap rendition" of 16th-century Venice: "There was a stock image of St Mark's, a couple of canals and a couple of sets set by water, and a not terribly convincing CGI reconstruction at the end – although some effort did seem to have been made on the interiors and certainly the costumes of the Venetians."

■ **Arcs in Space** The Doctor previously met (pseudo) vampires in **112** *State of Decay*, **154** *The Curse of Fenric* and **179** *Smith and Jones*. He references Napoleon (see **8** *The Reign of Terror*), Byron (see **294** *The Haunting of Villa Diodati*) and Houdini (see **74** *Planet of the Spiders*, **79** *Revenge of the Cybermen* and **304** *The Church on Ruby Road*). Rosanna and her kin ran from the Silence, "through a crack" (seen in **203** *The Eleventh Hour*).

208 Amy's Choice

by **Simon Nye**

Are Rory and Amy travelling with the Doctor, or have they settled down to married life as they await the birth of their first child?

Left
Amy dreams a future in which she's pregnant with Rory's child in *Amy's Choice*.

Below inset
The Dream Lord (Toby Jones).

■ **Where and When** Upper Leadworth in 2015 – or is it? The TARDIS control room – or is it?
■ **The Baddies** The sinister Dream Lord (Toby Jones) and the Eknodines, an ancient race of aliens possessing some of the elderly inhabitants of Upper Leadworth.
■ **Look out for...** The moving scene in which Rory realises that not only did Amy choose him over the Doctor, but that she preferred death to a life without him.
■ **Farewell to...** The Doctor-Amy-Rory love triangle. From now on, it's pretty much Rory all the way for Amy.
■ **Where else have I seen...** Nick Hobbs (playing Mr Nainby here) often popped up in 1970s episodes, but you wouldn't recognise him from his prominent role as royal beast Aggedor in **61** *The Curse of Peladon* and **73** *The Monster of Peladon*. Andy Jones (as a postman) was equally unrecognisable as a Hoix in **184** *The Pandorica Opens*. Leadworth OAP Huw Rees was previously the older Tim Latimer in **185** *The Family of Blood*.
■ **Arcs in Space** The Dream Lord knows that the Doctor has history with Elizabeth I – see **180** *The Shakespeare Code* and **240** *The Day of the Doctor*, that he's "the last of the Time Lords" (as the Doctor described himself in **158** *The End of the World*), and that he's known as "the Oncoming Storm" (the ancient Dalek name for him, according to **166** *The Parting of the Ways*). In fact, the Dream Lord turns out to be a manifestation of the darker aspects of the Doctor's persona – not unlike the Valeyard in **143** *The Trial of a Time Lord*.

Rosanna Calvierri (Helen McCrory) and her son Francesco (Alex Price) are just two of *The Vampires of Venice*.

Text by Jacqueline Rayner

209 The Hungry Earth/ Cold Blood

(two episodes) by Chris Chibnall

A drilling operation disturbs a group of warrior Silurians deep underground. Emerging onto the surface, the reptilians begin their campaign to reclaim the Earth by taking a human hostage.

■ **Where and When** Wales, "2020-ish", according to the Doctor.

■ **The Baddies** Homo reptilia? Homo sapiens? Or maybe both. These Silurians (aka Eocenes) are a different branch to the ones the Doctor met previously in **52** *Doctor Who and the Silurians* and **130** *Warriors of the Deep* – no third eye, but with the same ambivalence towards humans. They've been asleep for 300 million years and used to hunt apes for sport.

■ **Look out for…** Lone future Amy, waving at the TARDIS at the end, is a gut-wrenching moment.

■ **Introducing…** Rory's first death! Dying (or being presumed dead) will become a habit for Rory. On this occasion, he's wiped from existence too…

■ **Where else have I seen…** Neve McIntosh is Alaya and Restac here, later becoming another Silurian when she plays Madame Vastra from **218** *A Good Man Goes to War* onwards.

■ **Arcs in Space** We're told that 21 kilometres is further than anyone's ever drilled into the Earth, although the drill in **54** *Inferno* reached a depth of 20 miles (ie, 31 kilometres) – but perhaps the true extent of Professor Stahlman's operations were hushed up? People being pulled under the ground recalls **132** *Frontios*. Amy may have lost her memory of Rory, but her engagement ring survives; she'll find it in **211** *The Lodger*.

The Doctor and Amy share a drink with Vincent Van Gogh (Tony Curran) in *Vincent and the Doctor*.

210 Vincent and the Doctor

by Richard Curtis

Vincent Van Gogh saves the Doctor and Amy from an alien creature that only he can see. But will this mark the end of the struggling artist's torment?

■ **Where and When** The Musée d'Orsay, Paris, in 2010. In and around Auvers-sur-Oise in 1890.

■ **The Baddies** The Krafayis, a lone monster left behind by its pack – part of a scavenging race that will kill until they're killed.

■ **Introducing…** Vincent Van Gogh (Tony Curran) – who, along with his art, will reappear in **212** *The Pandorica Opens*.

■ **Look out for…** The Doctor, Amy and Vincent lying in the dark, looking up – with Vincent letting them see through his eyes and the sky becoming a *Starry Night*.

■ **What they said** "Not just the first five-star story of this series, but probably the single best episode ever of *Doctor Who*," claimed a letter published in *Radio Times*, noting also that Tony Curran's "was a performance of the sort that should be recognised with a BAFTA nomination."

■ **Arcs in Space** Invisible monsters have previously featured in such stories as **21** *The Daleks' Master Plan*, **23** *The Ark* and **68** *Planet of the Daleks*.

"Art can wait. This is life and death. We need to talk to Vincent Van Gogh." THE DOCTOR

The Silurian Alaya (Neve McIntosh) confronts the Doctor in *The Hungry Earth/ Cold Blood*.

211 The Lodger

by **Gareth Roberts**

A mysterious disturbance affects the TARDIS. While he investigates its source, the Doctor must adapt to life on 21st-century Earth – and to having a flatmate…

- **Where and When** Colchester, 2010.
- **The Baddies** The owners of the vessel hiding above Craig's flat, disguised as 79B Aickman Road. In 214 *The Impossible Astronaut/Day of the Moon*, we uncover their identity.
- **Introducing…** The Doctor's "mate" Craig Owens (James Corden) – who reappears, along with his love interest Sophie (Daisy Haggard), in 223 *Closing Time*, by which time they have a baby boy named Alfie.
- **Look out for…** While encroaching on Craig and Sophie's romantic evening, the Doctor spits red wine back into the glass in disgust; he does much the same in 214 *The Impossible Astronaut/Day of the Moon*, too. Previous incarnations seemed quite fond of the stuff, though – as demonstrated by the Third in 60 *Day of the Daleks*, 69 *The Green Death* and 70 *The Time Warrior*, the Fourth in 84 *The Brain of Morbius* and 101 *The Androids of Tara*, and the Ninth in 165 *Boom Town* (among others).
- **What they said** On 14 June 2010, the IGN website's Matt Wales wrote: "There was much to like about *The Lodger* and its domestic take on the Doctor, with some genuinely funny moments and a central conceit that delivered a welcome bit of feel-good fuzz."
- **Arcs in Space** At the end of the episode, the Doctor tells Amy to leave him a note containing Craig's address, completing the story's time loop. We witness Amy doing this during the Doctor's trip back through his own timeline in 212 *The Pandorica Opens/The Big Bang*.

Right
The Doctor has a message for the forces gathered above Stonehenge in *The Pandorica Opens*.

Below right
Stone Daleks in *The Big Bang*.

Bottom left
Craig (James Corden) and his flatmate the Doctor with Sophie (Daisy Haggard) in *The Lodger*.

212 The Pandorica Opens/ The Big Bang

by **Steven Moffat**

The crack in time is finally explained, the TARDIS finally explodes, the universe is finally destroyed, and Amy and Rory finally get married.

- **Where and When** Stonehenge, 102 AD. The National Museum, 1996.
- **The Baddies** The Alliance – a supergroup of baddies from confrontations gone by. Visible among them are Cybus Cybermen, Daleks, Sontarans, Silurians, Sycorax, Roboforms, Judoon, Hoix, Blowfish and Weevils from *Torchwood*, and Uvodni from *The Sarah Jane Adventures*. Unseen but mentioned are the Slitheen, Terileptils, Zygons, Drahvins, Atraxi, Draconians, Chelonians and Haemogoth. And Rory returns… as an unwilling Auton.
- **Introducing…** The Doctor's very first fez, which gets unceremoniously blown to smithereens by River Song. It's a style of hat that reappears in 213 *A Christmas Carol* and 283 *Kerblam!* – and in 240 *The Day of the Doctor*, Clara remarks: "Someday, you could just walk past a fez." Black marketeer Dorium Maldovar (Simon Fisher-Becker) makes his debut.
- **Look out for…** "I just don't want her growing up and joining one of those Star Cults," says Aunt Sharon (Susan Vidler). "I don't trust that Richard Dawkins."

Dawkins makes a brief appearance in 198 *The Stolen Earth/Journey's End*.
- **What they said** "*The Big Bang* was, ultimately, lots of things," wrote Simon Brew for Den of Geek on 26 June 2010. "It was puzzling, bold, triumphant and brilliant. And a more complex series finale for *Doctor Who* you may never see again (for a supposed children's programme too, remember)."
- **Arcs in Space** Back from earlier in the season: young Amelia Pond, Liz Ten, Winston Churchill and Edwin Bracewell, plus Vincent Van Gogh and Madame Vernet. There's a significant flashback to 206 *The Time of Angels/Flesh and Stone*. The Doctor receives a phone call about "an Egyptian goddess loose on the *Orient Express*" in space". We never get to see this adventure, but we do see a similar one in 249 *Mummy on the Orient Express*.

Singer Abigail (Katherine Jenkins) with the older Kazran (Michael Gambon), the Doctor and the boy Kazran (Laurence Belcher) in *A Christmas Carol*.

214 The Impossible Astronaut/Day of the Moon

by **Steven Moffat**

There's an elephant in the room – the Doctor just died, and everybody knows it but him. The TARDIS team takes on America in a story featuring the most forgettable villains yet.

■ **Where and When** Washington DC and Florida, 1969.
■ **The Baddies** The Silence. You're keeping a tally on your skin of the times you've encountered them. They've been on Earth since time immemorial, manipulating human development. You just can't seem to recall what they are.
■ **Introducing...** The TARDIS goes invisible, with a little help from River. This has happened before, in **46** *The Invasion*, but that time it was just a side-effect of the visual stabiliser circuit being removed.
■ **Look out for...** After the Doctor is rescued from Area 51, he finds time not only to shave his beard but to tidy up his hair too. The longer hair makes a comeback in **224** *The Wedding of River Song*.
■ **What they said** On 29 April 2011, the *Metro* newspaper declared that "This show has more oomph in the tip of its sonic screwdriver than half the proper, serious, adult dramas on TV have in their entire plodding runtimes."
■ **Arcs in Space** In **223** *Closing Time*, the Doctor catches up with his future self, and we discover that both the 'TARDIS blue' envelopes and the Doctor's Stetson originally belonged to Craig Owens.

213 A Christmas Carol

by **Steven Moffat**

Doctor Who *does* A Christmas Carol – *albeit with time travel, flying space sharks and opera singing.*

■ **Where and When** Sardicktown (planet unknown), circa 4398.
■ **The Baddies** This story's answer to Ebeneezer Scrooge is Kazran Sardick (Michael Gambon), an old miser refusing to save more than 4,000 passengers on a crashing spaceship – including Amy and Rory.
■ **Where else have I seen...** Pooky Quesnel, who plays the captain of the spaceship, later appeared in a recurring role as mysterious headteacher Dorothea Ames in the *Doctor Who* spin-off, *Class*.
■ **Look out for...** "It's this or go to your room and design a new kind of screwdriver. Don't make my mistakes. Now, go." A funny line, but also the first real reference to the Doctor *inventing* the sonic screwdriver, rather than just building his specific one.
■ **What they said** "From special effects to storyline to the actors themselves," enthused MTV's Rick Marshall on 26 December 2010, "*A Christmas Carol* fires on all cylinders and is as close to a perfect *Doctor Who* story as we've seen in a while."
■ **Arcs in Space** The Doctor's Santa-like entrance is a reminder of his claim to actually be him back in **164** *The Empty Child/The Doctor Dances*: "Who says I'm not? Red bicycle when you were 12?"

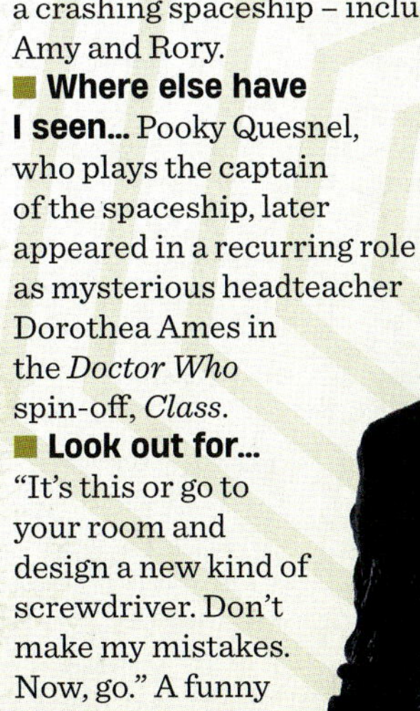

Far left
One of the Silence, in *The Impossible Astronaut/Day of the Moon*.

Left
River Song joins Rory (Arthur Darvill), the Doctor and Amy in Utah.

THE SARAH JANE ADVENTURES

The intrepid investigations of Sarah Jane Smith and her unlikely band of allies. **Richard Unwin** selects the highlights of *Doctor Who*'s CBBC spin-off series.

Below
Sarah Jane Smith (Elisabeth Sladen) had her own series of adventures after her travels with the Doctor came to an end.

Outstanding

Over the course of *The Sarah Jane Adventures*, there were several changes made to the roster of schoolkids aiding Sarah Jane Smith (Elisabeth Sladen), with Maria Jackson (Yasmin Paige) being written out during the second series and Sky (Sinead Michael) introduced for the fifth. But the majority of episodes feature the core trio of Clyde Langer (Daniel Anthony), Rani Chandra (Anjli Mohindra) and Luke Smith (Tommy Knight). For *The Wedding of Sarah Jane Smith* this dream team is also joined by K9 (voiced by John Leeson – the Mark III model having originally been gifted to Sarah Jane in the one-off Christmas 1981 Special, *K9 and Company: A Girl's Best Friend*). Having met someone special, Sarah Jane has decided to tie the knot – dismissing her friends' concerns about her choice of suitor. But when the big day comes, and the registrar gets to the "If any person can show just cause or impediment..." bit, the doors burst open and the Doctor himself (David Tennant) storms in, demanding that the wedding be halted immediately. And then – as if this wasn't already the most exciting cliffhanger of all time – Sarah Jane's fiancé (Nigel Havers) is revealed to be in thrall to her arch-nemesis the Trickster (Paul Marc Davis).

Essential

The gang's first encounter with the Trickster takes place in the first series story *Whatever Happened to Sarah Jane?* – in which reality is altered, and Maria Jackson must work out why she's the only one who remembers Sarah Jane when the latter is replaced by a very ordinary woman called Andrea Yates (Jane Asher). There's another guest appearance from the Doctor – this time played by Matt Smith – in *Death of the Doctor*, when Sarah receives a visit from UNIT and is given the terrible news that her Time Lord pal has passed away. All is not as it seems, however, so the gang team up with Jo Jones (Katy Manning) at the sham funeral and uncover a massive deception. The show's willingness to explore adult themes in a child-friendly manner is exemplified by *The Curse of Clyde Langer* – a powerful instalment that sees the lovable schoolboy cursed by an alien artefact and rejected by everyone he knows, to the extent that he becomes homeless.

Excellent

Poor old Clyde also faces a tough time in *The Mark of the Berserker*, when his father becomes possessed by a different alien artefact – a necklace that gifts unearthly powers to the person wearing it.

Another pesky pendant causes trouble in *Eye of the Gorgon*, which pits the gang against the race that inspired the Greek myth of women with snakes for hair. *The Mad Woman in the Attic* is an emotional Rani-focused piece that delves into issues of loneliness, while *Mona Lisa's Revenge* is a joyfully riotous serial that features a hugely entertaining guest performance from Suranne Jones. The team of kids all get to shine in *Lost in Time*, when they're split up for exciting adventures of their own and become scattered throughout history.

The Best of the Rest

The very first episode – the double-length *Invasion of the Bane* – is a good initiation into the adventures revolving around Sarah Jane's home in Bannerman Road. It also introduces the leader of the Bane, Mrs Wormwood (Samantha Bond), who returns to face Brigadier Lethbridge-Stewart (Nicholas Courtney) in *Enemy of the Bane*. *The Eternity Trap* and *The Empty Planet* are a great pair of serials focused on the popular pairing of Clyde and Rani, while *The Nightmare Man* is a terrifying tale that delves into Luke's fears of leaving home for university. *The Gift* spotlights returning adversaries the Slitheen, making a memorable finale to the third series. And for a dose of good old action-packed fun, *Warriors of the Kudlak* is a solid story of space-based derring-do.

"The things you've done, Sarah, they're pretty impressive. But oh, the things you're going to do."
THE DOCTOR, *THE WEDDING OF SARAH JANE SMITH*

215 The Curse of the Black Spot

by Steve Thompson

The crew of a 17th-century pirate ship are being menaced by a mysterious siren. Anyone receiving even the slightest injury soon acquires the mark of the black spot on their palm…

■ **Where and When** The *Fancy*, becalmed on the ocean, circa 1 April 1699; and inside a spaceship in an adjacent universe.

■ **The Baddies** The Siren (Lily Cole) – although her real purpose has been misconstrued. The real villain here is Captain Henry Avery (Hugh Bonneville) – who's gunned down "a thousand innocent men", according to his own boatswain (Lee Ross). Avery's probably the same man whose crew we met in **28** *The Smugglers*, still squabbling over what happened to his treasure.

■ **Look out for…** Avery's gun-waving prompts the Doctor to recall psychoanalytic pioneer Sigmund Freud: "Ever met Freud? No? Comfy sofa." The Eighth Doctor claimed to have known Freud in **156** the 1996 TV movie *Doctor Who*: "We got on very well…" So which Doctor needed therapy?

■ **What they said** *"Doctor Who* took a break from its main narrative with an episode displaying much me-heartiness aboard a haunted pirate ship," wrote Andrew Billen in *The Times* on 9 May 2011. "But two things: does this idea of the Doctor as gooseberry to Amy and Rory really work; and is it not time for Matt Smith to tone down his performance and let the Doctor mature a shade?"

■ **Arcs in Space** The TARDIS lands in the hold of an earthly seaship, just as it did in **66** *Carnival of Monsters* and **127** *Enlightenment* (although, oddly, this is the first time the ship it's landed in has been on the open sea, on Earth!). The Doctor is forced to walk the plank, as in **99** *The Pirate Planet*. Avery and his son Toby (Oscar Lloyd) will reappear, briefly, in **218** *A Good Man Goes to War*.

Text by Jamie Lenman

Idris (Suranne Jones) and the Doctor fly a TARDIS made from junk in *The Doctor's Wife*.

216 The Doctor's Wife

by Neil Gaiman

The time travellers arrive in a TARDIS graveyard, inhabited by a band of misfits… and someone who claims to be the living embodiment of the Doctor's beloved ship.

■ **Where and When** House, a sentient planetoid in a bubble universe; and aboard the TARDIS. The date is unclear.

■ **The Baddies** Also House (voiced by Michael Sheen).

■ **Look out for…** The 'junkyard TARDIS' – a console cobbled together by the Doctor from various bits of salvage, but in reality designed by 12-year-old *Blue Peter* competition winner Susannah Leah.

■ **Where else have I seen…** The hypercubes that gather on House were first seen in **50** *The War Games*, used by the Second Doctor to contact the Time Lords. TARDIS safety belts were first demonstrated in **141** *Timelash*.

■ **What they said** "Dressed in what appeared to be a cast off from Helena Bonham-Carter's wardrobe, Suranne Jones gave an energetic and zany performance as the TARDIS," said *The Independent*'s Neela Debnath on 16 May 2011. She concluded that: *"The Doctor's Wife* was a beautiful but tragic love story of two beings that could never truly be together."

■ **Arcs in Space** To find the energy to enter the bubble universe, the Doctor burns up various TARDIS rooms – which was just how the Fifth Doctor gained the energy to escape the Big Bang in **116** *Castrovalva*. Nephew (Paul Kasey) is an Ood, a species introduced in **174** *The Impossible Planet/The Satan Pit*. Idris

Above inset
The Siren (Lily Cole) delivers *The Curse of the Black Spot*.

Left
Amy picks up a cutlass aboard the *Fancy*.

The Jennifer Ganger (Sarah Smart) turns killer in *The Rebel Flesh/The Almost People*.

makes several references to the Doctor having stolen her, as eventually shown in **239** *The Name of the Doctor*. "I always liked it when you called me… 'old girl'," Idris tells the Doctor – after the pet name he gave her in **70** *The Time Warrior*, and on several occasions thereafter.

217 The Rebel Flesh/ The Almost People

(two episodes) by Matthew Graham
A freak accident in a futuristic industrial complex results in the goop-moulded avatars of factory workers evolving consciousness.

■ **Where and When** St John's Monastery, Earth, the 22nd century.
■ **The Baddies** Miranda Cleaves (Raquel Cassidy) and the 'Jennifer' Ganger monster (Sarah Smart).
■ **Introducing…** The Flesh, a self-replicating substance that can assimilate human form, for use in hazardous environments. Despite the issues raised in this adventure, the Flesh is still around in the 52nd century, where it'll be used to duplicate Amy and Rory's baby in **218** *A Good Man Goes to War*.
■ **Look out for…** The monstrous 'Jennifer' Ganger with the elongated neck was inspired by John Tenniel's drawing of Alice suffering the effects of a grow-potion, as seen in Lewis Carroll's 1865 novel *Alice's Adventures in Wonderland*.
■ **What they said** Writing after transmission of *The Almost People*, *Daily Telegraph* blogger Gavin Fuller thought "it was something of a pity that Jennifer's

ganger turned into a psychotic 'let's make war on humankind' staple monster… but this was the only thing that let down this impressive episode with its neatly realised psychological and body horror."
■ **Arcs in Space** The Doctor's duplicate spouts a torrent of his counterpart's catchphrases from **1** *100,000 BC* (aka *An Unearthly Child*), **62** *The Sea Devils*, **90** *The Robots of Death*, **129** *The Five Doctors* and **171** *The Girl in the Fireplace*. And we discover that Amy hasn't been herself for some time, since at least **214** *The Impossible Astronaut/Day of the Moon*.

218 A Good Man Goes to War

by Steven Moffat
The Doctor and Rory gather an army to do battle against Amy's captors. Meanwhile, River Song's true identity is at last revealed.

■ **Where and When** The asteroid Demon's Run, the 52nd century.
■ **The Baddies** The mysterious Eye Patch Lady, who's appeared and disappeared out of Amy's gaze several times since **214** *The Impossible Astronaut/Day of the Moon*, is at last named: she's Madame Kovarian (Frances Barber). The Headless Monks – seen following a mention in **206** *The Time of Angels/Flesh and Stone*.
■ **Look out for…** The Doctor's cot, which he claims to have slept in during his first incarnation. (We're assuming he means the one originally played by William Hartnell.) This cot will resurface in **236** *Journey to the Centre of the TARDIS*, when Clara stumbles across it.
■ **Introducing…** Silurian assassin Madame Vastra (Neve McIntosh), housemaid ninja Jenny Flint (Catrin Stewart) and Sontaran nurse Strax (Dan Starkey) – collectively known as the Paternoster Gang. These three will reappear in **231** *The Snowmen*, **237** *The Crimson Horror*, **241** *The Name of the Doctor* and **242** *Deep Breath*. Amy and Rory's baby, Melody Pond – even though it turns out we've met her grown-up self many times before!
■ **Where else have I seen…** Neve McIntosh had previously played Silurian Restac and her sister Alaya in **209** *The Hungry Earth/Cold Blood*, whereas Dan Starkey had appeared as both Sontaran Commander Skorr and the identical Lieutenant Skree in **192** *The Sontaran Stratagem/The Poison Sky*. He would later play Ian the Elf in **253** *Last Christmas* before reappearing as yet another Sontaran, Svild, in **297** *Flux*.
■ **Arcs in Space** Rory wears his Roman Centurion armour from **212** *The Pandorica Opens/The Big Bang*. River's convoluted origins will be further clarified in **219** *Let's Kill Hitler*.

Madame Kovarian (Frances Barber) in *A Good Man Goes to War*.

The Führer (Albert Welling) is a time travellers' target in *Let's Kill Hitler*.

219 Let's Kill Hitler

by Steven Moffat

The TARDIS is hijacked by an old friend of Amy and Rory, before an encounter with the Führer leads the Doctor to his own assassination – and a first meeting with an old flame.

■ **Where and When** Present-day Leadworth, with flashbacks to the village in preceding years. The Reichskanzlei and the Hotel Adlon in Berlin, 1938. The hospital of the Sisters of the Infinite Schism and Luna University in 5123.

■ **The Baddies** Adolf Hitler (Albert Welling) – who spends most of the episode locked in a cupboard. Turns out the leader of the Third Reich is a bit of a pushover in person. Mels (Nina Toussaint-White), whom Amy and Rory have known for decades, turns out to be their long-lost daughter Melody. Under orders from the Silence, Melody has been waiting to get close enough to the Doctor to kill him – but not before she regenerates into someone more recognisable (Alex Kingston).

■ **Introducing...** The Teselecta, a time-travelling shape-changing robot with a miniaturised crew and a mission to punish those who escaped justice. It will reappear in **224** *The Wedding of River Song*....

■ **Look out for...** Speaking of whom, the more familiar 'archaeology professor' incarnation of River Song makes her first chronological appearance here – striking a 'Mrs Robinson' pose as she does so, after the 1967 movie *The Graduate*: "Hello Benjamin..."

■ **What they said** Reviewing this episode for Canada's *Postmedia News* on 27 August 2011, Alex Strachan said: "There are few dramas on TV with the ability to be goofy and serious at the same time, but *Doctor Who* manages to pull it off with an almost breathtaking ease."

■ **Arcs in Space** The Doctor discovers the circumstances of his death, depicted in **214** *The Impossible Astronaut/ Day of the Moon,* and gives the newly renamed River Song her diary, first seen in **195** *Silence in the Library/ Forest of the Dead.*

220 Night Terrors

by Mark Gatiss

A psychic distress call lands the TARDIS in the most terrifying world imaginable – the nightmares of a seven-year-old boy.

■ **Where and When** A rundown block of flats in England, around the present day.

■ **The Baddies** Whatever force it is that's tormenting poor George (Jamie Oram) and trapping people in a strange wooden house – which turns out to be George himself. He's a Tenza, a cuckoo species that conforms to what his foster parents perceive, and his subconscious fear of rejection has locked him into a cycle of fear.

■ **Introducing...** The spooky nursery rhyme recited by the peg dolls that pursue people through the dolls' house – revealed at the end to have an ominous meaning – foreshadows **224** *The Wedding of River Song.* "Tick tock goes the clock, even for the Doctor..."

■ **Look out for...** Before leaving, the Doctor excitedly cooks a breakfast of kippers for George and his parents, adding another item to his list of eccentric culinary favourites.

■ **What they said** Gary Bushell, writing in the *Daily Star* on 4 September 2011, said this episode was "simple, effective and (for kids) genuinely scary."

■ **Arcs in Space** Another frightened child with awesome powers appeared in **176** *Fear Her*, while the Doctor's habit of guessing that people whose names he can't remember are called Brian will finally pay off in **227** *Dinosaurs on a Spaceship.*

The Doctor encounters scary peg dolls in *Night Terrors*.

An older Amy is locked out of the TARDIS in *The Girl Who Waited*.

221 The Girl Who Waited

by Tom MacRae
Amy is accidentally trapped in the wrong time stream at a hospital where the treatment will kill her, leaving the Doctor and Rory to face an impossible choice.

■ **Where and When** The Twostreams quarantine facility on Apalapucia, where victims of the planet-wide Chen-7 plague live out the single day between infection and death in compressed time, enjoying a lifetime in comfort before succumbing.
■ **The Baddies** Arguably the Doctor himself, for making the mistake of breaking into the other stream too late and finding a middle-aged Amy who's been hiding from the facility's well-meaning but deadly handbots for 36 years. His dilemma, and Rory's, is whether to rescue the younger Amy, erasing the older one and making her suffering meaningless, or rescue the older and condemn the younger to decades alone.
■ **Farewell to…** A final mention of Clom, home planet of the Abzorbaloff from **175** *Love & Monsters*. The planet's Disneyland has been faithfully replicated as part of the residents' leisure facilities.
■ **Look out for…** An outstanding performance from Karen Gillan as the two Amys come face to face.
■ **What they said** Interviewed in Sydney's *Sun-Herald* on 11 September 2011, Karen Gillan called her dual role "a challenge for me as an actress. I kind of begged everyone to let me do it… I was so curious about how I'd look old."
■ **Arcs in Space 3** *Inside the Spaceship* (aka *The Edge of Destruction*) is another adventure with a minimal cast and no clear villain, while **125** *Mawdryn Undead* sees two versions of the Brigadier share a fateful meeting. Rory angrily telling the Doctor he no longer wants to travel with him prefigures the following episode.

222 The God Complex

by Toby Whithouse
There is a hotel where every room contains someone's mortal fear, the thing they most dread. And in the middle of its maze of carpeted corridors is a minotaur…

■ **Where and When** An automated prison floating in space somewhere near the planet Tivoli. The prison resembles a hotel furnished in a style familiar from the 1980s. Also, a residential street – the Ponds' new home.
■ **The Baddies** The Minotaur, a being that replaces its captives' faith or superstition with worship of itself before killing them – even though this is also a function of the hotel/prison in which it's trapped.
■ **Farewell to…** Amy and Rory end their travels with the Doctor, the latter deciding he must depart the TARDIS while they have a chance of a life… although we'll see them again many times before their final farewell in **230** *The Angels Take Manhattan*.
■ **Look out for…** The greatest fear of gambler Joe (Daniel Pirrie) is ventriloquist's dummies, so he finds an entire dining room of them. Later, they're all neatly lined up beside his body, like mourners at a funeral.
■ **Where else have I seen…** Spencer Wilding, who plays the Minotaur, lends his imposing frame to a number of other roles, including Skaldak in **234** *Cold War* and the lead Dreg monster in **289** *Orphan 55*.
■ **Arcs in Space** The Weeping Angels first appeared in **186** *Blink*, while one of the past captives in the hotel was a Tritovore from **200** *Planet of the Dead*. The Minotaur is related to the Nimon from **108** *The Horns of Nimon*, while the contents of the Doctor's room is revealed in **241** *The Time of the Doctor*.

Ventriloquist's dummies are the stuff of nightmares in *The God Complex*.

Craig finds himself trapped in a long-buried Cybership in *Closing Time*.

223 Closing Time

by Gareth Roberts

Investigating strange electrical fluctuations after dropping in on his friend Craig, the Doctor takes a job in the toy section of a department store, where two of the staff have gone missing...

■ **Where and When** The Sanderson & Grainger department store, and Craig's new house – both in Colchester, in 2011.

■ **The Baddies** A Cybermen spaceship is buried beneath the department store, having crashed without any survivors. To provide it with a fresh crew, a single Cybermat – looking very different from when we last saw one of its kind, in **79** *Revenge of the Cybermen* – has been capturing and converting humans...

■ **Look out for...** 'Bitey' the Cybermat has teeth – and proves more than a match for the Doctor and Craig's frying pan and baking tray.

■ **What they said** In 2011, Steven Moffat told *Doctor Who Insider* magazine that "The single worst thing that could happen to a new dad having to look after a new baby on his own for the first time would be the arrival of the Doctor and the Cyberman invasion."

■ **Where else have I seen...** Lynda Baron, who plays Val, had previously been Captain Wrack in **127** *Enlightenment*. She'd also been heard in **25** *The Gunfighters*, singing *The Ballad of the Last Chance Saloon*.

■ **Arcs in Space** Craig (James Corden) and Sophie (Daisy Haggard) return from **214** *The Lodger*. The idea that the Doctor can speak to babies was introduced in **218** *A Good Man Goes to War* and recurs in **257** *The Girl Who Died*. The Doctor here acquires the blue envelope and Stetson hat for **214** *The Impossible Astronaut/Day of the Moon*.

224 The Wedding of River Song

by Steven Moffat

People from all of Earth's history co-exist on a world where it's always the same time on the same day in the same year – all because River Song has changed a fixed point, by refusing to kill the Doctor.

■ **Where and When** Earth, beginning in the Buckingham Senate and then shifting to the interior of a pyramid designated Area 52. The time is exactly 5.02pm on 22 April 2011.

■ **The Baddies** We're in another version of reality, where Madame Kovarian has been plotting with the Silence.

■ **Introducing...** Even as it resolves one arc, this story kicks off another, setting up **239** *The Name of the Doctor* and **241** *The Time of the Doctor*. As the decapitated head of Dorium Maldovar tells the Doctor: "It's all still waiting for you. The fields of Trenzalore, the fall of the Eleventh, and the question..."

■ **Farewell to...** As well as Madame Kovarian and Dorium, this episode also marks the final appearances of both Charles Dickens (seen being interviewed on BBC Breakfast) and Winston Churchill (here promoted to the office of Holy Roman Emperor).

■ **Look out for...** The bit where everyone is suddenly wearing eyepatches – or rather eyedrives, used to protect against the Silence – was inspired by an often-told anecdote about a prank during the recording of **54** *Inferno*, where members of the regular cast surprised Nicholas Courtney by suddenly adopting eyepatches of the same kind he was wearing in character as the parallel Earth's 'Brigade-Leader'.

■ **Arcs in Space** This story resolves the mysterious circumstances of the Doctor's 'death' in **214** *The Impossible Astronaut/ Day of the Moon*, and brings back the Teselecta from **219** *Let's Kill Hitler*. We also meet an alt-version of the Silurian scientist Malohkeh (Richard Hope) from **209** *The Hungry Earth/Flesh and Blood*. During his "farewell tour", the Doctor attempts to visit the Brigadier, last seen in **152** *Battlefield* – only to learn that he passed away, peacefully, in a nursing home, a few months earlier.

225 The Doctor, the Widow and the Wardrobe

by Steven Moffat

Madge Arwell helps the Doctor find his police box. During the war, her husband's plane goes missing. For Christmas, she takes her children to an old house, where the Doctor has several surprises in store.

The Doctor faces one of the Silence in the Area 52 pyramid in *The Wedding of River Song*.

Madge Arwell (Claire Skinner), the Doctor plus Arwell children Lily (Holly Earl) and James (Maurice Cole) in the forest of Androzani Minor, in *The Doctor, the Widow and the Wardrobe*.

■ **Where and When** England, 1938; Uncle Digby's house three years later; Androzani Major, 5345.

■ **The Baddies** Whoever's behind the fateful harvesting of the trees of Androzani remains unknown, but they employ hapless troopers Droxil (Bill Bailey), Ven-Garr (Paul Bazely) and Billis (Arabella Weir).

■ **Look out for...** The Doctor delighting in showing the Arwell children their new bedroom – "A window disguised as a mirror. A mirror disguised as a window!"

■ **Where else have I seen...** Alexander Armstrong, who plays Reg Arwell, provides the voice of Sarah Jane's computer, Mr Smith, in **198** *The Stolen Earth/Journey's End*.

■ **What they said** Writing in *The Guardian* on 25 December 2011, Dan Martin called this "the smallest – yet perhaps the most enchanting – Christmas special we've had to date... Any other time of year I would gnaw holes all over this, but it's Christmas, and today it felt perfect."

■ **Arcs in Space** The Doctor previously visited the Androzani System in **135** *The Caves of Androzani*. He also remembers Jabe from **158** *The End of the World*, and has acquired a copy of the Magna Carta (which was endangered in **129** *The King's Demons*).

226 Asylum of the Daleks

by **Steven Moffat**

The Daleks kidnap the Doctor, Amy and Rory and bring them to their parliament. A Starliner has crashed on their planet-sized Dalek asylum, and they're worried that the inmates will escape.

■ **Where and When** Skaro, then the Asylum. The date is unspecified, but as far as the Daleks are concerned it's after **224** *The Wedding of River Song*.

■ **The Baddies** The Daleks now have a Prime Minister (voiced by Nicholas Briggs) and have the ability to convert humans into their puppets (eg Darla, played by Anamaria Marinca). The planet's microscopic nanogenes can also convert humans, living or dead.

■ **Introducing...** This story sees the surprising first appearance of Jenna-Louise Coleman as souffle-maker Oswin, pre-empting her debut as Oswin's double Clara in **231** *The Snowmen*.

■ **Look out for...** The scene where Amy starts to succumb to the Dalek nanocloud and sees the Daleks as people, including a spinning ballerina.

■ **What they said** Steven Moffat was initially reluctant to bring back the Daleks, as he pointed out in the 31 May 2011 edition of *Radio Times*: "They are the most famous of the Doctor's adversaries and the most frequent, which means they are the most reliably defeatable enemies in the universe."

■ **Arcs in Space** Daleks in the Asylum include examples from Aridius (from **16** *The Chase*), Kembel (from **21** *The Daleks' Master Plan*), Vulcan (from **30** *The Power of the Daleks*), Spiridon (from **68** *Planet of the Daleks*) and Exxilon (from **72** *Death to the Daleks*). Dalek puppets again feature in **241** *The Time of the Doctor* and **254** *The Magician's Apprentice*.

Above inset Why is 'souffle girl' Oswin (Jenna-Louise Coleman) inside the *Asylum of the Daleks*?

Above Amy ventures into the Asylum.

227 Dinosaurs on a Spaceship

by **Chris Chibnall**

A Silurian space-ark packed with the last living dinosaurs is hijacked by an intergalactic freebooter. But now the ship is on a collision course with Earth…

■ **Where and When** A spaceship en route to Earth, 2367 CE.

■ **The Baddies** Solomon (David Bradley), a pirate and black-marketeer from an unnamed civilisation.

■ **Introducing…** The idea of the Doctor travelling with a gang – in this case Egyptian queen Nefertiti (Riann Steele), big-game hunter John Riddell (Rupert Graves) and Rory's dad Brian (Mark Williams) – rather than just his regular companions. It's something that writer Chris Chibnall will return to throughout the Thirteenth Doctor's time, when the TARDIS crew will often be supplemented by a few visitors.

■ **Look out for…** Solomon's robot servants (voiced by David Mitchell and Robert Webb). You'll be seeing one of these impressively hulking machines again, with a new paint job and some redesigned armour, playing the body of Hydroflax in **263** *The Husbands of River Song*.

■ **Where else have I seen…** Richard Hope, who plays the Silurian scientist Bleytal (seen in the ship's data records), is also the very similar-looking Silurian scientist Malokeh in **209** *The Hungry Earth/Cold Blood* and **224** *The Wedding of River Song*. (They must both be part of the same gene-chain.) David Bradley – Solomon here – would play the real William Hartnell in the 2013 making-of drama *An Adventure in Space and Time*, before assuming the mantle of the First Doctor in **276** *Twice Upon a Time*.

■ **Arcs in Space** We've seen homo reptilia using other saurians for defence or attack in **52** *Doctor Who and the Silurians* and **130** *Warriors of the Deep* – but this the first time we've seen a more caring approach to their fellow prehistoric reptiles.

Rory and the Doctor take a ride on 'Tricey' the triceratops – just one of the *Dinosaurs on a Spaceship*.

228 A Town Called Mercy

by **Toby Whithouse**

A frontier town in the Old West is under siege. A cyborg gunslinger demands the handover of an alien doctor – but probably not the one we were expecting.

■ **Where and When** Mercy, Nevada, USA, 1870.

■ **The Baddies** Is it the programmed killing machine Khaler-Tek (Andrew Brooke) or the hard-hearted scientist (Adrian Scarborough) who created him? You'll have to work that one out for yourselves.

■ **Look out for…** The words 'Doctor Who' in the opening titles. As with all the stories in the first half of series 7, the titles have been styled to match the story theme. This one is wood-effect punctured by bullet-holes.

■ **Farewell to…** The Doctor wearing a Stetson hat. He first wears one in **25** *The Gunfighters*, then in **214** *The Impossible Astronaut* and **224** *The Wedding of River Song*. He wears another, given to him by Craig Owens, in **223** *Closing Time*.

■ **What they said** Dan Martin, writing for *The Guardian* on 15 September 2012, called this story "a complex morality dilemma, fizzing with sharp dialogue… If anything *A Town Called Mercy* is more effective as a western than as a *Doctor Who* episode." Martin also nodded to a

The TARDIS team arrive in *A Town Called Mercy*.

Rory, the Doctor and Amy ponder what's in the boxes in *The Power of Three*.

Toby Whithouse script "full of paranoid philosophising of the kind we're used to from [Whithouse's] *Being Human*," concluding that "this was not really one for behind-the-sofa moments. The Gunslinger was cute as much as anything else."

■ **Arcs in Space** The last time the Doctor visited the Old West was in **25** *The Gunfighters* – but **49** *The Space Pirates* and **58** *Colony in Space* also play with themes drawn from Westerns.

229 The Power of Three

by **Chris Chibnall**
Billions of small black cubes mysteriously appear all over Earth, but as months go by and the cubes stay inert, the Doctor gets a glimpse into the day-to-day reality of ordinary human life.

■ **Where and When** London, England, present day. The year of the slow invasion.
■ **The Baddies** The Shakri (Steven Berkoff) – figures from Gallifreyan legend. They travel extra-dimensionally and eliminate species they consider to be pests.
■ **Introducing...** Kate Stewart (Jemma Redgrave), daughter of Brigadier Lethbridge-Stewart, puts in her first appearance as head of UNIT.
■ **Look out for...** The phone charger clasped in the Doctor's right hand as he hides under Henry VIII's bed, which must be the same one Rory left in Henry's

en-suite, briefly mentioned in **228** *A Town Called Mercy*.
■ **What they said** At the time of broadcast, it was well known that Karen Gillan and Arthur Darvill were leaving the programme, so reviewers noticed plenty of bittersweet moments foreshadowing Amy and Rory's departure. Writing in *The Independent*, Neela Debnath described this story as "the last moment of happiness before the darkness descends."
■ **Arcs in Space** The Doctor, Amy and Rory eat fish fingers and custard together, one last time. This was the first meal the Doctor and young Amelia shared when they met in **203** *The Eleventh Hour*.

230 The Angels Take Manhattan

by **Steven Moffat**
New York's statues have been possessed by Weeping Angels and everything's gone a bit timey-wimey. River is back, in film-noir mode, but it's the end of the road for Amy and Rory.

■ **Where and When** Manhattan, USA, in 2012 and 1938.

■ **The Baddies** The Weeping Angels in all shapes and sizes, from evil cherubs to the Statue of Liberty herself.
■ **Introducing...** Melody Malone, an alter-ego of River Song, styling herself as a gumshoe in the tradition of popular hardboiled detective stories of the 1930s. The character, created partly as a means of River communicating through time with the Doctor, has gone on to star in her own series of paperback thrillers, written by River and Amy.
■ **Farewell to...** The Ponds. They've hopped around the timelines, entered alternate realities, lived double-lives and even died (more than once). Now at last they embark on the big adventure of living one day after another.
■ **Look out for...** Amy and Rory's names on the gravestone. Rory has gained the middle name Arthur, as a link to the actor who plays him, but Amy's middle name Jessica (first mentioned in **204** *The Beast Below*) is missing.
■ **Arcs in Space** The final shot links right back to Amy's first meeting with the Doctor, as a little girl in her garden in Leadworth, in **203** *The Eleventh Hour*.

The Doctor and Amy visit Central Park in *The Angels Take Manhattan*.

Right
Victorian governess Clara Oswald (Jenna-Louise Coleman) comes face-to-face with the Doctor in *The Snowmen*.

Below inset
Dr Simeon (Richard E Grant).

231 The Snowmen

by Steven Moffat

The Doctor has retired to live on a cloud, but he's persuaded out of his sulk to investigate some homicidal snowmen – and an impossible mystery called Clara Oswald.

- **Where and When** London, 1892 (and, briefly, 2012).
- **The Baddies** The Great Intelligence, using the body of scientist Dr Simeon (Richard E Grant) to build an "army of ice" from sentient snow.
- **Introducing...** Clara Oswald (Jenna-Louise Coleman), both sassy cockney barmaid and cut-glass governess. And Clara Oswald, a children's nanny from 2012...
- **Look out for...** The sequence in which Clara follows the Doctor up a spiral staircase into the clouds – framed against the Moon, with a Dickensian Christmas card London laid out below – is truly enchanting.
- **What they said** "Douglas Adams pitched that story, *The Doctor Retires*, many years ago," Steven Moffat pointed out in the *Radio Times*, dated 22 December 2012. "I remember reading about it and thinking: that would be one hell of a story to tell."

- **Arcs in Space** The Great Intelligence appeared in **38** *The Abominable Snowmen* and **41** *The Web of Fear*. (The Doctor's London Underground map tin is a reference to – and may even have inspired – the latter.) It will return in **232** *The Bells of Saint John* and **239** *The Name of the Doctor*. Clara appears to be the same, yet not the same, person as Oswin Oswald, from **226** *Asylum of the Daleks*. The 'Paternoster Gang' of Madame Vastra, Jenny Flint and Strax were all first seen in **218** *A Good Man Goes to War*.

232 The Bells of Saint John

by Steven Moffat

The Doctor's search for Clara leads him to present-day London, where the Great Intelligence has hacked the wi-fi to upload human souls to the internet.

- **Where and When** London, 2013 – and a Cumbrian monastery in 1207.
- **The Baddies** The Great Intelligence and its latest human servant, tech boss Miss Kizlet (Celia Imrie) – assisted by robotic base station 'Spoonheads'.

- **Introducing...** Nanny Clara's charges, Angie and Artie Maitland (Eve De Leon Allen and Kassius Carey Johnson) – who'll become TARDIS travellers in **238** *Nightmare in Silver*.
- **Look out for...** The thrilling sequence in which the house lights of London are turned into a landing strip – and the switcheroo that sees Clara go from street to 'snog box' to cabin-of-crashing-plane in the blink of an eye.
- **Where else have I seen...** Richard E Grant – the Great Intelligence, still using the appearance of Dr Simeon from **231** *The Snowmen* – played an alternative Ninth Doctor in the 2003 BBC webcast *Scream of the Shalka*, whose features are briefly glimpsed in **310** *Rogue*.
- **What they said** Discussing this story's 'aliens in the wi-fi' plot, Steven Moffat noted in **Doctor Who Magazine** 458 (April 2013) that "It's the traditional *Doctor Who* thing of taking something omnipresent in your life and making it sinister, only it's time to update that a bit."
- **Arcs in Space** Artie is reading *Summer Falls* by Amelia Williams – aka Amy Pond. (According to Clara, chapter 11 will make you "cry your eyes out".) The 'woman in the shop' who gives her the Doctor's phone number is revealed to be Missy in **252** *Dark Water/Death in Heaven*.

A modern-day Clara Oswald runs into the Doctor in *The Bells of Saint John*.

Clara makes her first trip to an alien world in *The Rings of Akhaten*.

233 The Rings of Akhaten

by **Neil Cross**

For her first trip in the TARDIS, Clara asks to see "something awesome"… in a story that brings a whole new meaning to the term 'space opera'.

■ **Where and When** A bustling alien marketplace on the fabled rings of the planet Akhaten (exact date unknown). Clara's parents' first meeting, probably in England in 1981.

■ **The Baddies** Akhaten itself – a planet-sized parasitic creature that feeds off memories, stories and feelings. The telekinetic Vigil – a trio of aliens sent to seek out and sacrifice the Queen of Years.

■ **Look out for…** *The Long Song* – "a lullaby without end", sung by young Merry, the latest Queen of Years (Emilia Jones), to pacify the 'Old God' (ie, Akhaten) – sees *Doctor Who* go full-on rock opera.

■ **Where else have I seen…** Aidan Cook, as the Akhaten-waking Mummy, is one of modern *Doctor Who*'s go-to monster men, with roles including Zygons, Cybermen, the Crooked Man (in 235 *Hide*) and the Vlinx (in 303 *The Giggle* and 311 *The Legend of Ruby Sunday/Empire of Death*).

■ **What they said** "We thought, let's go to outer space and do the best alien planet *Doctor Who* has ever done," said Steven Moffat in an April 2013 BBC online preview. "Let's just go for it – have lots and lots of aliens."

■ **Arcs in Space** The Doctor mentions bringing his granddaughter – Susan, introduced in 1 *100,000 BC* (aka *An Unearthly Child*) – to Akhaten. An older version of Clara's dad Dave (Michael Dixon) appears in 241 *The Time of the Doctor*.

234 Cold War

by **Mark Gatiss**

When the crew of a Soviet submarine defrost an Ice Warrior in their hold, the Doctor and Clara find themselves in a Cold War hot spot…

■ **Where and When** The Soviet submarine *Firebird*, on manoeuvres near the North Pole in 1983.

■ **The Baddies** Grand Marshal Skaldak (Spencer Wilding, voiced by Nicholas Briggs), an Ice Warrior plotting revenge against humanity. The ship's blindly patriotic executive officer, Lieutenant Stepashin (Tobias Menzies).

■ **Look out for…** The *Alien*-riffing scenes when Skaldak escapes captivity by shedding his chitinous armour – the "gravest dishonour" in the Ice Warrior code, according to the Doctor.

■ **Where else have I seen…** Or rather, *heard* – since genre legend David Warner, here playing Ultravox-loving Ice Warrior excavator Professor Grisenko, had previously provided the voice of Viperox leader Lord Azlok in the 2009 BBCi animation *Dreamland*. (He also played an alternative Third Doctor in numerous stories for the audio company Big Finish.)

■ **What they said** "I'd been badgering Steven Moffat for years to let me bring back the Ice Warriors," Mark Gatiss wrote in the 13 April 2013 edition of *Radio Times*. "The episode is a love-letter to those Troughton stories that so often saw a group of desperate, frightened people under attack from an alien menace. A 'base under-sea' if you like… We had to 'Hollywood-ise' the amount of room on board, though. It would be hard to hide a seven-foot monster on a conventional submarine."

■ **Arcs in Space** The Ice Warriors previously appeared in 39 *The Ice Warriors*, 48 *The Seeds of Death*, 61 *The Curse of Peladon* (which the Doctor recalls here as the time he spent "pretending to be an Earth ambassador") and 73 *The Monster of Peladon*. They will return in 273 *Empress of Mars*. The Doctor mentions the TARDIS' Hostile Action Displacement System, first introduced in 47 *The Krotons*.

Ice Warrior Skaldak (Spencer Wilding) in chains aboard a Soviet sub in *Cold War*.

HOW TO WATCH...
THE TARDIS

The most dimensionally transcendental adventures of all, compiled by **Alan Barnes**.

Below
The Doctor (Tom Baker) and Adric (Matthew Waterhouse) aboard the TARDIS in *Logopolis*.

Outstanding

No one's shown a greater fascination with the TARDIS than Christopher H Bidmead, whose script for the Fourth Doctor's farewell, **115** *Logopolis* begins with an attempt to repair its most famous fault – the busted chameleon circuit that's kept it stuck in a police-box shape. The first episode swiftly descends into TARDIS horror, when the Doctor (Tom Baker) discovers that the real police box he thought he'd materialised his ship around was actually the Master's. Cue a trip through progressively gloomier TARDISes nested inside one another, like Russian dolls. Plus *Logopolis* introduces the ship's ivied cloister, with its tolling tocsin – a presentiment of disaster ever after.

Essential

Logopolis' direct sequel, the Bidmead-authored **116** *Castrovalva*, also begins with two almost entirely TARDIS-centric episodes – with the new Fifth Doctor (Peter Davison)

discovering its restorative zero room here at the start of his especially TARDIS-heavy era, full of arguments in its bedrooms. The sheer *wonder* of the ship's bigger-than-the-outside interior has never been better conveyed than in the first episode of the first-ever serial, **1** *100,000 BC* (aka *An Unearthly Child*); it doesn't roll along on wheels, you know. For some, that wonder was never fully recaptured until **156** the 1996 TV movie *Doctor Who*, with the ship reimagined, for one night only, as part-Jules Verne submersible, part-Notre Dame cathedral.

Excellent

The wood-panelled secondary control room is seen to its best effect in **87** *The Hand of Fear*, which ends with probably the most celebrated TARDIS scene of all – the Doctor's abrupt farewell to Sarah Jane Smith (Elisabeth Sladen). The TARDIS itself became a companion when it gained the form of Idris (Suranne Jones) in **216** *The Doctor's Wife*: "Did you wish really hard?" the Eleventh Doctor (Matt Smith) is asked. Simultaneously, its 'haunted' interior becomes dangerous, as it did in the early chamber piece **3** *Inside the Spaceship* (aka *The Edge of Destruction*). The ship's shocking destruction in the first episode of **132** *Frontios* – reduced to just its hatstand – sets up its startling reconstitution at the end of this third Bidmead adventure. It also disintegrates into bits in **45** *The Mind Robber*, a story that begins with the TARDIS caught in a weird all-white void.

The Best of the Rest

198 *Journey's End* reveals why the ship's console is hexagonal – an "Of *course!*" moment that proves the TARDIS can still surprise us, decades after its introduction. Meanwhile, **236** *Journey to the Centre of the TARDIS* does exactly what it says, with a salvage crew seeking to navigate the damaged ship's increasingly twisted interior. In commissioning the latter, showrunner Steven Moffat was supposedly seeking to make up for the final episode of **97** *The Invasion of Time*, with the Fourth Doctor chased by Sontarans through what look like the corridors of an abandoned Victorian institution – but maybe the TARDIS made itself look that way deliberately to confuse? There's much TARDIS action throughout the 1985 season – especially in **137** *Attack of the Cybermen*, with the chameleon circuit temporarily fixed prior to the Cybermen's assault on its interior. Also in Season 22, **139** *The Mark of the Rani* showcases the oh-so-1980s pastel pink, smoked grey and chrome TARDIS owned by the eponymous Time Lady (Kate O'Mara) – but it's still not as stylish as the "classic" all-white TARDIS stolen by the Twelfth Doctor (Peter Capaldi) in **262** *Hell Bent*; a thing of beauty. Finally, **239** *The Name of the Doctor* shows the TARDIS at the end of its days – at once the Doctor's giant gravestone, with its internal dimensions bleeding out, and his overgrown tomb.

"I'm certainly looking forward to having a properly functioning TARDIS."
THE DOCTOR, *LOGOPOLIS*

Paranormal investigators Alec Palmer (Dougray Scott) and Emma Grayling (Jessica Raine) join forces with Clara and the Doctor in *Hide*.

235 Hide

by **Neil Cross**

Professor Alec Palmer and his assistant Emma Grayling are investigating spectral sightings at Caliburn House – but their 'ghost' is actually a space traveller caught in an echo universe.

■ **Where and When** Caliburn House (on a moor somewhere in England) and the echo universe (same point in space, but in parallel) – beginning at 11.00pm on 25 November 1974, concluding the next morning.

■ **The Baddies** None. Hila Tacoran (Kemi-Bo Jacobs) is just a marooned explorer, and the monsters are creatures from another universe that merely wish to be reunited.

■ **Look out for...** The Doctor and Clara exploring the house, hearing a heavy thumping noise, and *something* holding Clara's hand...

■ **Where else have I seen...** The Caliburn House location, Margam Castle, was previously used for the Rattigan Academy in **193** *The Sontaran Stratagem/The Poison Sky*.

■ **What they said** In **Doctor Who Magazine** issue 464 (October 2013), writer Neil Cross confessed to being a "huge fan" of Quatermass creator Nigel Kneale: "In 1972 he did a TV play called *The Stone Tape*, which is why I set it in that period... Time-travel and ghosts are echoes of one another. What is a ghost, if not a fragment caught in time?"

■ **Arcs in Space** The Doctor uses a blue crystal from Metebelis III – last visited in **74** *Planet of the Spiders*. His trip into another dimension at the end of a rope gives him a chance to reuse skills acquired in **141** *Timelash*.

236 Journey to the Centre of the TARDIS

by **Steve Thompson**

The TARDIS is caught in the magnetic hobble-field of a salvage ship, whose crew members capture the Doctor. Clara, meanwhile, flees into the depths of the TARDIS, where terrifying zombies lurk.

■ **Where and When** The Van Baalan Bros salvage ship and inside the TARDIS (including a store room, the library, the engine room and the Eye of Harmony). Date unknown – though the events turn out to be part of a cancelled timeline.

■ **The Baddies** The Van Baalan brothers – Gregory (Ashley Walters), Bram (Mark Oliver) and Tricky (Jahvel Hall) – are ruthless but credulous. Bram is killed by one of the Time Zombies, which seem to act out of pure savagery.

■ **Introducing...** This is the only time the word 'TARDIS' has been used in the title of a TV story.

■ **Look out for...** Brief glimpses of the TARDIS observatory and swimming pool, and a spectacular tree-like structure in the Architectural Reconfiguration Room.

■ **What they said** "It's the visuals that really shine," wrote Jon Cooper in *The Mirror* on 27 April 2013. "From the (quite literal) opening as the TARDIS is swallowed by the gaping maw of a giant ship to the endless weirdness of the TARDIS interior, there's a lot to look at – and it all looks superb."

■ **Arcs in Space** Clara's journey through the TARDIS builds on previous corridor-wandering stories such as **98** *The Invasion of Time*, **115** *Logopolis* and **216** *The Doctor's Wife*. The Eye of Harmony looks rather different from its appearance in **156** the 1996 TV movie *Doctor Who*. The Doctor questions Clara about her other selves, from **226** *Asylum of the Daleks* and **231** *The Snowmen*, although the conversation is forgotten until **239** *The Name of the Doctor*.

Clara, the Doctor and Gregor Van Baalen (Ashley Walters) gaze upon the Eye of Harmony when they *Journey to the Centre of the TARDIS*.

237 The Crimson Horror

by Mark Gatiss

Nobody who goes to live in the factory town of Sweetville ever comes out – except as bright red corpses in the local canal. Madame Vastra, Jenny and Strax investigate…

■ **Where and When** Sweetville, somewhere in Yorkshire, 1893.

■ **The Baddies** Expert chemist and engineer Mrs Winifred Gillyflower (Diana Rigg) plans to wipe out most of humanity, rebuilding civilisation with her chosen few. She also has a symbiotic relationship with Mr Sweet, a large prehistoric leech.

■ **Introducing…** Strax's fondness for sherbet fancies introduces the notion that Sontarans have a new Achilles heel – sweeties.

■ **Look out for…** The reveal of the monster tended by Amy (Rachel Stirling) – it's the Doctor, bright red and frozen stiff, with his mouth wide open.

■ **What they said** "The original pitch was to have [Arthur] Conan Doyle in it," writer Mark Gatiss told the *Radio Times* website on 14 March 2023. "That's why there's the optigram at the beginning, because Doyle was an eye surgeon and that's that where all that was going to come from."

■ **Arcs in Space** The end of this story, with Artie and Angie discovering photographs of Clara from 231 *The Snowmen,* 234 *Cold War* and 235 *Hide,* leads directly into the next, 238 *Nightmare in Silver.* The Doctor recalls

Right
A chess-playing Cyberman precipitates a *Nightmare in Silver.*

Below right
The Doctor receives an unwanted upgrade.

trying to get Tegan back to Heathrow Airport – a theme running from 117 *Four to Doomsday* through to 122 *Time-Flight.* The idea of the eye retaining the image of the last thing it sees previously cropped up in 76 *The Ark in Space.*

238 Nightmare in Silver

by Neil Gaiman

The Doctor takes Clara's two charges, Artie and Angie, to the Hedgewick's World amusement park. But its only remaining attraction is filled with waxworks and three surviving Cybermen.

■ **Where and When** Hedgewick's World, located on the edge of what was once the

Tiberion galaxy. The date is unspecified, but it's a thousand years since the Cyberwars.

■ **The Baddies** The Cybermen survived the Cyberwars, using the unnamed planet as a 'tomb' for damaged units. Ever since, they've been quietly kidnapping visitors from the amusement park to use as spare parts.

■ **Introducing…** A brand-new Cybermen upgrade, with the capacity for super-speed, and a new Cyber-threat – the Cybermites.

■ **Look out for…** Clara taking charge of the motley members of the punishment platoon as they're besieged in the castle.

■ **What they said** According to Dan Martin in *The Guardian* on 11 May 2013, Matt Smith's Doctor "never looked more demented as he plays out the battle between the two forces inside his own brain; a physical feat as much as the delivery of the tongue-twisty dialogue."

■ **Arcs in Space** The Cybermen are directed by a Cyber-planner intelligence, last mentioned in 46 *The Invasion.* Their initial plan, to exploit the potential of children's brains, recalls both 148 *Remembrance of the Daleks* and 170 *School Reunion.* Waxworks owner Webley (Jason Watkins) describes his display Cyberman as "the 699th wonder of the universe". The 700th was destroyed in 72 *Death to the Daleks.*

Clara and the Doctor head north, to Sweetville – the province of Mrs Gillyflower (Diana Rigg) and her daughter Amy (Rachel Stirling), protectors of *The Crimson Horror.*

239 The Name of the Doctor

by **Steven Moffat**

The Doctor has many secrets. But one of them he'll take to his grave. And it's discovered.

■ **Where and When** Principally London (1893 and 2013), Glasgow (1893) and planet Trenzalore in the far-distant future. But temporal "splinters" of Clara show up everywhere – including on Gallifrey "a very long time ago", when "some idiot" is seen stealing a faulty TARDIS...

■ **The Baddies** The Great Intelligence, again using the form of Dr Simeon (Richard E Grant), as seen in **231** *The Snowmen* and **232** *The Bells of Saint John* – and now using screeching, fang-mouthed, dream-invading Whisper Men as muscle.

■ **Introducing...** John Hurt as the War Doctor. A hitherto unacknowledged incarnation who fought in the Time War. What he did, he did without choice. In the name of peace and sanity.

■ **Look out for...** In an episode that blows many kisses to the past, one of the best moments is something new. Clarence (Michael Jenn), terrified of the Whisper Men, mutters "They'll stop and look at you." And then looks at *us*.

■ **What they said** On 18 May 2013, *Guardian* blogger Dan Martin applauded "a fantastic new villain in the Whispermen [sic], effectively blank-faced and handy with a couplet. Their slow approach gives another chill addition to this gothic tale, even though it's not exactly clear what they actually do or how they're going to stop your heart." Summing up, he observed that "Here was a finale based on ideas, and the ideas were gigantic. Not just the best episode of the season, but possibly the best season finale we've seen."

■ **Arcs in Space** The question of "the impossible girl", running since **226** *Asylum of the Daleks*, is finally answered. Trenzalore, mentioned by Dorium Maldovar in **224** *The Wedding of River Song*, is where the Doctor is now buried – inside his now-giant TARDIS. Clara glimpses various past Doctors, in footage extracted from **6** *The Aztecs*, **13** *The Web Planet*, **35** *The Mind Robber*, **97** *The Invasion of Time*, **123** *Arc of Infinity*, **129** *The Five Doctors* and **147** *Dragonfire*. The Intelligence refers to the fact that the Doctor will one day be known as the Valeyard, from **143** *The Trial of a Time Lord*. We also see the First Doctor stealing a TARDIS and running away from his home planet, as originally described in **50** *The War Games*. A number of Clara's "splinters" appear on Gallifrey. Are they actually one "splinter" who is a Time Lord?

Right
The Eleventh and Tenth Doctors are united in *The Day of the Doctor*.

Below
The War Doctor with the Moment, which takes the form of Rose Tyler.

240 The Day of the Doctor

by **Steven Moffat**

The Tenth and Eleventh Doctors face their past, literally and figuratively, on the day that their War incarnation prepared to end the Dalek-Time Lord conflict by triggering a sentient weapon known as the Moment.

■ **Where and When** Rural England in 1572. London in 1572, and circa 2013. Gallifrey's second city, Arcadia, its desert, and the War Room in the final hours of the Time War.

■ **The Baddies** The Daleks, laying siege to Gallifrey. Zygons invading contemporary Earth from its own past.

■ **Look out for...** When 13 Doctors approach Gallifrey in their TARDISes,

Right
Dr Simeon returns in *The Name of the Doctor*, aided by the Whisper Men.

Above inset
The War Doctor (John Hurt) is revealed.

241 The Time of the Doctor

by **Steven Moffat**

The Time Lords are returning to the universe, endangering a small town on a hill and facing the Doctor with an impossible choice. The war on Christmas has begun.

■ **Where and When** Trenzalore, for around a thousand years, starting before (and eventually overwriting) **239** *The Name of the Doctor*. Also London on Christmas Day, circa 2013.

■ **The Baddies** Those laying siege to Trenzalore include Daleks, Cybermen, Sontarans and Weeping Angels. The relationship between the Church of the Papal Mainframe, security hub of the known universe (mentioned in **218** *A Good Man Goes to War*) and the Silence (introduced in **214** *The Impossible Astronaut/Day of the Moon*) is clarified, as are their motivations. The Silents themselves are established as "confessional priests" who allow you to forget your sins.

■ **Look out for...** One of the puppets in the Doctor's show represents a Monoid from **23** *The Ark*.

■ **Farewell to...** The Eleventh Doctor, after an astonishing speech about change, renewal and keeping moving. "Raggedy man, good night."

■ **What they said** "[Matt] Smith's conviction, and nuanced delivery of an old, brave man fighting against the odds," wrote the *Daily Mirror*'s Jon Cooper on 27 December 2013, "was what really made this episode special. Easily the highlight of this year's Christmas viewing... a careful, concise and emotional hour of top-quality entertainment."

■ **Arcs in Space** The Doctor circumvents the '13 lives' limit introduced in **88** *The Deadly Assassin* – but see also **295** *Ascension of the Cybermen*. It's confirmed that the aborted regeneration in **198** *The Stolen Earth/Journey's End* cost the Doctor an incarnation. The Eleventh Doctor still has the Seal of the High Council, pocketed by the Third in **129** *The Five Doctors*, on his person. Which, given he said he'd "return it at the first opportunity", is hilarious.

they appear via clips from **2** *The Mutants* (aka *The Daleks*), **37** *The Tomb of the Cybermen*, **58** *Colony in Space*, **81** *Planet of Evil*, **132** *Frontios*, **137** *Attack of the Cybermen*, **152** *Battlefield*, **156** the 1996 TV movie *Doctor Who* and **166** *Bad Wolf/ The Parting of the Ways*, plus additional audio from **48** *The Seeds of Death*, **65** *The Three Doctors* and **129** *The Five Doctors*. The Seventh Doctor is there twice, in two different costumes. (He must have popped back.) The Fourth Doctor doesn't speak here, but check out the walls of the Curator's undergallery.

■ **What they said** "Event TV is a hackneyed term," noted Ben Lawrence in *The Daily Telegraph* on 25 November 2013, "but this special anniversary episode really has inspired the same fervour as a World Cup final or a Royal wedding... [*Doctor Who* is] a unique part of our cultural life."

■ **Arcs in Space** Dalek Caan's "no more", from **198** *Journey's End*, turns out to have been a quote from the War Doctor, whose presence at "the fall of Arcadia" was established in **177** *Doomsday*. The General (Ken Bones) dismisses the High Council's scheme from **202** *The End of Time* – "To hell with the High Council, their plans have already failed" – and twice paraphrases the Brigadier from **65** *The Three Doctors*. After the War Doctor steals the Moment, he touches alien sands and sees birds wheeling in another sky, recalling **1** *100,000 BC* (aka *An Unearthly Child*).

Right
The Doctor and Clara discover a town called Christmas in *The Time of the Doctor*.

Above inset
The aged Eleventh Doctor regenerates.

The
TWELFTH
DOCTOR

Peter Capaldi
Stories 242–276, 2014–17

Was he a good man, this "big, grey-haired stick insect" with "attack eyebrows" and a permanently cross reflection? Did he really think we were all "pudding brains"? As it turned out, he'd spend billions of years battering an azbantium wall with his fists, and break all the laws of time, if it meant he might save a friend.

Left
Clara gets to know a new Doctor (Peter Capaldi) in *Deep Breath*.

Below inset
The Half-Face Man (Peter Ferdinando).

243 Into the Dalek

by **Phil Ford** and **Steven Moffat**
Is the Doctor a good man? Can there ever be such a thing as a good Dalek? To answer either question, you need to take a good look inside.

■ **Where and When** Coal Hill School, Shoreditch, circa 2014; the spaceship *Aristotle*, at some point in the future; and inside a Dalek.

■ **The Baddies** Daleks, laying siege to the *Aristotle*.

■ **Introducing...** The malfunctioning 'Good Dalek', which the Doctor nicknames 'Rusty', returns in **276** *Twice Upon A Time*. Soldier turned Coal Hill maths teacher Danny Pink (Samuel Anderson).

■ **Look out for...** Rusty chants the title of **72** *Death to the Daleks*. Other Daleks chant "Seek – Locate – Destroy!" – apparently after an episode of *Blake's 7* (1978-81) written by Dalek creator Terry Nation, and nearly a quote from **104** *Destiny of the Daleks*.

■ **What they said** Neela Debnath, writing in *The Independent* on 1 September 2014: "*Into the Dalek* reflects the darker and more adult tone that the makers of the show are now going for... the special effects... were nothing short of blockbuster."

■ **Arcs in Space** "Nobody guards the dead, mortuaries... always the easiest to break out of," mutters the Doctor – unintentionally foreshadowing season finale **252** *Dark Water/Death In Heaven*. He later recalls the events of **2** *The Mutants* (aka *The Daleks*), and says his first encounter with Skaro's machine creatures defined who he was because "The Doctor was not the Daleks." When he asks Clara "Am I good man?" he's returning to issues raised in **218** *A Good Man Goes To War* and *The Night of the Doctor* (see pages 112-113). His declared dislike of soldiers and the trauma of Danny's army days play out later in the season.

242 Deep Breath

by **Steven Moffat**
New Doctor. Old friends. A buried spaceship. A quest for paradise. Take a deep breath, and jump.

■ **Where and When** London, both in the late 19th century and circa 2014.

■ **The Baddies** The Half-Face Man (Peter Ferdinando) – a Clockwork Robot who's been repairing and replacing every component of himself and his time-ship for millions of years.

■ **Introducing...** The new Doctor is quicksilver and "properly... Scottish", while struggling with his memory after his "whopper" of a regeneration. Like the Half-Face Man, he's replaced every part of himself so often, he no longer knows if he's the same person he was to begin with. Clara remembers being cheeked by Courtney Woods (Ellis George) on her first day at Coal Hill; we'll be seeing her again. In the final seconds, a madwoman (Michelle Gomez) introduces herself to the Half-Face Man as 'Missy'; we'll be seeing her again, too.

■ **Farewell to...** 'The Paternoster Gang' comprising Madame Vastra, Jenny and Strax, first seen in **218** *A Good Man Goes To War*.

■ **Look out for...** Vastra affects a Scots accent (Paisley-born Neve McIntosh's own, in fact) to calm the Doctor when he complains "You all sound English."

■ **What they said** *Variety*'s Geoff Berkshire cited the "immediate rapport [Peter] Capaldi strikes with sparkling cast holdover Jenna Coleman", and praised a "skillful tonal balance that... exemplifies the ethos that keeps the series going strong, nodding to the past with all eyes on the future."

■ **Arcs in Space** The Doctor worries where he's seen his new face before; the reason why he resembles Caecilius from **190** *The Fires of Pompeii* is finally explained in **256** *The Girl Who Died*. Vastra's "here we go again" in the opening scene paraphrases the Brigadier in **74** *Planet of the Spiders*. The cyborgs' ship, the SS *Marie Antoinette*, is the sister vessel to the SS *Madame de Pompadour*, from **171** *The Girl in the Fireplace* (not that the Doctor can remember).

244 Robot of Sherwood

by Mark Gatiss

Clara wants to meet Robin Hood. The Doctor says he's not real. So who's that in Lincoln Green laughing on a log? When the myth becomes legend, print the legend.

- **Where and When** Sherwood Forest, near Nottingham, England, 1190.
- **The Baddies** Where there's a Robin Hood (Tom Riley), there's always a Sheriff of Nottingham (Ben Miller). But this one has ambitions to rule a much larger area, and he doesn't mean Worksop.
- **Where else have I seen...** Trevor Cooper (Friar Tuck) was Takis in **142** *Revelation of the Daleks*.
- **Look out for...** One of the images in the spaceship databank's history of Robin Hood is Second Doctor actor Patrick Troughton in the title role of BBC Television's *Robin Hood* (1953).
- **What they said** Michael Hogan writing in *The Daily Telegraph* on 6 September 2014 called this a "funny and thrillingly old-fashioned adventure... a deliriously daft, *Blackadder*-esque romp with a fizzing script... the episode in which Capaldi truly came into his own as The Doctor."
- **Arcs in Space** The spaceship hidden in Nottingham is headed to "the promised land... like the Half-Face Man" (see **242** *Deep Breath*). The Doctor speculates that he's in a miniscope (from **76** *Carnival of Monsters*). The Doctor claims to have duelled both Richard the Lionheart and Cyrano de Bergerac, but these must be separate occasions to his meetings with them in **14** *The Crusade* and **45** *The Mind Robber*, respectively. Continuing the early

Right
The Doctor goes in search of a theoretical horror in *Listen*.

Below inset
Astronaut Orson Pink (Samuel Anderson).

season theme of having guest characters who parallel and highlight aspects of the Doctor, Clara draws the Doctor's attention to the things he and Robin have in common.

245 Listen

by Steven Moffat

"What's that in the mirror, or the corner of your eye?... Perhaps they're all just waiting. Perhaps when we're all dead, out they'll come-a-slithering from underneath your bed."

- **Where and When** Shoreditch, circa 2014. A west country children's home, in the mid-1990s. The last planet at the end of the universe. And Gallifrey's past – in the same barn that the War Doctor took the Moment to in **240** *The Day of the Doctor*.
- **The Baddies** Evolution breeds survival skills. In a universe with perfect hunters, the Doctor theorises, there must be a creature that's perfected hiding. Being the Doctor, he decides to find it.
- **Where else have I seen...** Children's home janitor Reg is Robert Goodman's only credited *Doctor Who* role, but he made many background appearances in the 20th century series – among them as a Starliner citizen in **111** *Full Circle*, and as a colonist in **132** *Frontios*.
- **Look out for...** Time traveller Colonel Orson Pink (Samuel Anderson) wears a spacesuit first seen in **174** *The Impossible Planet/The Satan Pit*.

- **What they said** *Guardian* blogger Dan Martin called the episode "phenomenally good. A masterclass in fright. A litany of psychological set pieces."
- **Arcs in Space** Waking up in the TARDIS, the Doctor shouts "Sontarans! Perverting the course of human history!" – his fourth incarnation's first utterance, from **75** *Robot*. Clara invokes the Doctor's mantra "never cruel or cowardly", as heard in **240** *The Day of the Doctor*. Inadvertently, she also prompts something the First Doctor says in **1** *100,000 BC* (aka *An Unearthly Child*), when she tells his sleeping boyhood self: "Fear makes companions of us all."

Clara meets Robin Hood (Tom Riley) in *Robot of Sherwood*.

246 Time Heist

by Steve Thompson

After answering a mysterious phone call, the Doctor and Clara find themselves caught up in a plot to rob the most secure bank in the galaxy.

■ **Where and When** The Bank of Karabraxos, unspecified time period.

■ **The Baddies** The unscrupulous Ms Delphox (Keeley Hawes) and her various clones appear to be the antagonists here. But – plot twist – it turns out to be an older version of the character who's set the heist in motion. Her ultimate aim is to free the Teller creature (Ross Mullan), which her younger self kept captive, and reunite it with its mate.

■ **Farewell to...** The memory worm, making its second and final appearance after **231** *The Snowmen*. (As far as anyone can remember, at least.)

■ **Look out for...** When Psi (Jonathan Bailey) distracts the Teller from attacking Clara, he does so by accessing files on all the greatest criminals in history. Among the faces that flash up are glimpses of a Sensorite from **7** *The Sensorites*, a Terileptil from **119** *The Visitation*, a Slitheen from **160** *Aliens of London/World War III*, Kahler-Tek from **228** *A Town Called Mercy* and an Ice Warrior of the type seen in **234** *Cold War*. Also visible: the bodysnatcher Androvax and the Trickster, both from *The Sarah Jane Adventures*, Captain John Hart (James Marsters) and a Weevil, both from *Torchwood*, and Dalek-killer Abslom Daak, from the **Doctor Who Magazine** comic strip.

■ **What they said** "In *Time Heist*," observed *Guardian* blogger Dan Martin on 20 September 2014, "the Doctor is properly and completely the Doctor again, leading an intrepid group on a dangerous mission and saving the day through a combination of intelligence and empathy while having a proper adventure."

■ **Arcs in Space** When the TARDIS phone rings at the start of the story, the Doctor points out that they still don't know the identity of the 'woman in a shop' who gave the number to Clara – enabling her to call it in **232** *The Bells of Saint John*.

247 The Caretaker

by Gareth Roberts and **Steven Moffat**

In an effort to track down anomalous traces of alien technology in the vicinity, the Doctor goes undercover – as the caretaker at Coal Hill School...

■ **Where and When** Coal Hill School, 2014.

■ **The Baddies** The Doctor calls the Skovox Blitzer (Jimmy Vee) "one of the deadliest killing machines ever created", suggesting it's been drawn to the Coal Hill area by the high number of artron emissions over the years – presumably caused by the TARDIS' frequent visits, as seen in such stories as **1** *100,000 BC* (aka *An Unearthly Child*), **135** *Attack of the Cybermen*, **148** *Remembrance of the Daleks* and **243** *Into the Dalek*.

■ **Introducing...** The final scene features the first appearance of Seb (Chris Addison) – Missy's AI assistant in the Nethersphere.

■ **Look out for...** When the Doctor meets Clara's fellow teacher, Adrian (Edward Harrison), he assumes this is the man Clara is dating – an assumption based, egotistically, on Adrian's passing resemblance to his previous incarnation.

■ **What they said** In **DWM** issue 479 (December 2014), Graham Kibble-White described the Skovox Blitzer as "a *Robot Wars* creation with a name that will never trip off the tongue. The voice is set on 'generic automaton' and the head-up display does as little as it can get away with."

■ **Arcs in Space** The policeman killed by the Skovox Blitzer finds himself in the Nethersphere at the very end of the story. And we get another glimpse of the mysterious woman who first appeared in **242** *Deep Breath*. She'll eventually be revealed as Missy – a female incarnation of the Master – in **252** *Dark Water/ Death in Heaven*.

Above inset Bank security chief Ms Delphox (Keeley Hawes) in *Time Heist*.

Above The mind-reading Teller (Ross Mullan) is led across the floor of the Bank of Karabraxos.

248 Kill the Moon

by **Peter Harness**

The Doctor takes Clara and one of her students on a field trip to the Moon – where they discover that Earth's satellite isn't all it's cracked up to be...

- **Where and When** The Moon, 2049.
- **The Baddies** The 'Moon Spiders' are analogous to bacteria, so can't really be classed as villains. From Clara's perspective, the antagonist here is the Doctor; forcing her to take a decision on behalf of all humanity leads to her deciding to give up travelling with him.
- **Farewell to...** Courtney Woods, the troublemaking teen first glimpsed in Clara's subconscious during **242** *Deep Breath*.
- **Look out for...** Earth's Moon is revealed to be an egg. The fact that the dragon-like creature that hatches from it immediately lays another egg of the same size suggests that some sort of dimensional transcendentalism may be at play here.
- **Where else have I seen...** Tony Osoba plays expedition member Duke, killed by a Moon Spider. He was previously powered down as the dreadlocked Movellan android Lan in **104** *Destiny of the Daleks*, and killed by Kane's frozen touch as Iceworld officer Kracauer in **147** *Dragonfire*.
- **Arcs in Space** By the end, Clara is so furious with the Doctor that she tells him to leave without her, informing Danny Pink that she's finished with TARDIS travel. But Danny suggests that her level of emotion indicates she's not quite ready to cut ties with the Doctor – and she will indeed return in the next story, **249** *Mummy on the Orient Express*.

Right
The Doctor and Clara enjoying the luxury aboard the *Orient Express*.

Below inset
The Foretold (Jamie Hill) targets another victim.

249 Mummy on the Orient Express

by **Jamie Mathieson**

Passengers on board a space-faring version of the famous locomotive start seeing a terrifying mummy – and when they do, they have just 66 seconds to live.

- **Where and When** The *Orient Express*. In space! Unspecified time period.
- **The Baddies** The Foretold 'mummy' (Jamie Hill) turns out to be the remains of a soldier, forced to continue killing by his integrated battle technology. The real baddie is a computer called GUS – which is working for an unknown boss to discover the secrets of the Foretold. We've yet to find out who that mysterious employer was...
- **Look out for...** When the Doctor becomes the intended victim of the Foretold , meaning he's at last able to perceive it, he asks "Are you my mummy?" – a reference to the phrase used repeatedly in **164** *The Empty Child/ The Doctor Dances*. (This is a gag that no one else in the scene could possibly understand.)
- **Where else have I seen...** As Miss Hardaker in **154** *The Curse of Fenric*, Janet Henfrey was dispatched by creatures resembling vampires. Here, as Mrs Pitt, she's finished off by one that looks like a different horror-movie monster altogether.
- **What they said** According to Graham Kibble-White, writing in **DWM** issue 479, in 2014: "Jamie Mathieson's tale is the most delicious *Doctor Who* so far this year. So rich, so *plush* an experience, you can almost feel its velvety drag on your skin."
- **Arcs in Space** Having decided to end her travels with the Doctor in **248** *Kill the Moon*, Clara is back here for one final trip. By story's end, however, she's changed her mind and resolves to continue her adventures in time and space – even if it means lying to both the Doctor and Danny.

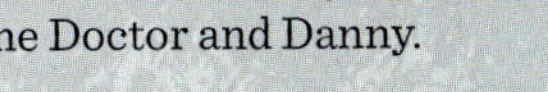

Above
A tight squeeze for the Doctor in *Flatline*.

Above right
Rigsy (Joivan Wade) sees the Boneless in an underpass.

250 Flatline

by Jamie Mathieson

The TARDIS exterior starts to shrink, trapping the Doctor inside. As Clara investigates a connection with missing people in Bristol, the threat takes on a new dimension…

■ **Where and When** Bristol, probably 2014.
■ **The Baddies** Creatures the Doctor names 'the Boneless' – beings from a two-dimensional plane of existence, trying to learn about the three-dimensional world and killing people in the process. Their 3D forms look rather like grim early generative AI art.
■ **Introducing…** Bristol. The city is mentioned in several previous stories, including **45** *The Mind Robber* and *Shada* (see page 77), but this is the first time we see the TARDIS land there. In **265** *The Pilot* we learn that the Doctor spends several decades teaching at a university in the city – so he's presumably across town while the events of *Flatline* take place.
■ **Look out for…** The *Addams Family* bit, where the Doctor extends his full-size hand out of the TARDIS' miniaturised exterior, so he can move his ship out of danger. Audacious, funny and tense all at once.

■ **What they said** Partway through scripting, *Flatline* became a 'Doctor-lite' episode. "I was asked to think of a clever way to lock the Doctor away in a single location," Jamie Mathieson recalled in **Doctor Who Magazine** issue 479 (December 2014), "because one location can be recorded relatively quickly in the schedule."
■ **Arcs in Space** The TARDIS is also shrunk, for a variety of reasons, in **9** *Planet of Giants*, **66** *Carnival of Monsters* and **115** *Logopolis*.

251 In the Forest of the Night

by Frank Cottrell-Boyce

The world wakes up to discover that planet Earth has been reclaimed by trees. One of Clara's pupils, who can hear the voices of the forest, has gone to find the Doctor…

■ **Where and When** London, probably 2014.
■ **The Baddies** There isn't a villain as such, although there is a tiger. The threat is a massive solar flare that has the potential to wipe out life on Earth.

■ **Introducing…** The TARDIS terrestrial navigation system. Basically, a sat nav. Which hasn't been heard from since. But then, the HADS wasn't mentioned for 44 years after **47** *The Krotons*, then suddenly came back in **234** *Cold War*.
■ **Look out for…** The Doctor's latest explanation of how the TARDIS can be bigger on the inside: "When you drink a glass of Coke, it's only [indicates small quantity] this big, but it's actually got [indicates huge quantity] this much sugar in it. It works a bit like that."
■ **What they said** In *The Independent* on 28 October 2014, Neela Debnath wrote that this episode has "a novel concept that starts off well but unravels fairly quickly… Perhaps it's a generational thing that grown ups just 'don't get'."
■ **Arcs in Space** This is surely the most extreme illustration of the Doctor's claims in stories like **148** *Remembrance of the Daleks* and **160** *Aliens of London/ World War Three* that humanity forgets or willingly ignores large-scale extraterrestrial or supernatural incursions.

252 Dark Water/ Death in Heaven

(two episodes) by Steven Moffat

Danny is killed in an accident. The Doctor tells the grief-stricken Clara that they'll try to find him in the afterlife – and to their surprise, they do. But an old enemy has plans for him…

■ **Where and When** London, probably 2014, and the Nethersphere.
■ **The Baddies** Missy, at last revealed to be the latest incarnation of the Master –

The Doctor discovers an overgrown Trafalgar Square… *In the Forest of the Night*.

Left
A new generation of Cybermen emerges from St Paul's Cathedral in *Dark Water/ Death in Heaven*.

Right
Missy (Michelle Gomez) reveals her scheme to the Doctor.

"Upload the mind, upgrade the body. Cybermen from cyberspace." MISSY

the first Time Lord to appear on screen in male and female incarnations. She's using the Nethersphere to create a new army of Cybermen from humanity's dead – but to what end?

- **Farewell to…** Petronella Osgood – or one of them, at least.
- **Look out for…** Michelle Gomez's gloriously baroque delivery of the simple line *"I'm in charge."*
- **What they said** In *The Guardian* on 8 November 2014, Dan Martin praised "how brilliant Michelle Gomez is in the role. This is how an instant classic is created; she preens with a perfect combination of madness and malevolence that is just so Master."
- **Arcs in Space** The Master and the Cybermen, previously only seen working together in **129** *The Five Doctors*, become a regular combo after this, teaming up again in **275** *World Enough and Time/ The Doctor Falls* and **295** *Ascension of the Cybermen/The Timeless Children*.

253 Last Christmas

by Steven Moffat

A research base at the North Pole is under attack from face-hugging aliens. If the Doctor can't help, maybe Santa Claus can?

- **Where and When** The North Pole and London, probably 2014.
- **The Baddies** The Kantrofarri, or Dream Crabs – creatures that cling to a victim's face and distract them with dreams while consuming their brains.
- **Farewell to…** Danny Pink, whose final appearance is in the form of a Dream Crab-induced vision experienced by Clara.
- **Look out for…** After Santa (Nick Frost) turns up at the base offering to help, and the Doctor, Clara and the crew insist he can't possibly be real, Shona (Faye Marsay) gets the best line: "If [the North Pole] was an actual pole, it would not be stripy."
- **What they said** "It's Santa meets *Alien* meets *The Thing from Another World* meets *Miracle on 34th Street*," said Steven Moffat in **DWM** issue 481 (January 2015), stressing also that "a lot of the main themes of *Doctor Who* are there. There's a base under siege, there's scary monsters…"
- **Arcs in Space** The Doctor claims to know Santa (and to know him as 'Geoff') in **213** *A Christmas Carol*, and implies he *is* Santa in **164** *The Empty Child/ The Doctor Dances*.

Two squabbling elves (Nathan McMullen and Dan Starkey) join Clara, the Doctor and Santa (Nick Frost) in *Last Christmas*.

TIMEY-WIMEY

The most temporally twisted tales, unscrambled by **Paul Kirkley**.

Above
The Tenth Doctor leaves time-twisting video messages for Sally Sparrow (Carey Mulligan) in *Blink*.

Outstanding

The story that coined the 'timey-wimey' phrase in the first place, **186** *Blink*, remains the high water mark of Steven Moffat's trademark Möbius strip plotting. From the opening teaser, in which Sally Sparrow (Carey Mulligan) unveils a message behind the wallpaper telling her to duck, to the scene in which the Doctor reads from a transcript of a conversation he's still having, it's a dizzyingly inventive puzzle box of an episode. The Weeping Angels – creatures of the abstract who "zap you into the past and let you live to death" – are a brilliantly terrifying creation, but Moffat doesn't just use time for scares and party tricks. Arguably the finest moment comes when the dying Billy Shipton (Louis Mahoney) tells Sally it was raining when they met. Her devastating reply? "It's the same rain."

Essential

In **212** *The Pandorica Opens/ The Big Bang*, Moffat turns the timey-wimeyness up to 11, with the Doctor zapping in and out of his own timeline, snatching drinks and leaving Post-It notes in order to nudge history along the right path. Its nearest 20th-century antecedent, **125** *Mawdryn Undead*, offers a time-travel spin on the Flying Dutchman myth, in which the Doctor meets Brigadiers from 1977 and 1983 (helpfully, only one of them has a moustache). And in **197** *Turn Left*, Russell T Davies examines the tiny human moments on which history turns and timelines diverge, cleverly woven through an alternative history of the show's own recent past.

Excellent

No one illustrates the crazy-paving nature of time travel better than River Song (Alex Kingston), whose personal chronology is as tangled as her corkscrew curls. And no story is more head-spinning than **224** *The Wedding of River Song*, in which "all of history happening at once" is only the start of it. **60** *Day of the Daleks* may feel straightforward by comparison, but the revelation that a group of 22nd-century guerrillas were responsible for starting the war they've travelled back in time to avert is an early paradoxical head-scratcher. **163** *Father's Day* depicts the terrible consequences of meddling in one's own personal history. **105** *City of Death* takes a delightfully playful approach to time, including the Doctor foiling an art forgery scam by nipping back to Renaissance Florence and giving Leonardo da Vinci a marker pen. For a more emotional sucker punch, try **221** *The Girl Who Waited,* in which Amy and Rory's marriage is tested by them ageing at different rates.

The Best of the Rest

15 *The Space Museum*, in which the TARDIS travellers arrive to discover they've been mounted as exhibits, is the show's earliest flirtation with timey-wimey (not that the First Doctor would have called it that). **149** *Remembrance of the Daleks* introduces the Seventh Doctor as a 'cosmic chess player', making moves across four dimensions – here catching up with his original incarnation's activities in London, prior to the series' first-ever episode. **171** *The Girl in the Fireplace* is the cautionary tale of why you should never fall in love with a time traveller. **213** *A Christmas Carol* contains perhaps the series' finest timey-wimey visual, as the Doctor exits the room where Kazran Sardick (Michael Gambon) is watching old home movies, only to reappear in the scratchy film footage. In **239** *The Name of the Doctor*, 'impossible girl' Clara Oswald (Jenna-Louise Coleman) leaps into the Doctor's own timeline, and the BBC archives, while **288** *Spyfall* plays the concept for LOLs as the Thirteenth Doctor (Jodie Whittaker) almost forgets to nip back in time to avert the air crash that, in her head, she's already sorted. And in **308** *73 Yards*, Ruby Sunday (Millie Gibson) is dogged every step of her adult life by a woman who isn't yet her 83-year-old self.... but will be one day. Confused? That's time travel for you.

"People don't
understand time.
It's not what you
think it is."
THE DOCTOR, *BLINK*

Left
The Doctor again finds himself captive on Skaro, in *The Magician's Apprentice/The Witch's Familiar*.

Below inset Missy returns.

254 The Magician's Apprentice/The Witch's Familiar

(two episodes) by Steven Moffat
The Doctor receives an invitation to meet Davros on the Dalek creator's dying day. It's an offer he can't refuse – even though he knows it's a trap.

■ **Where and When** Skaro, the Maldovarium, the Shadow Proclamation and Karn – all date unknown. Coal Hill School, UNIT HQ and "somewhere hot", all in 2015. A castle in Essex, 1138 AD.

■ **The Baddies** Davros, deviously plotting to prolong his life. The Daleks, in an impressive complement of variant models, headed by the Supreme from **198** *The Stolen Earth/ Journey's End*. Colony Sarff (Jami Reid-Quarrell), Davros' serpentine head of personal security. And Missy's certainly got it in for Clara – best friend or not.

■ **Introducing...** The Doctor's electric guitar, a Yamaha SGV 800 in Black Sparkle colourway. He plays this guitar

again in **255** *Under the Lake/Before the Flood*, **257** *The Woman Who Lived* and **258** *The Zygon Invasion/The Zygon Inversion*, then acquires a new one in **262** *Hell Bent*. After his previous sonic screwdriver is destroyed, the Doctor takes to wearing sonic sunglasses.

■ **Look out for...** The differing perspectives in the Doctor's interactions with Davros, only evident on a repeat viewing. The Doctor believes that Davros is accusing him of abandonment, but from Davros' point of view, he's actually accusing the Doctor of compassion.

■ **What they said** "Redemption is a pretty meaty theme for Saturday teatime viewing," noted Jon Cooper in *The Independent* on 26 September 2015, "and here it was deftly explored in an accessible yet intelligent way – hardly a bad way to get kids thinking critically about ethics."

■ **Arcs in Space** The Doctor's confession dial plays a more vital role in **260** *Face the Raven*, **261** *Hell Bent* and **262** *Heaven Sent*. Davros reveals his knowledge of a Gallifreyan prophecy about the Hybrid, a Dalek/Time Lord amalgam; this mystery resurfaces in **262** *Heaven Sent*.

255 Under the Lake/Before the Flood

(two episodes) by Toby Whithouse
Workers at the Drum, a mining base beneath a Scottish lake, are being terrorised by ghosts. The solution lies in an alien hearse that landed there 139 years earlier, before the area was flooded.

■ **Where and When** Caithness in Scotland, November 2119 and 1980.

■ **The Baddies** The Fisher King (voiced by Peter Serafinowicz and Corey Taylor), an evil alien warlord who's assisted by his Ghosts – the separated souls of the deceased given form by Earth's electromagnetic energy.

■ **Look out for...** The Doctor's guitar amplifier is seen here to have been manufactured by Magpie Electuca. Presumably this is a rebranding of Magpie Electricals, the company at the centre of **173** *The Idiot's Lantern*. Also, take a close look at the business card of Albar Prentis, Universal Funeral Director (Paul Kaye) – the slogan on it reads "May remorse be with you."

■ **Where else have I seen...** The unfortunate Moran is played by Colin McFarlane, who previously voiced the Heavenly Host in **188** *Voyage of the Damned*.

■ **What they said** "This is a story *about* time – about cause and effect, the intricacies of 'fate' and whether we can escape it," noted Digital Spy's Morgan Jeffrey on 10 October 2015, after the second half went out. "In one particularly brilliant moment, [Toby] Whithouse subverts the Doctor's 'hero moment' – the sort of scene we've seen dozens of time before – and catches the Time Lord in a time-loop."

The towering Fisher King (Neil Fingleton) in *Under the Lake/ Before the Flood*.

Clara, the Doctor and Ashildr (Maisie Williams) defend a Viking village in *The Girl Who Died*.

■ **Arcs in Space** In the remarkable fourth-wall-breaking pre-credits sequence, the Twelfth Doctor explains the concept of a bootstrap paradox. Further to the one he creates at the Drum, this iteration of the Doctor is also the catalyst for the creation of bootstrap paradoxes in **263** *The Husbands of River Song*, **275** *World Enough and Time/The Doctor Falls* and **276** *Twice Upon a Time*.

256 The Girl Who Died

by Jamie Mathieson and Steven Moffat
Captured by Vikings, the Doctor and Clara arrive in the Norsemen's village just as it comes under attack from a troop of warmongering aliens.

■ **Where and When** England and Norway, circa 850 – exact date unknown, but some 800 years before 1651.
■ **The Baddies** The Mire, one of the deadliest warrior races in the galaxy, according to the Doctor's 2000 Year Diary. Their leader uses holography to masquerade as the Viking god Odin (David Schofield).
■ **Introducing…** Viking teenager Ashildr (Maisie Williams), daughter of Einarr, aka 'Chuckles' (Ian Connigham). She dies during the rout of the Mire, but the Doctor uses the aliens' medical technology to restore her to life, making her "functionally immortal".
■ **Look out for…** The Doctor suddenly remembers that the face he has now is that of Caecilius, the marble trader he saved from the eruption of Vesuvius in **190** *The Fires of Pompeii*. He realises that he subconsciously chose Caecilius' face as a

reminder, to hold him to the mark – he's the Doctor and he saves people.
■ **What they said** "*The Girl Who Lived* is the show doing historical episodes as they're meant to be done," wrote IndieWire's Kaite Welsh on 17 October 2015. "It's like *Fires of Pompeii, Robin of Sherwood* [sic] and classic Third Doctor adventure *The Time Warrior* all mixed into one – literally – electrifying episode."
■ **Arcs in Space** The Doctor last met Vikings in **17** *The Time Meddler* – and briefly tried out a Viking look in **75** *Robot*! Ashildr's story is continued in the following episode…

257 The Woman Who Lived

by Catherine Tregenna
The Doctor is reunited with Ashildr, now calling herself 'Lady Me' and masquerading as a notorious 17th-century highwayman. But Ashildr harbours a dark secret that threatens all life on Earth…

■ **Where and When** Hounslow and Tyburn, London, 1651.
■ **The Baddies** Leandro (Ariyon Bakare), a fire-breathing lion-man from Delta Leonis who secretly plans to invade Earth using a jewelled amulet called the Eyes of Hades.
■ **Look out for…** The Doctor uses a Curioscanner to track exoplanetary energy. As they close in on the location of the Eyes of Hades, he explains to Ashildr that the device scans for curios. "I'm just realising how it got its name," he adds.
■ **Where else have I seen…** Lady Me's half-blind and "deaf-as-a-post" servant, Clayton, is played by Struan Rodger, who previously voiced the Face of Boe in **168** *New Earth* and **181** *Gridlock*. He'll also voice the Kasaavin in **288** *Spyfall*.
■ **What they said** As Me, *Game of Thrones* star Maisie Williams mightily impressed *Daily Express* blogger Neela Debnath on 24 October 2015. "Her performance was nothing short of brilliant as she graduated from scared little Viking girl to full blown villain… She went from all-knowing and untouchable to vulnerable within the space of 45 minutes and at no point did it feel unnatural."
■ **Arcs in Space** The Doctor tells Ashildr that the forthcoming Great Fire of London was caused by the Terileptils, as seen in **119** *The Visitation*. While they're hiding in the chimney at Fanshawe's manor house, Ashildr warns the Doctor that Clara will eventually die on him and "blow away like smoke" – words foreshadowing the tragic events of **260** *Face the Raven*.

The former Ashildr has adoped the guise of a highwayman when the Doctor catches up with her in *The Woman Who Lived*.

258 The Zygon Invasion/ The Zygon Inversion

(two episodes) by **Peter Harness** and **Steven Moffat**

Twenty million Zygons are living peacefully on Earth, disguised as humans. But a splinter group believes they shouldn't have to hide who they are. Can the peace deal hold?

■ **Where and When** London. Truth or Consequences, New Mexico, USA. Turmezistan. Probably 2015.
■ **The Baddies** Bonnie (Jenna Coleman), leader of the Zygon rebels, who takes on the form of Clara with the aim of sabotaging the Doctor and UNIT. Her group also kidnaps Osgood…
■ **Farewell to…** It turns out that Osgood's Zygon twin continued to take her form and personality. Though one of them was killed by Missy in 252 *Dark Water/Death in Heaven*, they made a pact not to reveal whether the human or Zygon Osgood survived. This is Osgood's final appearance to date, though she gets a shout-out in 264 *The Return of Doctor Mysterio*.
■ **Look out for…** This story deals with some thorny issues, coming to a head in an excellent speech from the Doctor to Bonnie: "How are you going to protect your glorious revolution from the next one?"
■ **What they said** Following transmission of the second half, Den of Geek's Simon Brew described how:

"*Doctor Who* has just blasted a 45 minute lesson in tolerance, the state of the world, war and the futility of conflict straight into people's living rooms while *The X Factor* was on the other side."
■ **Arcs in Space** The fictional country of Turmezistan, where UNIT have a base, features again in 271 *The Pyramid at the End of the World*. One of the two Osgood boxes in the climactic UNIT scene supposedly contains 'Sullivan's Gas' – seemingly concocted by former companion Harry Sullivan, last seen in 83 *The Android Invasion*.

The Doctor helps Clara disconnect from a Morpheus pod in *Sleep No More*.

259 Sleep No More

by Mark Gatiss

Professor Gagan Rassmussen, inventor of sleep-compressing pods, has made a video documenting the deadly creatures who've infested his lab. He warns you not to watch it…

■ **Where and When** The Le Verrier space station, in orbit around Neptune, on a Tuesday in the 38th century.
■ **The Baddies** The Sandmen, creatures created out of rheum and stimulated into sentience by the Morpheus pods. They've consumed the crew of the station and intend to do the same to the rescue mission that's just arrived.
■ **Introducing…** Due to its 'found footage' nature, this is the first *Doctor Who* episode to have no opening title sequence at all (though the title does flash up as part of a mass of letters and numbers), and the first to put its title and writer credit at the end.
■ **Look out for…** The moment when we see things from Clara's point of view.
■ **What they said** Mark Gatiss in **Doctor Who Magazine** issue 493 (Winter 2015/2016): "I was conscious that, obviously, 'found footage' has been done before, in movies, not so much on TV, and certainly not in *Doctor Who* – but hopefully I've twisted it a bit, brought something new to the idea."
Arcs in Space This is the second *Doctor Who* story to feature the song *Mr Sandman*. It was previously heard playing over the camp's PA system in 146 *Delta and the Bannermen*.

Clara flanked by rebel aliens in *The Zygon Inversion*.

Text by Eddie Robson

260 Face the Raven

by Sarah Dollard

The Doctor and Clara help an old friend who stands accused of a murder said to have been committed on a trap street – a hidden thoroughfare that's become a refuge for aliens on Earth.

■ **Where and When** London, the 2010s.
■ **The Baddies** The Quantum Shade, known as the Raven. Trap Street's Mayor Me – last seen in **257** *The Woman Who Lived* – has a deal with the creature, to dispense justice and maintain law and order.
■ **Farewell to…** This is the second and final appearance of Rigsy (Joivan Wade) from **250** *Flatline*, who's moved to London and started a family. He's the one who calls the Doctor and Clara after a tattoo appears on his neck and starts counting down – and together they the investigate the murder he's been accused of.
■ **Look out for…** "Sometimes Jane Austen and I prank each other," says Clara. "Oh, she is the worst. I love her. Take that how you like." Sadly, this relationship was never seen on screen.
■ **What they said** "This feels like an episode of television you could only ever see on *Doctor Who*," Jon Cooper wrote in *The Independent* on 21 November 2015. "A heady mixture of science fiction, Gothic whodunnit and emotional rollercoaster, it doesn't just leave you breathless – it leaves you wanting more."
■ **Arcs in Space** Me has a deal with unknown persons to capture the Doctor, and teleport him away to an unknown location; their identity will be confirmed in **262** *Hell Bent*.

The Doctor struggles to evade the unstopping Veil (Jami Reid-Quarrell) in *Heaven Sent*.

261 Heaven Sent

by Steven Moffat

The Doctor has been teleported to a strange mechanical castle surrounded by water. The layout shifts, and he finds himself pursued by a shrouded figure. The only escape is to confess…

■ **Where and When** A castle, date and time unknown.
■ **The Baddies** The unspeaking Veil (Jami Reid-Quarrell), who follows the Doctor, is an interrogation tool, its form drawn from the Doctor's own nightmares, with the ultimate aim of getting him to tell what he knows about the Hybrid. But the Doctor isn't going to talk that easily.
■ **Farewell to…** The Doctor. In a sense.
■ **Look out for…** The stunning montage sequence, in which the truth of the situation dawns on the Doctor… repeatedly. "If I didn't know better, I'd say I've travelled seven thousand years into the future…"
■ **What they said** "*Heaven Sent* is brilliant," Morgan Jeffrey wrote for Digital Spy on 28 November 2015, adding the caveat that "its rejection of the standard *Doctor Who* trappings might be too much for some. But if you're willing to see past that and embrace the weirdness, then you'll end up captivated. Because this is demanding and intelligent science-fiction, the likes of which BBC One should be commended for airing."
■ **Arcs in Space** "Nothing is half Dalek," says the Doctor, musing on the nature of the legendary Hybrid. "The Daleks would never allow that." We see this in their initial extermination of Davros in **78** *Genesis of the Daleks*, the purity conflicts in **142** *Revelation of the Daleks* and **148** *Remembrance of the Daleks*, and the fate of Dalek Sec in **182** *Daleks in Manhattan/ Evolution of the Daleks*.

The Doctor watches, horrified, as Clara goes to *Face the Raven*.

Left
Clara heads off in a stolen TARDIS in *Hell Bent*.

Below left
The Doctor plays guitar in a strange diner.

262 Hell Bent

by Steven Moffat

The Doctor steps into a diner in the Nevada desert and tells the waitress a story about the time he returned to his home planet of Gallifrey…

■ **Where and When** Gallifrey and Nevada, date unknown in both cases; and in the last hours at the end of the universe.

■ **The Baddies** Rassilon (Donald Sumpter) is ultimately responsible for the Doctor's recent suffering – but in this, the Doctor is also up against the very Laws of Time.

■ **Look out for…** We get to see the Doctor in a different light when Rassilon orders his execution and the firing squad hesitates. "Lord President, he's a war

hero," the General points out. "Some of these men served with him."

■ **Farewell to…** This marks the final appearances to date for Rassilon, Ohila and the General – plus Clara and Me, seen taking the long route back to Gallifrey in a very unconventionally shaped TARDIS.

■ **What they said** "This episode is far more about [the Doctor and Clara's] relationship than it ever was about Gallifrey," wrote Alasdair Wilkins for The AV Club on 6 December 2015. "It's fair to say that *Hell Bent* delivers something rather different from what it and the episodes building up to it appear to promise."

■ **Arcs in Space** We learn a lot more about exactly why the Doctor first ran away from Gallifrey. The reason why Missy put the Doctor and Clara together – a thread dating back to 232 *The Bells of Saint John* – is finally explained, and the nature of the Hybrid is finally revealed (although the prophecy about two warrior races standing in the ruins of Gallifrey actually seems a pretty good fit for the CyberMasters of 295 *Ascension of the Cybermen/The Timeless Children*).

263 The Husbands of River Song

by Steven Moffat

The Doctor is summoned to perform surgery on an angry despot. Is this a case of mistaken identity? If so, it's a huge coincidence, because the patient is married to River Song…

■ **Where and When** The planets Mendorax Dellora and Darillium, as well as the cruise ship *Harmony and Redemption*, Christmas 5343.

■ **The Baddies** King Hydroflax (Greg Davies), a cyborg who ruthlessly conquers and pillages all he surveys. A recent raid on the Halassi Vaults ended with the Halassi Androvar, the most valuable diamond in the universe, becoming lodged in Hydroflax's head. The Shoal of the Winter Harmony – direct descendants of a species of disembodied brains who encounter the Doctor in New York in his next adventure, 264 *The Return of Doctor Mysterio*.

■ **Farewell to…** This is the last appearance to date of River Song, who has seduced and married Hydroflax with the intention of stealing the Halassi Androvar. It slots in chronologically just before her first appearance, 195 *Silence in the Library/Forest of the Dead* – and we finally see the Singing Towers of Darillium.

■ **Look out for…** River's book aimed at time travellers looking for a free meal, *History's Finest Exploding Restaurants*.

■ **What they said** "We need to cheer up the Doctor," said Steven Moffat, discussing this episode in **Doctor Who Magazine** issue 494 (January 2016). "He was in a right old state by *Hell Bent*, so you sort of need someone proactive to come into his life… and remind him that he has a laugh sometimes."

■ **Arcs in Space** The Doctor and River list each other's spouses. The Doctor's include Queen Elizabeth I (seen in 240 *The Day of the Doctor*), Marilyn Monroe (seen in 213 *A Christmas Carol*) and Cleopatra (mentioned by the

River and the Doctor aboard a space liner in *The Husbands of River Song*.

Text by Eddie Robson

Superhero the Ghost, aka Grant Gordon (Justin Chatwin), in *The Return of Doctor Mysterio*.

Doctor in **86** *The Masque of Madragora* and **171** *The Girl in the Fireplace*, and impersonated by River in **212** *The Pandorica Opens/The Big Bang*). River's include Stephen Fry (who later played C in **288** *Spyfall*).

264 The Return of Doctor Mysterio

by **Steven Moffat**
One Christmas, the Doctor accidentally turns a young boy into a superhero. Their paths cross again when zip-headed aliens threaten the Earth.

■ **Where and When** New York City, at various times between the 1990s and 2010s.
■ **The Baddies** The Harmony Shoal, seen in their future in the previous episode, are plotting to colonise the Earth by inhabiting heads of state – a plan that's caught the attention of the Ghost (Justin Chatwin), known to the Doctor as Grant Gordon.
■ **Introducing...** A new body for Nardole (Matt Lucas), introduced in **263** *The Husbands of River Song*, in which he was beheaded. The Doctor has reassembled him and taken him on as a travelling companion.
■ **Look out for...** Lucy Lombard (Charity Wakefield) infiltrating Harmony Shoal's HQ, then turning to find the Doctor hiding next to her, eating sushi. "Yeah, I brought snacks," he says. "Mark of a pro."
■ **What they said** "It was comforting and heartfelt, especially with the nods to the

Doctor mourning his wife," wrote Hanh Nguyen for IndieWire on 25 December 2016. "It felt like the grounding transition we needed for the new adventures that will come in Season 10."
■ **Arcs in Space** Significant events that took place between this episode and **263** *The Husbands of River Song* are related in **270** *Extremis*.

265 The Pilot

by **Steven Moffat**
The Doctor has become a university lecturer, and offers personal tuition to a young woman who works in the canteen. But she needs extracurricular assistance when something starts to follow her...

■ **Where and When** St Luke's University, Bristol, 2016 and 2017. Also: Sydney, Australia in 2017, the "other end of the universe, 23 million years in the future", and somewhere in the thick of the Dalek-Movellan war, in the past.
■ **The Baddies** A puddle of sentient oil.
■ **Introducing...** Bill Potts (Pearl Mackie), a young woman who's been in foster care and always wanted to go to university. In her spare time, while working at St Luke's, she went to lectures – including ones given

"If you're from another planet, why would you name your box in English?" BILL

by the Doctor, who's been teaching there for over 70 years.
■ **Look out for...** Bill guessing the TARDIS is a time machine when in fact it's just gone to Australia – then discovering it *is* a time machine.
■ **What they said** "If the companion is meant to be a surrogate for the audience, Bill is perfect at this juncture in the show's life," wrote *Entertainment Weekly*'s Nivea Serrao on 15 April 2017, "because not only have viewers become more sophisticated... but we're more aware of the Doctor's history – especially with the show's recent run, which has been making a lot of references to classic *Who*."
■ **Arcs in Space** The Dalek-Movellan war was originally described in **104** *Destiny of the Daleks*. The 'Out of Order' sign on the TARDIS is the one used in **27** *The War Machines*. Mystery surrounds the occupant of a high-security vault in the depths of the university, guarded by the Doctor and Nardole...

Above inset Nardole (Matt Lucas) is the Doctor's batman in *The Pilot*.

Left Bill Potts (Pearl Mackie) joins the TARDIS crew.

The Doctor and Bill encounter emojibots in *Smile*.

266 Smile

by Frank Cottrell–Boyce

Bill is thrilled when the TARDIS lands in a bucolic landscape, with a futuristic building on the horizon. Which is good. Because she doesn't want to be unhappy. Not where she and the Doctor are going.

■ **Where and When** One of the Earth's first colonies... many thousands of years in the future, during the third industrial revolution, when the settlers have cracked the secret of human happiness.

■ **The Baddies** The nano robot "vardies" and their android interfaces. They've started interpreting their mission to keep humans happy in a rather unusual way.

■ **Look out for...** "I'm happy, hope you're happy too," mutters the Doctor, quoting David Bowie's (thematically appropriate) 1980 hit *Ashes to Ashes*. Mentions of the Doctor's inability to "pass by" refer to the Parable of the Good Samaritan in the Gospel of Luke.

■ **Where else have I seen...** Mina Anwar (playing Goodthing) was Gita Chandra in *The Sarah Jane Adventures*. (See pages 154-155.)

■ **What they said** Describing Bill as a "scene-stealing character", *The Daily Telegraph*'s Michael Hogan praised this story on 22 April 2014 for being "light of touch, packed with ideas and neat gimmicks, lovely writing, lots of heart and just scary enough. Textbook *Doctor Who*."

■ **Arcs in Space** Bill notices the TARDIS' police-box outer shell invites calls for assistance, realising that the Doctor will never refuse one. She also notes "alien birds" in the sky, referencing **1** *100,000 BC* (aka *An Unearthly Child*). The Doctor says that "Earth was evacuated. There were a number of ships. I've bumped into a few of them over years" – referencing **23** *The Ark*, **132** *Frontios* and **158** *The End of the World*. He also admits that he cheats at chess, as seen in **154** *The Curse of Fenric*.

267 Thin Ice

by Sarah Dollard

Landing in the wrong city at the wrong time, the Doctor faces something strange beneath the frozen Thames – and a dilemma that cuts to the heart of an empire.

■ **Where and When** Regency London, 4 February 1814. The day before the end of the "last great frost fair", with stalls and attractions on the ice-locked Thames. There's even an elephant!

■ **The Baddies** Lord Sutcliffe (Nicholas Burns), aristocratic exploiter of all he surveys.

■ **Introducing...** The Doctor redefines his mission for a new age: "I serve at the pleasure of the human race." (Bill will remind him of this in **276** *Twice Upon a Time*.) This would seem to be the start of a loose trilogy of stories with anti-capitalist themes.

■ **Look out for...** The Doctor and Bill's conversation about situational ethics while on the ice is phenomenally written and played. Also: the Doctor turning round and punching Sutcliffe for being racist to Bill, after first advising her to watch her temper.

■ **What they said** Writing for *New York* magazine on 29 April 2017, Ross Ruediger was impressed. "Racism, climate change, income inequality, and redistribution of wealth: It's rare enough for *Doctor Who* to tackle one such issue in an episode, let alone *four* hot-button topics of the day... It's simultaneously fantastical and disturbing, a triumph of idea and execution coming together flawlessly."

■ **Arcs in Space** The Doctor admits to having been at this specific frost fair before – with River Song, according to **218** *A Good Man Goes To War*, and he offered Clara a trip "to see the Thames frozen over" in **247** *The Caretaker*. The Doctor's joke when Bill asks about

The Doctor dons diving gear as he and Bill find something strange beneath the Thames in *Thin Ice*.

The Landlord (David Suchet) is desperate to preserve his daughter Eliza (Mariah Gale) in *Knock Knock*.

changing history by treading on a butterfly (see also **180** *The Shakespeare Code*) finds even greater expression in **305** *Space Babies*. The Doctor reuses his 'Dr Basil Disco' pseudonym from **258** *The Zygon Invasion/The Zygon Inversion*. He also says his screwdriver is sonic because "it makes a noise", as in **199** *The Next Doctor*.

268 Knock Knock

by Mike Bartlett

To let: large, six-bedroomed house. Great location. Reasonable rent. Strict conditions apply. Landlord's family on site. Beware things that go knock in the night.

■ **Where and When** Suburban Bristol, where Bill and her friends have rented a new place to stay.

■ **The Baddies** Their unnamed, genially sinister landlord (David Suchet), who seems to be protecting something. Plus alien parasites, dubbed "dryads" by the Doctor because "I can't just call them lice."

■ **Where else have I seen…** Not a person, but a place. Bill's digs are, in part, the same Newport pile used for Wester Drumlins in **186** *Blink*.

■ **Look out for…** The similarity between the two equally spooky domiciles is underlined when Shireen complains about "this freaky *Scooby-Doo* house" – when Larry (Finlay Robertson) described the deserted Wester Drumlins as "Scooby-Doo's house" in *Blink*!

■ **What they said** "The ordinary is made terrifying: there's pace, chills, suspense, a charismatic villain and – dear god – a house that eats people," quaked Dan Martin for *The Guardian* on 6 May 2017. "This is a mystery that works within its own logic – a beautiful, tragic story about

the things a boy will do for his mother."

■ **Arcs in Space** Bill pretends the Doctor is her grandad, but he insists on the full 'grandfather', which is what Susan called him all the way from **1** *100,000 BC* (aka *An Unearthly Child*) to **10** *The Dalek Invasion of Earth*. The Doctor derides sleep as being "for tortoises", as in **71** *The Talons of Weng-Chiang*.

269 Oxygen

by Jamie Mathieson

With Nardole in tow, the Doctor and Bill set out on an urgent rescue mission that will bring them into brutal conflict with the darkness and emptiness of both outer space and a whole civilisation.

■ **Where and When** Chasm Forge, a copper ore mining space station operated by Ganymede Systems. The human crew have to buy oxygen from their employers in order to work.

■ **The Baddies** Ganymede Systems, as represented by powered robot spacesuits that have killed their occupants and are now marching around as a visual pun on 'zombie capitalism'. Or, as the Doctor puts it: "We're fighting an algorithm, a spreadsheet. Like every worker, everywhere, we're fighting the suits."

■ **Introducing…** The Doctor is injured on Chasm Forge, an injury that plays out across the next two stories.

■ **Look out for…** As the zombies in suits hand out oxygen, Ivan (Kieran Bew) briefly believes that Ellie (Katie Brayben) might still be alive. It's not even done with dialogue, just through Bew's facial expressions. Magnificent work.

■ **What they said** "Oh *Oxygen* is good… a treat of an episode that nails the funny/quirky/scary Venn Diagram of what *Doctor Who* is," wrote the *Daily Mirror*'s Daniel Jackson on 13 May 2017.

■ **Arcs in Space** This story cliffhangers into **270** *Extremis*. The TARDIS leaves Earth, despite the Doctor having sworn not to, and Nardole's erroneous belief that it can't move without fluid link K57, the latter having proved essential in **2** *The Mutants* (aka *The Daleks*). "Fear keeps you fast," says the Doctor – returning to his theme that "Fear is a superpower", as expressed in **245** *Listen*.

The Doctor faces peril outside a space station in *Oxygen*.

270 Extremis

by **Steven Moffat**

A mysterious document known as the Veritas triggers the self-destruction of everyone who reads it. The Doctor must discover its terrible secret, even if it means ruining Bill's hot date.

■ **Where and When**
Earth, 2017 – apparently. (All is not as it seems!) And the unknown planet where Missy faces her executioners.

■ **The Baddies** The Monks – robed, corpse-like creatures who are meticulously workshopping their planned invasion of Earth.

■ **Introducing...** The super-creepy Monks; this and the two following episodes comprise a trilogy focused around them.

■ **Look out for...** The Doctor refers to Pope Benedict IX – a controversial historical figure, assumed to be male – as a "lovely girl" who "wove a spell with her castanets".

■ **What they said** *Radio Times* reviewer Patrick Mulkern noted how *Extremis* "only fully makes sense at the end, and then – if your head isn't hurting too much – it's hard to resist the impulse to go back and watch again from the start."

■ **Arcs in Space** The Doctor, still blind after the events of **269** *Oxygen*, is asked by an unknown humanoid species to guard Missy's remains by placing her body in a quantum fold chamber, designed to prevent the occupant from 'relapsing' into life, "for no less than a thousand years". He has some form in this area: when the Master was executed by the Daleks in **156** the 1996 TV movie *Doctor Who*, the Seventh Doctor agreed to transport the Master's ashes to Gallifrey.

271 The Pyramid at the End of the World

by **Peter Harness** and **Steven Moffat**

A huge pyramid suddenly appears in an area disputed by three world superpowers. Meanwhile, in London, a lab leak is about to release a devastating biohazard.

■ **Where and When** Earth, 2017.

■ **The Baddies** The Monks again, putting their plan into real-world action. To save itself, will humanity accept their 'benign' dictatorship? Really, though, the zombie-like creatures just want to be loved. (Aww.) So why do they look like corpses? To fit in with humans, apparently: "You *are* corpses to us," they explain.

■ **Farewell to...** the Doctor's visual impairment. Although he finds several ways to get around it, it's nearly the cause of his demise until Bill asks the Monks to step in and cure him. Inevitably, this creates even bigger problems...

■ **Look out for...** The Monks land their pyramid in Turmezistan – the site of the radicalised Zygons' training camp when the Doctor visited it in **258** *The Zygon Invasion*. (Apparently, it sits "on the strategic intersection of the three most powerful armies on Earth" – the US, Russia and the People's Republic of China.)

■ **What they said** "Under the current *Doctor Who* regime," *Guardian* blogger Dan Martin observed on 27 May 2017, "Earth tends to get invaded less in favour of smaller, emotional stories. This was certainly no *Christmas Invasion*. But when they go for it, they *go* for it. My only real criticism is that the philosophical soliloquies don't half go on a bit."

■ **Arcs in Space** The Doctor is President of Earth in times of crisis; see **252** *Death in Heaven* and **258** *The Zygon Invasion*. He also assumes that role via the Gold Protocol in **303** *The Giggle*. Oh, and he's also technically Lord President of Gallifrey from time to time, as seen in many stories from **88** *The Deadly Assassin* to **262** *Hell Bent*.

272 The Lie of the Land

by **Toby Whithouse**

The Monks have rewritten humanity's memory of Earth history – and their chief cheerleader appears to be the Doctor!

■ **Where and When** Earth, 2017.

■ **The Baddies** A handful of Monks. That's all it takes to rule the world when

Above inset
One of the creepy monks in *Extremis*.

Above
Nardole, the Doctor and Bill explore the depths of the Vatican.

The UN Secretary General (Togo Igawa) and Col Brabbit (Eben Young) join the Doctor and Bill to gaze upon *The Pyramid at the End of the World*.

you've established psychic control over the entire population.

■ **Look out for…** The manner in which Bill passes the Doctor's "test" of true intentions is surprising, to say the least. Nardole neutralises an enemy with a "Tarovian neck pinch" and explains that he won his hand in a game.

■ **Farewell to…** The Monks – for now, at least. They erase themselves from Earth's history; as the Doctor bitterly reflects, humanity is doomed to never learn from its mistakes.

■ **What they said** *Daily Mirror* blogger Daniel Jackson described how Missy's "game of hot and cold with her sparring partner" – ie, the Doctor – together with her "mentions of pushing a small girl into a volcano and piano interludes create a *Silence Of The Lambs* [sic] vibe that I could watch an entire episode of."

Inside the Monks' London pyramid in *The Lie of the Land*.

The Doctor meets warrior turned manservant Friday (Richard Ashton) in *Empress of Mars*.

■ **Arcs in Space** At last we learn it's Missy – "going cold turkey from being bad" – in the quantum fold chamber, aka the Vault, originally established in **265** *The Pilot*. Bill's fixation on the idea of the mother she never knew becomes a powerful psychic force, capable of defeating evil. Ruby Sunday experiences a similar phenomenon in **311** *Empire of Death*.

273 Empress of Mars

by **Mark Gatiss**

Visiting NASA, the Doctor, Bill and Nardole are shocked to see the words "God Save the Queen" written in English on the surface of Mars… in 1881, apparently.

■ **Where and When** Earth in the 21st century, and Mars in 1881.

■ **The Baddies** Colonialism, mostly, as embodied by Neville Catchlove (Ferdinand Kingsley). This British Army captain is an utter rotter – greedy, cowardly, narcissistic, scheming and cruel. By contrast, the noble Ice Warriors stand on the brink of the "Martian golden age", in which they will become a galactic force for peace.

■ **Introducing…** Iraxxa, Ice Warrior Queen. Played by Adele Lynch, she's the first female of the species to appear on televised *Doctor Who*.

■ **Look out for…** The portrait of Queen Victoria. It's Pauline Collins, who played the Empress in **169** *Tooth and Claw*.

■ **Where else have I heard…** Ysanne Churchman, who'd just turned 92 when this story was screened, reprised her voice role as Alpha Centauri from **61** *The Curse of Peladon* and **73** *The Monster of Peladon*. (She'd also provided arachnid voices for **74** *Planet of the Spiders*.)

■ **Arcs in Space** The Doctor helps Iraxxa to establish contact with other space-going nations, and the call is answered by a being from Alpha Centauri. Is this the very same ambassador who will go on to work with the Ice Warriors in **61** *The Curse of Peladon*? In another tribute to the Third Doctor's era, Sergeant Major Peach (Glenn Speers) observes that "RHIP" – 'rank has its privileges' – echoing Mike Yates' words to Benton in **60** *Day of the Daleks*.

Queen Iraxxa (Adele Lynch).

274 The Eaters of Light

by **Rona Munro**

Bill has always wanted to know what happened to the Ninth Legion of the Roman Empire. The dangerous truth lies on the other side of a gate inside a cairn…

■ **Where and When** Aberdeen – or what *will* be Aberdeen – in the 2nd century AD.

■ **The Baddies** The Eaters of Light – extradimensional locusts that intrude into other dimensions to feed on their light.

■ **Introducing…** When Bill becomes aware of the TARDIS translation system, she's the first person to note that it also tweaks the listener's perceptions (and ours), so the words match the movements of the speaker's mouth.

■ **Look out for…** Bill awkwardly breaking it to Lucius (Brian Vernel) that she only likes women, only to discover the Romans regard bisexuality as 'normal'.

■ **What they said** "What's often rewarding about *Doctor Who* is that – beyond rewrites, budget constraints, casting and performance – it allows an authorial voice to sing through," Patrick Mulkern wrote for *Radio Times* on 17 June 2017. "It happened for [Rona] Munro in 1989's *Survival* and does so again in *The Eaters of Light*."

■ **Arcs in Space** The Doctor refers to having lived in Roman Britain. This has never been seen on TV, but the Doctor visited 2nd-century Britain in **212** *The Pandorica Opens/The Big Bang*, as well as 1st-century Rome (in **12** *The Romans*) and Pompeii (in **190** *The Fires of Pompeii*), where he met someone strongly resembling his twelfth incarnation.

Right
Bill's awful fate is revealed to the Doctor in *World Enough and Time/The Doctor Falls*.

Below right
Missy and the Master form an uneasy alliance.

275 World Enough and Time/The Doctor Falls

(two episodes) by **Steven Moffat**

As a test, the Doctor sends Missy to save a spaceship that's falling into a black hole. But terrible things are occurring further down the ship – as Bill discovers to her cost…

■ **Where and When** A vast colony ship, about 400 miles long, date unknown. The time-dilation effects of the black hole mean that time passes much more slowly at one end of the ship than the other.

■ **The Baddies** The colony ship originated on Mondas – which, as we know, was destroyed during the events of **29** *The Tenth Planet*. It took off before the Cybermen were created – but parallel evolution means the Cybermen are being created here again, in their Mondasian design.

■ **Farewell to…** Two versions of the Master. It happens that the ship chosen for Missy's test has another incarnation of the Master (John Simm) stranded on it, and this is the last we see of both.

■ **Look out for…** The interplay between the two Masters is superb, particularly when they both get into the shuttlecraft and use the same line on Nardole.

■ **What they said** "It was an immensely satisfying, packed, heart string tugging conclusion," wrote Daniel Jackson for the *Daily Mirror* on 2 July 2017. "Capaldi simply shines this week. His Doctor has never had a better episode, filled with emotion and defiance."

■ **Arcs in Space** When taking on the Doctor's mantle, Missy introduces herself as 'Doctor Who' and the Doctor decides he likes it and uses it. It's previously been suggested this may indeed be the Doctor's name: WOTAN uses it in **27** *The War Machines* and the Doctor signs his name as 'Doctor W.' in **32** *The Underwater Menace*.

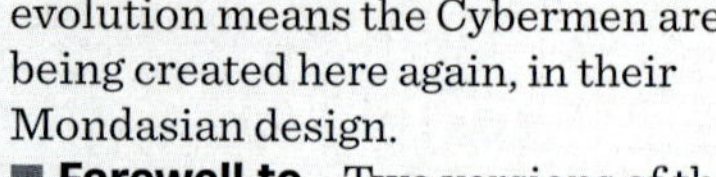

Legionnaire Kar (Rebecca Benson) runs into Nardole and the Doctor in *The Eaters of Light*.

Left
Ben (Jared Garfield), the First Doctor (David Bradley) and Polly (Lily Travers) at Snowcap Base in *Twice Upon a Time*.

Above
Two Doctors on a First World War battlefield.

276 Twice Upon a Time

by Steven Moffat

On the verge of regeneration, but also on the verge of giving up altogether, the Doctor stumbles upon his first incarnation – and both are swept up by a vast spaceship…

■ **Where and When** The South Pole, 1986 – crossing over with the final few scenes of **29** *The Tenth Planet*. Villengard in the far future. Ypres, 1914.

■ **The Baddies** The glass avatars, created on New Earth (seen in **168** *New Earth* and **181** *Gridlock*). They insist on taking the Captain (Mark Gatiss), a displaced First World War soldier, back to the moment of his death – which the Doctors refuse to allow.

■ **Farewell to…** It's the end of the road for the Twelfth Doctor, as he grapples with the question of whether to go on. We also get our last glimpses of Bill, Nardole and Clara.

■ **Look out for…** The Captain saying that he'd made his peace with death, but that, after being reprieved, "I'm not ready any more. I've lost the idea of it. That's the trouble with hope. Makes one awfully frightened."

■ **Where else have I seen…** David Bradley, as the First Doctor, previously played Solomon in **227** *Dinosaurs on a Spaceship*.

The new Doctor (Jodie Whittaker).

> ## "The silly old universe. The more I save it, the more it needs saving."
> ### THE DOCTOR

(He was cast in this episode due to having already played William Hartnell in the 2013 docudrama *An Adventure in Space and Time*.)

■ **Arcs in Space** The Doctor travels to Villengard to consult Rusty, the 'Good Dalek' created by his intervention in **243** *Into the Dalek*.

The Captain (Mark Gatiss), the Doctor and Bill in the original TARDIS (complete with astral map).

The Doctor is reunited with 'Rusty'.

The THIRTEENTH DOCTOR

Jodie Whittaker
Stories 277–300, 2018–22

"Oh, brilliant!" She started out her new life by falling into a train – and into the lives of the 'fam' that she gathered around her. She ate danger for breakfast. (Well, cereal. Or croissants. Never mind, it's not important.) And everything she thought she knew about her past would come unravelled, when the story of the Timeless Child was finally told.

The new Doctor (Jodie Whittaker, far left) and her 'fam': Yaz (Mandip Gill), Ryan (Tosin Cole), Graham (Bradley Walsh) and Grace (Sharon D Clarke).

277 The Woman Who Fell to Earth

by Chris Chibnall

The Doctor falls into a train, sees a lot of Sheffield, and finds herself a new family while trying to come to terms with no longer being a white-haired Scotsman – or any sort of man.

■ **Where and When** Sheffield, 2018.

■ **The Baddies** Tim Shaw, aka Tzim-Sha of the Stenza (Samuel Oatley), the wannabe scavenger-hunt winner who sticks his molar trophies into his face. (Bleurgh.)

■ **Introducing…** The Thirteenth Doctor. Her homemade, Sheffield-steel-manufactured "Swiss army knife without the knife" sonic screwdriver. Her charity-shop-sourced outfit. Her 'fam': Graham O'Brien (Bradley Walsh), his step-grandson Ryan Sinclair (Tosin Cole) and his former schoolfriend turned police constable Yasmin Khan (Mandip Gill). Plus Grace O'Brien (Sharon D Clarke) – Ryan's grandmother, and Graham's wife (formerly his chemo nurse).

■ **Look out for…** The saddest moment might not be the most obvious; it's Rahul (Amit Shah) dying before he can get closure about his sister's disappearance. But will viewers ever get closure? Will the Doctor find Asha and rescue her from stasis? Let's hope so.

■ **What they said** "The new Doctor and her team… have heart and soul, and are set against a comforting background of South Yorkshire women – especially Ryan's nan – talking common sense as alien life and electrical pulses erupt around them. Think of it as Happy Uncanny Valley. I hope intersectionalist feminist propaganda is always this much fun." So said Lucy Mangan in *The Guardian* on 7 October 2018.

■ **Arcs in Space** The Doctor has a Northern accent again – as did her ninth incarnation, something that was queried in 157 *Rose*. "My ship uses a particular type of energy," the Doctor explains, hoping to track her disappeared TARDIS. Probably she means artron energy, first mentioned in 88 *The Deadly Assassin*. Whereupon she and the fam teleport into…

278 The Ghost Monument

by Chris Chibnall

The Doctor and her fam, caught up in the final stage of the last ever rally of the 12 galaxies, have to cross a deserted planet to get to the eponymous Ghost Monument… aka the TARDIS.

■ **Where and When** Desolation, a world with three suns. Date unknown.

Ryan, Yaz, the Doctor and Graham on the planet Desolation in *The Ghost Monument*.

■ **The Baddies** The planet itself – "turned cruel" by the Stenza, with a toxic atmosphere and killing water. Deadly SniperBots.

■ **Introducing…** The Timeless Child. We don't know what it is. The Doctor doesn't know what it is. But the deadly living-bandage-things (aka 'Remnants', though not named within the story) know it's deep inside her, hidden even from the Doctor herself. Plus: a reformed, redecorated TARDIS, with no St John's Ambulance badge on the outside and a new custard-cream dispenser on the inside.

■ **Look out for…** It seems slightly odd that smoking, in the form of the cigar flourished by Epzo (Shaun Dooley), saves the day. At least younger viewers will learn a bit of chemistry in the process.

■ **Where else have I seen…** Ian Gelder, out of vision here as the Remnants' voices, will be seen in 293 *Can You Hear Me?* as the strangely fingered pseudo-god Zellin.

Civil rights campaigner Rosa Parks (Vinette Robinson) in *Rosa*.

■ **Arcs in Space** The Doctor's been in a race in space before; see **127** *Enlightenment*. She uses a Venusian martial arts move against Epzo – as originally practiced by her third incarnation, beginning with **54** *Inferno*. The Stenza (from **277** *The Woman Who Fell to Earth*) kidnapped scientists and forced them to find new ways of destruction, destroying this planet in the process.

279 Rosa

by **Malorie Blackman** and **Chris Chibnall**

The fam get swept up in one of the most important moments of the American civil rights movement: when African-American Rosa Parks refused to give up her seat on a bus for a white passenger.

■ **Where and When** Montgomery, USA, 1955.

■ **The Baddies** Space-racist Krasko (Joshua Bowman) is the headliner, but he's supported by millions of everyday Earth racists.

■ **Look out for...** Previously SS *Pentallian* crewember Abi in **184** *42*, Vinette Robinson's performance as Rosa Parks is both powerful and real. Look out, too, for Graham's pain when he's forced into a 'baddie' role on the bus, realising that as a white man he can't make this about him or his comfort.

■ **Where else have I seen...** Morgan Deare (playing Arthur) was last seen as CIA Agent Hawke in **146** *Delta and the Bannermen*.

■ **What they said** On 21 October 2018, *The Independent*'s Ed Power observed:

"it's easy to imagine teachers years from now screening *Rosa* to their students, as a primer to a tumultuous period in US history. It gladdens the heart – but diehard Dalek devotees may be relieved when the series reverts to having the Time Lord tangle with rubber monsters."

■ **Arcs in Space** Krasko was imprisoned in the Stormcage Containment Facility – which once held River Song, too, as established in **212** *The Pandorica Opens*. Again like River, he has a vortex manipulator – as originally worn by Captain Jack Harkness in **164** *The Empty Child/The Doctor Dances*. The Doctor can show moments from history through the TARDIS, recalling the Time and Space Visualiser last seen in **16** *The Chase*.

280 Arachnids in the UK

by **Chris Chibnall**

Something's wrong with the spider ecosystem in South Yorkshire.

■ **Where and When** Sheffield, 2018.

■ **The Baddies** Would you prefer to go up against businessman Jack Robertson (Chris Noth) or the giant mother spider? Take your pick...

■ **Introducing...** Yaz's family: Hakim (Ravin J Ganatra), Najia (Shobna Gulati) and Sonya Khan (Bhavnisha Parmar).

■ **Look out for...** "A giant spider just smashed through my bathtub and took out my bodyguard, Kevin!" Now that's what you call a *Doctor Who* moment.

■ **What they said** "I've always relished a monstrous menace in the now, a few shivers and jump scares, a bit of social comment – and a smattering of mirth. *Arachnids in the UK* has it all," wrote *Radio Times*' Patrick Mulkern, giving the episode a five-star review on 2 November 2018.

■ **Arcs in Space** The Doctor has brought the fam home to a point half an hour after they left in **277** *The Woman Who Fell to Earth*. The spiders turn out to be mutants created after big business fills a disused coal mine with waste; the mutant maggots in **69** *The Green Death* were created in much the same way. Spiders previously cocooned people in their larders in **74** *Planet of the Spiders*. Jack Robertson will return in **296** *Revolution of the Daleks*.

Above inset Jack Robertson (Chris Noth) is responsible for some unusual *Arachnids in the UK*.

Left The Doctor and her fam go spider-hunting.

Left
The Doctor is attended to by Chief Medic Astos (Brett Goldstein) in *The Tsuranga Conundrum*.

Below inset Beware the P'Ting!

281 The Tsuranga Conundrum

by **Chris Chibnall**

Waking up on a hospital spaceship after getting too close to a sonic mine, the fam has to deal with an intruder that threatens to eat the vessel from underneath them…

■ **Where and When** Seffilun 27 in one of the junk galaxies, and a quad zone rescue craft heading from the border with the Constant Division to its docking point at space station Resus One. The 67th century, which the Doctor says is a "bit tricky in the middle."

■ **The Baddies** A P'Ting, a gremlin-like creature that can survive in space, eats anything inorganic and hungers for power sources. Imagine the Xenomorph crossed with Disney's Stitch and you're getting close.

■ **Introducing…** This is the first story to depict a character giving birth – Amy having had Melody just before we join the events of 218 *A Good Man Goes to War*.

■ **Look out for…** The Doctor sets out her credentials by listing all the things she's a doctor of: "Medicine, science, engineering, candyfloss, Lego, philosophy, music, problems, people, hope. Mostly hope."

■ **What they said** Chris Chibnall noted in **Doctor Who Magazine** issue 531 (December 2018) that the P'Ting was christened by writer Tim Price: "He came up with a brilliant and unusual name for the alien and we all loved it… [but] Tim was ultimately too busy to work on the show."

■ **Arcs in Space** Ryan continues to be troubled by his relationship with his estranged father, whom we will meet in 287 *Resolution*. The Doctor previously encountered a hostile alien invasion of a pristine Earth facility containing 'medtechs' in 76 *The Ark in Space*.

282 Demons of the Punjab

by **Vinay Patel**

Investigating a family mystery, Yaz leads the fam back to the Partition of India to discover the truth about her grandmother, while unrest brews and aliens wait for the bloodshed to start…

■ **Where and When** Present-day Sheffield, and the area around the new border between Pakistan and India on 17 and 18 August 1947.

■ **The Baddies** The Thijarians, legendary assassins who appear to be disrupting the mixed-faith marriage between Umbreen (Amita Suman) and Prem (Shane Zaza). But this is a red herring – the race has reformed to watch over those who die alone. The real issue here is the violence that arose from Partition.

■ **Introducing…** This marks the Doctor's first on-screen visit to Southern Asia, although a reference to the TARDIS disguised as a howdah in 17 *The Time Meddler* suggests an earlier trip to India.

■ **Where else have I seen…** Leena Dhingra, who plays the older version of Yaz's grandmother Umbreen, previously appeared as housemaid Miss Chandrakala in 194 *The Unicorn and the Wasp*.

■ **Listen out for…** A special version of the theme music plays over the end credits, following the motifs and style of the episode's emotional score by Segun Akinola.

■ **Arcs in Space** After being party to a wedding being called off in 178 *The Runaway Bride* and being the groom in 224 *The Wedding of River Song*, this time the Doctor gets to officiate. Despite her claim, regarding her ceremonial henna tattoo, that she "never did this when I was a man," the snake motif on the Third Doctor's arm in 51 *Spearhead from Space* suggests otherwise.

283 Kerblam!

by **Pete McTighe**

A call for help from the galaxy's biggest retailer finds Team TARDIS getting jobs at a near-automated fulfilment centre – and uncovering a plot to make the next delivery the last post.

■ **Where and When** The headquarters of Kerblam! on the moon of human colony world Kandoka, hundreds of years in the future.

■ **The Baddies** Though the computer system running Kerblam! is the prime

The *Demons of the Punjab* are actually alien Thijarians.

Special deliveries from some deadly robots in *Kerblam!*

suspect, assisted by sour-faced exec Jarva Slade (Callum Dixon), the real culprit is cleaner Charlie Duffy (Leo Flanagan), an anti-automation terrorist who plans to deliver thousands of packages containing explosive bubble wrap simultaneously and undermine Kandoka's reliance on robotic systems.

■ **Farewell to…** The last appearance to date of a fez, the Eleventh Doctor's signature headgear, finally delivered by the Kerblam! delivery robot – presumably ordered after his first one was destroyed by River Song in **212** *The Pandorica Opens/The Big Bang*.

■ **Look out for…** Ryan delightedly popping the bubble wrap from the Doctor's package, little realising the danger he might be in.

■ **What they said** Julie Hesmondhalgh, appearing as Kerblam!'s head of people, Judy Maddox, told *TV and Satellite Week* on 17 November 2018: "Sometimes you get what I call 'one-line anxiety'. Jodie [Whittaker] is reeling off all this dialogue and then you come to your one line and you worry you're going to mess it up."

■ **Arcs in Space** The Doctor namedrops Agatha Christie in reference to **194** *The Unicorn and the Wasp*, while the design of the Kerblam! delivery robots and TeamMates is reminiscent of the Dums, Vocs and SuperVocs in **90** *The Robots of Death*.

284 The Witchfinders

by **Joy Wilkinson**

The TARDIS arrives amid the 17th-century witch trials. With King James taking personal charge, the Doctor must fend off sentient mud and a fanatical landowner.

■ **Where and When** The village of Bilhurst Cragg, near Pendle Hill in Lancashire, sometime in the early 17th century.

■ **The Baddies** Becka Savage (Siobhan Finneran), the local landowner and obsessive witch-hunter, who's intent on covering her connection to the Morax, sentient mud that plans to fill the bodies of the whole human race.

■ **Introducing…** With the Thirteenth Doctor taking her first steps into pre-20th-century history, this marks the first time her gender becomes a major stumbling block, leading to an appointment with the ducking stool.

■ **What they said** Joy Wilkinson felt a personal connection to the material, telling *TV and Satellite Week* on 24 November 2018 that she'd "always been interested in heroines who aren't bound by ideas of what women should do… So I've been in my element on *Doctor Who*."

■ **Look out for…** Having taken on the mantle of Witchfinder General, Graham (Bradley Walsh) inherits the impressive hat that goes with the job – something of which the Second Doctor would be envious, judging by his taste for millinery in **31** *The Highlanders*.

■ **Arcs in Space** The Tenth Doctor had past encounters with Elizabeth I in **180** *The Shakespeare Code* and **240** *The Day of the Doctor*, so maybe it's for the best that the TARDIS was drawn off-course this time; instead, the Thirteenth Doctor meets James I (Alan Cumming). The ducking stool echoes another time the Doctor was almost executed for witchcraft – in **59** *The Dæmons*.

Yaz, the Doctor and Willa Twiston (Tilly Steele) in *The Witchfinders*.

Left
The Doctor finds a world beyond a mirror in *It Takes You Away*.

Below inset
The Solitract adopts an amphibian disguise.

285 It Takes You Away

by Ed Hime

Young Hanne's father has gone missing from their log cabin. There's a creature in the woods, and a strange other dimension behind the bedroom mirror…

■ **Where and When** A creepy house in rural Norway, 2018; the alpaca farm close by; the Anti-zone; the Solitract Plane.

■ **The Baddies** None as such, but Ribbons of the Seven Stomachs (Kevin Eldon) is a shady denizen of the Anti-zone, trading information. Flesh moths eat just that, and the Solitract is "the maddest, most beautiful thing" the Doctor has ever experienced. A conscious universe expelled from existence, the Solitract's desire to be part of the normal universe will destroy the fabric of spacetime – and it manifests as a frog on a chair.

■ **Introducing…** An emotional air-punch as Ryan calls Graham "grandad" for the very first time – and means it.

■ **Look out for…** The revelation that Graham always packs a cheese-and-pickle sandwich whenever he leaves the TARDIS.

■ **What they said** "*It Takes You Away* is thoughtful and big-hearted, blending scares and surrealism with aplomb," said *The Independent*'s Ed Power on 2 December 2018.

■ **Arcs in Space** Being presented with a Solitract-generated avatar of Grace brings Graham and Ryan to an understanding, following her death in 277 *The Woman Who Fell to Earth*. The Doctor's delight at the nearby alpaca farm having a gift shop (little or otherwise) echoes the Tenth Doctor's retail enthusiasms, first expressed in 168 *New Earth*. Ryan's spikiness with Hanne (Eleanor Wallwork) on the subject of missing parents will be clarified when we meet his own absent father in 287 *Resolution*.

286 The Battle of Ranskoor Av Kolos

by Chris Chibnall

Nine planetary distress calls bring Team TARDIS to a barren world, where an old enemy waits… and Graham contemplates stepping over a line that will change him forever.

■ **Where and When** The planet Ranskoor Av Kolos ('Disintegrator of the Soul'), 5425.

■ **The Baddies** Thought to have perished in 277 *The Woman Who Fell to Earth*, Tim Shaw… sorry, Tzim-Sha, cruel Stenza warrior, survived his first run-in with the Doctor and pitched up on Ranskoor, 3,407 years later. He has a collection of miniaturised worlds, not unlike the Captain in 99 *The Pirate Planet*.

■ **Farewell to…** With Tzim-Sha taking a very long sleep in a very small stasis pod, this is the final time a Stenza warrior darkens the Doctor's door.

■ **Look out for…** "None of us know for sure what's out there. That's why we keep looking. Keep your faith. Travel hopefully. The universe'll surprise you… constantly." The Doctor's parting homily is a perfect mission statement for the entire Whoniverse.

■ **What they said** "There's a curiously old-school feel to much of the episode," said **Doctor Who Magazine** reviewer Paul Kirkley in issue 534 (February 2019). "Take the opening scene. Not only is it filmed in a (be still my beating heart) proper *Doctor Who* quarry, it features two random aliens with funny names and hairstyles having an intense theological debate about their space religion and saying things like 'It cannot be!'"

■ **Arcs in Space** Plotlines aplenty come home to roost with the return of Tzim-Sha. After coming to an understanding with Ryan in 285 *It Takes You Away*, Graham is almost consumed by his thirst for revenge, after Grace's murder by the Stenza warrior in *The Woman Who Fell to Earth*. The Doctor calls the TARDIS her

Paltraki (Mark Addy) joins the fam on a world of crashed spaceships in *The Battle of Ranskoor Av Kolos*.

Left
The Doctor in *Spyfall*.

Right
A new look for the Master (Sacha Dhawan).

Below inset
Traitorous tech magnate Daniel Barton (Lenny Henry).

"ghost monument", its mythical name in **278** *The Ghost Monument*, and recalls how her beloved ship once towed Earth across the universe (in **198** *The Stolen Earth/Journey's End*) and regressed a Slitheen to an egg (in **165** *Boom Town*).

287 Resolution

by **Chris Chibnall**
An unlikely army of friends comes together to face an impossible opponent from the planet Skaro.

■ **Where and When** Earth, 1 January 2019 – the same date *Resolution* was broadcast.
■ **The Baddies** "The mutated remnants of a warring race, genetically created and housed within a metal case, designed to be a relentless killing machine." In other words, a recon scout Dalek, lying dormant on Earth since its defeat in the ninth century by the Order of the Custodians.

The recon scout Dalek in *Resolution*.

■ **Look out for...** Call Centre Polly (Laura Evelyn), breaking the news to the Doctor that UNIT operations have been suspended due to "financial disputes". It seems those five rounds rapid don't help the bottom line.
■ **Introducing...** The recon scout Dalek, its resident mutant and grungy, re-engineered casing providing both DNA and blueprint for Jack Robertson's 'Defence Drone' scam in **296** *Revolution of the Daleks* (the events of which start exactly 367 minutes after the end of *Resolution*).
■ **Arcs in Space** Ryan's wayward dad Aaron (Daniel Adegboyega) arrives unexpectedly to see his son, his absence from Grace's funeral in **277** *The Woman Who Fell to Earth* being noted. The Doctor wonders how long a rel is, a unit of time measurement first used by the Daleks in **177** *Army of Ghosts/Doomsday*. The TARDIS fam have experienced 19 New Year's Eve celebrations across time and space. On other New Year's celebrations, the TARDIS landed in Trafalgar Square in **21** *The Daleks' Master Plan*, the Eighth Doctor got a kiss from Grace Holloway in **156** the 1996 TV movie *Doctor Who*, and the Doctor, Yaz and Dan will spend New Year's 2021-22 with Daleks again in **298** *Eve of the Daleks*.

288 Spyfall

(two episodes) by **Chris Chibnall**
Engaged on Her Majesty's Secret Service, the Doctor and co investigate the death of British secret agents in an espionage epic hinting at deep-buried secrets.

■ **Where and When** A globe-trot around space and time, from contemporary London, the Australian Outback, San Francisco, London 1834, Paris 1943, and the sinister realm of the Kasaavin. Oh, and for good measure – the devastation of Gallifrey.
■ **The Baddies** Tech bro and compromised secret agent Daniel Barton (Lenny Henry), allied with the extradimensional Kasaavin to transform humanity into biological hard drives. However, a big "Oh!" is reserved for the reveal that agent 'O' (Sacha Dhawan) is the Master. Or should that be Spy Master?
■ **Look out for...** Graham's laser shoes, featuring all the usual refinements, provide a delicious moment of deadly slapstick. Unavailable in all good toy shops.
■ **Where else have I seen...** Computing pioneer Charles Babbage is played by Mark Dexter, previously 'Dad', a parental avatar created for Charlotte Lux, in **195** *Silence in the Library/Forest of the Dead*.
■ **What they said** "Breathless, a bit silly and featuring both Nazis and 19th-century amateur inventors, this is *Doctor Who* blazing on all cylinders," decreed Ed Power in *The Independent* on 5 January 2020.
■ **Arcs in Space** The Doctor's affinity for mechanical engineering, seen in **277** *The Woman Who Fell to Earth*, is in evidence again when she gets the TARDIS up on blocks to drain the water slides, boating lake and rainforest – parts of the lido that Clara ran past in **236** *Journey to the Centre of the TARDIS*, perhaps? The Doctor and the Master's face-off atop the Eiffel Tower takes place 36 years before the Doctor and Romana ostentatiously discuss lunch there in **105** *City of Death*.

THE MASTER

They are the Master and you will obey them. The best of the Doctor's best frenemy, chosen by **Jamie Lenman**.

Below
The Master (Roger Delgado) surrenders in *Terror of the Autons*... or does he?

Outstanding

55 *Terror of the Autons* – the original and best. With its blank-faced policemen, killer troll dolls, strangling telephone cords and suffocating daffodils, this would've been a world-beater anyway. The fact that it's also the Master's debut just makes it unassailable. Roger Delgado delivers a tour de force performance here, laying out every trick in the bearded baddie's arsenal. He shrinks people! He disguises himself! He allies himself with an immensely powerful alien race and only realises his superfluousness at the last minute! The sight of factory boss McDermott (Harry Towb) being smothered by a plastic chair might easily look risible – but it's Delgado who sells it, watching on with a cold, heavy-lidded gaze.

Essential

Having possessed the body of caring Trakenite councillor Tremas, the Master (Anthony Ainley) nearly causes the unravelling of the entire causal nexus in **115** *Logopolis* – a jaw-dropping change of character. The Master was again reborn (twice!) in **187a** *Utopia*, with Derek Jacobi giving an electrifying five minutes as the villain, having shrugged off his 'Professor Yana' persona, before regenerating into the form of John Simm. As British Prime Minister 'Harold Saxon' in the subsequent story, **187b** *The Sound of Drums/Last of the Time Lords*, the Master is crueller and more insane than he's ever been, and his rejection of the Doctor's help at the last is possibly the deepest wound he's ever inflicted.

Excellent

The last thing anyone expected was an American-accented Master, but that was what we got. And it was brilliant, thanks to Eric Roberts' reptilian performance in **156** the 1996 TV movie *Doctor Who* – which emphasised the zombified nature of his predicament, taking over an ambulance driver named Bruce. **88** *The Deadly Assassin* had Peter Pratt as a skeletal wraith, skulking in the shadows instead of spinning in the spotlight, like a grinning spider in a temporal web. Michelle Gomez gave us the playful yet dangerously amoral Missy in **252** *Dark Water/Death in Heaven*, before going completely off the deep end. Then, in **275** *World Enough and Time/The Doctor Falls*, we got our longed-for multi-Master story... which went about as well for Missy and her predecessor (the Simm model) as might be expected. Finally, it's wonderful to watch Sacha Dhawan's incarnation get everything he's ever dreamed of in **300** *The Power of the Doctor* – namely, the Doctor's question-mark pullover.

The Best of the Rest

Roger Delgado's Master makes a surprisingly good vicar in **59** *The Dæmons*, while **62** *The Sea Devils* reminds us that he and the Doctor used to be friends (and possibly still could be) via a couple of touching prison scenes and a very tasty swordfight. Despite some of his appearances bordering on pantomime, Anthony Ainley's Master gets some cracking material in **129** *The Five Doctors* and proves a great foil for Michael Jayston's Valeyard in **143** *The Trial of a Time Lord*, before enjoying arguably his finest hour in **155** *Survival*. If you're a fan of John Simm's portrayal you might enjoy **202** *The End of Time*, in which he turns everyone on the planet into himself. And there's no denying the shocking impact of Sacha Dhawan's debut in **288** *Spyfall*.

“You see, Doctor, you’re my intellectual equal. Almost. I have so few worthy opponents.”
THE MASTER, *TERROR OF THE AUTONS*

289 Orphan 55

by Ed Hime

Graham has been collecting tokens for a free luxury holiday. But if something seems too good to be true, it probably is.

■ **Where and When** Tranquility Spa, a luxury holiday resort unwisely located on Orphan 55, an otherwise uninhabitable planet.

■ **The Baddies** Within hours of the fam's arrival, the Dregs – Orphan 55's surviving indigenous life forms – break through the ostensibly impregnable force barrier separating the resort from a nuclear winter.

■ **Farewell to…** Human life on Earth, if the Doctor's words in the final scene aren't heeded.

■ **Look out for…** The Doctor invokes her second incarnation's occasional catchphrase, "When I say run… Run!" – introduced in **30** *The Power of the Daleks* and also used by other Doctors, such as the Fifth in **116** *Castrovalva*.

■ **What they said** "Sprinkled with innovation, tension and food for thought," enthused *Radio Times* critic Patrick Mulkern on 12 January 2020. "It smacks of *Benidorm* meets *Aliens* with perhaps a tiny touch of *The Truman Show*."

■ **Arcs in Space** The Doctor deduces their true location from the signage in a disused underground railway, as in **143** *The Trial of a Time Lord*. Yaz has noticed that the Doctor has been "mardy" since she discovered that the Time Lords have been wiped out in **288** *Spyfall*. (Not that she's told the fam.)

The Dregs have inherited a ruined planet in *Orphan 55*.

Right
The Skithra Queen (Anjli Mohindra) in *Nikola Tesla's Night of Terror*.

Below inset Nikola Tesla (Goran Višnjić).

290 Nikola Tesla's Night of Terror

by Nina Metivier

Aliens have come to Earth to find the greatest human inventor of the early 20th century, and you'd better believe Thomas Edison is unhappy it's not him they want.

■ **Where and When** 1903, starting at Niagara Falls and moving to "New York… where the modern world begins", then Earth's orbit.

■ **The Baddies** The Skithra, a ship of scavengers led by their murderous "queen of shreds and patches" (Anjli Mohindra), flying a stolen ship and using second-hand guns, including some stolen from space-faring Silurians (as in **227** *Dinosaurs on a Spaceship*).

■ **Look out for…** The scenes between Bradley Walsh and Anjli Mohindra are a fun role-reversal. In *The Sarah Jane Adventures: Day of the Clown, she* was a heroic companion and *he* was the big bad under heavy make-up. (See pages 154-155.)

■ **Where else have I seen…** Robert Glenister (Edison) was both Major Salateen and his android duplicate in **135** *The Caves of Androzani*.

■ **What they said** Devan Cogan of *Entertainment Weekly* (19 January 2020) was delighted with this story, claiming to be "a sucker for insane interstellar scorpions who can shoot lasers from their tails and want to kidnap Nikola Tesla so he can help them conquer the galaxy. Inject that nonsense directly into my veins!!!"

■ **Arcs in Space** "Have you ever seen a dead planet?" teases the Skithra Queen. "More than you can possibly imagine," replies the Doctor, perhaps remembering, in particular, the burned Gallifrey (which she saw in **203** *Spyfall*) and the lifeless future Earth (which she saw in **204** *Orphan 55*). The phrase also recalls the title of the first episode of **2** *The Mutants* (aka *The Daleks*).

291 Fugitive of the Judoon

by Vinay Patel and Chris Chibnall

Judoon scour Gloucester for a fugitive in the unlikely form of local tour guide Ruth Clayton. Then the Doctor discovers a police box-shaped TARDIS buried outside Ruth's childhood home…

■ **Where and When** Gloucester, circa 2020. A stolen Cybership on the run. A Judoon spaceship heading out into neutral space.

■ **The Baddies** A Judoon platoon – privately contracted by Division, represented by Commander Gat (Ritu Arya), to bring in the titular fugitive from "the far backside of a tiny galaxy". We learn more about the mysterious Division in **295** *Ascension of the Cybermen/ The Timeless Children* and **297** *Flux*.

Left and right The Doctor helps her mysterious earlier incarnation (Jo Martin) to evade capture in *Fugitive of the Judoon*.

■ **Introducing…** That fugitive is an unknown incarnation of the Doctor, hiding on Earth under the identity of Ruth Clayton (Jo Martin), thanks to a chameleon arch (see **185** *Human Nature/ The Family of Blood*).

■ **Look out for…** The Judoon Captain (Paul Kasey) is named Pol-Kon-Don, after *Doctor Who* fan and writer Paul Condon (1970-2019).

■ **What they said** In *The Daily Telegraph* (26 January 2020), Michael Hogan called this "The best episode of the series, with surprise returns and killer twists… In a dizzying development, Ruth turned out to be… well, the Doctor. Viewers were left scratching our heads, but in a good way."

■ **Arcs in Space** Captain Jack Harkness – returning for the first time since **202** *The End of Time* – warns the Doctor about "the lone Cyberman" (whom she'll encounter in **294** *The Haunting of Villa Diodati*), and ruefully comments that "It's always the nanogenes" (after **175** *The Empty Child/The Doctor Dances*). The Doctor and Commander Gat make mental "contact", in the way two Doctors do in **75** *The Three Doctors*. "Platoon of Judoon near the Moon," says the Doctor, paraphrasing herself from **179** *Smith and Jones*.

292 Praxeus

by **Pete McTighe** and **Chris Chibnall**
British astronaut Adam Lang's ship has crashed in the Indian Ocean – and his estranged husband receives a mysterious text from Hong Kong, begging for help. The fam are already on the scene…

■ **Where and When** The UK, Peru, Hong Kong and Madagascar, early in the third decade of the 21st century.

■ **The Baddies** Praxeus is an alien bacteria latching onto life forms. Designed to target plastics, it was inadvertently brought to Earth by aliens looking for a cure.

■ **Introducing…** This is the first Thirteenth Doctor episode to mention Liverpool, which will be the setting for much of **297** *Flux*.

■ **Look out for…** The Doctor telling Ryan that he smells of dead bird. "I thought you'd changed your shower gel!"

■ **What they said** "To see a science fiction franchise lean into a same-sex romance is obviously heartening," said *The Independent*'s Ed Power on 1 February 2020. "Adam and Jake's love blooms anew, humanity is saved from a killer bug, the aliens are repelled. And *Doctor Who* ticks all the boxes in a standalone instalment that ranks as one of the series' finest."

■ **Arcs in Space** The earlier history of the British space programme is explored in **53** *The Ambassadors of Death*, **83** *The Android Invasion* and **167** *The Christmas Invasion*, among others. The Doctor speculates on, and seems disappointed to dismiss, the presence of Autons (introduced in **51** *Spearhead from Space*).

Adam Lang (Matthew McNulty), Warren Brown (Jake Willis), Graham, the Doctor and Ryan in *Praxeus*.

Immortals Zellin (Ian Gelder) and Rakaya (Clare-Hope Ashitey) in *Can You Hear Me?*

293 Can You Hear Me?

by **Charlene James** and **Chris Chibnall**

Immortal creatures terrorise a hospital in Aleppo, feeding off the fear and pain in people's nightmares, ranging from small insecurities to full-scale horrors.

■ **Where and When** A mental hospital in Syria in 1380; modern-day Sheffield; a craft in deep space in the distant future.

■ **The Baddies** Zellin (Ian Gelder) and Rakaya (Clare-Hope Ashitey), immortals with an air of superiority and calm malice. They detach their own fingers to plug into sleeping people so they can feed off their nightmares.

■ **Look out for...** Rakaya explains her history to the Doctor in a dream – a fabulous animated sequence set against the starry backdrop of space.

■ **Where else have I seen...** Graham's late wife, Grace (Sharon D Clarke), taunts him in his miserable dream. She also appears in 277 *The Woman Who Fell to Earth*, 280 *Arachnids in the UK*, 285 *It Takes You Away* and 296 *Revolution of the Daleks*.

■ **What they said** In *The Guardian* (9 February 2020), Dan Martin observed that "A story based around nightmares would do well to deliver some proper nightmare fuel. And *Can You Hear Me?* does not disappoint, the claw-around-the-face moment proving a particular standout, while Zellin's creepy detachable fingers persistently unsettle."

■ **Arcs in Space** Zellin refers to the Immortals from 127 *Enlightenment*, the Guardians from, among others, 98

The Ribos Operation and 125 *Mawdryn Undead*, and the Toymaker from 24 *The Celestial Toymaker* and 303 *The Giggle*. The Doctor interrupts a reflective moment between Ryan and Yaz with an excitable suggestion involving *Frankenstein*, leading straight into the next story.

294 The Haunting of Villa Diodati

by **Maxine Alderton**

The Doctor and her fam visit famous Romantic poets on what should be an auspicious evening for world literature, but turns out to be notable for quite different, and deadly, reasons.

■ **Where and When** The shores of Lake Geneva, 1816.

■ **The Baddies** The Lone Cyberman, Ashad (Patrick O'Kane). A human whose cyber-conversion failed, leaving him cruelly and monstrously part-human but with a Cyberman's ruthless drive – and determination to wipe out humans.

■ **Introducing...** Again: Ashad, who can remember his life before conversion. Has a Cyberman ever looked more menacing? With half his human face visible and a human hand at the end of a Cyber arm, he's horrific. A real Frankenstein's monster.

■ **Look out for...** Having walked in circles trying to find a bathroom, seen silent spooky figures that disappear into thin air, and watched Dr Polidori (Maxim Baldry) sleepwalk through a wall, Graham says, "There's something seriously wrong with this gaff." No one else sees the woman and the girl that he sees. Are they ghosts?

■ **What they said** "Lustrous, spooky, hitting every note, this episode is finely directed by Emma Sullivan," wrote *Radio Times* reviewer Patrick Mulkern, "and has enough confidence and generosity to unwind with an almost minute-long poetry reading." That would be *Darkness*, written by Lord Byron (Jacob Collins-Levy) in 1816.

■ **Arcs in Space** Captain Jack's warning from 291 *Fugitive of the Judoon* – to "beware the Lone Cyberman" – suddenly makes sense. The Doctor and friends go straight from this story into the next...

295 Ascension of the Cybermen/The Timeless Children

(two episodes) by **Chris Chibnall**

The last humans flee from the Cybermen, seeking refuge via a portal that should lead to safety. But it leads to the ruins of Gallifrey, the Master and revelations about the Doctor's past.

■ **Where and When** Unknown planets in the far future, at the end of the

Ashad (Patrick O'Kane), a modern Prometheus, in *The Haunting of Villa Diodati.*

The Master and his new allies on Gallifrey in *Ascension of the Cybermen/ The Timeless Children*.

Cyberwar. Gallifrey, date unknown. Also, rural Ireland in the early 20th century – although it turns out to be a creation of the Matrix aimed specifically at the Doctor.

■ **The Baddies** Warrior-class Cybermen designed especially for war and equipped with personal transmats, led by the Lone Cyberman. The Master (Sacha Dhawan), deranged as ever, plans to create hybrid Cyber Masters with the ability to regenerate.

■ **Introducing…** The Timeless Child, first mentioned by the Remnants in 278 *The Ghost Monument*, turns out to have been the Doctor. The Doctor's own backstory is revealed in the Matrix: they were an abandoned, then adopted child, exploited for their genetic secrets and drafted into the Division against their will, with their memories wiped.

■ **Look out for…** A flashback sequence as the Doctor projects her memories in order to break free of the Matrix. Here we see all the (known) previous incarnations of the Doctor, including those from the Doctor's mind-bending contest in 84 *The Brain of Morbius*.

■ **What they said** According to the critics' consensus on the Rotten Tomatoes review site: "Its relentless plotting and exposition teeter on overwhelming, but a bold daringness to reinvent Whovian lore coupled with Jodie Whittaker's dynamic performance make *The Timeless Children* a successful season finale."

■ **Arcs in Space** As the Doctor gathers her thoughts in the TARDIS at the end, a Judoon cold-case unit materialises – she is, after all, still wanted from 291 *Fugitive of the Judoon* – and transports her to prison, where we'll find her at the beginning of the next story.

296 Revolution of the Daleks

by Chris Chibnall

A corrupt entrepreneur unwittingly enables the breeding of an army of Daleks intent on taking over the Earth. With the Doctor imprisoned by the Judoon, her friends prepare to fight without her.

■ **Where and When** Sheffield and Osaka, around 2020 – ten months after 295 *Ascension of the Cybermen/The Timeless Children*. And the Judoon prison, date unknown.

■ **The Baddies** Unethical American businessman Jack Robertson (Chris Noth) returns from 280 *Arachnids in the UK*. It turns out he stole the remains of the recon scout Dalek from 287 *Resolution*, and used it to develop familiar-looking 'security drones' for the UK government. Now thousands of vat-grown Dalek clones in a Japanese laboratory are ready to transport into the 3D-printed drone casings…

■ **Farewell to…** Ryan decides it's time to leave, feeling that his mates, and his planet, need him. This isn't a big surprise, as he's been thinking about it since 293 *Can You Hear Me?* Graham leaves, too, so he can spend time with his grandson. A double whammy for the Doctor and Yaz. It's also the last appearance to date by the Doctor's fellow prisoner Captain Jack Harkness (John Barrowman).

■ **Look out for…** When the Dalek possessing Leo (Nathan Stewart-Jarrett) explains how it has built the factory, Robertson is concerned about how he got the purchase order numbers. And when he hears that the clone Daleks are being fed on liquidised humans, he mutters, "This is a PR disaster!"

■ **What they said** *Independent* reviewer Sean O'Grady, writing on 2 January: "Well, everyone's been hoping that 2021 might be a bit of an improvement on 2020, and in its own small, intertemporal way, the *Doctor Who* festive special is an encouraging start to a better future for Earth, menaced as it has been by a virus every bit as lethal as the Daleks. Everything about this *Doctor Who* is superb."

■ **Arcs in Space** This story follows 287 *Resolution* in Earth's timeline. Ryan asks the Doctor what happened on Gallifrey at the end of 295 *Ascension of the Cybermen/ The Timeless Children* and Jack mentions Gwen Cooper from 198 *The Stolen Earth/ Journey's End*.

Jack Robertson's 'security drones' launch their invasion in *Revolution of the Daleks*.

Yaz, the Doctor, Dan (John Bishop) and Vinder (Jacob Anderson) become avatars, exploring past events in *Flux*.

297 Flux

(six episodes)

Where and When Almost everywhere, whenever...

On Earth: Liverpool (in 1820); outside Sevastopol (1855); Medderton Village (1901 and 1967); Mexico, Constantinople, the ocean and Nepal (1904); the Great Wall of China and Liverpool (1905); countryside, exact location unknown (1958); UNIT HQ, London (1967 and 2017); a government office, London (1987); Liverpool, Iceland and Chile (2021); UNIT control centre, London (2023).

Exact dates unknown: A planet of acid oceans; a barren prison world; Observation Outpost Rose in deep space; the planet Arnvarius; Vinder's home world and star system; a red planet; Puzano Quadrant and the planet Puzano; the world of Angels; abandoned space fortress; space sector 21CZ4 TN 179QP; a Sontaran ship, three trillion light years away; deep space, 30 trillion light years away.

No time: The Temple of Atropos on planet Time; a creepy house; the Vinculum Biodome; an alien landscape within Passenger.

Other: A Lupari spaceship in the solar system, 2021.

Chapter One: The Halloween Apocalypse

by **Chris Chibnall**

Following Division operative Karvanista to Earth, the Doctor and Yaz arrive just as he abducts Dan Lewis. Meanwhile, the evil Swarm escapes captivity, and Vinder witnesses the arrival of the Flux.

■ **The Baddies** Swarm (Sam Spruell), a murderous crystalline psychopath who's an old enemy of the Doctor's (though she doesn't remember). Azure (Rochenda Sandall), Swarm's equally psychopathic other half. And briefly: the Sontarans and the Weeping Angels.

■ **Introducing...** Dan Lewis (John Bishop), wannabe museum guide and the Doctor's latest companion.

■ **Look out for...** Halloween shivers as a Weeping Angel targets Claire Brown (Annabel Scholey), who's met the Doctor and Yaz before (but they haven't met her yet).

■ **What they said** In *The Independent* on 1 November 2021, Isobel Lewis wrote: "It's refreshing to see [Chris] Chibnall attempt to shake things up for one of Whittaker's last spells in the TARDIS."

■ **Arcs in Space** The TARDIS heralds the coming of the Flux by sounding its Cloister Bell, first heard in 115 *Logopolis*. The Doctor refers to Nitro-9, an explosive favoured by the Seventh Doctor's companion Ace... whom she'll be reunited with in 300 *The Power of the Doctor*.

Chapter Two: War of the Sontarans

by **Chris Chibnall**

The Doctor, Yaz and Dan arrive in the Crimean War, where the British are fighting Sontarans, and meet nurse Mary Seacole.

■ **The Baddies** Sontarans, who are launching a temporal offensive on Earth, plus Swarm and Azure.

■ **Introducing...** Passenger (Jonny Mathers), the sinister skull-faced new member of Swarm's posse.

■ **Look out for...** The doors of the corrupted TARDIS disappear, and the Doctor is unable to enter.

■ **What they said** In the **Doctor Who Magazine** 2022 Yearbook, Sara Powell (who plays Mary) said, "Mary Seacole was an astonishing, extraordinary human. So to have her with the Sontarans in the middle of a Welsh quarry... Only in *Doctor Who*!"

■ **Arcs in Space** The mission undertaken by Svild (Dan Starkey) – to monitor "the weak and pathetic human resistance" – recalls Styre's in 77 *The Sontaran Experiment*. Skaak (Jonathan Watson) references Commander Linx from 70 *The Time Warrior*, and the vulnerability of the Sontaran probic vent is exploited again (see 70 *The Time Warrior*, 97 *The Invasion of Time* and others). The Doctor says she's a former President of Gallifrey, harking back to 97 *The Invasion of Time*.

Chapter Three: Once, Upon Time

by **Chris Chibnall**

Leaping into a time storm, the Doctor hides Dan, Yaz and Vinder in their pasts, while, in a reflection of her own history, she sees the Fugitive Doctor looking back at her.

Claire Brown (Annabel Scholey) is pursued by a Weeping Angel.

Text by David Richardson

Sontaran Commander Skaak (Jonathan Watson).

Above Azure (Rochenda Sandall) and Swarm (Sam Spruell).

Below inset Tecteun (Barbara Flynn).

The Baddies Swarm, Azure and Passenger, plus the Daleks and Cybermen both seizing the opportunity to expand their empires. The Weeping Angels, meanwhile, keep their stone-cold eyes on the TARDIS…

■ **Introducing…** Bel (Thaddea Graham), a refugee from the Flux who's desperately seeking her husband Vinder (Jacob Anderson), and the Grand Serpent (Craig Parkinson), a dangerous tyrant from Vinder's past.

■ **Look out for…** The intriguing scenes on Atropos as the Doctor, Yaz, Dan and Vinder live out the history of the Fugitive, Karvanista (Craige Els) and their team.

■ **What they said** On the *Radio Times* website (14 November 2021), Patrick Mulkern declared *Once, Upon Time* "blatantly confusing" and "tricky to engage with."

■ **Arcs in Space** We've encountered the Fugitive Doctor before, in both **291** *Fugitive of the Judoon* and **295** *Ascension of the Cybermen/The Timeless Children*.

Chapter Four: Village of the Angels

by **Chris Chibnall** and **Maxine Alderton**
The Doctor wrests control of the TARDIS from the Angels and arrives in a coastal village in 1967 – on the very day when, history relates, everyone in the village will disappear…

■ **The Baddies** The Weeping Angels, who are revealed to be working for Division and hunting down one of their own.

■ **Introducing…** Professor Eustacius Jericho (Kevin McNally), a scientist investigating parapsychology, who will spend three years travelling with Yaz and Dan.

■ **Look out for…** The 'quantum extraction' of the Doctor – as she turns to stone, grows wings and becomes an Angel.

■ **What they said** In DWM issue 575 (March 2022), executive producer Matt Strevens declared this "a really complete, perfect episode".

■ **Arcs in Space** The Angels again manifest from an image of themselves, a concept introduced in **206** *The Time of Angels/ Flesh and Stone*.

Chapter Five: Survivors of the Flux

by **Chris Chibnall**
The Doctor meets an important figure from her past, and the Grand Serpent spends decades on Earth preparing his masterplan.

■ **The Baddies** The Grand Serpent, out to destroy the Earth. Tecteun, out to destroy the universe. On the sidelines: Swarm and Azure, and the Sontarans.

■ **Introducing…** Tecteun (Barbara Flynn), the Doctor's adopted mother. She's currently the leader of Division, and has decided to shut down the universe in order to erase the Doctor's interference.

■ **Look out for…** Brigadier Lethbridge-Stewart making an out-of-shot cameo appearance with the line: "Lethbridge-Stewart here, I want a call to the RAF please."

■ **What they said** In the DWM 2022 Yearbook, Jodie Whittaker said: "For the Doctor the revelation of Tecteun is heartbreaking."

■ **Arcs in Space** We discover the origins of UNIT, which was established by General Farquhar (Robert Bathurst), prior to **35** *The Invasion*. The Post Office Tower is mentioned, a reference to **27** *The War Machines*. The Doctor discovers the fob watch containing her lost memory; the biodata module was introduced in **187a** *Utopia*. Kate Stewart returns, and Osgood is mentioned; both last appeared in **258** *The Zygon Invasion/The Zygon Inversion*. Division employ the services of an Ood; the species first appeared in **174** *The Impossible Planet/The Satan Pit*.

Chapter Six: The Vanquishers

by **Chris Chibnall**
As the Sontarans aim to be the ultimate vanquishers, the Ravagers prepare for universal dissolution. Can three versions of the Doctor defeat her enemies?

■ **The Baddies** Swarm and Azure, who now have the resources of Division. The Sontarans, who are working with the Grand Serpent and offering an alliance with Daleks and Cybermen – though it's actually a plan to destroy them.

■ **Farewell to…** Professor Jericho, whose "awfully big adventure" comes to a dramatic end.

■ **Look out for…** The three Thirteenth Doctors have a mental communion, uttering the word "contact" – a callback to **65** *The Three Doctors*.

■ **Arcs in Space** The Flux is anti-matter, a force the Doctor previously battled in **65** *The Three Doctors* and **81** *Planet of Evil*. Stenck (Jonathan Watson) mentions Rutans, last seen on screen in **92** *Horror of Fang Rock*. As she bids farewell to the Doctor, Kate says "I like this regeneration. Hope I meet it again". She will, in **300** *The Power of the Doctor*.

Above
The Doctor challenges some upgraded foes in *Eve of the Daleks.*

Right
Elf Storage manager Sarah (Aisling Bea).

298 Eve of the Daleks

by Chris Chibnall
When the TARDIS malfunctions, its crew find themselves trapped in a storage facility with a Dalek. But after it exterminates them, time rolls back, giving them a chance to do things differently…

■ **Where and When** Elf Storage in Manchester, during the last nine minutes of 31 December 2021. Repeatedly.
■ **The Baddies** A single Dalek, determined to kill the Doctor in revenge for her causing the Flux to destroy the Dalek fleet.

Yaz, the Doctor and Dan are trapped in a time loop triggered by the TARDIS.

■ **Introducing…** The Dalek has improved firepower, with a rapid-fire gunstick that can't be jammed by the sonic screwdriver (as it was in **287** *Resolution*).
■ **Look out for…** The first time around the loop, when the Doctor thinks she's really going to be exterminated and says "Not like this."
■ **What they said** "Funny, scary, inventive and the best episode in years," was the headline of Michael Hogan's review in *The Telegraph* on 1 January 2022. "It combined high-octane thrills with time-loop trippyness and a sweet romcom subplot. A stripped-back single setting provided narrative simplicity, tightness of focus, and lent propulsive momentum to the plot."
■ **Arcs in Space** The Doctor was previously caught in a time loop in **110** *Meglos*, while a similar 'shortening' time loop featured in **103** *The Armageddon Factor*. The Doctor considers using the sonic to resonate concrete, referring back to **164** *The Empty Child / The Doctor Dances*, while Karl (Jonny Dixon) from **277** *The Woman Who Fell to Earth* makes a surprise cameo.

299 Legend of the Sea Devils

by Ella Road and Chris Chibnall
Seeking the lost treasure of the Fol de la Mar, pirate queen Madame Ching unwittingly reanimates the Sea Devils – who intend to flood the world, to rid it of the "land crawlers".

■ **Where and When** The action begins in a Chinese fishing village in 1807, before shifting to Madame Ching's ship, then Ji-Hun's ship in 1533, and then back to 1807 and the Sea Devil undersea base.
■ **The Baddies** Despite being a pirate queen, Madame Ching (Crystal Yu) is no killer, which can't be said for her bloodthirsty predecessor Ji-Hun (Arthur Lee) or the equally bloodthirsty Sea Devil Chief (Craige Els).
■ **Introducing…** The Sea Devils' new weapons – glowing cutlasses that can kill with a single touch via hexo-toxic poison.
■ **Look out for…** The scene with the Doctor and Yaz on the ocean floor boasts everything you could ask for, from heartbreak to an enormous sea monster.
■ **What they said** "We had been intending to do a pirate story during *Flux* and we didn't manage to make it work for all sorts of reasons," explained co-writer Chris Chibnall in a promotional interview released on 13 April 2022. "So when it came to thinking about the final specials that was one of the things I really wanted to revisit, to do a big, thrilling Bank Holiday romp of an adventure for Jodie's penultimate story, featuring a warrior pirate queen."

Pirate queen, Madame Ching (Crystal Yu) in *Legend of the Sea Devils*.

Left
Tegan (Janet Fielding) and Ace (Sophie Aldred) in *The Power of the Doctor*.

Below inset
The Master adopts the guise of Rasputin.

■ **Arcs in Space** This could be regarded as the third part of a Sea Devils trilogy with `62` *The Sea Devils* and `130` *Warriors of the Deep*. The TARDIS can open its doors underwater by creating an oxygen bubble, as previously demonstrated in `245` *Listen*. Like Captain Avery in `215` *The Curse of the Black Spot*, Madame Ching is based on a real-life pirate – Zheng Yi Sao, aka Ching Shih.

The Chief Sea Devil (Craige Els).

`300` The Power of the Doctor

by Chris Chibnall

When the Cybermen kidnap a Qurunx from a space train, it's merely the opening act of the Master's elaborate scheme to not merely defeat the Doctor, but to take her place.

■ **Where and When** From a space train in the distant future to the Winter Palace in St Petersburg and a Cyberplanet in 1916, to UNIT HQ and beneath a Bolivian volcano in the present day.

■ **The Baddies** The Master has enlisted the help of the Daleks, the Cybermasters, the Cyberium and the Lone Cyberman, Ashad (last seen in `295` *Ascension of the Cybermen/The Timeless Children*).

■ **Farewell to…** Ian Chesterton – part of an ex-TARDIS travellers' support group. The Thirteenth Doctor, Yaz, Dan, Graham, Ace, Tegan and Jo all make their final appearances to date (not to mention manifestations of the Doctor's first, fifth, sixth, seventh and eighth incarnations, too). But not Mel. She will return!

■ **Look out for…** Pretty much every scene has a reason for fans to punch the air, but it's hard to top the Master dancing in the Winter Palace to *Rasputin* by Boney M, with the Daleks and Cybermen watching on incredulously.

■ **What they said** "For *Doctor Who* fans, I think it's a real treat," Jodie Whittaker told **Doctor Who Magazine** in issue 583, (November 2022). "It couldn't have more carrots, more homages, more involvement of past, present and future. And if you've never seen *Doctor Who* before, then you're getting an absolute dose. I really feel like it has something for everyone."

■ **Arcs in Space** As well as numerous past companions, and six past Doctors, the story has some 'deep cut' links too, such as the mention of the Toraji system from `184` *42*, the Master paraphrasing his earlier incarnation from `156` the 1996 TV movie *Doctor Who* ("Must dress for the occasion"), the mention of Tegan's Aunt Vanessa from `115` *Logopolis*, and Ace remembering the Master being half-cat in `155` *Survival*.

The Doctor undergoes the Master's "forced regeneration".

The FOURTEENTH DOCTOR

David Tennant
Stories 301–3, 2023

"What? What?! *What?!*" Same old teeth, new old Doctor: the Fourteenth was a man on a mission – to discover why he'd been given a face he'd worn before. He wouldn't learn the reason until he ran into his old friend Donna Noble once again, and had embarked on the biggest adventure of all: a normal life.

Left
A redecorated TARDIS and fresh adventures for the Doctor (David Tennant) and Donna (Catherine Tate).

301 The Star Beast

by **Russell T Davies**
The freshly minted Fourteenth Doctor bumps into former companion Donna Noble once more – and learns that her daughter Rose is harbouring an alien in the garden shed…

■ **Where and When** London, 2023.
■ **The Baddies** The Meep made its first appearance in the 1980 *Doctor Who Weekly* comic strip *Doctor Who and the Star Beast* – and this episode is a loose adaptation of that story. While seeming cute and cuddly at first glance, the Meep (voiced by Miriam Margolyes) is a deranged tyrant.
■ **Introducing…** Donna's daughter Rose Noble (Yasmin Finney), who'll eventually wind up working for UNIT in **221** *The Legend of Ruby Sunday/Empire of Death*. Shirley Anne Bingham (Ruth Madeley) is UNIT's 56th scientific adviser; she'll reappear in **303** *The Giggle*. The vast new TARDIS control room, with circulating ramps leading to multiple doorways off and a console with an integrated coffee machine.

■ **Look out for…** When Donna realises that Rose has inherited her memories of travelling with the Doctor, it becomes clear that all of Rose's handmade cuddly toys are based on creatures they met. There's a Dalek mutant and a Judoon, as seen by Donna in **198** *The Stolen Earth/ Journey's End*, an Adipose from **189** *Partners in Crime*, and an Ood from **191** *Planet of the Ood*. We also see a Cyberman, and a Lupari from **297** *Flux* – both of which suggest off-screen adventures for Donna.
■ **What they said** "Yasmin Finney as Rose was a bright and kindly presence," noted Martin Belam in *The Guardian* on 25 November 2023. "The bores who thought the Whittaker era was too 'woke' – whatever that means in the context of a science fantasy show that has always pushed stories with progressive values – will be choking on the scene where the Doctor is chastised by her for assuming the Meep's pronouns."

■ **Arcs in Space** Donna finally gets back her memories of travelling with the Doctor, which he took from her to save her life in **198** *The Stolen Earth/ Journey's End*. She agrees to a brief trip in the TARDIS, but almost immediately spills coffee on the console, and sends the ship careering out of control into the next story.

302 Wild Blue Yonder

by **Russell T Davies**
A malfunctioning TARDIS deposits the Doctor and Donna on a spaceship at the outer limits of the universe – where they discover that they're not alone…

■ **Where and When** A spaceship, the edge of the universe, unspecified time period.
■ **The Baddies** The 'Not-Things' are curious creatures inhabiting the void at the distant extremes of reality. They're able to replicate the bodies and minds of the beings they encounter, but have no real comprehension of shape or scale.
■ **Look out for…** Before arriving on the ship, the TARDIS makes a brief pit-stop to visit Isaac Newton (Nathaniel Curtis), who mishears the Doctor and Donna saying "gravity". The word has been "mavity" ever since – which may or may not be resolved at some point in the future…
■ **Introducing…** Newton's maid Mrs Merridew (Susan Twist) is the first manifestation we meet of multiple versions of the same woman. She'll be revealed in **311** *The Legend of Ruby Sunday/Empire of Death* to have been planted across space and time by Sutekh in order to unleash his gift of death.
■ **Farewell to…** Bernard Cribbins as Wilf Mott – the old soldier, waiting for the TARDIS at Camden Lock in the final scene.

Wrath Warriors (right) hunt the Meep (left) in *The Star Beast*.

Right
The Toymaker (Neil Patrick Harris) in *The Giggle*.

Below inset
Bi-generation creates the Fifteenth Doctor (Ncuti Gatwa).

■ **What they said** "Set aboard a haunted starship, this second adventure featuring the reunited Doctor and Donna tips its hat to Ridley Scott's original *Alien*," said *Independent* critic Ed Power on 2 December 2023. "Meanwhile, its plunge into claustrophobic body horror suggests a familiarity with the *Dead Space* video games."

■ **Arcs in Space** The Not-Donna knows everything the real Donna knows, and reveals that in 301 *The Star Beast* she saw into the Doctor's mind and glimpsed all that happened to him since they parted ways. She's aware that he's not originally from Gallifrey – as discovered in 295 *Ascension of the Cybermen/The Timeless Children*. She also mentions the events of 297 *Flux*, which the Doctor confirms destroyed half the universe. This story ends with the TARDIS returning to an Earth gone bananas, leading directly into the next adventure.

303 The Giggle

by **Russell T Davies**

Arriving back on Earth, the Doctor and Donna find that the whole planet has gone insane, with everyone convinced that only their opinions are the correct ones…

■ **Where and When** Soho in 1925 and 2023; the UNIT Tower in 2023; and inside the bizarre domain of…

■ **The Baddies** The extremely powerful extradimensional entity known as the Toymaker (Neil Patrick Harris) – back for the first time since 24 *The Celestial Toymaker*. There are even brief flashbacks to the original version of the character (played by Michael Gough) confronting the First Doctor.

■ **Look out for…** The Toymaker puts on a puppet show to demonstrate to Donna what happened to the people who travelled with the Doctor after he left her. Using marionettes of former companions, he references the 'deaths' of Amy Pond in 230 *The Angels Take Manhattan*, Clara Oswald in 260 *Face the Raven* and Bill Potts in 275 *World Enough and Time/The Doctor Falls*. He follows this up with a sequence representing the destruction of half the universe in 297 *Flux*.

■ **Introducing…** Although the exterior was briefly glimpsed in 301 *The Star Beast*, this is our first trip inside the swanky new UNIT Tower, where we're introduced to handsome soldier Colonel Ibrahim (Alexander Devrient) and alien entity the Vlinx (Aidan Cook) – both of whom will be back in 311 *The Legend of Ruby Sunday/Empire of Death*. Most significantly, the Fourteenth Doctor's battle with the Toymaker leads to an unprecedented 'bi-generation' – which sees his next incarnation (Ncuti Gatwa) joining him to defeat the troublesome trickster.

■ **Farewell to…** To date, these are the final appearances of the Fourteenth Doctor, Donna Noble, Sylvia Noble, Shaun Temple, Shirley Anne Bingham and US news presenter Trinity Wells.

■ **Arcs in Space** Mel Bush (Bonnie Langford) explains that, after departing Iceworld with Sabalom Glitz in 147 *Dragonfire*, they travelled the stars together. Then, after Glitz died by falling over a whiskey bottle at the age of 101, she got a lift back to Earth from a Zingo. (It's a thing you get a lift off.) The Master is now housed in a gold tooth belonging to the Toymaker – which is retrieved by a mysterious hand after the latter's defeat. After a conversation that touches upon many aspects of their former lives, the exhausted and damaged Fourteenth Doctor settles into 'retirement' with Donna and her family, while the brand-new Fifteenth Doctor wooshes off for further adventures in time and space.

The Doctor and Donna investigate an eerie spaceship in *Wild Blue Yonder*.

The FIFTEENTH DOCTOR

Ncuti Gatwa
Stories 304–??, 2024–??

The product of an unprecedented bi-generation, the Fifteenth Doctor doesn't have a home, or a job, or a boss, or bills to pay. Or a purpose, or a cause, or a mission. What he does have is freedom – freedom to keep moving on, to see the next thing, and the next, and the next. That, and the most amazing wardrobe in all of time and space...

Left
Ruby Sunday (Millie Gibson) gets tied up with the Doctor in *The Church on Ruby Road*.

Below inset
The Goblin King.

304 The Church on Ruby Road

by Russell T Davies

Orphan Ruby Sunday, dogged by a string of seemingly deadly coincidences, bumps into the newly bigenerated Doctor – a meeting that leads them into a huge dance number on board a goblin airship.

■ **Where and When** London, December 2023, and outside the eponymous church on Christmas Eve, 2004.
■ **The Baddies** Baby-eating goblins, and their King (he's not a myth, he's an actual thing).
■ **Introducing…** Ruby Sunday (Millie Gibson), her adoptive mother Carla Sunday (Michelle Greenidge), Carla's mother Cherry Sunday (Angela Wynter) and their mysterious neighbour Mrs Flood (Anita Dobson). The Doctor's new-look sonic screwdriver also debuts in this episode.
■ **Look out for…** *The Goblin Song*, written by Murray Gold and sung by Christina Rotondo in character as Janis Goblin (with accompaniment from Ncuti Gatwa and Millie Gibson), was released on 11 December 2024 and topped the UK iTunes chart.
■ **Where else have I seen…** Susan Twist, who plays an unnamed audience member at Ruby's gig, played Merridew in **302** *Wild Blue Yonder* and would go on to play at least one different character in every episode of the 2024 season – for reasons explained in the finale.

■ **Arcs in Space** The Doctor mentions that he once spent "a long hot summer" with Harry Houdini, having previously alluded to their meeting in **74** *Planet of the Spiders*, **79** *Revenge of the Cybermen* and **284** *The Witchfinders*.

305 Space Babies

by Russell T Davies

The Doctor and Ruby arrive on Baby Station Beta… and find themselves in a bedtime story gone mad, complete with toddler pilots and an actual Bogeyman.

■ **Where and When** The prehistoric Earth, circa 150 million years BC. But mostly in a space station oribiting Pacifico Del Rio in 21506.
■ **The Baddies** The Bogeyman (Robert Strange) – a creature manufactured by a very literal-minded computer.
■ **Look out for…** A demonstration of the so-called butterfly effect, whereby stepping on a Cretaceous-era butterfly causes changes to human evolution so massive that Ruby temporarily becomes an acutely defensive lizard-person.
■ **Introducing…** The TARDIS' butterfly compensation switch – see above.
■ **What they said** "It was more 'cute factor' than 'fear factor' in *Space Babies*," said *The Guardian*'s Martin Belam on 11 May 2024, "although the Bogeyman was an effective enough minor monster-of-the-week, and there was just a little moment where you thought surely

they are not going to start killing these babies off?"
■ **Arcs in Space** The Doctor tells Ruby to ask her mother not to slap him; he's previously been slapped by Jackie Tyler in **160** *Aliens of London/World War Three*, Francine Jones in **183** *The Lazarus Experiment* and Sylvia Noble in **301** *The Star Beast*. He also confirms that he's an orphan himself (as revealed in **295** *Ascension of the Cybermen/The Timeless Children* and mentioned in **304** *The Church on Ruby Road*), as well as explaining about the TARDIS' translation circuits – a subject he previously explored with Sarah Jane Smith in **86** *The Masque of Mandragora*, Rose Tyler in **158** *The End of the World* and Donna Noble in **190** *The Fires of Pompeii*. Snow falls around Ruby in a corridor, like a memory of the day of her is birth breaking through; it will continue to do so, on occasion, throughout the 2024 season.

306 The Devil's Chord

by Russell T Davies

The Doctor takes Ruby to meet the legendary Beatles, only to discover that their music has been stolen by a powerfully malevolent being who lives on unsung songs.

■ **Where and When** England, 1925; EMI's Abbey Road recording studios, 1963; and an alternative, devastated 2024.
■ **The Baddies** Maestro (Jinkx Monsoon) – one of the all-powerful Pantheon of Discord.
■ **Look out for…** Ruby's trip to a devastated 2024 echoes a similar trip taken by the Doctor and Sarah in **82** *Pyramids of Mars* – again making the point that established history can indeed be changed.

Eric and his fellow *Space Babies* fear the Bogeyman.

Maestro (Jinkx Monsoon) emerges from a piano in *The Devil's Chord*.

■ Where else have I seen… The actual Beatles (John Lennon, Paul McCartney, George Harrison and Ringo Starr) appeared in *Top of the Pops* footage seen on the Time and Space Visualiser in **16** *The Chase*.

■ What they said "It's almost difficult to hate them [Maestro] because it's clear how much [Jinkx] Monsoon relished bringing such a camp, theatrical and, in the best way, completely ridiculous villain to mainstream TV," said Louise Griffin on the *Radio Times* website (6 May 2024). "Is *The Devil's Chord* a perfect *Doctor Who* story? Absolutely not. But it's vivid, silly, gripping, and sees our brand new Doctor battle a larger than life villain across the streets of 1960s London. We could certainly be doing a lot worse."

■ Arcs in Space Maestro is revealed to be the child of the Toymaker, who debuted in **23** *The Celestial Toymaker* and returned in **303** *The Giggle*. Being set in 1963 London, the story features numerous references to **1** *100,000 BC* (aka *An Unearthly Child*), including ruminations on the whereabouts of the Doctor's granddaughter Susan, mentions of their Shoreditch address, and even a billboard for Chris Waites and the Carollers, a pop group featuring Susan's favourite singer.

307 Boom

by Steven Moffat

Amid a colossal war, the Doctor accidentally steps on a landmine that threatens to destroy half the planet. How can he disarm it without moving, and avoid being smelted by a trigger-happy AI?

■ Where and When The battlefield on Kastarion 3, 5 October 5087.

■ The Baddies The Villengard Corporation – inventors of the "acceptable casualty rate algorithm".

■ Look out for… The Doctor singing *The Skye Boat Song* to calm himself – a tune his second incarnation played on the recorder in **41** *The Web of Fear*, and which the Master had a crack at in **300** *The Power of the Doctor*.

■ Where else have I seen… If you're reading this in 2025, you will have seen Mundy actor Varada Sethu playing Belinda Chandra in the second series of Fifteenth Doctor adventures…

■ What they said "Put through the emotional wringer, Gatwa and Gibson really come into their own here as the Doctor and Ruby move beyond their Millennial-meets-Gen Z bestie dynamic into more emotionally rich, complicated territory," wrote Jordan King on the *Empire* website, on 4 June 2024. "Sharply written, superbly acted, and laser-focused, *Boom* sees Steven Moffat take *Doctor Who* back to basics and, in the process, deliver an instant classic."

■ Arcs in Space The Fourth Doctor also stepped on a landmine in an outer-space battlefield in **78** *Genesis of the Daleks*. It's worth noting that other stories in the 2024 season begin with a TARDIS traveller accidentally stepping on something, and causing disaster: **305** *Space Babies* (when Ruby treads on a butterfly) and **308** *73 Yards* (when the Doctor breaks a fairy circle).

The Doctor steps on a mine in *Boom*.

Pub landlady Lowri Palin (Maxine Evans) fills Ruby in on the local lore in *73 Yards*.

308 73 Yards

by Russell T Davies

After breaking a fairy circle, the Doctor is gone. But who is the woman following Ruby, always at a distance of 73 yards – and what terrors is she whispering to those close enough to hear?

■ **Where and When** South Wales, from 2024 to some decades after 2046. Other parts of the UK in the intervening years.

■ **The Baddies** Roger ap Gwilliam (Aneurin Barnard) – an intense but genial-seeming Welshman and closet nuclear holocaust enthusiast, described by the Doctor "the most dangerous Prime Minister in history". Which is good going, considering the others included the Master, aka Harold Saxon, in 187b *The Sound of Drums/Last of the Time Lords*.

■ **Introducing…** The title distance, and its metric equivalent of 66.7m, will become relevant again in season finale 311 *The Legend of Ruby Sunday/Empire of Death*.

■ **Look out for…** Heavily made-up BBC journalist Amol Rajan, playing a future version of himself interviewing Prime Minister ap Gwilliam.

■ **What they said** According to *Guardian* blogger Martin Belam, writing on 25 May 2024, the series got "cranked up to full-on horror in *73 Yards*, with an episode destined to be remembered as one of the all-time great companion performances."

■ **Arcs in Space** Roger ap Gwilliam's authoritarian, data-gathering government, and its fall, will become significant in *Empire of Death*. Ruby meets Kate Lethbridge-Stewart – but with the timeline wiped clean, they'll meet for the first time again later, also in the season finale. The dizzying, magical atmosphere seems to be a result of the Doctor's spilling of salt in 302 *Wild Blue Yonder* – which may have changed the rules of reality, as he feared.

309 Dot and Bubble

by Russell T Davies

Happy in your bubble? Why not look outside it? What might you learn? That there are creatures out there in the real world that are monsters, and they're coming to get you.

■ **Where and When** Finetime – a human colony in the future, after the year "five dash five". There the young adult children of Finetime's Homeworld do two hours of data entry "work" a day before playing hard. It's also a post-genocidal racist ethno-state after an unspecified "decontamination".

■ **The Baddies** Unnamed within the episode, giant slug-like 'Mantraps' are eating the population of Finetime in alphabetical order. But are they the real monsters?

■ **Look out for…** The extraordinary slow build-up of racist microaggressions from Lindy Pepper-Bean (Callie Cooke) and her visually homogeneous friends. Her dismissal of the Doctor's warning is because of the colour of his skin. She then doesn't recognise him when he returns, and is disgusted that he's in the same room as Ruby. On and on it goes. Until the end.

■ **Where else have I seen…** After 309 story entries, this heading finally becomes a plot point! The face of Susan Twist – here playing Lindy's "Mummy", Penny Pepper-Bean – first appeared in 302 *Wild Blue Yonder,* then reappeared in every episode since 304 *The Church on Ruby Road*… and now the Doctor and Ruby have *noticed*.

■ **What they said** "I'm all for bleakness in *Who*, and *Dot and Bubble* gives it to us," wrote Vicky Jessop of the London *Evening Standard* on 1 June 2024, praising "the ending scene, where [Lindy] and her fellow survivors essentially doom themselves".

■ **Arcs in Space** Like 305 *Space Babies*, this is a story about children isolated from their parents, who don't understand the world they live in, and who need to be saved. But *these* children refuse to be saved (and don't deserve to be).

Lindy (Callie Cooke) is forced to face reality in *Dot and Bubble.*

Text by James Cooray Smith

Bounty hunter Rogue (Jonathan Groff).

310 Rogue

by **Kate Herron** and **Briony Redman**

A Regency romance. A bounty hunter. A case of mistaken identity. The world doesn't end if the Doctor dances.

■ **Where and When** Bath, England, 1813 – the same year as **139** *The Mark of the Rani*.

■ **The Baddies** The Chuldur – alien shape-shifters cosplaying as humans for the fun of it. Unfortunately that fun also involves a lot of killing the thing they profess to love. (Like the more proprietorial forms of fandom, some might say.)

■ **Introducing...** The titular Rogue (Jonathan Groff) – an alien bounty hunter and a man of mystery to whom the Doctor takes quite the shine.

■ **Look out for...** The parade of 'past Doctor' heads flashed up by the scanner in Rogue's spaceship includes both the War and Fugitive variations – from **240** *The Day of the Doctor* and **291** *Fugitive of the Judoon*, respectively – plus a less familiar likeness: that of Richard E Grant, who played the Doctor in the 1999 Comic Relief sketch *The Curse of Fatal Death* and the 2003 webcast *Scream of the Shalka* before returning as Dr Simeon, host of the Great Intelligence, firstly in **231** *The Snowmen*. (Foreshadowing? A bit of fun? Time will tell.)

■ **What they said** Writing on 8 June 2024, Tom Fordy of *The Daily Telegraph* insisted: "Compared to the show's progressive ideals, the Time Lord's romantic affairs have always seemed rather chaste – until now. The new series is bold and gleefully diverse. There's a sense of telling *Doctor Who* fuddy-duddies to get onboard or have it rubbed in their faces."

■ **Arcs in Space** A familiar likeness (that of Susan Twist) appears in a portrait of the Duke's late mother. Rogue says bounty-hunting involves paperwork "ever since we got that new boss". Is this the same unrevealed "boss" alluded to by Beep the Meep in **301** *The Star Beast*?

Right
The Doctor and Mel watch Sutekh's *Empire of Death* take shape.

Below inset
Sutekh controls the TARDIS.

311 The Legend of Ruby Sunday/Empire of Death

(two episodes) by **Russell T Davies**

A dust of death blows over all reality.

■ **Where and When** London, 2024 and 2046. Aqua Santina, date unknown.

■ **The Baddies** Sutekh the Destroyer, last of the Osirans – who's been haunting the TARDIS since **59** *Pyramids of Mars*, and turns out to have been the "one who waits" mentioned by the Toymaker in **303** *The Giggle* and Maestro in **306** *The Devil's Chord*.

■ **Introducing...** UNIT's 57th scientific adviser (probably) – 13-year-old Morris Gibbons (Lenny Rush), his genius accelerated by a passing asteroid.

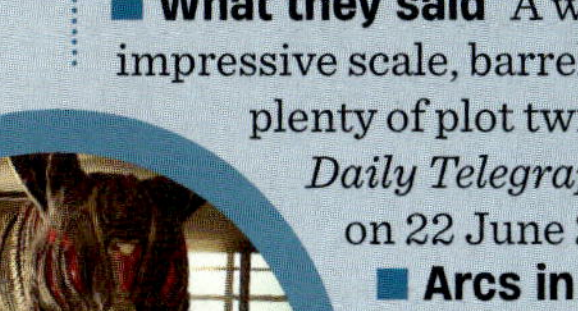

Susan Triad (Susan Twist) in *The Legend of Ruby Sunday*.

■ **Look out for...** In the Memory TARDIS, Mel reaches for a familiar multicoloured coat and question-mark pullover.

■ **What they said** "A wild ride with impressive scale, barrelling pace and plenty of plot twists." So said *The Daily Telegraph*'s Michael Hogan on 22 June 2024.

■ **Arcs in Space** In addition to those we know about, it turns out that the Doctor and Ruby have encountered many other individuals who look like just like 'S Triad' Technology boss Susan Triad (Susan Twist) in off-screen adventures: a Sloogma on Sloog, a Griffin on Varsitay and a Bleet of the Fivefold Configuration. (All of whom, it transpires, were created by Sutekh, using the TARDIS.) The riddle of Ruby's mum – set up in **304** *The Church on Ruby Road* – is solved. Planets apparently destroyed by Sutekh, then resurrected, include the Dalek homeworld of Skaro, the Cybermen's second home of Telos, Karn (introduced in **84** *The Brain of Morbius*), the Ood Sphere (introduced in **191** *Planet of the Ood*), Vortis (aka **13** *The Web Planet*), Tigella (seen in **110** *Meglos*), Spiridon (visited in **68** *Planet of the Daleks*), Calufrax (formerly the second segment of the Key to Time in **99** *The Pirate Planet*) and Shan Shen (seen in **142** *Turn Left*). But does that reverse the damage to reality left after the **297** *Flux*, too? Before she's killed by the dust, the strangely sinister Mrs Flood (Anita Dobson) says "But I had such plans." Of course, she too is resurrected, so she'll have a chance to play them out... perhaps.

Title Index

Principal page references for every story broadcast from 1963 to 1996, and every full-length episode broadcast from 2005 to 2024.